Decolonizing Freedom

Studies in Feminist Philosophy is designed to showcase cutting-edge monographs and collections that display the full range of feminist approaches to philosophy, that push feminist thought in important new directions, and that display the outstanding quality of feminist philosophical thought.

STUDIES IN FEMINIST PHILOSOPHY

Linda Martín Alcoff, Hunter College and the CUNY Graduate Center
Elizabeth Barnes, University of Virginia
Lorraine Code, York University, Toronto
Penelope Deutscher, Northwestern University
Ann Garry, California State University, Los Angeles
Sally Haslanger, Massachusetts Institute of Technology
Alison Jaggar, University of Colorado, Boulder

Serene Khader, Brooklyn College and CUNY Graduate Center
Helen Longino, Stanford University
Catriona Mackenzie, Macquarie University
Mari Mikkola, Humboldt University, Berlin
Sally Scholz, Villanova University
Laurie Shrage, Florida International University
Lisa Tessman, Binghamton University
Nancy Tuana, Pennsylvania State University

Published in the Series:

Ecological Thinking: The Politics of Epistemic Location
Lorraine Code

Self Transformations: Foucault, Ethics, and Normalized Bodies
Cressida J. Heyes

Family Bonds: Genealogies of Race and Gender
Ellen K. Feder

Moral Understandings: A Feminist Study in Ethics, Second Edition
Margaret Urban Walker

The Moral Skeptic
Anita M. Superson

"You've Changed": Sex Reassignment and Personal Identity
Edited by Laurie J. Shrage

Dancing with Iris: The Philosophy of Iris Marion Young
Edited by Ann Ferguson and Mechthild Nagel

Philosophy of Science after Feminism
Janet A. Kourany

Shifting Ground: Knowledge and Reality, Transgression and Trustworthiness
Naomi Scheman

The Metaphysics of Gender
Charlotte Witt

Unpopular Privacy: What Must We Hide?
Anita L. Allen

Adaptive Preferences and Women's Empowerment
Serene Khader

Minimizing Marriage: Marriage, Morality, and the Law
Elizabeth Brake

Out from the Shadows: Analytic Feminist Contributions to Traditional Philosophy
Edited by Sharon L. Crasnow and Anita M. Superson

The Epistemology of Resistance: Gender and Racial Oppression, Epistemic Injustice, and Resistant Imaginations
José Medina

Simone de Beauvoir and the Politics of Ambiguity
Sonia Kruks

Identities and Freedom: Feminist Theory between Power and Connection
Allison Weir

Vulnerability: New Essays in Ethics and Feminist Philosophy
Edited by Catriona Mackenzie, Wendy Rogers, and Susan Dodds

Sovereign Masculinity: Gender Lessons from the War on Terror
Bonnie Mann

Autonomy, Oppression, and Gender
Edited by Andrea Veltman and Mark Piper

Our Faithfulness to the Past: Essays on the Ethics and Politics of Memory
Sue Campbell
Edited by Christine M. Koggel and Rockney Jacobsen

The Physiology of Sexist and Racist Oppression
Shannon Sullivan

Disorientation and Moral Life
Ami Harbin

The Wrong of Injustice: Dehumanization and Its Role in Feminist Philosophy
Mari Mikkola

Beyond Speech: Pornography and Analytic Feminist Philosophy
Mari Mikkola

Differences: Between Beauvoir and Irigaray
Edited by Emily Anne Parker and Anne van Leeuwen

Categories We Live By
Ásta

Equal Citizenship and Public Reason
Christie Hartley and Lori Watson

Decolonizing Universalism: A Transnational Feminist Ethic
Serene J. Khader

Women's Activism, Feminism, and Social Justice
Margaret A. McLaren

Being Born: Birth and Philosophy
Alison Stone

Theories of the Flesh: Latinx and Latin American Feminisms, Transformation, and Resistance
Edited by Andrea J. Pitts, Mariana Ortega, and José Medina

Elemental Difference and the Climate of the Body
Emily Anne Parker

Racial Climates, Ecological Indifference: An Ecointersectional Approach
Nancy Tuana

On Taking Offence
Emily McTernan

Decolonizing Freedom
Allison Weir

Decolonizing Freedom

ALLISON WEIR

Oxford University Press is a department of the University of Oxford. It furthers the University's objective of excellence in research, scholarship, and education by publishing worldwide. Oxford is a registered trade mark of Oxford University Press in the UK and certain other countries.

Published in the United States of America by Oxford University Press
198 Madison Avenue, New York, NY 10016, United States of America.

© Oxford University Press 2024

All rights reserved. No part of this publication may be reproduced, stored in a retrieval system, or transmitted, in any form or by any means, without the prior permission in writing of Oxford University Press, or as expressly permitted by law, by license, or under terms agreed with the appropriate reproduction rights organization. Inquiries concerning reproduction outside the scope of the above should be sent to the Rights Department, Oxford University Press, at the address above.

You must not circulate this work in any other form
and you must impose this same condition on any acquirer.

Library of Congress Cataloging-in-Publication Data
Names: Weir, Allison, author.
Title: Decolonizing freedom / Allison Weir.
Description: First edition. | New York : Oxford University Press, [2024] |
Series: Studies in Feminist Philosophy series | Includes index.
Identifiers: LCCN 2023054372 | ISBN 9780197507957 (pb) |
ISBN 9780197507940 (hb) | ISBN 9780197507971 (epub)
Subjects: LCSH: Decolonization. | Free will and determinism. | Liberty. |
Ethnoscience. | Indigenous peoples—Ethnic identity. | Reparations for
historical injustices. | Feminist theory. | Critical theory.
Classification: LCC JV185.W45 2024 | DDC 325/.3—dc23/eng/20240116
LC record available at https://lccn.loc.gov/2023054372

DOI: 10.1093/oso/9780197507940.001.0001

Contents

Acknowledgments	vii
Introduction: Decolonizing Freedom	1
1. Noninterference, Nondomination, and Colonial Unknowing: Mis-Encounters with Indigenous Relational Freedom	38
2. For Love of the World: Relational Political Freedom as Love of Land	80
3. Dancing Resistance, Re-creating the World: *Philoxenic* Relational Freedom	115
Excursus: Freedom and Love: A Speculative Genealogy	145
4. Colonial Unknowing and Heterogeneous Relationalities: Alternative Formations of Power, Knowledge, and Freedom	155
5. Indigenous Feminisms and Relational Rights	203
Conclusion: Critical Theory and the Spirit of Freedom	243
References	271
Index	289

Acknowledgments

This book took far too long, and I'm grateful to so many people who supported its various incarnations. I especially thank my wonderful colleagues in the Institute for Social Justice in Sydney, Australia: Kiran Grewal, Naser Ghobadzadeh, Emilian Kavalski, Nikolas Kompridis, and Magdalena Zolkos, as well as Linda Martin Alcoff, Paul Apostolidis, Rajeev Bhargava, Akeel Bilgrami, Joe Carens, Rom Coles, Costas Douzinas, Lia Haro, Jeanne Morefield, Jenny Nedelsky, and Jacqueline Rose. Working with this most fabulous community of scholars made the years in Sydney feel like a working holiday. I'm especially grateful to the luminous Paula Gleeson, who exemplifies creative intellectual freedom and engaged critique, and who sustained me through the early drafts of this book. And to Jennifer Newman, Wiradjuri elder, teacher, academic and storyteller extraordinaire for her friendship, guidance, and patience. I also thank Lisa Tarantino, the many participants in our public Decolonizing Feminism seminars, and our PhD students, especially Riikka Prattes, Ayah Abubasheer, Semra Mese, Tina Dixson, and Julie Macken. More thanks to Jess Whyte, Ihab Shalbak, Moira Gatens, Dany Celermajer, Lucia Sorbera, Raewyn Connell, Aileen Moreton-Robinson, Irene Watson, Murrumu Walubara Yidinji, Tani Bhargava, Sheila Clancy, and Rinku Lamba.

The book changed a lot when I returned to Canada, in a very different context of colonization, and through the isolation of pandemic lockdowns. I appreciate the support of the Centre for Ethics at the University of Toronto, and I particularly thank Lauren Bialystok, Markus Dubber, and Sergio Tenenbaum, as well as Ben Davis and Shannon Hoff. More thanks to Rahel Jaeggi and Eva von Redecker at the Center for Humanities and Social Change at the Humboldt University in Berlin, and to Nividita Menon at the Centre for Developing Societies in Delhi.

My thanks to Amy Allen, Peg Birmingham, John Borrows, Kristie Dotson, Tanja Dreher, Ann Ferguson, Duncan Ivison, Serene Khader, Rauna Kuokkanen, Kiera Ladner, Bonita Lawrence, Johnny Mack, Lorraine Mayer, Margaret McLaren, Johanna Meehan, Tamara Metz, Anshuman Mondal, Ella Myers, Dory Nason, Robert Nichols, Jana Sawicki, Margaret Toye, Jim Tully, Charles Taylor, Shay Welch, Kyle Powys Whyte, and Cindy Willett. And to a wide and diverse network of Indigenous scholars, activists, and land protectors, whose work of resurgence and resistance sustains the world.

Once again I thank Lucy Randall and Cheshire Calhoun, editors extraordinaire, as well as the lovely Egle Zigaite at Oxford, and Gigi Clement at Newgen.

I am especially grateful to Nathalie Bertin, whose beautiful work, *Round Dance*, graces the book cover.

I began writing this book in the subtropical rainforest of Lavender Bay and Quibaree Park, overlooking Sydney Harbour. I'm grateful to the artists and activists of Lavender Bay, especially Jan Allen, Peter Kingston, and Wendy Whitely, and to the bush turkeys, kookaburras, lorikeets, magpies, tawny frog-mouth owls, the frangipani, jacarandas, bottle brush, jasmine, palm trees and fig trees, and everyone else in this magical place, for keeping me company. I am forever grateful to Cassandra Missio and the Earth and Sky kula. In Toronto, the Singing Out 2SLGBTQIIA+ choir has sustained the joy of life beyond academia.

Finally, as always, I thank all my relations, and especially Rebekah, who knows everything, Lori and Sandra and Waya, for the beach walks and so much more, Kia and Jerry, for ideas and art, and Susan, for the art of life. Carolyn, Mike, Greg, and Tom, for being there always. And Nick and Kaelen, for the most challenging yet sustaining relationships. In memory of my mother, whose commitment to social justice was unwavering, and my father, who always wanted me to do something useful.

Introduction

Decolonizing Freedom

In New York Harbor, at the entrance to the United States of America, stands the Statue of Liberty: *Liberty Enlightening the World*. Liberty stands as a beacon welcoming all to the land of the free, holding a torch and a tablet inscribed with the date of American Declaration of Independence. At her feet lies a broken chain. The ideal of freedom is celebrated as the definitive ideal of modern Western civilization, and it is exported to the world, often by force. Wars and invasions are justified with the claim that we must free the foreign people, whom we will then turn away at our borders. Many are excluded from the ideal of freedom: the American Declaration of Independence was signed by slave owners, and the land that was declared independent was stolen from Indigenous peoples. Indigenous lands and peoples around the world remain colonized, and the practice of Black slavery continues in practices of mass incarceration. The land of the free, like other "developed" nations, polices its borders to keep out unwanted foreigners. Walls are not really necessary. Worldwide, the freedom of some depends on the exploitation and oppression and exclusion of most of the world's people.

None of this should be surprising: in Western thought and practice, freedom has consistently been defined through opposition to the unfreedom of slaves, barbarians, foreigners, and women. The concept of freedom in ancient Greek and Roman societies was defined in opposition to slavery, and those ancient "democracies" excluded women, slaves, and foreigners. The fathers of modern Western philosophy—Hobbes, Locke, Rousseau, Kant, Mill—all defined human freedom through explicit opposition to the "savage peoples" of the Americas and Africa, thus legitimizing colonization and slavery by constructing raced others as not fully human.[1] And as many feminist theorists have pointed out, the freedom of men in the public realm has been enabled by the imprisonment of women, as housewives, and as servants and slaves, in the private realm: women have done the work of caring for children and households so that free men could be free.[2] Thus, as Nancy Hirschmann writes, there is a tension in modern theories of

---

[1] See Mills, *The Racial Contract*; Tully, *Strange Multiplicity*; Williams, Jr., *Savage Anxieties*.
[2] See, for example, Davis, *Women, Race and Class*; Jaggar, *Feminist Politics and Human Nature*; Okin, *Justice, Gender, and the Family*.

freedom between "the theoretical need to define freedom as a universal concept and the political need to exclude most people, including laborers and women, from its expression and enactment."[3] But it's more than a tension. And it's not just a tragic failure of politics to live up to lofty ideals. These are arguably *constitutive exclusions*: in other words, these exclusions are not contingent or secondary to a prior concept of freedom, but they have shaped the ways in which we define what freedom is

The claim that our conceptions of freedom have been produced through constitutive exclusions can be taken to mean that the ideal of freedom is indelibly shaped by exclusions, and that it is therefore irretrievable. That is a metaphysical conception of constitutive exclusions. I do not believe that constitutive exclusions are essential to the concept of freedom. The exclusions that have shaped our conceptions of freedom are historical, and our conceptions of freedom themselves are historical, dynamic, and subject to change. They are also multiplicitous, complex, and conflictual. So I don't agree with those who argue that the concept of freedom is only a justification for domination and exclusion, nor do I think that the concept is owned by Western modernity. That would require that we negate all of the struggles for freedom through history and throughout the world today. We still need to struggle for freedom, but in our struggles, we need to reimagine—and remember—what freedom might be.

Freedom is a contested concept, and it is particularly embattled now. I've opened with the image of the Statue of Liberty because it is a powerful symbol. *Give me your tired, your poor, your huddled masses yearning to breathe free.* Those words are still stirring, and still beckon. But it would be difficult to imagine many of the leaders of the Western world holding the lantern on the Statue of Liberty today. How can we explain the proliferation and popularity of autocratic, sexist, racist, rich, and stupid leaders around the world in the twenty-first century of the Common Era? We need to look very closely at the conceptions of freedom that uphold and perpetuate white male supremacy, the exclusion of foreigners, and capitalist plutocracy. We can begin by considering the common understanding of freedom as negative freedom. We still live in the world of Hobbes, who argued that a strong leader is necessary to the preservation and protection of private freedom—more to the point, that government by authority is preferable to republican democracy, because freedom is defined not as participation in democratic self-governance but as noninterference: the freedom of each individual from any direct constraint, or any support. So dictatorship is fine, as long as I have my private freedom.[4] And private freedom has historically been raced

---

[3] Hirschmann, *The Subject of Liberty*, 70.
[4] In a recent interview, Wendy Brown remarked that the combined emphasis on nondemocratic liberty and authority in the populist politics of the Trump administration was "a peculiar political

and gendered, and propertized: exclusions of women, slaves, and foreigners have been essential to the private freedom of the head of the household.⁵

Freedom from interference in one's private affairs and private property, in conjunction with authoritarian leadership, is the conception of freedom that has been claimed by the right. According to this conception, freedom is fundamentally opposed to equality: freedom and equality can be held together only in a tenuous balance of constant conflict. In contrast, egalitarian movements for freedom from heteropatriarchal ,white supremacist, colonial, and imperial domination and oppression are propelled by an understanding of freedom in relationship with others: no one is free unless all are free. These movements of resistance to oppression appeal to an alternative tradition of political freedom as participation in the social and political life of a society.⁶ And we can find the tradition of freedom in relationship in a wide range of philosophies worldwide, including the European tradition of critical theory.⁷ All of these philosophies are indebted to Indigenous understandings of relational freedoms.

This book takes up Indigenous political theories of decolonization grounded in theories of relationality and resurgence, to re-encounter and reconstruct a tradition of freedom as participation in social and political relations, through a series of dialogic encounters between Indigenous and Euro-American formulations of freedom. I begin by tracing an historical legacy of identification, misperception, and disavowal of Indigenous relational freedoms in modern Western conceptions of freedom. In the context of this history, I re-encounter a tradition of Indigenous relational freedom as a distinctive *political* conception of freedom: a mode of engagement and participation in social and political relations with an infinite range of strange and diverse beings perceived as free agents in interdependent relations in a shared world. As I understand it, Indigenous relational freedom involves meeting strangeness, danger, and conflict with a

---

formation that we've not had before." (Brown, "Where the Fires Are"). But, of course, this peculiar political formation is exactly the one Hobbes envisioned. I discuss this further in Chapter 1.

⁵ The raced and gendered construction of freedom as private property has been complex: in settler colonies, the partial freedom of white women, and their "protection" in the household, has depended on the racialization of populations who threaten the household property. That protection has been complicated, as household property has historically included both white women and Black slaves. On the coloniality of gender, see Lugones, "Heterosexualism and the Colonial/Modern Gender System"; Mendez, "Notes Toward a Decolonial Feminist Methodology"; Wynter, "Unsettling the Coloniality of Being/Power/Truth/Freedom"; McClintock, Imperial Leather; Stoler, Carnal Knowledge and Imperial Power.

⁶ There is, of course, an extensive literature of debates on positive versus negative freedoms in Anglo-European philosophy. My own views have been shaped through readings of the European critical theory tradition, in particular Hegel, Marx, Arendt, and the Frankfurt School, and by Charles Taylor and James Tully, along with feminist, antiracist, postcolonial, and decolonial literatures.

⁷ An earlier incarnation of this book began to explore philosophies of relational freedom in Eastern teaching traditions, Africana philosophies, and Islamic feminist philosophies.

philoxenic ethic oriented toward relations of reciprocity. This is a performative conception of freedom as *world-creation*, guided by an ethic of *grounded normativity* that is learned from *land as pedagogy*, where *land* refers to a system of relationships among interdependent beings in an animate universe.[8] It is learned, then, from engaging with free agents in interdependent relations, and from an interpretation of values inherent in and emergent from this world of relations of power and cooperation among free beings. This is a conception of democratic participation that goes far beyond an understanding of democracy as a politics of contestation, or as rational discourse in a public realm walled off from the private, guided by an ethic of *philia politikē:* friendship among equal citizens united in their sameness. This more expansive conception of democratic participation includes formal rituals of rational discourse and contestation, but it also includes embodied, affective rituals explicitly oriented toward the inclusion of diverse and strange others, employing techniques that address conflict and hostility. This *philoxenic* model extends to all social and political relations as democratic practices: world-creating performances guided by an ethic of exemplarity and an understanding of knowledge as polycentric. Within this worldview, all relations among all beings are social and political relations. Democratic participation includes all beings in a radically heterogeneous and constantly changing world.[9]

The guiding argument of this book is that decolonization, for all of us, depends upon a revaluation of Indigenous philosophies of relational freedom. For many Indigenous theorists and activists, those philosophies guide a politics of decolonization through resurgence. For the rest of us, decolonization involves learning from and with the philosophies and practices of relational freedom in the work of Indigenous philosophers and political theorists, not to appropriate but to encounter a deeply democratic conception of freedom. All of us need to

---

[8] The term *world-creation* is taken from Arendt; *grounded normativity* from Coulthard (*Red Skin, White Masks*); *land as pedagogy* from Betasamosake Simpson (*As We Have Always Done*). The concept of *land* as a system of relationships is arguably definitive of Indigenous philosophies. See, for example, Waters, ed., *American Indian Thought*; McPherson and Rabb, *Indian from the Inside*; LaDuke, *All Our Relations*. Thomas Norton-Smith argues that relatedness and circularity are world-ordering principles in American Indian philosophy, and that performances, including stories and ceremonies, are world-creating acts. "In American Indian traditions, the action, procedure, or performance is the principal vehicle of meaning and the way by which the world is made" (Norton-Smith, *The Dance of Person and Place*). Shay Welch draws on Norton-Smith to analyze Indigenous philosophy as a performative knowledge system (Welch, *The Phenomenology of a Performative Knowledge System*).

[9] McPherson and Rabb argue that polycentrism is "fairly pervasive in Indigenous philosophy" (McPherson and Rabb, *Indian from the Inside*, 121–122). They cite Cree scholar Michael A. Hart's account of the "sharing circle" as a practice of community knowledge production (Hart, "Sharing Circles"). See also Tuhiwai Smith, *Decolonizing Methodologies*; Battiste and Youngblood Henderson, *Protecting Indigenous Knowledge and Heritage*; Kovach, *Indigenous Methodologies*. I discuss the relation between an understanding of knowledge as polycentric and an ethic of exemplarity, and the relation of both to democratic practice, in Chapter 3. See Williams, Jr., *Linking Arms Together*; Ladner, "Governing within an Ecological Context"; Alfred, *Wasáse*.

intelligently combine these formulations with Western and other discourses of freedom, to reimagine what freedom might be.

Indigenous philosophies and political theories of relationality offer modes of addressing difference, conflict, and violence, to develop more democratic relations with each other and with the earth. Relational freedom is a radical democratic practice of engagement in a field of uncertain, unpredictable, changing relations, resisting the will to master and control, resisting the violence toward the other that is a consequence of that will. Indigenous philosophies of relational freedom, then, are central to all forms of decolonization, linking the decolonization of Indigenous lands and people with the decolonization of racialized and gendered economic, social, and political systems of domination.[10]

---

[10] A note on terminology and scope: in this book I generally use the term *Indigenous* but also follow Indigenous scholars' uses of the terms Native, Aboriginal, Amerindian, Indian, and NDN, to refer to people, politics, and philosophies. While all of these terms are problematic generalizations, I follow Indigenous scholars' usages of the terms, and their own generalizations about indigeneity. I draw on a range of scholarship in Indigenous critical theory, including work by philosophers, political theorists, and cultural and social theorists, focusing mainly on work by theorists in Canada but also considering the contributions of theorists in the United States, Finland, Australia, and New Zealand. As Dale Turner notes, given the great diversity of Indigenous knowledge, Indigenous critical theory is developed through a community of Indigenous intellectuals from many nations, all of them in dialogue with one another (Turner, *This Is Not a Peace Pipe*, 10).

The category of the Indigenous is a social construction, produced through colonization, which falsely generalizes and collapses the specificities of thousands of diverse social groups, nations, tribes, communities, and societies around the world. The binary categories of Indigenous and settler are constructions of colonization that obscure histories of "mixing" and interrelations among diverse peoples. These constructions have also produced divisions between status and nonstatus Indians which, of course, did not exist prior to contact. The category of the Indigenous is nevertheless a useful category, used and developed by diverse Indigenous peoples to form solidarities, to develop knowledge, and to make political claims. It is a category taken up in a politics of resistance to a common system of colonization.

The United Nations Working Group on Indigenous Populations, which eventually produced the United Nations Declaration of the Rights of Indigenous Peoples, accepted a preliminary definition by José R. Martínez-Cobo, Special Rapporteur on Discrimination against Indigenous Populations: "Indigenous communities, peoples, and nations are those that, having a historical continuity with pre-invasion and pre-colonial societies that developed on their territories, consider themselves distinct from other sectors of the societies now prevailing in those territories, or parts of them. They form at present non-dominant sectors of society and are determined to preserve, develop, and transmit to future generations their ancestral territories, and their ethnic identity, as the basis of their continued existence as peoples, in accordance with their own cultural patterns, social institutions and legal systems" (Martínez-Cobo, "Study of the Problem of Discrimination Against Indigenous Populations," UN Final Report, 1982).

There is, then, no simple definition of indigeneity. As the Canadian Royal Commission on Aboriginal Peoples affirms, "Aboriginal peoples are not racial groups; they are organic political and cultural entities [that can] change and evolve over time." M. Annette James Guerrero writes: "In a literal sense *indigenism* means to be born of a place, but for Native peoples, it also means to live in relationship with the place where one is born" (Guerrero, "'Patriarchal Colonialism' and Indigenism"). This is an important interpretation. It does not, however, entirely account for the situations of people who have been displaced from their land. Most Indigenous people now live in urban centers—though many do still maintain connections to land. Dian Million writes: "indigenism as both political identity and as lived ways of life includes myriad peoples in all the continents excepting Antarctica, whose societies predate the nation-states that came to surround them." Million understands indigenism as "a current articulation that brings a multitude together in our times.... It is an alternative, active, and

I write as a nonindigenous descendant of settlers—a treaty land inhabitant[11]—and as a critical theorist. Critical theory has been defined as social and political theory oriented toward the realization of freedom.[12] While this book focuses on Indigenous theories of freedom and decolonization, I stress the links to decolonization in its broadest sense: freedom from all forms of colonization and domination. All of us are bound together in the chains of interlocking systems of domination. And while we are all very differently positioned in those systems, no one within those systems is free. The colonizer is not free. The power of wealth and privilege bought at the cost of enslavement of others is a power that enslaves our minds and souls. For all of us, then, the motivation for decolonization can be the desire for freedom. As a settler, I think we have to start with the recognition that we live on stolen land. The response to this recognition is not to wallow in white guilt, but to confront and unsettle what Mishuana Goeman calls *settler creation myths*, to acknowledge that our properties and rights and state are founded on injustice.[13] So we have to work in the present to (re)create relationships. Decolonization involves freeing ourselves from unjust relations, to find our freedom through transformative re-creations of relations of freedom among humans, and among all of the strange beings that inhabit the earth.

Indigenous Relational Freedom

This book aims toward freedom through engagement in dialogical encounters oriented toward mutual recognition and transformative reconciliation, in the spirit of relational freedom. I draw together diverse conceptions of relational freedom in the work of Indigenous philosophers and critical political theorists who articulate individual and political freedoms rooted in attachment to and responsibility for land, in contrast to conceptions of freedom based in ownership of property. In these theories, individual freedom is not located in a binary opposition of private versus public freedom. Individual freedom is not "private," but is found in relations of freedom that connect individual freedoms to political freedoms. Political freedom is not just public but permeates through all relations.

---

mobile set of meanings available in the midst of present globalization, mass diasporas, and multiplicity" (Million, *Therapeutic Nations*, 13).

[11] Cree/Mohawk podcaster Shawn Cuthand has argued that we should all define ourselves as Treaty Land Inhabitants, to avoid rigidifying hierarchical positions. https://www.cbc.ca/news/canada/saskatoon/calling-yourself-a-settler-pov-1.6151582

[12] I discuss this lineage in the Conclusion.

[13] Goeman, *Mark My Words*, 28. For the concept of unsettling, see Tuck and Yang, "Decolonization Is Not a Metaphor."

These freedoms are central to forms of relational sovereignty that ground resistance to colonization.

Indigenous theorists, including Taiaiake Alfred, Glen Coulthard, and Leanne Betasamosake Simpson, argue that freedom from colonization can be found only through a politics of Indigenous *resurgence:* through reconnecting with relations to land.[14] In these formulations, *land* refers to a system of interdependent relationships among all beings. As Winona LaDuke puts it, defining relations with land include "all our relations."[15] Leanne Betasamosake Simpson writes that *Indigenous freedom* is "freedom to establish and maintain relationships of deep reciprocity."[16] This is a freedom forged through love for, attachment to, and responsibility for land: "freedom as a way of being, as a constellation of relationship, freedom as world making, freedom as a practice."[17]

John Borrows writes, "In Anishinaabe tradition, freedom can be characterized by healthy interdependencies, with the sun, moon, stars, winds, waters, rocks, plants, insects, animals and human beings. Freedom is holistic and does not just exist in an individual's mind. It is much more than a product of an individual's will; it is lived."[18] This definition will strike many as a romantic idealization of static harmony ill-suited to modern life, dangerously inattentive to individual freedom, denying the reality of relations of power, and inadequate to theories and practices of freedom in political participation, and in struggles of resistance to oppression.

But they would be wrong. This conception of relational freedom does not affirm a static harmony. It's dependent on an ontology of an animate universe in which all beings are in a constant state of change. Freedom is understood as engagement in change, movement, recalibration, and self-transformation in relationship with all others in an animate universe. This is a *political* conception of freedom that connects individual liberty with public participation and with collective freedom, and grounds politics of resurgence and resistance to colonization.

---

[14] See Simpson, *Dancing on Our Turtle's Back*; Alfred, *Peace, Power, Righteousness*; Coulthard, *Red Skin, White Masks*; Borrows, *Recovering Canada*.

[15] LaDuke, *All Our Relations*. See also Johnston, *Ojibway Heritage*; Wall Kimmerer, *Braiding Sweetgrass*. This understanding of relation to land contrasts starkly with the colonial understanding of land as property. Patrick Wolfe distinguishes settler colonization as the form of colonization that is founded primarily on the acquisition of territory, rather than the extraction of labor. "The primary object of settler-colonization is the land itself rather than the surplus value to be derived from mixing native labour with it" (Verancini, *Settler Colonialism*, 8). Settler colonization works by eradicating the peoples indigenous to the land, through extermination and/or assimilation. Wolfe points out that settler colonization is a defining structure of relations, not an historical event that can be located in the past. See Wolfe, *Settler Colonialism and the Transformation of Anthropology*. See also Deloria Jr., *God Is Red*; Littlebear, "Jagged Worldviews Colliding."

[16] Simpson, *As We Have Always Done*, 163.

[17] Simpson, *As We Have Always Done*, 18.

[18] Borrows, *Freedom and Indigenous Constitutionalism*, 6.

"Within Anishinaabe tradition," Borrows writes, "freedom is not just the absence of coercion or restraint: it is the ability to work in cooperation with others to choose, create, resist, reject, and change laws and policy that affect your life."[19] This understanding of freedom is central to the self-understanding of democracies. James Tully calls this *public autonomy*: the democratic freedoms of members to participate in their society and to enter into democratic negotiations to change the conditions that can be shown to be unjust.[20] In Indigenous relational philosophies, democratic freedoms are not separate from individual liberty, but are connected to a conception of individual freedom that is itself relational. As Borrows writes, "there is no relationship-free place."[21]

Relational freedom is rooted in Indigenous philosophies of *relationality*. For Aileen Moreton-Robinson, Indigenous relationality is an experience of "*the self as part of others and others as part of the self*; this is learnt through reciprocity, obligation, shared experiences, co-existence, co-operation and social memory."[22] Yet this is not a communitarian model in which the individual is embedded in the community and fixed in relationships, as opposed to a liberal model of individual freedom that values autonomy and capacities for change. The imaginary of the Native as fixed in traditional relations in opposition to the liberal subject of freedom is a fantasy of Western modernity. Just as the mature freedom of the modern contracting individual has been constructed against the background of the unfreedom, or merely natural freedom, of barbarous savages, the cosmopolitan freedom of unfixed modern and postmodern individuals has been constructed through an opposition with the idea of the fixed and unchanging Native, who is rooted in place and tradition.[23] Indigenous relationality is a philosophy and politics rooted in relation to land. But relation to land includes relation to the living enspirited world, in all of its diversity and processes of change. The rooted subject is not fixed but is radically heterogeneous, fluid, and in movement *through* its connections. So this is a conception of relational freedom that includes heterogeneity and change while maintaining rootedness in relation to land. Relational freedom is intersubjective: it is rooted in a philosophy of radical relationality and intersubjectivity with all beings in relations of interdependence. This is a philosophy of *rooted dynamism* that supports transformation. Relational freedom includes the ability to transform oneself and to transform

---

[19] Borrows, *Freedom and Indigenous Constitutionalism*, 12.
[20] Tully, *Democracy and Civic Freedom*, 193, 196.
[21] Borrows, *Freedom and Indigenous Constitutionalism*, 10.
[22] Moreton-Robinson, "Towards an Australian Indigenous Women's Standpoint Theory," 341. See also Wilson, *Research Is Ceremony*; Martin, *Please Knock Before You Enter*; Starblanket and Stark, "Towards a Relational Paradigm"; Cajete, *Native Science*.
[23] Denise Ferreira da Silva argues that the modern Western ideal of the self-determined subject is posited against racialized "affectable others" who are subject to both nature and the power of the self-determining subject. See Ferreira da Silva, *Toward a Global Idea of Race*. See also Smith, "Queer Theory and Native Studies."

social relations. Borrows writes: "Freedom is an embodied experience and is evidenced in public settings. It is relational. In Anishinaabemowin such freedom can more particularly be described as *dibenindizowin*, which can mean a person possesses liberty within themselves and their relationships."[24]

Relational freedom is a *political* conception of freedom as participation in relations of interdependence, in a radically diverse and heterogeneous democratic culture. These relations are, of course, not necessarily harmonious. Relational freedom involves engagement in conflict, risk, and danger, in relations of power and relations of oppression. Relations of oppression are, however, understood as violations of ethical relations of reciprocity. A politics of relational freedom, then, is a politics of resistance to colonization.

Glen Coulthard theorizes a decolonial politics of Indigenous freedom through the revaluing and resurgence of ethical and practical relations to land, following an ethic of *grounded normativity*:

> the theory and practice of Indigenous anticolonialism, including Indigenous anticapitalism, is best understood as a struggle primarily inspired by and oriented around the *question of land*—a struggle not only *for* land in the material sense, but also deeply *informed* by what the land *as a system of reciprocal relations and obligations* can teach us about living our lives in relation to one another and the natural world in nondominating and nonexploitative terms—and less around our emergent status as "rightless proletarians." I call this place-based foundation of Indigenous decolonial thought and practice *grounded normativity*, by which I mean the modalities of Indigenous land-connected practices and longstanding experiential knowledge that inform and structure our ethical engagements with the world and our relationships with human and nonhuman others over time.[25]

Isaiah Berlin would have said that the idea of relational freedom is a confusion of values: the only true freedom is negative freedom. Participation in relations of interdependence is something else altogether. From the perspective of negative freedom, an ethics of reciprocity can exist only in tension with freedom. The concept of freedom should not be burdened with other values. From the standpoint of Indigenous relational freedom, the ideal of freedom as only noninterference is an ideal situated within and burdened by an ethics of self-interest rooted in the ownership of self as property and in an understanding of relations as threats: as Hobbes acknowledged, this is a freedom based in fear.

---

[24] Borrows, *Freedom and Indigenous Constitutionalism*, 6.
[25] Coulthard, *Red Skin, White Masks*, 13.

Freedom has been defined in many ways. Others have argued that true freedom is autonomy, or action, or capacities for choice, or agonistic participation in relations of power, or in public discourse and governance, or engagement in resistance, or solidarity, or self-transformation, or realization of an ideal. Some have argued that true freedom is the realization of an ideal of equality, or collective emancipation, or unity with divine spirit. Through this book I shall consider the ways in which the vision of freedom in relations of interdependence in Indigenous relational philosophy includes a range of freedoms, including a form of individual freedom from interference very different from the one that Hobbes imagined, not as the end point but as a component of a more expansive freedom. This more expansive vision supports practices of freedom in diverse powers of embodied action and participation, in collective practices of public freedom, just as it has grounded democratic systems. It grounds a powerful critique of the violation of relationships, which motivates and sustains struggles of resistance to oppression. It supports struggles for individual rights to inclusion and participation, and theories of distinct and overlapping national sovereignties understood as relations of responsibility. Finally, it offers a normative ideal of freedom in nonoppressive mutually supporting relationships, and it affirms reparative practices of freedom through engagement in relations of power. It's this conception of relational freedom that grounds a critique of colonization and state sovereignty, a critique of colonial regimes of racialized heteropatriarchal capitalism, a politics of resurgence and a politics of transformative reconciliation.

Relational freedom is perhaps the only conception of freedom that will allow us to survive, and to flourish, as a species. Environmentalists have shown that the species that have gained power through competitive struggles for domination are the ones that are dying out. The species that are surviving are those that rely on interdependence.[26]

Genealogies of Freedom

So far I've told two stories: modern Western ideals of freedom have been produced, in part, through constitutive exclusions; in contrast, Indigenous philosophies describe a distinctive conception of relational freedom, which is the source of a politics of resurgence. This contrast is complicated by two important theories of the development of modern Western concepts of freedom, both of which trace that development to the influence of the exemplary politics of subjugated peoples.

---

[26] I thank Sheila Clancy for this argument from Brown, *Emergent Strategy*, 2017. See also Red Nation, *The Red Deal*.

Contrary to the claim that the ideal of freedom has been bestowed upon backward peoples by modern Westerners, Orlando Patterson has argued that the Western ideal of freedom is an ideal born of slavery. Patterson traces the concept of individual freedom, which he argues is a definitively Western ideal, to the slave societies of classical Greece and Rome. "Who were the first persons to get the unusual idea that being free was not only a value to be cherished but the most important thing that someone could possess? The answer, in a word: slaves. Freedom began its career as a social value in the desperate yearning of the slave to negate what, for him or her, and for nonslaves, was a peculiarly inhuman condition."[27] More recently, Susan Buck-Morss has argued that Hegel's narrative of the master-slave dialectic as the definitive account of the human struggle for freedom was influenced by the news of the Haitian revolutions, first against slavery and then against French colonization. These uprisings were unprecedented: for the first time in history, a slave society successfully overthrew its ruling class.[28]

These arguments suggest that the ideal of freedom prized as the definitive modern Western ideal actually originated with those who were enslaved, and who struggled against the system of slavery. In other words, Marx's understanding of revolutionary freedom may have been influenced by the actual rebellions of subjugated peoples. Our ideals of freedom, then, are not the products of an enlightened progression to a more advanced civilization, but are the effects of struggle within relations of power. The ideal of freedom is born of oppression, and of resistance to oppression. And philosophies of freedom develop out of these struggles.

Patterson argues that prior to the institution of slavery, the ideal of freedom did not exist in most of the world's ancient societies, which valued communal belonging: individual freedom could be understood only as licentiousness, as an aberration, and a threat to the cohesion and survival of the community. Patterson's narrative, then, is still a narrative of progress from a state of unfreedom to an ideal of freedom. While it is probably true that the conception of freedom as freedom from bondage arose in slave societies, and that the ideal of freedom as personal liberty without constraint is a definitively Western European ideal, Indigenous philosophies suggest that a distinctive understanding of freedom in relationship is embodied in individual and collective practices not dependent on the contrast with slavery.

Political historians have argued that the Indigenous peoples of the Americas were *exemplars of liberty*, confronting European settlers with forms of individual and political freedom unprecedented in the Western world, and that these models strongly influenced the new American and European ideals of

---

[27] Patterson, *Freedom in the Making of Western Culture*, 10.
[28] Buck-Morss, *Hegel, Haiti, and Universal History*. See also Olson, *Imagined Sovereignties*.

individual freedom and democratic freedom.[29] Reports of Jesuit missionaries and "travellers' tales" that were widely disseminated and extremely popular in Europe described peoples whose individual freedom and democratic forms of governance were quite startling to European observers. Such reports shifted uneasily between horror at licentiousness, violence, and depravity, and admiration of autonomous individuation, nonhierarchichal orders, reasoned discourse, and democratic governance. Also reported were Amerindians' perceptions of the vulgarity of the Europeans, some of whose skills of reasoning, discourse, and conflict resolution were found to be lacking.[30]

The influence of these encounters with Indigenous freedoms on American settlers and Europeans is well documented—but typically disavowed. The encounters certainly influenced modern Western conceptions of freedom. The encounter with Indigenous democracies clearly influenced American democratic ideals, practices, and institutions, and clearly influenced the framing of the U.S. Constitution.[31] European philosophers, including Engels and Montesquieu, cited the influence of Indigenous egalitarian freedoms on their own thinking, as did American suffragists, including Matilda Joslyn Gage and Elizabeth Cady Stanton.[32] But the influence of encounters with Indigenous freedoms on the history of philosophy and political theory, and on popular American and European conceptions of freedom, is more complicated.

If modern Western ideals of freedom have been influenced both by resistance to oppression and by encounters with forms of positive freedom, this complicates the story of the development of the ideal of freedom through constitutive exclusions. This book argues that Euro-American ideals of freedom are produced in part through identifications with the (typically misperceived) freedom of Indigenous peoples, along with a disavowal of that emulation: a disavowal of the freedom of Indigenous peoples as anything other than savage freedom. If Indigenous freedoms have been misperceived as primitive, savage freedoms, then Euro-American ideals of freedom have been produced in part through a peculiar combination of emulation, romantic idealization, fear, and disavowal. This is the complicated history of colonial unknowing.[33]

---

[29] Grinde and Johansen, *Exemplar of Liberty*.

[30] Some of this is documented in Graeber and Wengrow, *The Dawn of Everything*, published just as I was completing final revisions to this book. Graeber and Wengrow argue that historical records leave no doubt that Western conceptions of freedom are indebted to encounters with Indigenous societies in the Americas.

[31] For a review of the evidence, see Stubben, "The Indigenous Influence Theory of American Democracy."

[32] Grinde and Johansen, *Exemplar of Liberty*; Wagner, ed., *The Women's Suffrage Movement*.

[33] The concept of colonial unknowing draws on analyses of epistemic ignorance as an active disavowal of conquest and of systems of domination. As Charles Mills writes, "*white misunderstanding, misrepresentation, evasion, and self-deception on matters related to race* are . . . in no way *accidental*, but *prescribed* by the terms of the Racial Contract, which requires a certain schedule of

Critical Theories, Contract Theories, and Colonial Unknowing

Critiques of negative, atomistic, and liberal conceptions of individual freedom have, of course, been central to the traditions of continental philosophy and critical theory, as well as feminist theory. As critics of liberal individualism since Hegel have noted, the early modern social contract theories are based on a strange conception of history: society is born of freely contracting individuals, who are fundamentally atomistic, independent, and competitive. Feminist theorists have pointed out that such individuals seem to have been born without mothers, and without dependency.[34] The critique of the Hobbesian assumption that individuals are fundamentally competitive, and rationally agree to social contracts to ensure their own survival, and the critique of the Lockean conception of the self as property, in contractual conceptions of self-ownership—what C. B. Macpherson has called *possessive individualism*—was central to Marx's critique of capitalism. Marx argued that these modern understandings of the individual were products of capitalist relations of power.[35] Critical theories draw on this legacy to analyze the social and political constitution of modern individuals, and to theorize the freedoms of interdependent social and political beings.

Yet the traditions of European critical theory have been insufficiently attentive to the grounding of modern and liberal theories of the individual and of individual freedom in constitutive exclusions of the savages and barbarians of the world beyond Europe. Hence they have been insufficiently attentive to the ways in which these theories work to justify colonization and slavery, through racialized discourses that justify white possession.[36] Hobbes's inaugural image of the state of nature was inspired by stories of the "savages in many places in America." The image of wild unconstrained freedom in the state of nature—the

---

structured blindnesses and opacities in order to establish and maintain the white polity" (Mills, *The Racial Contract*, 19). See also Sullivan and Tuana, eds., *Race and Epistemologies of Ignorance*. Vimalassery, Hu Pegues, and Goldstein argue that "Colonial unknowing endeavors to render unintelligible the entanglements of racialization and colonization, occluding the mutable historicity of colonial structures and attributing finality to events of conquest and dispossession" (Vimalassery, Hu Pegues, and Goldstein, "On Colonial Unknowing," 1). See also Dotson and Whyte, "Environmental Justice, Unknowability, and Unqualified Affectability" and Whyte, "Settler Colonialism, Ecology, and Environmental Injustice." Here I am arguing that colonial unknowing is a practice of disavowal of relationship to peoples designated as savages. This practice produces colonial conceptions of freedom through disavowing the relation of conquest, and disavowing relational freedom. I develop this argument in Chapters 1 and 4.

[34] For example, Jaggar, *Feminist Politics and Human Nature*; Held, "Non-contractual Society"; Benhabib, *Situating the Self*; Kittay, *Love's Labor*.
[35] Macpherson, *The Political Theory of Possessive Individualism*.
[36] See Moreton-Robinson, *The White Possessive*. See also Robinson, *On Racial Capitalism*; Gilmore, *Change Everything: Racial Capitalism and the Case for Abolition*; Bhambra, "Decolonizing Critical Theory?"

condition that *could* be produced in a lawless state, and that *did* exist (he thought) among the savages in America—was one of the threats that motivated Hobbes's argument that freedom must be constrained by a strong sovereign authority. As Charles Mills has argued, each of the contract theories, as well as the liberal theories of Kant and Mill, similarly relied on constructions of the savage as the negative background, contrasting with and hence shaping ideals of civilized freedom. Robert Nichols argues that contract theories work to erase the actual violence of colonization, erasing the relationship between conquest and sovereignty, to produce the myth of the *settler contract*. The settler contract, he argues, is "the strategic use of the fiction of a society as the product of a 'contract' between its founding members when it is employed in these historical moments to displace the question of that society's actual formation in acts of conquest, genocide and land appropriation."[37] In other words, contract theories disavow colonial relations of conquest and domination.

In his powerful argument for American freedom from monarchist rule, Locke had to somehow justify the theft of the lands already inhabited by the Amerindians. He did this by arguing that ownership of property—an extension of ownership of self—depended upon working the land—or, as he put it, mixing one's labor with the land. And he argued that the Amerindians did not do this. Here he invoked the fantasy (which in fact he knew to be untrue) of a lawless freedom of wild roaming people who did not cultivate the land. While he acknowledged that they did do a bit of cultivation, he argued that what they did was insufficient to qualify for property claims. He argued, further, that since they had no property, and hence no property disputes, such people had no need for European forms of political government, and hence no political liberty and no claims to sovereignty. Thus, as James Tully has argued, Locke's conceptions of political freedom and sovereignty rely on contrasts with Indigenous savagery.[38]

By now it should not be necessary to point out that these images were inaccurate. At the time of colonial encounter, Indigenous peoples did have sophisticated systems of local and international political governance.[39] And they did in fact work the land, cultivating crops, and working with a systematic and detailed knowledge of land far more sophisticated than the rudimentary understanding of the settlers. In a memorable scene in Kate Grenville's novel *The Secret River*, the

---

[37] Nichols, "Indigeneity and the Settler Contract Today," 168. For a different argument, see Pateman, "The Settler Contract."

[38] Tully, *An Approach to Political Philosophy: Locke in Contexts*. See also Williams, *The American Indian in Western Legal Thought*.

[39] See, for example, Warrior, *Tribal Secrets: Recovering American Indian Intellectual Traditions*; Wilkins and Kiiwetinepinesiik Stark, *American Indian Politics and the American Political System*; Borrows, *Recovering Canada*; Bell and Val Napoleon, *First Nations Cultural Heritage and Law*; Asch, *On Being Here to Stay*; Cameron, Sari Graben and Val Napoleon, *Creating Indigenous Property*; Watson, *Aboriginal Peoples, Colonialism, and International Law*; Alfred, *Peace, Power, Righteousness*.

Aborigines watch, incredulous and disgusted, as the settlers tear out all of their food, to grow English potatoes. Unable or unwilling to listen to the Aborigines' attempts to explain, the settlers spend days and weeks laboring in the hot sun, only to find that the crops, unsuited to the land and its climate, fail.[40]

While Locke understood land as property, Indigenous peoples have had very different understandings of land. In Indigenous philosophies, individuals do not own the land; they belong to the land. And land is understood expansively to encompass all of the relationships among humans and all beings in the natural world. So in contrast to an understanding of individual freedom in self-ownership, Indigenous conceptions of individual freedom are based in an understanding of belonging to land as relationality. And this conception of freedom grounds decolonial struggles. As Coulthard writes, contemporary Indigenous struggles for freedom from colonization are rooted in an understanding of *land as a system of reciprocal relations and obligations*—land as relationality.

Just as Locke's justification of settler colonization was predicated on a disavowal of the reality of Indigenous inhabitation and cultivation of land, and of Indigenous political governance, contractualist conceptions of individual freedom are predicated on a disavowal of Indigenous freedom in relation to land: a disavowal of Indigenous relational freedom, which is misrecognized and reimagined as primitive natural freedom. The early European settlers were in fact very much impressed by the individual and political freedoms of the people they encountered in the "new world." Those freedoms were variously idealized and emulated, feared and disavowed. But they have been very poorly understood.

The failure to attend to this history of disavowals and constitutive exclusions has produced a repetition of this history in the long tradition of critiques of liberal freedoms in critical theory and continental philosophy since Hegel. These critiques advance conceptions of freedom situated in social and political relations; many are relational theories that betray a nostalgia for but disavow an imagined primitive past. We can see this in Hegel's attraction to the worldviews of ancient cultures, and in his insistence on a progressive model of history, and on individual freedom, in the form of autonomy, as the achievement of the modern West. We can see this in the continuation of this insistence in the work of Habermas and Honneth—and in their claims that the regulative norms of Western modernity must be used to adjudicate among contesting claims among people of "other cultures."[41] We can see it when neorepublican and democratic

---

[40] Kate Grenville's novel, *The Secret River*, tells a story of encounter between convict settlers and Aboriginals on the Hawkesbury River in New South Wales, Australia. In Australian law, colonization was justified with the doctrine of *terra nullius*: the land was empty of human inhabitants. This doctrine remained in place until it was successfully challenged by the Mabo case in 1992. For a settler account of Aboriginal agriculture in Australia, see Gammage, *The Biggest Estate on Earth*.

[41] Allen, *The End of Progress*.

theories draw on the ancient Greeks and Romans, but ignore the models of democratic constitutionalism in Indigenous societies. And we can see it also in critiques of Indigenous arguments for political self-determination, when such arguments are uncritically dismissed as essentialist "origin stories," as politics of return to primitive traditions and ethnic nationalisms. In many of these theories it's possible to trace a fear of regression: a dialectic of attraction and repulsion, nostalgia for and disavowal of an imagined primordial past.

Modern theories of freedom typically engage with ancient Greek and Roman understandings of human sociality, citizenship, republicanism, and democracy. Ancient Indigenous thought has rarely been considered. But we cannot understand the transition from ancient conceptions of social being to racialized capitalism and neoliberalism without understanding the disavowal of Indigenous philosophies of relationality: the disavowal of forms of freedom that resist, and continue to resist, regimes of colonization.[42] In Grenville's story, the colonists stubbornly refused to consider a different way of being. To survive, they needed to listen.

Politics of Freedom from Colonization: Resurgence and Reconciliation as Forms of Relational Freedom

Settler states, including Canada, the United States, and Australia, are founded on histories of colonization through genocide and theft of land, through the attempted erasure of relations among people and land, through systems of containment and assimilation, including reservations and residential schools isolating children from families and communities, through banning language and ceremony, through systemic violence and abuse, criminalization and incarceration, through legal doctrines of *terra nullius* and white supremacy, through legislated raced and gendered status categories, replacement of legal and political formations, refusal to make or honor treaties, and subjugation under regimes of state sovereignty and racialized capitalism. Settler states have attempted to displace Indigenous legal systems and nation-to-nation treaties with the sovereignty of the settler state over Indigenous nations and peoples. In legal struggles to reclaim land, Indigenous groups with long histories of relationship to land, where relation to land has been understood as responsibility for land, are forced to comply with the state understanding of land as property, and forced to prove traditional ownership to the state. Under the assumption of state sovereignty, the

---

[42] For accounts of racialized capitalism, see Robinson, *On Racial Capitalism, Black Internationalism, and Cultures of Resistance*; Quijano, "Coloniality of Power, Eurocentrism, and Latin America."

colonizing state that has stolen land and failed to honor treaties decides whether to recognize Indigenous land claims. Against these forms of state colonization, the politics of decolonization involve a wide range of strategies, ranging from direct actions to legal change, some of which can be divided into the categories of politics of reconciliation and politics of resurgence.

Politics of Reconciliation

Politics of reconciliation include *treaty constitutionalism*: negotiations and renegotiations of treaties understood as founding political documents. The practice of treaty constitutionalism has a long history among Indigenous nations on Turtle Island (North America) prior to contact with settlers. For Indigenous nations, treaty constitutionalism is ideally a practice of nation-to-nation recognition, to determine forms of governance and adjudicate claims to land and resources, as well as fulfilment of treaty obligations, including economic and social supports. Treaty constitutionalism can allocate separate territories as well as overlapping sovereignties, and shared as well as sovereign powers.[43] Crucially, a practice of treaty constitutionalism includes the retrieval, revaluation, reinterpretation, and reformulation of Indigenous law, and the recognition of Indigenous law by treating nations.

Politics of reconciliation include many forms of *rights politics*, in appeals to states and to international bodies for recognition. For example: struggles for rights to collective self-determination in appeals to states and to international bodies; struggles for rights to land, resources, economic supports, and autonomous governance; struggles of Indigenous women, 2SQ people, and nonstatus groups for civil and political rights to status, inclusion, and participation in Indigenous communities and organizations. While appeals for recognition of rights are directed to states and to international organizations, these appeals often coexist with an assertion of the primacy of Indigenous natural rights

---

[43] Histories and policies of treaty constitutionalism between Indigenous nations and colonizing states vary significantly in Canada, the United States, Australia, and New Zealand. In Canada and the United States, early treaties recognized the independence of Indigenous nations, but this understanding was overturned in the United States with the Marshall decisions in 1823–1832 and the Indian Appropriations Act in 1871, and in Canada with a series of policies culminating in the Indian Act of 1876. In the United States, Indigenous nations are now recognized as sovereign nations with powers of self-governance, subject to federal law. According to this paradoxical understanding, Indigenous nations are both autonomous nations and "domestic dependent nations." Yet as John Borrows argues, despite the recognition of Aboriginal and treaty rights in the Canadian Constitution Act of 1982, Indigenous tribes have much more autonomy in the United States than in Canada (Borrows, *Freedom and Indigenous Constitutionalism*, chapter 5). Australia made no treaties, and the legal doctrine of *terra nullius* was overturned only in 1992, with the Mabo decision.

that are not dependent on recognition by colonizing regimes. This primacy is affirmed in the United Nations Declaration of the Rights of Indigenous People.

Politics of reconciliation include participation in rituals of reconciliation with the state, oriented toward policy changes. In Canada, these have included The Royal Commission on Aboriginal Peoples (1991–1996), the Truth and Reconciliation Commission focused on the legacy of the residential school system, and the ensuing Apology (2008–2015), and the National Inquiry into Missing and Murdered Women and Girls (2016–2019). These rituals culminate in the production of reports outlining essential policy changes, but they do not typically produce substantial changes in state policy or practice.

Politics of Resurgence

The politics of *resurgence* are opposed to asymmetrical politics of "reconciliation" with states that refuse to relinquish sovereignty.[44] Against forms of "reconciliation" that involve subsumption within the colonizing state, the politics of resurgence can take the form of politics of critique and refusal, rejecting the authority of the state, and refusing the struggle for recognition by the state. Freedom is claimed through a turning away from the state, through an assertion of sovereignty or a transformative praxis, and can be oriented toward abolition of the state. A politics of refusal, however, can still be oriented toward the state, through a focus on negation, separatism, or a politics of resistance. Audra Simpson resists the problematic concept of reconciliation, and advocates a politics of "thoughtful antagonism and contention"—a politics of freedom through engagement in relations of power.[45]

While resistance is essential, resurgence theorists stress that the central focus of a politics of resurgence is the location of freedom in the retrieval and reconstruction and practice of a relational way of being. The focus of resurgent politics is on rebuilding communities, rebuilding ways of life and institutions, rebuilding relations with each other and with land. Resurgence politics include the retrieval and reconstruction of systems of Indigenous law. This shift in focus is central to an effective resistance to colonization. Yet these politics shift the focus away from the state—away from either appeals to state recognition or resistance to the state—toward a transformative ethics and politics of relational freedom.

---

[44] See Coulthard's critique of the politics of recognition, in *Red Skin, White Masks*.
[45] Simpson, "The State Is a Man," 3. On the politics of refusal, see Simpson, *Mohawk Interruptus*. On the politics of turning away from the state, see Coulthard, *Red Skin, White Masks*.

Transformative Reconciliation and Transformative Resurgence

The challenge for settlers is to follow the lead of Indigenous politics of resurgence and reconciliation, to engage in decolonial politics of (re)conciliation with Indigenous peoples, guided by the ethics of reciprocity that is central to grounded normativity: an ethics grounded in an experience and understanding of land not as property but as a system of relations of responsibility that support relational freedoms. John Borrows and James Tully argue for a politics of *transformative reconciliation* empowered by robust practices of resurgence.[46] Against the polarized discourses of a state-centric and state-dominated "reconciliation" and a separatist resurgence that resists engagement with the state, Borrows and Tully argue for a politics of transformation of unjust relationships of dispossession, domination, exploitation, and patriarchy. For Borrows, transformative reconciliation includes the retrieval and reformulation of Indigenous law in combination with the systems of law introduced by European settlers. Borrows argues that Canadian law is already a hybrid of Indigenous, European, and new legal traditions, and that reconciliation requires an expansion and formalization of this hybrid tradition. Transformative reconciliation is not an end state. A politics of transformative reconciliation is an ongoing practice of building and rebuilding relationships. For Borrows and Tully, transformative reconciliation is grounded in the resurgence of Indigenous philosophies of relationship with land. Reconciliation between settlers and Indigenous peoples, then, must be grounded in practices of reconciliation with the living earth.

Transformative reconciliation will need to be informed by a theory and politics of *critical* and *transformative resurgence*. In *Violence on the Land, Violence on Our Bodies: Building an Indigenous Response to Environmental Violence*, the Women's Earth Alliance and the Native Youth Sexual Health Network call for a *transformative resurgence* that foregrounds resistance to all forms of heteropatriarchal colonization, linking the destruction of land to heteropatriarchal violence. A politics of transformative resurgence creates paths to justice through community-based organizing.[47] As Leanne Simpson and Glen Coulthard argue, a *critical* resurgence resists legitimating heteropatriarchal power and racist status definitions as Indigenous traditions, and foregrounds critical interpretation, contestation, and evaluative judgement in the retrieval and reformulation of traditions.[48]

Together, transformative resurgence and transformative reconciliation constitute transformative politics of relational freedom: freedom is found in rebuilding and transforming relations among humans and with the living earth.

---

[46] Borrows and Tully, Introduction to *Resurgence and Reconciliation*, ed. Asch, Borrows, and Tully.
[47] Women's Earth Alliance and the Native Youth Sexual Health Network, *Violence on the Land, Violence on Our Bodies*.
[48] See Coulthard, *Red Skin, White Masks*; Simpson, *As We Have Always Done*.

Contemporary Indigenous activists and political theorists draw on social and political traditions of relational freedom to practice and to theorize alternative presents and futures: formations of social and political governance that resist the specific historical forms of individual freedom and state sovereignty produced through heteropatriarchal and racialized colonization.

Entangled Relations of Colonization

Discourses of reconciliation and resurgence can convey the false impression of a simple binary between colonizer and colonized, settler and Indigenous. Reality, of course, is much more complex. The histories of settler states include multiple waves of migration, including the forced migrations of economic and political refugees and of people traded as slaves. Settler states include diverse peoples with very different relations to the power and sovereignty of the nation, divided by a complexity of power relations along dimensions that include class, gender, ethnicity, religion, citizenship, and racialized status. Indigenous peoples are similarly divided. All of these divisions are crossed by interrelations, mixing, and hybridities among settlers and Indigenous peoples, all of whom are subject to regimes of colonization.[49] Given this complexity, the project of freedom through the resurgence and self-determination of Indigenous nations with particular relations to land can appear to critics as naïve and dangerous nativisms, anachronistic identity politics resistant to modern hybridity and cosmopolitanism, deaf to the competing claims of migrants and racialized groups, and antagonistic toward feminist and queer critiques.

It is certainly true that Indigenous politics of self-determination can be all of these things. Claims to traditional identity are too often used to justify oppression, marginalization, and exclusion on the basis of essentialist gendered and racialized status categories. Essentialist understandings of identity and defensive sovereign borders have been the basis of blood quantum policies used to exclude Indigenous people without official status, as well as racialized ethnic groups and migrants.[50] In Canada, self-determination has been framed by

---

[49] As Mahmood Mamdani argues, colonization has worked through defining difference in order to manage it. See Mamdani, *Define and Rule*. Vimalassery, Hu Pegues, and Goldstein argue that an essentialized settler/native binary obscures the colonial constitution of these categories and occludes the entanglement of settler colonization with broader imperial formations. See Vimalassery, Pegues, and Goldstein, "On Colonial Unknowing." For distinctions between settlers and immigrants, see Mamdani, "When Does a Settler Become a Native?" and Tuck and Yang, "Decolonization Is Not a Metaphor." Tuck and Yang write: "Settlers are not immigrants. Immigrants are beholden to the Indigenous laws and epistemologies of the lands they migrate to. Settlers become the law, supplanting Indigenous laws and epistemologies."

[50] For critiques of these positions and policies, see, for example, Simpson, *Mohawk Interruptus*; Palmater, *Beyond Blood*; Lawrence, *"Real" Indians and Others*; Barker, *Native Acts*; Byrd, *The Transit of Empire*.

Indigenous patriarchal leaders as a struggle for collective rights in opposition to claims of Indigenous women's rights. Sovereignty has been framed as noninterference by the state in the affairs of Indigenous communities.⁵¹ As feminists are too well aware, this understanding of sovereignty has historically supported the right of patriarchal control over women, children, and slaves in the household. In line with this history, male-dominated Indigenous organizations and bands have too often defended their collective rights *over* women and children in their communities. They have defended their arguments with claims to traditional gender roles and authentic Indigenous traditions. They have too often failed to address male violence and abuse in Indigenous communities.⁵²

In response to these injustices, theories and policies of liberal pluralism often assume that any claim to social and political recognition of Indigenous self-determination rooted in collective "tradition" or cultural identity must be subject to liberal normative principles adjudicated by state law, to ensure that individual rights and freedoms are upheld, and that exclusions and oppressions on the basis of gender and race are disallowed.⁵³ For Indigenous peoples, such claims can seem bitterly ironic: as we've seen, the European ideals of individual rights and freedoms have been constituted through modern Western philosophy, political theory, and legal systems through the constitutive exclusion of non-European savages and barbarians.⁵⁴ Colonizing states have been established through denial of the rights and freedoms of Indigenous peoples. And colonial settler states have worked through gendered and racialized systems of governance that have undermined Indigenous women's power and divided populations according to essentialized gendered and racialized status identities, in an attempt to break

---

⁵¹ Joanne Barker argues that since the 1970s, male-dominated Indigenous organizations have defended a conception of Indigenous self-government and sovereignty defined as noninterference by the Canadian government, in resistance to the struggles of Indigenous women for legal rights to belong to their communities. See Barker, "Gender, Sovereignty, and the Discourse of Rights in Native Women's Activism."

⁵² Native Women's Association of Canada, *Aboriginal Women, Self Government and The Canadian Charter of Rights and Freedoms*; McIvor, "Aboriginal Women Unmasked"; Green ed., *Making Space for Indigenous Feminism*; Napoleon, "Aboriginal Discourse: Gender, Identity and Community"; Barker, "Gender, Sovereignty, and the Discourse of Rights in Native Women's Activism"; Sayers et al., *First Nations Women, Governance, and the Indian Act*; Snyder, Napoleon, and Borrows, "Gender and Violence."

⁵³ In Canada, while Section 35 of the 1982 Constitution Act recognizes that Aboriginal peoples have an inherent right to self-governance, Aboriginal self-governance is subject to the Charter of Rights and Freedoms. Self-governance does not include a right of sovereignty. At this point, self-governance is very limited, and it is still subject to the provisions of the Indian Act. As noted earlier (note 37), Indigenous tribes in the United States are recognized as having tribal sovereignty and have extensive powers of self-governance, but these are subject to federal law. Originally recognized as independent nations, Indigenous tribes are now recognized as both autonomous nations and "domestic dependent nations."

⁵⁴ See Coulthard's critique, in *Red Skin, White Masks*, of Benhabib's argument, in *The Claims of Culture: Equality and Diversity in the Global Era*, that the protection of individual rights requires that self-governance must be subject to universal normative conditions adjudicated by state law.

relations among Indigenous people and between people and land.[55] The view that affirmations of traditional collective identities are responsible for problems of oppression and exclusion, and that addressing these problems requires that Indigenous communities must adopt Western rights adjudicated by the state, disavows the agency of the colonizing state that has produced the exclusive and divisive status identities, and transfers that agency to the identities themselves. The argument that state regulation is the solution to Indigenous identity politics assumes that the state is neutral, failing to acknowledge the history of the colonizing state, and the constitution of modern Western values through the explicit exclusion of racialized, primitivized, and gendered others. This argument naturalizes Indigenous traditions and collective identities as oppressive, such that the only solution is Western norms, adjudicated by a Western state. It relies on the assumption of historical progressivism: the assumption that original peoples are backward and primitive, fixed in a historical position of *preexistence*, in the sense of existing in anticipation of and requiring what came later: modern Western civilization and values. Thus their preexistence is naturalized, construed as deficiency in relation to the civilization that they preexist. The view that Indigenous communities must be subject to Western rights relies on the assumption that individual freedom and democracy, equality and inclusion of diversity, are distinctively modern Western values. Against this claim, Indigenous historians, political theorists, and legal scholars are reconstructing long histories of Indigenous democratic and legal systems that systematize rights and responsibilities.[56] Indigenous philosophers argue that individual freedom is a central value in Indigenous ethics.[57] Indigenous feminist and queer critical theorists trace histories of women's power, acceptance of gender fluidity, and inclusion of diversity in Indigenous communities.[58]

If liberal pluralists fail to recognize the historical production of Indigenous identities, many critical theories, including critical legal theories and postcolonial theories, recognize that divisive identities have been produced through regimes of colonization. Theorists who are critical of discourses of individual

---

[55] See all the references in note 50. See also Maracle, *I Am Woman*; Monture, *Thunder in My Soul*; Guerrero, "'Patriarchal Colonialism' and Indigenism"; Suzack, Huhndorf, Perreault, and Barman, eds., *Indigenous Women and Feminism. Politics, Activism, Culture*; Simpson, "The State Is a Man"; Ladner, "Gendering Decolonisation, Decolonising Gender"; Smith and Kauanui, "Native Feminisms Engage American Studies"; Goeman and Denetdale, "Native Feminisms: Legacies, Interventions, and Indigenous Sovereignties"; Deer, "(En)gendering Indian Law"; Kuokkanen, *Restructuring Relations*; Rifkin, *When Did Indians Become Straight?*; Morgensen, "Settler Homonationalism"; Smith, "Queer Theory and Native Studies"; Driskill, Finley, Gilley, and Morgensen, eds., *Queer Indigenous Studies*.
[56] See note 39.
[57] See Brundige, "Ungrateful Indian: Continuity of Native Values"; Cordova, "Ethics: The We and the I"; McPherson and Rabb, *Indian from the Inside*; Welch, "Radical cum Relational."
[58] See all the references in note 52. See also Anderson, *A Recognition of Being*; *Reconstructing Native Womanhood*; Anderson and Lawrence, *Strong Women Stories*; Roscoe, *Changing Ones*; Jacobs, Thomas, and Lang, eds., *Two-Spirit People*.

rights and of the power of the nation state do not affirm Western norms, individual rights, or state power as solutions to the exclusions and internal oppressions of Indigenous nations. But like liberal pluralists, Western critical theorists often perceive claims to Indigenous tradition as claims to false origin stories, and see the politics of self-determination as nativist identity politics, ethnic nationalisms that essentialize and reify identity categories, misconstrue the true sources of domination, and divide and fragment resistance.[59] As Nancy Fraser has argued, these kinds of identity politics are simple affirmations of historically produced identities and are therefore not transformative.[60] As Wendy Brown and Judith Butler argue, identity politics must be resisted in favor of sustained critique.[61]

Indigenous theories and politics of resurgence affirm Indigenous identities—and surely politics of revaluation and affirmation are necessary and important for people whose existence and ways of life have been attacked, suppressed, and reviled as primitive and barbaric. Yet the affirmative/transformative binary is inadequate to account for the politics of resurgence. Contemporary Indigenous critical theorists argue for a critical resurgence that revalues, reinterprets, and reformulates tradition to ground a politics of radical transformation of economies and of social and political life: "a resurgent politics of recognition that seeks to practice decolonial, gender-emancipatory, and economically nonexploitative alternative structures of law and sovereign authority grounded on a critical refashioning of the best of Indigenous legal and political traditions."[62] Critical resurgence resists and transforms the binary of affirmation and critique. Against a simply affirmative politics, and against a politics of critique without a constructive project of transformation, Indigenous resurgence is a politics of transformation rooted in philosophies and practices of relationality and grounded normativity.

Contemporary Indigenous critical theorists reject a politics of self-determination understood as the uncritical affirmation of timeless traditions. They criticize claims to Indigenous traditions that invoke idealized origin stories, recognizing that such stories obscure complex histories and reinscribe colonial fantasies of a state of nature as a state of lost innocence and purity. They reject claims to Indigenous nationhood and self-determination that

---

[59] See Alcoff, *Visible Identities*, for an incisive critique of the antagonism toward identity politics in left critical theories. See also Weir, *Identities and Freedom*. The antagonism toward identity politics can be based on the old leftist understanding of "culture" as mere "superstructure," relative to the economic base. Identity politics are blamed for fragmenting united resistance, for undermining norms of universal equality, for redeploying categories that have been instituted to divide and oppress populations, for fanning the flames of ethnic hostilities and resentments.

[60] Fraser, "From Redistribution to Recognition?" Fraser has developed and modified this argument in multiple dialogues with Axel Honneth, Judith Butler, and others, in her subsequent work.

[61] See, e.g., Butler, *Gender Trouble*; Brown, *States of Injury*.

[62] Coulthard, *Red Skin, White Masks*, 179.

reaffirm Westphalian forms of nation state sovereignty with borders that exclude migrants and raced others. They reject claims to sacred traditions and collective identity that defend heteropatriarchal power and gender norms, and that are used to mask violence against women, children, and 2SQ people. And they reject claims to authority over land as property that are used to defend the construction of gas pipelines as a source of revenue on reserves. They affirm politics of critical resurgence that draw on Indigenous traditions and Indigenous modernities to resist interlocking systems of colonization and oppression.[63]

As Indigenous feminist and queer critical theorists have pointed out, claims to tradition need to be critically analyzed to consider the power relations embedded in those claims. Regimes of patriarchal power, heteropatriarchal gender norms, and racialized status categories are not traditional but have been internalized and reproduced by many Indigenous leaders and organizations. Ironically, Indigenous antifeminist critiques of women's rights as Western rights are based on the same assumption as liberal pluralist and feminist critiques of collective rights: both assume an incommensurability between Indigenous traditions and Western rights and freedoms. Indigenous policies that exclude raced and nonstatus others have taken over the essentialist identity categories that have been used to legitimate colonization. As Audra Simpson points out in her discussion of identity politics in Kahnawà:ke, identities became an issue when tied to resources. "Race became an issue at the time when being Mohawk became being Indian and being Indian carried rights."[64]

The politics of settler colonization are situated within the entangled relations of global racialized patriarchal capitalist imperialism that constitute the nation state. These entangled relations are the formations of what Byrd et al. call *economies of dispossession*: "those multiple and intertwined genealogies of racialized property, subjection, and expropriation through which capitalism and colonialism take shape historically and change over time."[65] As Harsha Walia points out, state borders are instruments of conquest and control that have served historically to contain and discipline Indigenous and racialized populations, and to exclude the unwanted. The policing of these borders is central to the carceral state.[66] This means that the colonization of Indigenous peoples is intimately connected with the modern system of racialized slavery and

---

[63] See Starblanket and Stark, "Towards a Relational Paradigm"; Aikau, Arvin, Goeman, and Morgensen, "Indigenous Feminisms Roundtable"; Simpson and Smith, *Theorizing Native Studies*; Barker, "Critically Sovereign"; Barker, *Native Acts*; Lyons, *X-Marks*; Simpson, *As We Have Always Done*; Altamirano-Jiménez, *Indigenous Encounters with Neoliberalisms*; Vimalassery, Pegues, and Goldstein, "On Colonial Unknowing"; The Red Nation, *The Red Deal*.
[64] Simpson, *Mohawk Interruptus*, 59.
[65] Byrd, Goldstein, Melamed, and Reddy, "Predatory Value."
[66] Walia, *Border and Rule*.

with the establishment of nation states that exclude, marginalize, commodify, and incarcerate racialized migrants. The system of containment of Indigenous populations on reservations and the high rates of incarceration of Indigenous people are central to these systems. And these are deeply connected with heteropatriarchal regimes of gendered and racialized capitalism that claim women and racialized workers and land as property.[67] These entangled relations require integrated critiques to theorize the connections among settler colonization and imperialism abroad, the propertized relations of global capitalism, racial systems, heteropatriarchal dominance, state borders, and techniques of control.

While critique is essential, transforming those relations requires more than critique. Decolonization involves coalitional theorizing and coalitional organizing. Entangled relations of colonization require what Leanne Betasamosake Simpson calls *constellations of co-resistance and freedom* that "refuse and reject dispossession and settler colonialism and the violence of capitalism, heteropatriarchy, white supremacy, and anti-Blackness that maintains them.... to create networks of reciprocal resurgent movements with other humans and nonhumans radically imagining their ways out of domination, who are not afraid to let those imaginings destroy the pillars of settler colonialism."[68] The transformative project of decolonization requires new imaginaries and politics of freedom that can address factional conflicts, to create movements that address the complex and entangled relations of colonization, to imagine and create decolonial futures. To develop these new imaginaries and politics, theorists and activists can draw on Indigenous theories of relational freedom. Transformative theories and transformative *constellations of co-resistance and freedom* can be grounded in critically analyzed traditions of heterogeneous relational freedoms.

Transformative Theories: Heterogeneous Relational Freedoms

Indigenous critical theories, often led by Indigenous women, feminists, and queer theorists, offer relational accounts of several interlinked forms of freedom: theories of the freedom of Indigenous nations, freedom as democratic participation, individual freedoms, and freedom as decolonization. All of these theories constitute freedom in transformative relations, in performative practices of world-creation.

---

[67] von Redecker, "Ownership's Shadow."
[68] Simpson, *As We Have Always Done*, 10. See also Maynard and Simpson, *Rehearsals for Living*.

Relational Freedoms of Nations

Against an understanding of Indigenous nationhood on the model of the Westphalian state as a right to noninterference, with policed borders that protect property rights and exclude noncitizens, Indigenous critical theories led by Indigenous women and queer theorists offer alternative conceptions of nation rooted in theories of relationality and relational freedom. Leanne Betasamosake Simpson draws on elder Doug Williams's understanding of nation as a web of connections to theorize nationhood as *a series of radiating responsibilities*.[69] Kiera Ladner argues for an understanding of collective self-determination that emphasizes taking on relations of responsibility and care for the wellbeing of interdependent individuals and communities.[70] For Patricia Monture, Indigenous struggles for rights to self-determination are struggles for rights to be responsible for land. "I do not know of anywhere else in history where a group of people have had to fight so hard just to be responsible."[71] Nationhood, for these theorists, is a custodial relation to land and to the people and other beings who belong to the land. Rauna Kuokkanen argues for a conception of self-determination—of both nations and individuals—as the restructuring of relations of domination to create more reciprocal relations.[72]

This understanding of nation in terms of responsibility and belonging does not preclude a politics of rights to territory.[73] Kiera Ladner argues that self-determination must combine treaty constitutionalism *and* responsibility for wellbeing. Nor is the custodial conception of nationhood necessarily opposed to ownership of property. Some argue that rights to property can be found in systems of Indigenous law. But this is a very different conception of property from the one that is central to the system of commodity capitalism.

These understandings of nation are rooted in long histories of political relations among polities. Treaties among nations—including the treaties with British settlers—were and are understood as the formal institution of social and political relations. These can be seen as similar to the contractual agreements that are central to Western legal traditions. But Indigenous treaty traditions are grounded in an ontology of the primacy of relations of interdependence rather than of atomistic individual states. The primary emphasis is on creating political

---

[69] Simpson, *As We Have Always Done*.
[70] Ladner, "Understanding the Impact of Self-Determination on Communities in Crisis."
[71] Monture-Angus, *Journeying Forward*, 36.
[72] Kuokkanen, *Restructuring Relations*. See also Bruyneel, *The Third Space of Sovereignty*.
[73] Robert Nichols addresses the apparent contradiction between Indigenous critiques of the understanding of land as property and Indigenous claims of dispossession with a reconstruction of the concept of *dispossession*. In the colonial context, he argues, the concept of dispossession specifies a unique process of the constitution of property through theft. The process of dispossession is one of transference, transformation, and retroactive attribution, according to a logic that he calls *recursive dispossession*. Nichols, *Theft Is Property!*

relations of reciprocity rather than allocating rights of noninterference. Treaties are agreements to be responsible for land, understood capaciously as a system of relations among interdependent beings. Such treaties do allocate areas of noninterference but also allow for nested or overlapping sovereignties.

Against the understanding of the nation as a homogeneous ethnic state, Indigenous critical theorists trace histories of inclusion of heterogeneous relations, organized by kin relations not based on "blood" and marriage. Audra Simpson argues that Indigenous nations are not ethnic or cultural groups but *polities*. Many Indigenous communities were organized around kin systems that included heterogeneous relations: Kahnawà:ke—a community that has instituted blood quantum policies—was historically a heterogeneous community of refugees. "Thus identity was not a problematic, ethical issue, a matter to be confused by. It was not confused with political membership. It was political membership."[74] Jodi Byrd traces systems of *kinship sovereignties* inclusive of *arrivants* as traditions that can accommodate contemporary claims of forced migrants and their descendants.[75] Against understandings of nations founded on sexist, homophobic, and racialized exclusions, Indigenous feminist and queer critical theories trace histories of queer kinship that mirror the heterogeneous relations among diverse beings in Indigenous understandings of land. All of these understandings of the freedom of nations are rooted in philosophies and politics of relationality and relational freedoms.

Relational Democratic Freedoms

Against the assumption that the cradle of democracy can be found in ancient Greece, and that its development is best, if inadequately, realized in European and North American states, Indigenous constitutional theorists and political historians trace traditions of democratic governance and constitutional law that were both intranational and international. Practices of freedom as participation in democratic self-governance include many examples of formal democratic councils in small communities, as well as international treaties and agreements.[76] Indigenous democratic politics also include political systems in which power is dispersed among different groups and individuals. In Chapters 2 and 3, I argue that Indigenous democracy encompasses not just the relations of political friendship among equals that Aristotle called *philia politikē*, but *philoxenic* engagements with diverse and strange beings. Democratic practice combines

---

[74] Simpson, *Mohawk Interruptus*, 48.
[75] Byrd, *The Transit of Empire*.
[76] See the references at note 39.

both reasoned discourse and embodied rituals of philoxenia that consciously address conflict and danger. Democracy can be seen more expansively as a way of life in which formal practices of democratic governance are supported by performative rituals of world-creation, which include both formal rituals and daily relations that are understood as ceremony. Democratic politics are, moreover, supported by the education and socialization of individual agents as participants in interdependent relations. Children are raised to understand themselves as social and political beings who are responsible for relations.

Relational Individual Freedoms

Against the understanding of individual freedom as an intrinsically Euro-American or modern Western liberal ideal, Indigenous philosophers argue that many Indigenous communities have supported the development of individual freedom and autonomy through forms of education and socialization that support social responsibility and nonconformist individuation. Individual freedoms are relational freedoms—neither liberal nor communitarian, neither rootless nor fixed—enacted through participation in changing relations.[77] This understanding of individual freedom is the basis of unique conceptions of rights: in Chapter 5, I argue that Indigenous feminist theorists and activists in Canada have drawn on long traditions of relationality to formulate *relational rights*: rights to inclusion and participation in their communities. Relational rights also support individual bodily sovereignty and resistance to heteropatriarchal violence, through critiques of violations of relationship.

Relational Freedom as World-Creation

These understandings of nationhood, democratic governance, and individual freedom are interrelated forms of *political* freedom. Freedom is understood as a transformative performance that creates relationships, to re-create the world. This world-creative conception of freedom is rooted in the ontology and ethic of a gift economy: an understanding of the world as a circle of relations forged through acts of generosity. Dance, ritual, and story are exemplary performances that create and re-create meaning, create and re-create the world, through risking connection with strange and often hostile others.[78]

---

[77] See the references at note 57.
[78] See the references at note 8. These arguments are developed in Chapters 2 and 3.

Encountering Indigenous Relational Freedoms

This book takes the form of a series of encounters between Indigenous relational freedoms and definitive "Western" conceptions of freedom, engaging these diverse conceptions in dialogue, to shift and rethink our collective understandings of what freedom might mean. Chapter 1 traces a legacy of the Hobbesian conception of freedom as noninterference, arguing that this is a tradition of colonial unknowing rooted in a disavowal of relational freedoms. Chapter 2 takes up conceptions of relational freedom as collective participation in social and political life. For Hannah Arendt, freedom as collective participation was motivated by *amor mundi*: love of the world. This chapter argues that the understanding of love of land articulated by Leanne Betasamosake Simpson can be seen as the expression of a more radical form of political freedom as democratic participation. Chapter 3 develops a conception of freedom as a performative practice of world-building, focusing on the round dance as a ritual of embodied, affective collective love—philoxenia—that enacts a radically democratic practice through techniques of inclusion of the other. In a brief Excursus, I trace the etymological lineage of the connection between freedom and collective love. Chapter 4 addresses misperceptions of Indigenous relational freedom. Against the understanding of relational traditions as fixed essentialisms rooted in homogeneous communitarian regimes, and against racialized and heteropatriarchal identity politics, this chapter draws on critical Indigenous theories of rooted dynamisms and polycentric knowledges that ground democratic freedoms characterized by the dispersal of power and inclusion of diversity and otherness, to address entangled relations of colonization. Chapter 5 argues that Indigenous women struggling for rights to belong to their communities and to participate in governance have developed unique conceptions of relational rights that bridge the opposition between theories of rights and theories of resurgence. In the Conclusion, I propose a model of critical theory as a practice of freedom through transformative encounters with the other. Throughout, I employ a model of argument as dialogue, to facilitate transformative relations of knowledge and freedom.

In Chapter 1, I take up the legacy of the Hobbesian conception of freedom as noninterference, to situate it in relation to Indigenous relational freedom. Hobbes's formulation of freedom inaugurated a long tradition of colonial unknowing: defining a central concept of modern Western social and political thought through a disavowal of relations to Indigenous peoples. Freedom is formulated in a way that disavows conquest, disavows relations of power, and disavows Indigenous knowledge and politics of relationality and relational freedom.

The concept of freedom as noninterference has dominated modern Western understandings of individual and political freedom since Hobbes argued that it was the only true form of freedom. His conviction was echoed by Isaiah Berlin, who wrote that noninterference is the only form of freedom worthy of the name. In this tradition, individual freedom is opposed to relations of equality, and to democracy. As Quentin Skinner and Philip Pettit have pointed out, the irony is that Hobbes argued for the conception of freedom as noninterference against British republicans, in support of monarchist rule. The work of Skinner and Pettit has sparked a revival of republican theories of freedom, affirming an understanding of individual and political freedom as a status in a relation of nondomination. But while they trace a history that situates Hobbes's conception of freedom as an act of resistance to early British republicanism, Skinner and Pettit do not consider the significance of Hobbes's argument as a response to another competing ideal of freedom: the popular ideal of Indigenous relational freedom.

Drawing on Michel Foucault and Robert Nichols, and on William Brandon, Robert A. Williams Jr., and Grinde and Johansen, I suggest that the concept of freedom as noninterference works for Hobbes both to disavow the conquest of the Amerindians, and to disavow Indigenous relational freedom. It does this by disavowing relationship with the savages, and by disavowing relationship altogether. And I suggest that modern American ideals of individual freedom as noninterference are shaped in part through both romantic idealization and constitutive exclusion of the perceived natural freedom of the Amerindians.

For the early American settlers and European missionaries, Indigenous peoples were exemplars of unprecedented freedoms: their practices of individual freedom and democracy served as models for these "new" American values, which became definitively Western Euro-American ideals. In two late essays, Iris Young recognized this influence and argued that contemporary Indigenous claims for self-determination are grounded not in a conception of freedom as noninterference but in conceptions of freedom in relationship. To explicate this form of freedom, Young turns to Pettit's neorepublican theory of nondomination. I argue that both Young and Pettit, while explicitly arguing against a conception of freedom as noninterference, ultimately reduce freedom as nondomination to noninterference. This reduction, I argue, is an effect of a failure to seriously consider and learn from Indigenous philosophies and political theories of relational freedom.

As I understand Indigenous relational theories, noninterference is not the endpoint or essence of freedom, but is one aspect of a philosophy and practice of freedom as participation in interdependent relations. Individual autonomy, democratic governance, and the sovereignty of nations within international relations are interrelated forms of social and political participatory freedoms. For understandings of Indigenous relational freedom, I turn to Indigenous philosophy and political theory, including theories of relational autonomy and individual freedom (Dennis McPherson, Douglas Rabb, and Lorraine Mayer), relational traditions of democratic governance and law (Robert A. Williams Jr., John Borrows, and Val Napoleon), relational conceptions of sovereignty (Patricia Monture, Leanne Betasamosake Simpson, Robert A. Williams Jr., Robert Warrior, Wallace Coffey, and Rebecca Tsosie) and conceptions of freedom as resurgence (Taiaiake Alfred, Glen Coulthard, and Leanne Betasamosake Simpson). All of these theorists elucidate conceptions of relational freedom that ground struggles of first peoples for resistance to colonial rule.

Indigenous relational theories, practices, and institutions support understandings of political freedom as participation in relations of interdependence. This alternative understanding of freedom can be found in a long tradition of European critical theories of freedom as participation in democratic relations. Against conceptions of freedom as noninterference, and against freedom as a status of mastery or equality, Hannah Arendt argued that human beings are most free when they act creatively together in public political life. For Leanne Betasamosake Simpson, Indigenous freedom is a practice of engagement in relations with land, where land is the web of relations that connect all beings. Simpson describes Indigenous resurgence as a practice of freedom grounded in love for land. Chapters 2 and 3 consider relational freedom as a practice and politics of love for land, understood as a web of relations among an infinitely diverse range of strange and free beings. Relational freedom, then, is a world-creative *philoxenic* freedom that facilitates radically democratic participation in interdependent relations.

In Chapter 2, I consider the connections between Leanne Simpson's formulation of freedom through love for land and the concept of *amor mundi*—love of the world—as the spirit of political freedom in the work of Hannah Arendt. To mediate between Arendt's and Simpson's conceptions of love and freedom, I take up Ella Myers's linking of democratic politics to an ethic of care for the world. Myers draws on Arendt's *amor mundi* to define a *worldly ethics* as the ethos or spirit of care for the world that animates political engagement in contesting and associative relations concerning matters of concern in the public world. Myers expands Arendt's conception of world to displace human beings from the center, and rejects the distinction between world and earth, to include the webs of relations among beings and things that constitute the conditions of life on earth. But she rejects Latour's and Bennett's extension of agency to include nonhuman actants, and retains a focus on the world as it appears for human beings. In Simpson's conception of *land as pedagogy*, humans develop knowledge and ethics by learning from land—from nonhuman agency. Love as the ethos of freedom doesn't originate in humans but circulates in gift relations among radically heterogeneous beings. Love of land as active participation in reciprocal relations of gift giving expands the mediating role of world to include a plurality of agentic relations.

Political contestations between Indigenous people and colonizing states over the meanings of *land* challenge divisions between human and nonhuman agency, and between public and private care. They also challenge what we mean by nation, by love of nation, and by freedom as national sovereignty. Against Arendt's understanding of love of nation as merely self-interest, and against state freedom as a propertized freedom that assumes the right to destroy, Simpson formulates nationhood as *a series of radiating responsibilities*. I suggest that transformative reconciliation requires an ethics of philoxenic solidarity among heterogeneous beings, a risky politics of care for the wellbeing of diverse others and for the web of relations that connect us.

In a brief *coda*, I consider Arendt's resistance to James Baldwin's connection between freedom and love. Arendt's ambivalence about the role of love in politics is perhaps typical of a common failure to clearly distinguish among forms of love and their relations to freedom. Baldwin's essay offers a distinction between a privatizing and destructive love and a love of freedom.

If love of land is a practice of freedom, it's a practice of *philoxenic* freedom: freedom through love of the strange others with whom we share and co-create the world. Chapter 3 considers the histories and meanings of the round dances that are often performed as part of Indigenous resistance movements, to argue that the dance works to support political resistance by enacting philoxenic relational freedom. Round dances, along with other forms of dance, ritual, and ceremony, were banned by settler states for a good reason: they challenged the order of colonization by performing another way of being. Danced rituals are world-creating performances that challenge hierarchy and domination to enact a dangerous political freedom: freedom in relationality.

Hannah Arendt had originally sought the grounding for a politics of public freedom in philosophies of love.[79] But while love of the world continued to be a touchstone in her work, she ultimately rejected most forms of love as unpolitical and unworldly, and dangerous. The exception was *philia politikē*, or political friendship, which Arendt supported as the public bond that could sustain democracy. Yet the political friendships among equals in the Greek polis were highly exclusive, in a way that is too often mirrored in modern democracies. In contrast to *philia politikē*, *philoxenia* is a form of political friendship that includes the stranger, the normally excluded, the marginal and oppressed. Rituals of relationality can be understood as rituals of an embodied and affective philoxenic freedom: a freedom that includes a diverse range of strange others. Against a naïve view of democratic discourse as honorable contestation among friendly and equal individuals—and against a cynical view of democracy as only a game of power—the danced rituals directly address and work through fear and

---

[79] See Arendt, *Love and Saint Augustine*.

hostility toward the other, to work through conflict and forestall violence, domination, and exclusion. Such rituals are supportive of and in some ways more effective than the rituals of agonistic discursive politics.

Round dances can be located within a larger history of circle dance rituals common to ancient and continuous cultures throughout the world. Barbara Ehrenreich draws on Victor Turner's understanding of ritual as a form of *communitas* that creates and sustains social bonds, to theorize rituals as practices of collective love. But this analysis misses the distinctive forms of love and freedom that characterize the round dance. And it misses the performative role of ritual emphasized by Thomas Norton-Smith: ritual is a practice of world-creation. It misses, then, the political role of the dance as a creation of relations among free beings who are strange to each other—and to themselves.

I consider Cree stories of the meanings of the round dance in light of Julia Kristeva's Kleinian psychoanalytic theory, to analyze how the round dance works to bridge the worlds of the living and the dead, and to repair the division between good and bad objects, to enact the inclusion of the mother, and the other, in public political life. The inclusion of the other is performed also in masked dances in which the dancer dances the dance of another being—a spirit or animal. This is an embodied practice of shifting perspective by becoming the other: it performs a decentering of the self, both to experience the world from the body of the other, and to experience the otherness, the strangeness of oneself. Such rituals enact an ethics of exemplarity: being the change by becoming the other. And all of the dances are skilled techniques of the ethics of exemplarity—being the change by performing the creation of the world. They are practices of *philoxenic solidarity* that involve not just welcoming others in—not just hospitality—but opening out, to displace oneself, to locate oneself in a larger world.

Chapters 2 and 3 develop connections between a politics of freedom and exemplary practices of love of land. Following these chapters, in a brief *Excursus*, I take up a surprising and generally unremarked connection in the genealogy of the concept of freedom: the etymological connection between freedom and love.

Chapter 4 argues that colonial unknowing works to delegitimize Indigenous claims to land in part by disavowing philosophies and political systems of relationality and relation to land as alternative formations of knowledge, power, and freedom. If colonization is dependent on a disavowal of legitimate claims to land, then it is tied also to dismissal and rejection of the philosophies and politics of rooted relationality that ground those claims. This chapter addresses misperceptions of Indigenous philosophies and politics of relation to land as essentialist affirmations of fixed and homogeneous traditions. Against these misperceptions, Indigenous critical theories formulate relations to land in philosophies and politics of heterogeneous relationalities and rooted dynamisms. This chapter takes up formulations of heterogeneous relationalities in interrelated theories of knowledge, freedom, identity, and political governance, to argue that a polycentric understanding of knowledge as dispersed among interdependent beings and an understanding of freedom as participation in relations of interdependence support a radically democratic politics. Decolonization, then, involves revaluing and regenerating Indigenous knowledges and politics of heterogeneous relationalities.

This chapter is divided into four parts. The first part argues that undermining systems of relationality is central to breaking relations to land. As Indigenous feminist and queer scholars have shown, the establishment of patriarchal regimes of governance that undermine the political power of women in relation to land, the racialized and gendered division of populations, the institution of the manageable heteropatriarchal nuclear family, and the calculated destruction of intimate relationships have served as policies of elimination to undermine alternative political orders of relationality in which power is dispersed and heterogeneous.

The second part takes up polycentric conceptions of knowledge, and the normative knowledge practices and values grounded in an understanding of the world as a system of interdependent relations. In contrast to conceptions of knowledge and intellectual freedom as dependent on skeptical and disembedded critique, an understanding of knowledge as dispersed among a diversity of interdependent beings supports a radically democratic politics.

The third part addresses the understandings of self and collective identity that emerge from relational understandings of knowledge and world, to distinguish between fixed essentialisms and rooted dynamisms. The assumption that freedom is opposed to rootedness legitimates the propertized freedom of settlers who relate to land only as commodity, while denying the basis of Indigenous claims to land: relational freedom. Against conceptions of individual freedom that are opposed to rootedness, I draw on feminist and queer critical Indigenous theories to articulate a relational conception of self that is both rooted in place and heterogeneous and in process, precisely because it is rooted in the radical relationality of an entirely animate universe. Against assumptions that Indigenous collective identities are necessarily rooted in racialized essentialisms and patriarchal traditions, Indigenous critical theories formulate Indigenous nations as heterogeneous polities.

The fourth part addresses the entangled politics of colonization, heteropatriarchal domination, racialized capitalism, and exclusive state borders, to argue that a coalitional politics can be grounded in Indigenous political traditions of heterogeneous relationalities. Against the claim that Indigenous traditions are essentially patriarchal and homogeneous, Indigenous critical theorists point to Indigenous political traditions of inclusion of heterogeneity and diversity. Traditions in which power is dispersed can challenge hierarchical regimes, and traditions of inclusion of strangers can support negotiations of relations with racialized and migrant *arrivants*. These histories can guide the formation of alliances in coalitional struggles for decolonization.

Chapter 5 considers the struggles of Indigenous women against the historical violation of their rights to belong to their communities in Canada, to argue that Indigenous women have formulated unique conceptions of relational rights. In Canada, the "Indian problem" has historically been managed through governance practices that divide populations by racialized identities and by gender. The systematic disempowerment of Indigenous women has been central to the strategy of erosion of Indigenous relations to land, and the weakening of capacities for resistance to colonial power.

Indigenous women leaders and organizations, including the Native Women's Association of Canada, have asserted and struggled for women's rights to belong to their communities and to participate in governance, and have won these legal rights through appeals to federal courts and to the United Nations Human Rights Committee. These assertions of rights have often been interpreted by liberal multiculturalists and feminists as critiques of Indigenous self-determination. And they have been interpreted by antifeminist Indigenous leaders as appeals to Western rights that undermine Indigenous self-determination. Both the liberal feminist and the Indigenous antifeminist positions assume an opposition between individual and collective rights, and between women's rights and Indigenous solidarity. Indigenous resurgence theorists also assume an opposition between struggles for rights and the politics of resurgence.

Against the liberal feminist position that individual rights and gender equality rights must supersede Indigenous claims to tradition and to collective self-determination, Indigenous feminists argue that any affirmation of individual rights or women's rights without a critique of state colonization fails to grasp the centrality of racialized gendered colonization in the oppression of Indigenous women. Indigenous feminists affirm the centrality of women's power in Indigenous communities and Indigenous history, and argue for rights to belong to those communities and to exercise that power in the context of struggles for collective self-determination, resurgence, and decolonization.

Against the Indigenous antifeminist position that individual and gender equality rights undermine collective self-determination, Indigenous feminists argue that this claim denies the history of state-legislated heteropatriarchal dominance and its perpetuation in Indigenous organizations and communities. This ongoing history of the undermining of women's power has violated Indigenous traditions and undermined Indigenous sovereignty. If relationality is the ground for a politics of Indigenous resurgence, the continued violation of relationships between Indigenous women and their communities will continue to thwart Indigenous freedom.

While they recognize the limitations of rights claims, and while no one claims that legal rights—especially in the context of colonization—will end violence and domination, Indigenous feminists have developed hybrid discourses, rejecting the binary of pure and opposed traditions. Indigenous feminist and queer theorists and activists have mobilized unique formulations of rights rooted in principles of Indigenous relationality, in struggles for inclusion in Indigenous communities, in struggles against heteropatriarchal violence, and in struggles for Indigenous sovereignty. These formulations have been central to Indigenous resurgence: to the critical revaluation of Indigenous law in struggles for individual and community wellbeing, and for resistance to all forms of domination.

As Kiera Ladner writes, "colonialism is a gendered enterprise defined by racialized sexual violence perpetuated by the church and state as a means of securing control over a nation and its land—and it is increasingly being perpetuated from within as a result of neo-colonialism, institutionalised sexism and the internalisation of sexual violence." Thus, she argues, decolonization must be reframed as a gendered project. "Gender must be decolonized and decolonization must be gendered."[80]

In a concluding chapter, I reflect on the possibility of a critical theory of freedom from relations of colonization. Such a theory would require a model of critique as a practice of encounter with the other, oriented toward transformation of our selves and our relations, guided by an ethos of freedom in relations of reciprocity. This method informs a practice of freedom from colonial unknowing through reparative encounters between Euro-American and Indigenous critical theories, and among a constellation of critical theories of resistance to multiple and intersecting forms of domination. This is a method of critical theory as a practice both *of* and *for* freedom: a practice of critique that is both engaged in resistance and oriented toward an ideal of relational freedom emergent from our shared and intersecting histories.[81]

---

[80] Ladner, "Gendering Decolonisation, Decolonising Gender," 66, 63. Ladner's essay includes a discussion of debates over the (in)compatibility of Indigenous sovereignty and feminism. See also Mayer, "A Return to Reciprocity."

[81] I take the formulation of practices *of* and *for* freedom from Tully, "The Struggles of Indigenous Peoples for and of Freedom," to thematize the interconnection between practices of freedom and a substantive ideal of freedom. I should clarify, however, that in this essay Tully does not affirm a substantive ideal of freedom. He distinguishes between struggles *of* freedom as "practices of freedom on the rough ground of daily colonisation"—arts of resistance that include a "diverse range of possibilities of thinking and acting differently," and struggles *for* freedom as "a non-colonial relation between Indigenous and non-Indigenous peoples." The ideal of freedom in this essay, then, is defined minimally as a relation of noncolonization. This is not a purely negative image of absence of colonization, but a more positive ideal of a *relation* of noncolonization, similar to a republican ideal of a relation of nondomination. In other work, Tully affirms a more substantive conception of this relationship, as involving collective reconciliation with the living earth. See Tully, "Earth-Bound: Indigenous Resurgence and Environmental Reconciliation" and "Reconciliation Here on Earth."

While Eurocentric critical theories tend to resist substantive conceptions of freedom, political movements have always affirmed ideals of relational freedom. Contemporary activist movements, including Idle No More and Black Lives Matter, have developed politics of transformative justice that bind critique to a sense of what critique is *for*: action against domination is motivated and sustained by love for the world, and love for an ideal of relational freedom: love for land, love for a beloved community. Transformative justice includes embodied, affective practices of care for selves and each other, care for the world, as vital *political* practices that enact the relations that counter violence and domination.

For Michel Foucault, the spirit of modernity was critique as a practice of self-transformation. Central to this practice was what Pierre Hadot called *spiritual exercises*. For Hadot, these were the defining practices of ancient philosophy. They were *spiritual* because they involved one's entire spirit, or way of life, and because they focused not just on the self, but on the self in relation to a shared world. Hadot argues that modern philosophy can continue that project. We could say that modern critical theory could be a practice of self-transformation that creates and enacts relations of freedom.

I draw on Eve Sedgwick's method of reparative theorizing to propose a mode of critical theory that could repair the relation between critique and freedom, by practicing a reparative relation to a substantive ideal of relational freedom. By giving up both the dream of a perfect freedom and a dreamless critique, we can enact a world-creative freedom grounded in love for the world.

1
Noninterference, Nondomination, and Colonial Unknowing

Mis-Encounters with Indigenous Relational Freedom

In his classic essay, "Two Concepts of Liberty," Isaiah Berlin noted that historians of ideas have recorded more than two hundred different conceptions of freedom. He proceeded, famously, to argue that only one of these conceptions is worthy of the name: negative freedom, or individual freedom from interference.[1] A glance at the contemporary global political economy appears to indicate that Berlin has won the argument: noninterference has won out as the definitive conception of freedom governing global capitalism, which operates on the principle of possessive individualism, or "free trade." Neoliberal governance preserves the ideology of noninterference as the essence of freedom, protecting private interests with a system of surveillance and control. More generally, the Hobbesian definition of freedom as "freedom to act unobstructed by others" can be said to have found its full expression in American popular culture and is fairly successfully exported to the world.[2] Right-wing movements assume a monopoly on freedom, while leftists are left with equality. The opposition between these two values is often taken for granted. To many, it appears evident that the principle of noninterference has triumphed as the definitive *political* conception of freedom. Thus, democratic movements such as the uprisings of the "Arab Spring" in 2011, along with anticolonial and anti-imperialist movements through the past several centuries, are very often hailed as movements for freedom American-style: noninterference.

But, of course, democracy movements are not reducible to movements for freedom as noninterference. Berlin saw this clearly: his argument for the

---

[1] Berlin, "Two Concepts of Liberty," 168. So convinced was he, and so intolerant of other views, that he was reduced to arguing: "Everything is what it is. Liberty is liberty" (172). (Berlin used the terms *freedom* and *liberty* interchangeably.)

[2] "I am normally said to be free to the degree to which no man or body of men interferes with my activity. Political liberty in this sense is simply the area within which a man can act unobstructed by others" (Berlin, "Two Concepts of Liberty," 169). Berlin quotes Hobbes in support of this view: "'A free man', said Hobbes, 'is he that . . . is not hindered to do what he has a will to'" (*Leviathan*, chapter 21, quoted by Berlin, "Two Concepts of Liberty," 170). American freedom is typically understood as Lockean; here I'm emphasizing the Hobbesian roots.

Decolonizing Freedom. Allison Weir, Oxford University Press. © Oxford University Press 2024.
DOI: 10.1093/oso/9780197507940.003.0002

understanding of freedom as noninterference was posited explicitly against the understanding of freedom as collective participation in democratic self-government. He argued that this latter understanding of freedom—rooted in ancient Greece and revived in the Kantian tradition of political philosophy that runs through the work of Hegel, Rousseau, and Marx—led inexorably to totalitarian regimes. Berlin's attempt to purify the idea of freedom, to eliminate the taint of totalitarianism, led to absurdity: he argued that there was no necessary connection between individual freedom and democracy. For freedom could *only* be freedom from interference.[3]

Quentin Skinner has argued that movements of resistance against colonial rule were understood by Berlin to be invoking a third type of freedom: the demand for status and recognition for a "class, race, or nation." Such movements puzzled Berlin, who could not understand why people would choose a government of corrupt bullies of their own nation when they could choose to be governed by kind and benevolent colonists who would allow their individual freedom from interference. He did not seem to imagine an alternative to these two options.[4] Skinner argues that this third conception of freedom is "freedom from subjection to the dominion of someone else," and he argues that this is the understanding of freedom that is central to republican movements in a long history that has its origins in ancient Rome.[5] For Skinner, republicanism, or freedom from dependence, is a different form of negative freedom, characterized by the absence of slavery or servitude to a master.[6]

In this chapter, I argue that the type of political freedom that grounds resistance to settler-colonial rule is not simply negative freedom—the absence of slavery—but a positive conception of relational freedom, rooted in the recognition of interdependence. I trace a history of colonial unknowing in modern theories of freedom that have disavowed and misrecognized Indigenous relational freedom. This story begins with Hobbes, whose conception of freedom as noninterference works, I suggest, to disavow Indigenous relational freedom. And it continues with contemporary republican and critical theories that repeat this

---

[3] Charles Larmore argues that Berlin had no intention of arguing that negative liberty forms the whole of freedom, and that he recognized the importance of positive freedom. (Larmore, "A Critique of Philip Pettit's Republicanism," 233.) But in "Two Concepts of Liberty," Berlin is very clear: he argued that while (negative) freedom may sometimes be sacrificed for other values, these other values are not forms of freedom. To claim that they are is simply a "confusion of values" (172).
[4] See James Tully's trenchant critique of Berlin in Tully, "'Two Concepts of Liberty' in Context."
[5] Skinner, "A Third Conception of Liberty," 248.
[6] Others understand the third conception of freedom differently, in terms of relations of mutual recognition and solidarity. See, for example, Willett, "Three Concepts of Freedom," who argues that negative freedom corresponds to "first generation" rights to individual liberty, free speech, voting rights, and ownership of property positive, positive freedoms are aimed at "second generation" social rights to basic necessities, education, social security, fair labor conditions, and the third form of freedom is freedom of belonging and solidarity rooted in an assumption of interdependence. See also Wellmer, "Models of Freedom in the Modern World."

legacy, affirming noninterference as the essence of freedom, even as they criticize that conception. I tell the story of colonial unknowing backward, beginning with contemporary theorists, and tracing the legacy of freedom as noninterference back to Hobbes. Finally, I contrast these conceptions with understandings of relational freedom in contemporary Indigenous political philosophies.

I begin with Iris Marion Young's attempt, in her late essays, to develop a relational interpretation of freedom and self-determination that would support Indigenous claims. Young is inspired by the argument that the encounter with Indigenous people and with their systems of democratic self-governance influenced American and European understandings of freedom. Yet for a relational theory of freedom and self-determination she turns not to Indigenous political theory, but to feminist theories of relational autonomy, and to Philip Pettit's understanding of republican freedom as nondomination.[7] I argue that while their theories are directed against the conception of freedom as noninterference, both Young and Pettit follow the Hobbesian tradition of ultimately reducing freedom as nondomination to noninterference. And I argue that this understanding of freedom reproduces a failure to account for the relations of power and domination that structure conflicts between Indigenous nations and the state.

I trace the Hobbesian concept of noninterference through Skinner's argument that it was introduced to support the British monarchy against the republicans, through Foucault's argument, in *Society Must Be Defended*, that the abstraction of contract theory served, for Hobbes, to disavow the reality of the Norman conquest, and through Robert Nichols's argument that contract theory continues to work to disavow the conquest of the Amerindians, and that this disavowal constitutes the Settler Contract. And I juxtapose these critiques with arguments that the Amerindians served as *exemplars of liberty* for Europeans influenced by popular "travelers' tales," and for the American settlers. I suggest that the concept of freedom as noninterference works for Hobbes both to disavow the conquest of the Amerindians and to disavow Indigenous relational freedom. It does this by disavowing relationship with the savages, and by disavowing relationship altogether. And I suggest that modern American ideals of individual freedom as noninterference are shaped through both identification with and constitutive exclusion of the perceived natural freedoms of the Amerindians.

For understandings of Indigenous relational freedom, I turn to Indigenous philosophy and political theory, including theories of relational autonomy and individual freedom (Dennis McPherson and Douglas Rabb, Lorraine Mayer), relational traditions of democratic governance and law (Robert A. Williams Jr.,

---

[7] Pettit has suggested that Aboriginal struggles for what he calls "special minority rights" could draw on the republican model. (Pettit, "Minority Claims Under Two Conceptions of Democracy.")

John Borrows, Val Napoleon), relational conceptions of sovereignty (Patricia Monture, Leanne Betasamosake Simpson, Robert A. Williams Jr., Robert Warrior, Wallace Coffey and Rebecca Tsosie) and conceptions of freedom as resurgence (Taiaiake Alfred, Glen Coulthard, and Leanne Betasamosake Simpson). All of these theorists elucidate conceptions of relational freedom that ground struggles of first peoples for resistance to colonial rule.

Iris Young: From Relational Freedom to Noninterference?

In some of her late essays, Iris Young sought an understanding of freedom and of self-determination that could support Indigenous claims for self-determination in the face of the continued colonization of first peoples in the Americas. Young argues in support of contemporary Indigenous conceptions of self-determination as relational, in contrast to conceptions of self-determination as only noninterference. But Young's argument ultimately reaffirms noninterference as the endpoint of freedom.

Young advocates an understanding of self-determination in terms of relationship, rather than noninterference, and argues that "peoples can be self-determining only if the relations in which they stand to others are nondominating."[8] Young contrasts conceptions of self-determination as sovereignty grounded in a principle of noninterference with an alternative understanding of "self-determination as relationship and connection."[9] To illustrate this conception of self-determination, Young cites Craig Scott's contribution to the discussion of the draft of the United Nations Declaration of the Rights of Indigenous Peoples: "We need to begin to think of self-determination in terms of peoples existing in relationship with each other. It is the process of negotiating the nature of such relationships which is part of, indeed at the very core of, what it means to be a self-determining people."[10] Roger Maaka and Augie Fleras argue for a model of "soft" sovereignty: they "explicitly eschew a notion of sovereignty as noninterference, and instead articulate a model of the relations of distinct peoples in which they engage with one another as equals on an ongoing basis."[11] Taking these claims as her starting point, Young asks "What is a meaning of the concept of self-determination that would correspond to the claims of Indigenous peoples?"[12]

---

[8] Young, "Two Concepts of Self-Determination," 40.
[9] Young, "Two Concepts of Self-Determination," 39.
[10] Scott, "Two Concepts of Self-Determination," 819. Cited by Young, "Two Concepts of Self-Determination," 39. The *United Nations Declaration on the Rights of Indigenous Peoples* was adopted by the General Assembly in 2007. Canada, the United States, Australia, and New Zealand voted against the decision, but they have since reversed their positions.
[11] Young, "Two Concepts of Self-Determination," 31.
[12] Young, "Two Concepts of Self-Determination," 44.

Young begins by drawing on the extended argument made by Donald Grinde and Bruce Johansen, in *Exemplar of Liberty*, that American and European conceptions of freedom were influenced by their encounters with the Indigenous peoples of America. Grinde and Johansen argue that American political institutions were directly influenced by the British colonists' observations of the democratic practices and the constitution of the Iroquois Confederacy. While their argument that the American constitution was directly influenced by the Iroquois Great Law of Peace has met with opposition, this influence has been affirmed and commemorated in a resolution passed by the U.S. Congress.[13] The broader thesis is that the conceptions of freedom and self-determination embraced by the American settlers and their descendants were influenced and partly shaped by their interactions with and observation of Indigenous peoples, who were regarded as "exemplars of liberty." This claim, as Young points out, is well supported.[14]

Drawing on Homi Bhabha's hybrid model for an understanding of colonial history in terms of encounters of cultural difference, Young writes:

> By proposing that Indians served for American revolutionaries as exemplars of liberty, Grinde and Johansen deconstruct the modern Western discourse which positions the Native Americans as the excluded Other in comparison with which the Europeans confirmed their cultural superiority. On this hybrid interpretation, the Indians regard the Europeans as obsequious servants to distant lords and social conventions, while they know freedom. On this interpretation, Native Americans stand for an alternative to monarchist European structures, an alternative internalized in a plural European-American discourse.[15]

Young notes that in Western discourses, democracy is assumed to be a Western value. The history of democratic governance in Indigenous societies is typically ignored. Yet Indigenous peoples had complex systems of democratic governance both within communities and among federated nations, and histories of dialogue and negotiation with diverse peoples. The Great Law of Peace of the Iroquois Federation (the Haudenosaunee Confederacy) exemplifies the valuation of "deliberation, an orientation to collective problem solving, and local self-governance in the context of a strong federation."[16] Young argues that contemporary models for self-government and societal cooperation should draw on the history of Indigenous governance practices. And she argues for a model of

---

[13] In 1988, the United States Congress passed Concurrent Resolution 331 to recognize the influence of the Iroquois Constitution upon the American Constitution and Bill of Rights.
[14] Young, "Hybrid Democracy," 22.
[15] Young, "Hybrid Democracy," 23.
[16] Young, "Hybrid Democracy," 24.

decentered diverse democratic federalism to envision governance based on local self-determination without sovereignty.

A growing body of Indigenous political theory and legal theory draws on long histories of Indigenous constitutionalism, and on Indigenous models of decentered diverse democratic federalisms, to develop contemporary models for Indigenous self-determination.[17] And a growing body of Indigenous philosophy and political theory explicates Indigenous self-determination and sovereignty in terms of relationality. Unfortunately, Young does not turn to this literature. To explicate a theory of self-determination that could support the claims of Indigenous peoples, Young turns not to Indigenous philosophy and political theory but to two theories of individual freedom in contemporary Anglo-American philosophy: feminist theories of relational autonomy and to Philip Pettit's neorepublican theory of freedom as nondomination.

Young points out that feminist critics of the equation of freedom with noninterference argue, with other critics of liberal individualism, that "the idea that a person's autonomy consists in control over a domain of activity independent of others and from which others are excluded except through mutual agreements is a dangerous fiction."[18] Feminist theorists argue that the appearance of independence of the male head of household and property holder is in fact produced by a system of domination. Feminist arguments for relational autonomy assume that agents are not atomistic individuals, but are embedded in and constituted through social relations of interdependence, but continue to value individual choices, arguing that all agents should have the capacity and support to pursue their own ends. Young writes that that this conception of autonomy entails a "presumption of noninterference." Recognizing that within the relationships in which we are embedded agents are able either to thwart or to support one another, "relational autonomy consists partly, then, in the structuring of relationships so that they support the maximal pursuit of individual ends."[19]

Not all feminist theorists agree with Young's claim that relational autonomy entails a presumption of noninterference, or a focus on the maximal pursuit of individual ends. Jennifer Nedelsky explicitly criticizes these positions.[20] Young's conception of freedom is similar to that of many contemporary liberal theorists who understand positive freedom procedurally as the capacity and opportunity to pursue one's own ends or choices, and, recognizing that choices are shaped and made in social contexts, affirm the importance of providing social conditions that can support that pursuit.[21]

---

[17] See, for example, the work of Borrows, Watson, and Tully.
[18] Young, "Two Concepts of Self-Determination," 46.
[19] Young, "Two Concepts of Self-Determination," 47.
[20] Nedelsky, *Law's Relations*.
[21] Nancy Hirschman writes that her theory has a core of negative freedom but is positive insofar as it affirms social constitution and embeddedness. "Like classic negative-liberty theorists, I maintain

Young goes on to cite Pettit's account of freedom as nondomination in support of her own claims:

> In Pettit's account, noninterference, while related to freedom, is not equivalent to it. Instead, freedom should be understood as nondomination. An agent dominates another when he or she has power over that other and is thus able to interfere with the other *arbitrarily*. Interference is arbitrary when it is chosen or rejected without consideration of the interests or opinions of those affected. An agent may dominate another, however, without ever interfering with that person. Domination consists in standing in a set of relations which makes an agent *able* to interfere arbitrarily with the actions of others.[22]

Young's argument, then, is that self-determination assumes a "presumption of noninterference" in the maximal pursuit of one's own aims, but that this presumption of noninterference entails a commitment to restructuring relations so that they support, rather than thwart, this pursuit. And, following Pettit, she argues that domination should be understood not as interference but as a relationship in which one has the *capacity* for *arbitrary* interference in the choices and actions of another. The point is that the criterion for domination is shifted from actual interference to social relations that enable interference. Thus domination can exist even without active interference. It is the power to interfere arbitrarily that constitutes domination. And freedom requires the absence of this power to interfere.

But it is not clear to me how this argument does not define freedom, fundamentally, as freedom from interference.[23] In fact, it reasserts the basic definition of freedom as freedom from interference in an individual's choices and actions. The understanding of domination as "standing in a set of relations which makes an agent *able* to interfere arbitrarily with the actions of others" broadens the understanding of freedom and domination to include a relational context, but still

---

that the ability to make choices and act on them is the basic condition for freedom. However, like positive-liberty theorists, I maintain that choice needs to be understood in terms of the desiring subject, of her preferences, her will, and identity. For subjectivity exists in social contexts of relations, practices, policies, and institutions that affect and shape desires, will, and identity" (Hirschmann, *The Subject of Liberty*, 30).

[22] Young, "Two Concepts of Self-Determination," 48. Note that this understanding of arbitrary interference as interference "without consideration of the interests or opinions of those affected" would allow for paternalism: as long as one "considers" the interests or opinions of those affected, interference would not count as domination. Pettit makes this point, and argues that nonarbitrary interference by the state must be guided by interests and ideas that are shared by those affected, and the assumption of shared interests must be open to contestation by those affected, who have the capacity to change policy. See Pettit, *Republicanism*, 60–63.

[23] This argument with regard to Pettit's theory has also been made by Robert Goodin (Goodin, "Folie Républicaine") and by Matthew Kramer (Kramer, "Liberty and Domination").

ultimately reduces freedom to the freedom of the individual from interference. It adds to this definition a recognition that humans exist in relationships, and it recognizes that those relationships may or may not support the individual in the pursuit of her ends. Thus social relations should be structured to facilitate the maximal pursuit of individual ends.

In taking up the understanding of domination as a set of relations in which an agent is able to interfere arbitrarily with the actions of others, Young seems to have forgotten her own early work on domination. In that work, domination was defined as the opposite of democracy, and it was understood in terms of systemic and structural conditions. Young defined justice, in opposition to oppression and domination, as "the institutional conditions necessary for the development and exercise of individual capacities and collective communication and cooperation."[24] She explicitly criticized the understanding of oppression and domination in terms of intentional acts or policies, and she argued instead that oppression is "embedded in unquestioned norms, habits, and symbols, in the assumptions underlying institutional rules" and in the "often unconscious assumptions and reactions of well-meaning people."[25] This understanding of domination could have been developed in combination with the arguments for collective self-determination rooted in theories of relational freedom in Indigenous philosophy. Here, Young follows Pettit, who argues that domination must be defined as intentional arbitrary interference, and freedom as nondomination, or the absence of the capacity for interference.[26] This, I think, was a mistake.

Philip Pettit and the Republican Model of Freedom: Noninterference Again?

Pettit's argument for a republican model of freedom as nondomination is developed in his 1997 book, *Republicanism: A Theory of Freedom and Government*.[27] Along with Quentin Skinner, Pettit traces the republican conception of freedom from ancient Rome through modern thought and revolutionary movements, arguing that the focus of this tradition was on relations of domination, exemplified by the relation of master and slave, rather than on an individual right of noninterference. Liberty is thus seen as a status. As both Pettit and Skinner note, the conception of political liberty or freedom as simple noninterference was introduced only in the early modern period, by Thomas Hobbes. The irony

---

[24] Young, *Justice and the Politics of Difference*, 38–39.
[25] Young, *Justice and the Politics of Difference*, 41.
[26] Pettit, *Republicanism*, 52.
[27] The argument for freedom as nondomination remains unchanged, and it is restated in Pettit's *Just Freedom* (2014).

is that this conception of freedom, which has been taken up as the quintessential conception (in Berlin's words, the only conception of freedom worthy of the name), was originally introduced in support of an authoritarian regime—in support of the British monarchy. Against the long-standing republican view that political freedom was secured through relations of nondomination between citizens and the state, maintained by just laws, and explicitly against the republican use of this argument to challenge the British monarchy, Hobbes argued that freedom should be defined simply as noninterference, and thus that any state, and any laws, serve to constrain freedom. Thus, as Pettit writes, "Hobbes used his conception of liberty to argue that the subjects of his *Leviathan* are going to be no worse off in terms of liberty—he thought they would be much better off in other terms—than the citizens of republican regimes."[28] Like the English republican resistance to the monarchy, the American Revolution was supported not by the ideal of freedom as noninterference but by the republican conception of liberty as nondomination.

Pettit writes that the Hobbesian conception of freedom had little political influence until British loyalists revived this idea to do "important, ideological work: to help in silencing complaints of servitude and domination—complaints of unfreedom—from those in Britain's American colonies." But the idea "quickly attained a respectable status, not just among authoritarians and reactionaries, but also among those who saw themselves as advancing the cause of democracy and freedom."[29] The idea of liberty as noninterference, Pettit argues, has triumphed as the definitive modern liberal conception of freedom, displacing the republican ideal, which had been largely forgotten.[30]

So what is the understanding of freedom as nondomination according to Pettit? For Pettit, a relationship of domination has three aspects. Someone dominates another to the extent that "1. They have the capacity to interfere; 2. on an arbitrary basis; 3. in certain choices that the other is in a position to make."[31] The point, for Pettit, is that domination doesn't have to involve actual interference but exists wherever one party has the capacity or power to interfere with another. Thus a person is not free so long as another has the *capacity* to interfere with their choices. This means that domination can exist even in the absence of actual interference.

---

[28] Pettit, *Republicanism*, 42. See Skinner, *Liberty before Liberalism*; Skinner, *Hobbes and Republican Liberty*.

[29] Pettit, *Republicanism*, 44–45.

[30] It has, of course, been revived since Pettit wrote this. As Larmore notes, in reducing the liberal tradition to the doctrine of noninterference, Pettit displaces Locke, who with other republicans argued that law is constitutive of freedom, and includes Rawls, along with, presumably, all of the liberal theorists of positive freedom. Skinner has argued that Pettit's claim that republicanism integrates negative and positive freedom is based on a misconstrual of positive freedom (Skinner, "A Third Conception of Liberty," 262).

[31] Pettit, *Republicanism*, 52.

But clearly, for Pettit, as for Young, freedom from interference is the *prima facie* assumption of an ideal of freedom as nondomination. While Pettit argues that republican freedom is a "third, radically different way of understanding freedom" (after negative and positive freedoms), in fact his understanding of republican freedom is grounded in the assumption that domination is *essentially* the capacity or power to *interfere* intentionally and arbitrarily with an individual's choices and actions. Republican liberty, Pettit writes, is "negative to the extent that it requires the absence of domination by others, not necessarily the presence of self-mastery, whatever that is thought to involve. The conception is positive to the extent that, at least in one respect, it needs something more than the absence of interference; it requires security against interference, in particular against interference on an arbitrary basis."[32] In other words, freedom is *essentially* negative freedom from interference, or freedom to make certain choices free of arbitrary interference. Freedom is the absence of interference with the addition of "something more": the security against interference on an arbitrary basis. In this formulation of nondomination, the protection against interference is *strengthened* to include not only actual interference but even the threat of it. As Pettit writes: "To enjoy non-domination . . . is to be possessed, not just of non-interference by arbitrary powers, but of *a secure or resilient variety of such non-interference.*"[33]

Like Young, Pettit explicitly argues against the equation of freedom with noninterference. And yet he continues to use the Hobbesian language of noninterference as the basis of freedom as nondomination. Pettit's argument is motivated by the need to conceive of freedom in a way that does not conflict with our ideals of equality and social justice. He wants to convince his fellow citizens that a state social welfare system that aims toward equality is compatible with freedom.[34] This means, for Pettit, that freedom must be situated in a relationship of equality: a capacity to look the other in the eye. With Locke, he argues that freedom should be understood as civic freedom, supported and secured within a framework of laws. Against the Hobbesian and libertarian belief that any involvement of the state constitutes an infringement on individual freedom, that any laws constrain freedom, Pettit argues for a conception of freedom that is compatible with state social welfare provisions: thus state "interference" does not conflict with individual liberty so long as the interference is in our interests, and justified with reasons that we would endorse, namely, the support of well-being, of equality and social justice. Thus, only *arbitrary* interference, defined as interference that is subject only to the agent's choice, without reference to interests or choices of

---

[32] Pettit, *Republicanism*, 51. Note that Pettit conflates absence of domination with absence of interference.
[33] Pettit, *Republicanism*, 69, my italics.
[34] The fellow citizens requiring persuasion are primarily American, Australian, and British.

those affected, and that does not support their well-being, counts as domination, or an infringement of our liberties.[35]

Pettit wants to distance republican freedom from the understanding of freedom as democratic participation in collective self-government—the version of positive freedom that so frightened Berlin. Against the collectivist orientation toward consensus in many theories of mutual recognition and democratic participation, Pettit argues that the "ultimate form of arbitrariness" is the tyranny of a majority: thus individual freedom from interference should be maintained, and not collapsed into a conception of freedom as democratic participation. Pettit argues for a conception of democracy that stresses contestability rather than consent. But it is not necessary to fall back on an understanding of freedom as noninterference in order to argue for a practice of democracy that upholds contestability.

An understanding of freedom situated in a relationship of equality would not be reducible to an absence of interference. Such an understanding would acknowledge that humans exist in relationships, would define freedom in relational terms, and would reject the claim of an opposition between equality and freedom. This conception of freedom could support an argument for the liberal welfare state, and for governance by rule of law. But this understanding of freedom in terms of a relationship, in fact, contradicts Pettit's definition of freedom as nondomination: as the absence of arbitrary or uncontrolled interference. Pettit's understanding of freedom returns to an ontology of atomistic individuals who are free in the absence of interference. While he resists this understanding, and asserts that humans are not atomistic individuals but social beings, Pettit defines nondomination as "the absence of domination in the presence of other people."[36] But freedom *in the presence* of other people is very different from freedom *in relation* with other people. This conception misses any understanding of humans as essentially relational beings. It misses, then, the *republican* understanding of freedom as a *relationship*—and of domination as a relationship between master and slave. With the definition of nondomination as freedom from the threat of arbitrary interference, Pettit projects the Hobbesian conception of noninterference back into the republican tradition. But this tradition did not rely on the mediation of the concept of noninterference. This was

---

[35] Pettit has suggested that "arbitrary" could be replaced with "uncontrolled" interference. (Pettit, On the People's Terms). But this makes no real difference to my argument here. Pettit has also argued for a broader conception of discursive freedom, but he always returns to the conception of political freedom outlined here as the definition of republican freedom as nondomination, and as the most basic understanding of freedom. The reduction of freedom to noninterference contradicts Pettit's distinction between republican theories and liberal theories. I agree with Charles Larmore that Pettit's is a liberal theory, but I agree with Pettit that the liberal tradition is rooted in the ideal of noninterference. Like Locke, Pettit situates an understanding of freedom as noninterference in a context of equality and law (see Larmore, "A Critique of Philip Pettit's Republicanism").

[36] Pettit, Republicanism, 66.

an understanding of freedom and domination as relations of power, and as relational statuses.

Quentin Skinner describes republicanism somewhat differently. "The nerve of the republican theory," he writes, is that "freedom within civil associations is subverted by the mere presence of arbitrary power, the effect of which is to reduce the members of such associations from the status of free-men to that of slaves."[37] He does not define this arbitrary power in terms of a capacity to interfere. "But I am not talking about . . . interference or non-interference of any kind. I am talking about the predicament of those who recognize that they are living in subjection to the will of others, and I am following my classical and early-modern authorities in claiming that the mere fact of living in such a predicament has the effect of placing limits on our liberty. If freedom is construed as absence of interference, this is unquestionably to speak of an alternative theory of liberty, since it is to claim that freedom can be restricted and constrained in the absence of any element of interference or even any threat of it."[38] And this is because the relations of domination in themselves preclude freedom. Skinner argues, moreover, that the point of the neo-republican theory of liberty is that it is possible to be a free individual only in a free state.[39]

Colonial Unknowing and Indigenous Self-Determination

Pettit's model is designed primarily to justify the right of state power to protect equal rights and justice, against libertarian resistance. But because he has no analysis of relations of power, his understanding of nondomination includes no analysis of systems and structures of domination, assuming the freedom of individuals who are not embedded in and constituted through those systems and structures. In defining domination as interference that is intentional, and that is recognized as such by both parties, Pettit misses the complexity of systems of power and domination.[40]

---

[37] Skinner, *Hobbes and Republican Liberty*, ix.
[38] Skinner, "A Third Conception of Liberty," 263. Skinner argues that republican nondomination is a negative conception of freedom, distinct from noninterference, and thus distinguishes two rival and incommensurable theories of negative liberty ("A Third Conception of Liberty," 255). In *Liberty Before Liberalism*, Skinner argues that the British republicans—"neo-romans" in debate with Hobbes—fully accepted the equation of liberty with lack of constraint, and believed that "to live in a condition of dependence is in itself a source and a form of constraint" (82–84). In *Hobbes and Republican Liberty*, he writes that for republicans "a free-man is someone who lives independently of the will of others, and is free in consequence from the possibility of being arbitrarily impeded in the pursuit of their chosen ends. . . . it is the mere existence of arbitrary power, not its exercise in such a way as to stop us from acting, that takes away our liberty and leaves us as slaves" (152).
[39] Skinner, *Liberty Before Liberalism*, 60.
[40] In assuming arbitrary or uncontrolled interference as the model of domination, this model accepts nonarbitrary, controlled interference as appropriate to relations of nondomination. This model is developed to justify state "interference" in the lives of citizens, in the interests of individual

This model for relations between states and citizens assumes a sovereign power that has rights to interference with dependent citizens. Young accepts this model when she argues for a principle of collective self-determination for Indigenous peoples. Here again she draws on Pettit. She writes: "Self-determining peoples morally cannot do whatever they want without interference from others.... Pettit argues that states can legitimately interfere with the actions of individuals in order to foster institutions that minimize domination. A similar argument applies to actions and relations of collectivities. In a densely interdependent world, peoples require political institutions that lay down procedures for coordinating action, resolving conflicts, and negotiating relationships."[41] Young's model of Indigenous self-determination entails a "prima facie right of noninterference with participatory rights in collective decision-making in those many cases when the prima facie autonomy is justifiably overridden."[42] Young's model begins with a principle of noninterference, with the understanding that that principle cannot be absolute: cases of conflict require negotiation, and sometimes the enforcement of laws that have been established through democratic and inclusive procedures.

To illustrate this principle, Young takes up the case of the conflict between the Skull Valley Goshutes and the State of Utah over the storage of toxic waste. As she describes it, the Goshutes had agreed to the temporary storage of high-level civil nuclear waste on their reservation, while the State of Utah opposed this decision on the grounds that the state has the responsibility to protect the health and welfare of the citizens of Utah. Young opposes the state's challenge to the Goshutes' legal right of self-determination. But she argues that if this right is understood in the terms of relational autonomy, it is not an unlimited right of noninterference. So the Goshutes are obliged to consider the claims of the State of Utah and the U.S. federal government.[43]

Unfortunately, Young's analysis betrays a very poor understanding of the relations of power involved in this case, and it exemplifies the poverty of understanding of those relations in a model that relies on an understanding of domination as arbitrary interference. In fact, the toxic waste dump was facilitated by the U.S. government, which offered a large payoff that was accepted

---

and collective welfare. In other words, Pettit is assuming what Hobbes assumed: freedom is equated with noninterference, but interference is justified so long as it's in your interest.

[41] Young, "Two Concepts of Self-Determination," 51.
[42] Young, "Hybrid Democracy," 34.
[43] Young's model supports democratic negotiation rather than the authority of the sovereign state. But because she defines state authority as nonarbitrary interference, she accepts the state's power to override the right of noninterference in the interest of the wellbeing of its citizens. Young's model of *prima facie* noninterference that can be overridden assumes the understanding of Indian nations as "domestic dependent nations" rather than independent nations. (But to be fair, she supports this model for global relations among nations.)

by a corrupt tribe leader, against the opposition of many members of the tribe. His justification was that the payment in exchange for the dump would alleviate the extreme poverty of tribe members. Young's understanding of the case fails to thematize the U.S. government's use of the reserve and surrounding lands to test and dump toxic chemicals. It fails to thematize the government practice of bribing corrupt or desperate tribe leadership, rather than engaging in fair negotiations that would provide economic support as compensation for the decimation of those tribes. Young's account appears to accept the moral superiority of the State of Utah and the American environmental protection board in recognizing the need to protect citizens from hazardous waste, rather than recognizing the history of destruction of Indigenous peoples and lands, and of ways of life that respected and cultivated the land, as asserted by the group of seventy-one tribes that, along with a majority of Goshute band members, opposed the waste dump.[44]

Young's account begins with the right of Indigenous peoples to noninterference. But it fails to situate that right within an understanding of the history of relations of power that have produced the current situation. The concept of *arbitrary interference* isn't quite adequate to describe genocide: the attempted decimation of a people and their way of life. The problem is that the normative principle of a right to noninterference with negotiation in cases of conflict gets it backward, in three ways. It elides the history of domination. It fails to recognize that conflict and relations of power are the ever-present context of any right to noninterference. And it reverses the frame within which Indigenous peoples understand freedom as relational freedoms, situated in relations of interdependence. Within this frame, the history of colonial domination is understood not just as a violation of rights to noninterference, but as a violation of relations of interdependence.

Young's failure to seriously consider the philosophy and political theory of Indigenous relational freedom, Pettit's and Skinner's failure to look beyond Roman republicanism to consider a history of relational freedoms that have grounded resistance to colonial rule, and Pettit's and Young's inability to conceive of a model of freedom that is not reducible to noninterference: all of these failures belong to a long tradition of obfuscation of colonial relations of power. The failure of the Anglo-American imagination to conceive of freedom as something other than *prima facie* interference must be located within a history of colonial unknowing: a history of disavowals of Indigenous relational freedom.

---

[44] Again, I recognize that Young was usually much more sensitive to relations of power. I'm arguing that the influence of Pettit's theory of nondomination as freedom from arbitrary interference is implicated in this careless reading.

The Constitution of Freedom through Colonization: Disavowals of Relational Freedom

While Pettit and Skinner trace the history of Hobbes's argument for an understanding of freedom as noninterference in opposition to the republican conception, and trace the ways in which these two opposed understandings of freedom were deployed in British and American political conflicts, they leave out an important part of that history: the history of settler colonization.[45] Both argue that the republican model of a relationship of nondomination was the commonly accepted conception of liberty, until Hobbes introduced the novel idea of freedom as only noninterference. And they argue that this was motivated by resistance to republicans, in support of the monarchy. Pettit argues that any conception of freedom will include some idea of noninterference, and this is probably true. Against Benjamin Constant's classic contrast between the liberty of the ancients (democratic participation) with the liberty of the moderns (noninterference), Pettit, with Skinner, argues that republicans very much valued noninterference. But, as Pettit himself argues, this is very different from a conception of freedom as *reducible to* noninterference. So where did the new idea of freedom as *only* noninterference come from? And what work did it do?

As theorists of race and of settler colonization have pointed out, Hobbes's conception of the state of nature was directly influenced by his image of "the savage people in many places of America."[46] As Hobbes puts it:

> It may peradventure be thought, there was never such a time, nor condition of warre as this; and I believe it was never generally so, over all the world: but there are many places, where they live so now. For the savage people in many places of *America*, except the government of small Families, the concord whereof dependeth on natural lust, have no government at all; and live at this day in that brutish manner, as I said before.[47]

Hobbes is not certain that modern civilization actually did originate in the state of nature. Yet clearly the image of the state of nature was influenced by Hobbes's perception of the savages in America. As Robert Nichols writes, "The 'savage' of the Americas thus becomes the symbolic negative—the embodiment of the state of nature itself" in contrast to civil society.[48]

---

[45] They leave out also the history of racialized capitalism. Hobbes's understanding of freedom introduces the new understanding of the atomistic competitive individual, and the abstraction of the contracting individual in contract theories—the idea of possessive individualism that supported the development of capitalism. Hobbes also introduces the image of the state of nature populated by savages that supported the racialization of capitalism.
[46] Mills, *The Racial Contract*, 65; Nichols, "Realizing the Social Contract."
[47] Hobbes, *Leviathan*, Part 1, chapter 13, 63.
[48] Nichols, "Realizing the Social Contract," 47.

I shall argue that the new conception of freedom as noninterference was produced in part through this image of the savage as symbolic negative of civilization. This conception was a product of Hobbes's disavowal of the possibility of a different way of life—a life of freedom—that was being popularized in the tales of encounter with the Amerindians. The Hobbesian ideal of freedom as noninterference assumes an imagined state of nature in which people experience natural freedom. And this imagined state of nature was influenced by a distorted perception of the "savages," who were seen to be living in a state of natural freedom that was feared and repudiated, but that was also romanticized, desired, and envied.

In numerous accounts, settlers and missionaries described the Indigenous peoples as living "a life lived free of toil and tyranny, free of masters, free of greed and the struggle for gain." William Brandon writes that this image "became so much the key picture presented by the first historian of the New World, Peter Martyr of Anghiera, that his English translator summed it up in the repeated word *liberty*."[49] Richard Eden, the translator, writing in the 1550s, referred to this way of life as *aunciente libertie*. The image of a golden age that had been fantasized in pre-Columbian literature was now seen to be realized among the Amerindians. Brandon points out that this image persisted in numerous reports that were eagerly taken up by a wide audience in Europe. He argues, however, that the pre-Columbian image of the golden age did not include the ideal of *liberty*. This ideal was new: it was seen and imagined for the first time among the Amerindians. So the new European ideal of "a life lived free of toil and tyranny, free of masters, free of greed and the struggle for gain" was a product of the encounter with the Amerindians, who actually did appear to be living that life.

While Hobbes did not devote much space to a consideration of the savages in America—there are only a few lines—the image was clearly in his mind. He offers three examples to convince us of the reality of the threat of the state of nature: thieves in our midst, state warfare, and the savages in America. F. W. Maitland argued that Hobbes "was led to exaggerate his account of man's naturally unsocial character by a desire to bring 'the state of nature' into discredit."[50] And Hobbes's attack on the state of nature was an attack on the idea of *liberty* that was allied with it. "If a man should talk to me of . . . *a free subject; a free will;* or any *free* but free from being hindered by opposition, I should not say he were in error, but that his words were without meaning, that is to say, absurd."[51] As Brandon writes: "But the forcefulness of his attack on the very idea of liberty . . . and the forcefulness of his attack on a felicitous picture of natural man . . . seems to

---

[49] Brandon, *New Worlds for Old*, 6.
[50] F. W. Maitland, "A Historical Sketch of Liberty and Equality," in *The Collected Papers*, ed. H. A. L. Fisher (Cambridge, 1911). Cited by Brandon, *New Worlds for Old*, 85.
[51] Hobbes, *Leviathan*, chapter V.

bespeak an exasperation that might have sprung from the saturation of his time with such irritating ideas."[52]

Against the popular image of a golden age of liberty realized among the Amerindians, Hobbes argued that savage freedom—and all freedom—was simply absence of constraint, and produced only his dystopic image of the state of nature. This was not an entirely new idea. Hobbes was drawing on earlier ideas of natural liberty as absence of constraint. We could say that Hobbes's conception of individual freedom was still ancient: for the ancients, the idea of freedom as unconstrained self-interest was condemned as licentiousness. And licentiousness was recognized as a part of what human beings can be. Perhaps it became the essence of what we are as free beings, for Hobbes, only when he saw it realized in the savages. Certainly the stories of the savages were not all stories of utopia. There were many tales of violence and cannibalism, and the images of naked humans living without law could be horrifyingly dystopic. What many of the stories—both utopian and dystopian—shared was an image of a people living in the *absence* of European laws. So the idea of noninterference perhaps reflected what was most salient for Europeans, and what was most shocking and exciting in those stories: the possibility of the absence of rule.[53]

So what work does the idea of freedom as noninterference do for Hobbes? As Pettit and Skinner argue, it provides a conception of freedom opposed to the republican understanding of freedom—and domination—as a relationship. We will still be just as free, Hobbes is arguing, under a sovereign leader. I think he is able to make this argument by disavowing the possibility of a different way of life—a new image of substantive freedom and a real alternative to authoritarian rule.

But the concept of freedom as noninterference also does other work. In the lectures, *Society Must Be Defended*, Foucault argues that "*Leviathan*'s invisible adversary is the Conquest."[54] In other words, Hobbes was disavowing the historical reality of struggle, conquest, and domination as the basis of monarchist rule in England, and inaugurating what Alison Jaggar and Charles Mills have called "ideal theory." By imagining a state of nature in which relative equality produces only fear and insecurity in the face of the constant threat of violence, Hobbes is able to imagine a resolution in which all consent to be ruled. "Basically, it is as though, far from being the theorist of the relationship between war and political power, Hobbes wanted to eliminate the historical reality of war, as though he wanted to eliminate the genesis of sovereignty."[55] So Hobbes is not saying

---

[52] Brandon, *New Worlds for Old*, 85.
[53] This image persists in contemporary popular understandings of Indigenous peoples: primitive peoples without law, who have benefited from civilized settler governance.
[54] Foucault, *Society Must Be Defended*, 98.
[55] Foucault, *Society Must Be Defended*, 97.

that war is everywhere. He is being reassuring: it's what you wanted. And the king is basically "a right-thinking man."[56] As Robert Nichols writes, Hobbes is shifting the *register of argumentation* from analysis of history to abstraction, to ideal theory. And as Nichols argues, this is the strategy of the *settler contract* in all of the contract theories, and in liberal theories today.[57] The settler contract disavows the historical reality of the violent conquest of the Amerindians and replaces this history with a story of the state as a product of voluntary consent.

We could say, then, that the idea of freedom as noninterference—as reducible to the freedom of an atomistic individual from constraint by all others—works to disavow the relationship of domination. And it disavows the possibility of an alternative, nondominating way of life. These two disavowals are accomplished by disavowing relationship altogether. Hobbes invents a new ontology of the individual: we are all atoms. The only relationship is the relation of contract, voluntary consent.

The argument that Hobbes disavows relationship runs through the history of continental philosophy, and in critical theories drawing on Hegel and Marx. This argument is also made by contemporary feminist theorists, who note that there seem to be no mothers and no relations of dependency in the state of nature.[58] Hobbes disavows our dependency, and the possibility of freedom in relations of interdependence. I'm suggesting that this disavowal of relationships of dependency and interdependence, and hence of freedom and domination, was in part an effect of a disavowal of the images of freedom among the savages in the state of nature. And that this disavowal is central to the idea of freedom as noninterference.

For Foucault, the modern discourse of injustice—the assumption that domination is unjust, and that progress entails a struggle for freedom—displaces the premodern discourse, stretching from the Romans through the Middle Ages, of the glory of sovereignty. "Can we not say that until the end of the Middle Ages and perhaps beyond that point, we had a history—a historical discourse and practice—that was one of the great discursive rituals of sovereignty, of a sovereignty that both revealed and constituted itself through history as a unitary sovereignty that was legitimate, uninterrupted, and dazzling."[59] This history is now challenged by a counterhistory: a new discourse of division between what Foucault, following French historians of the sixteenth and seventeenth centuries, calls "races"—meaning nations, or what we might call identity groups. And between what Marx and Engels were later to call classes. (Foucault cites a letter from Marx, writing to Engels, in which he attributes the concept of class struggle

---

[56] Foucault, *Society Must Be Defended*, 98.
[57] Nichols, "Indigeneity and the Settler Contract Today."
[58] See Held, "Non-Contractual Society"; Benhabib, Situating the Self.
[59] Foucault, *Society Must Be Defended*, 73.

to the French historians' concept of race struggle.) And this counterhistory is a history of rebellion and prophecy: "the twin and simultaneous declaration of war and of rights."[60] The modern discourse of struggle against domination "definitively detached us from a historico-juridical consciousness centred on sovereignty, and introduced us into a form of history, a form of time that can be both dreamed of and known, both dreamed of and understood, and in which the question of power can no longer be dissociated from that of servitude, liberation, and emancipation."[61] The transition from premodern to modern discourse, then, was the transition from an understanding of "history as the praise of Rome" to a discourse of history as the call for revolution, and the fear of revolution.

Foucault suggests that there is a certain "boomerang effect" when the colonial practice in the West Indies is brought back to the West, such that "the West could practice something resembling colonization, or an internal colonialism, on itself."[62] And this internal colonialism can now be recognized and criticized as a regime of domination, because it is seen as a reflection of or analogous to the colonization of the West Indies. The parallel is drawn, Foucault says, by Blackwood in 1581, who says, essentially that "the Normans acted in England as people from Europe are now acting in America."[63] The implication is that the discourse of critique of colonization at home is inspired by seeing colonization elsewhere. Foucault does not suggest—but I do suggest—that the discourse of critique of internal colonization is partly inspired not only by seeing and recognizing colonization elsewhere but also by the stories of an encounter between domination and something that looks like actual liberty. We know that the positive image of a different way of life among the Amerindians did inspire many theorists, including theorists of revolution—for example, Montaigne, Rousseau, and Engels. So we could say that Hobbes is not only disavowing domination but also disavowing that new discourse of freedom: the image of freedom in a different way of life, represented by the tales of Amerindians.

Hobbes, as he tells us, was born and lives in fear, and so he is prone to disavowal. He sees in the stories not the utopia of liberty but its opposite: the dystopic image of the state of nature. This image of people living in a state of lawless noninterference producing constant fear helped to persuade him that a certain kind of domination is just fine, and not really domination at all. We could say, following Foucault, that Hobbes is still clinging to the premodern discourse of sovereignty and is resisting not just the reality of historical struggle, but the new history—the

---

[60] Foucault, *Society Must Be Defended*, 73.
[61] Foucault, *Society Must Be Defended*, 83.
[62] Foucault, *Society Must Be Defended*, 103. The concept of the boomerang effect comes from Hannah Arendt.
[63] Foucault, *Society Must Be Defended*, 102.

new story—of domination and freedom. Of struggles against domination in the name of a vision of a world where people live together in relations of freedom. So he is disavowing both relations of domination and relations of freedom. And he does it by disavowing relationships of dependency and interdependence, and imagining a society in which men spring like mushrooms alone from the earth. And so he disavows the understanding of freedom as a relationship—as relation of power and interdependence.

Noninterference as an Ideal: Exemplars of Liberty

But how do we make sense of the transition from Hobbes's dystopia to the embrace of freedom as noninterference as an *ideal*? How is it that, as Pettit argues, this idea that was used to defend the monarchy became popular even among many settlers who saw themselves as advancing the cause of democracy and freedom in America?[64]

In *Exemplar of Liberty*, Grinde and Johansen argue that the early colonists of North America were profoundly influenced by their interaction with the natives, who were exemplars of both democracy and individual freedom. "The American Indian was so tightly intertwined with images of liberty in the colonists' minds . . . that both the Puritan and Jamestown colonists passed statutes against 'Indianizing.' "[65] "During the almost one hundred seventy years between the first enduring English settlement in North America and the American Revolution, the colonists' perceptions of their native neighbors evolved from the Puritans' devil-man, through the autonomous 'noble Savage,' to a belief that the native peoples lived in confederations governed by natural law so subtle, so nearly invisible as to be an attractive alternative to monarchy's overbearing hand."[66] Grinde and Johansen argue that the colonists saw the values of life, liberty, and happiness in practice in Indigenous societies, and saw also a model of government by consensus, with relative equality of property. "The fact that native peoples in America were able to govern themselves in this way provided

---

[64] In *Republicanism*, Pettit attempts an explanation. He suggests that the revival of the conception of freedom as absence of interference was made possible because the republican conception of civil liberty was explicitly contrasted with natural liberty in the social contract theories of the early modern period. The republicans saw natural liberty as licentiousness, and civil liberty as true liberty. But the contrast with natural liberty made the category of natural liberty as noninterference "available" to be taken up by others. This doesn't explain why it *was* taken up. Pettit also suggests that "progressives" who advocated for the inclusion of women and servants in democratic citizenship would have found the argument for nondomination too radical to be accepted, and so turned to the less challenging argument for freedom as noninterference—presumably because it was available.

[65] Grinde and Johansen, *Exemplar of Liberty*, 2.

[66] Grinde and Johansen, *Exemplar of Liberty*, 3.

advocates of alternatives to monarchy with a practical model for a philosophy of government based on the rights of the individual, which they believed had worked, did work, and would work for them in America."[67] And they offer extensive evidence that the American Revolution, the Albany Plan of Union, the Declaration of Independence, and the U.S. Constitution were influenced by the colonists' interactions with the natives and observation of their practices of democracy. In their acknowledgments they thank all of the scholars of American history "who have insisted, with straight faces that the Iroquois and other native confederacies could not possibly have helped shape democracy in the United States and Europe."[68]

But while the Amerindians served as exemplars of democratic freedoms, they were also, for the settlers, exemplars of individual freedom from constraint. Grinde and Johansen quote numerous examples of colonists who wrote that the American Indians lived lives of freedom and scoffed at coercive authority. Among the Jesuits in New France, Father le Jeune wrote that attempting to Christianize and civilize the natives was a challenge: "All these barbarians have the law of wild asses. They are born, live and die in a liberty without restraint. They do not know what a bridle is."[69] Others were more admiring: "There is nothing for which these people have a greater horror than restraint."[70] Thomas Morton spoke of "the more happy and freer life, being voyde of care."[71] Thus we could say that many of the colonists were impressed by and strongly identified with the individual freedom of the Amerindians, who were regarded as exemplars of democratic forms of governance but also as exemplars of a freedom as absence of constraint. And these contradictory forms of freedom became combined in the American imagination. So the American settlers saw and valued Indigenous democratic freedom, yet this was powerfully conflated with the romantic fantasy of freedom as absence of constraint—as noninterference.

Perceiving a new form of freedom combining natural freedom and democracy, the settlers argued, radically, that it wasn't necessary to be "civilized" like the Europeans. The example of the Amerindians living without rule provided a powerful motivation for resistance to the Europeans still in thrall to distant kings. So resistance to monarchy is motivated through not just distinguishing from but romantic emulation of and identification with the natural savages: we are free like them. But this romantic identification also works to disavow the reality of conquest, the reality of relations of power and domination of the Amerindians.

---

[67] Grinde and Johansen, *Exemplar of Liberty*, 3.
[68] Grinde and Johansen, *Exemplar of Liberty*, xv.
[69] Grinde and Johansen, *Exemplar of Liberty*, 17.
[70] Grinde and Johansen, *Exemplar of Liberty*, 16.
[71] Grinde and Johansen, *Exemplar of Liberty*, 2.

Constitutive Exclusions and Romantic Identifications: Ambivalent Freedoms

This ambivalence runs through the history of contract theories. Contrary to Pettit's claim that Hobbes's conception of individual freedom as noninterference was not generally taken up by others, this conception was in fact extremely influential: subsequent contract theories begin with the picture of the individual that Hobbes introduced, and with the conception of natural freedom as absence of constraint. The conception of the individual as an atomistic individual who rationally chooses to join with other individuals to establish a social contract in order to protect his self-interest relies on the assumption that natural freedom is essentially absence of constraint. While for Hobbes individual freedom remains the same in both the state of nature and the state of civilization, subsequent contract theorists drew on the contrast between natural freedom and civilized states and on this new picture of the natural individual living in the absence of law to argue that *civilized* freedom requires, and is produced by, the rational consent to law and governance by the social contract. The idealized understanding of individual freedom as rational consent to law still relies on the new model of *Homo economicus*: man as self-interested calculator. This image of man was certainly shaped by the new mercantile economy and the development of capitalism.[72]

It was also shaped by colonization. The picture of individuals living in a state of absence of constraint before they rationally consent to a contract (or before they recognize the law that constitutes their civilized freedom) works through both *constitutive exclusion* and *romantic identification* to shape modern ideals of freedom. The reliance of the social contract theories on the device of the state of nature, and on natural freedom as a contrast with rational civilized freedom, makes sense of the fact that conceptions of freedom in modern European and Anglo-American philosophies and worldviews (along with many of the ideals that are taken to be definitive of modern Western humanity—equality, rights, universal citizenship) were developed alongside the colonization, enslavement, and attempted annihilation of a large proportion of the world's peoples. This contradiction cannot be explained as simply a tragic failure of practices to live up to ideals. These ideals developed through constitutive exclusions: the modern ideal of freedom acquired its meaning through opposition to the unfreedom of the colonized and enslaved.[73] The social contract theories of the early modern

---

[72] While political theorists of history have argued, against Macpherson's thesis of possessive individualism, that the political motivations for theorists in the social contract tradition cannot be reduced to economic motivations, it remains true that the new economy did play a powerful role in shaping the thought of the social contract theorists, regardless of their intentions.

[73] In this they drew on ancient Greek and Roman understandings of freedom as mastery in opposition to slavery.

Anglo-European philosophers conceptualized modern society through an explicit contrast with an imagined state of nature populated by savages who lived either in a condition of abject unfreedom or in a state of primitive freedom, which is in turn either romanticized as idyllic or feared as lawless and chaotic. The civilized freedom of the modern Western world, founded on rational agreements to respect individual rights, is the product of both a nostalgia for an imagined state of nature and a horror of the primitive savagery of that state. We know that slavery and colonization were rationalized and justified by most of the modern Anglo-European philosophers, who dealt with the rather glaring contradiction between these practices and their espoused ideals of freedom and equality by defining those peoples as not fully human. Thus the category of whiteness was constructed in opposition to blackness, and civilized humans were defined as white in opposition to the black savages and slaves. The category of civilization was defined in opposition to the colonized.[74] And it followed that only those who were fully human were capable of exercising rights and freedoms in civilized society, and hence only they could be recognized as free citizens.[75]

James Tully has shown how constitutive exclusions worked to shape Locke's justifications of settler colonization. "First, Locke defines *political society* in such a way that Amerindian government does not qualify as a legitimate form of political society. Rather, it is construed as a historically less developed form of European political organization located in the later stages of the 'state of nature' and thus not on a par with modern European political formations. Second, Locke defines *property* in such a way that Amerindian customary land use is not a legitimate type of property."[76] These exclusions were central to Locke's conceptions of individual rights of self-ownership and collective rights of land ownership and sovereignty.

As Charles Mills writes: "The evolution of the modern version of the contract, characterized by an antipatriarchalist Enlightenment liberalism, with its proclamations of the equal rights, autonomy, and freedom of all men, thus took place simultaneously with the massacre, expropriation, and subjection to hereditary slavery of men at least apparently human. This contradiction needs to be reconciled; it is reconciled through the Racial Contract, which essentially denies their personhood and restricts the terms of the social contract to whites."[77] The

---

[74] Of course, humans were defined also as male, and as property owners: the logic of colonization and exclusion is repeated along lines of gender, class, and sexuality.
[75] For accounts of this history see Tully, *Strange Multiplicity*; Mills, *The Racial Contract*.
[76] Tully, *An Approach to Political Philosophy*, 139.
[77] Mills, *The Racial Contract*, 63–64. As Mills points out, the racial contract continues to construct the opposition between human and subhuman, black and white, on a global scale. "Ironically, the most important political system of recent global history—the system of domination by which white people have historically ruled over and, in certain important ways, continue to rule over nonwhite people—is not seen [by white people] as a political system at all" (Mills, *The Racial Contract*, 1–2).

social contract is, then, a racial contract. "From the inception, then, race is in no way an 'afterthought,' a 'deviation' from ostensibly raceless Western ideals, but rather a central shaping constituent of those ideals."[78] The social contract relies on the racial contract: relies on the contrast between humans and racialized others in the state of nature to shape the meaning of civilized freedom. But Mills vacillates between arguing that the ideals were shaped through constitutive exclusions and arguing that the exclusions were secondary, introduced into the ideals to justify historical exclusions.

Robert Nichols defines the *settler contract* as "the strategic use of the fiction of a society as the product of a 'contract' between its founding members when it is employed . . . to displace the question of that society's actual formation in acts of conquest, genocide and land appropriation."[79] Following Foucault, Nichols argues that this displacement is effected by the shift from attention to actual history to abstraction, ideal theory. Its strategic function is in "relieving the burden of the historical inheritance of conquest."[80] Since contract theories have traditionally relied on the fiction of the state of nature to displace the question of the society's actual formation by disavowing the reality of conquest, the social contract relies on the settler contract. Nichols argues that the strategy of the settler contract works even without a negative evaluation of the colonized. As I've shown, it can also work through an identification with a romanticized image of the freedom of the Amerindians as absence of constraint. And this identification also works to disavow the relation of domination.

So modern American ideals of individual freedom are shaped by paradoxical and ambivalent evaluations of the natural freedom of the Amerindians. On one hand, the ideal of freedom is shaped by *constitutive exclusion*: they don't work and so have no right to property, or to self as property; their freedom is only natural, and barbaric, whereas ours is shaped by laws and contracts. On the other hand, the ideal of freedom is shaped by *identification*: they are truly free, without rule, without constraint, and that's what we want. We could say that American ideals of freedom are shaped by complicated relations of ambivalence between desire and disavowal, identification and disidentification, in relation to Indigenous peoples. Both the identifications and the exclusions have worked to disavow domination, to deny the structure of a power relation between colonists and natives, and to deny similarity between the resistance struggles of the natives as struggles for freedom from colonization with the settlers' own resistance to

---

[78] Mills, *The Racial Contract*, 14.
[79] Nichols, "Indigeneity and the Settler Contract Today," 168.
[80] Nichols, "Indigeneity and the Settler Contract Today," 169. In earlier work Nichols argues that the use of a state of nature in social contract theories served a dual purpose: to lend rhetorical weight to the contractarian thesis by warning that shared or cooperative sovereignty would degenerate into anarchy, and to deny the Amerindians a right of sovereignty (Nichols, "Realizing the Social Contract").

British rule. The irony is that the understanding of freedom as absence of constraint also works to support a tolerance for their own domination. To the extent that individual freedom is defined by a romanticized absence of constraint, and hence privatized—rather than being understood as a relation of power, or as a relationship of interdependence—power relations are denied and disavowed, and rule by a strong leader is tolerated, even desired: if we are all atoms in competition, we need a strong patriarch to preserve us, to contain our natural freedom in the private realm. This is Hobbes's legacy.

So the colonization of savages can be justified not only because of constitutive exclusions—they do not labor, they do not reason, they are not educated—but also because the colonizers are good masters and protectors, who do not interfere with the natural freedom of the colonized. This is the understanding of freedom that allows Isaiah Berlin to dismiss resistance to colonization with the claim that the colonized will be more free under a benevolent colonizer than in a barbarous state: as long as each individual is not physically constrained, he is vastly better off under colonization than in the state of nature. So Berlin, obsessed as he was with the threats to freedom posed by communism, and democracy, was happy to support colonization of the natives. Not only because the natives are barbarous, but because freedom as noninterference is entirely compatible with domination. And this brings us to the ongoing appeal of Trump's America, where a significant proportion of the populace craves a strong leader, and walls, because we are all really savages in need of a patriarch who will protect us from the invading barbarians and from the savages within. And we are still free, as long as he doesn't stop us from doing what we want in our private lives. Americans have exported this model of freedom to the world, such that strong leaders are increasingly compelling.

And so we arrive at neoliberalism, defined by free trade: freedom of the market from interference by governments, and freedom of individuals from constraint—except for the management of populations and the disciplining of individuals, within a system of capitalist imperial domination.[81] The popularity of the ideal of freedom from interference, with little concern for domination, provides some understanding of the contemporary desire for strong leaders in neoliberal states. And the motivation is the same: the specter of the savage people who are *still* in many places in America, and of the barbarians who are invading our borders, underlies the white supremacist desire for strong leaders who will preserve our freedom from interference.

In a recent interview, Wendy Brown remarks that the libertarian authoritarianism of neoliberalism is a novel political formation produced by a libertarian

---

[81] As Wendy Brown notes, privatized freedom is spreading to displace the public realm altogether. Brown, "Neoliberalism's Frankenstein."

regime of freedom that attacks social bonds, creating the need for strong authority to secure order and boundaries. "What brings someone like Trump to power was the combined emphasis on non-democratic liberty and authority. . . . Again, this is a peculiar political formation that we've not had before."[82] It may be that that this political order is unprecedented in practice, but it is certainly not unprecedented in political philosophy. This peculiar political formation is exactly the one Hobbes envisioned.

Freedom, Eurocentrism, and Historical Progress

As James Tully writes, the conceptions of modern freedom and modern constitutions espoused by the social contract theorists and by liberal philosophers up to the present ignore the histories of sophisticated forms of government in Indigenous societies. "To presuppose that the initial conditions of popular sovereignty are a state of nature, a veil of ignorance, a set of European traditions and institutions, or an already existing national community is to beg the question of the politics of recognition. It dispossesses Aboriginal peoples of their constitutions and authoritative traditions without so much as a hearing and inscribes them within the Eurocentric conventions of modern constitutionalism."[83]

In his *History of the Five Indian Nations Depending on the Province of New York in America* (1747), Cadwallader Colden claimed that the republican government of the Iroquois was superior to that of the Romans. Colden believed that the Indians, particularly the Iroquois, provided the new Americans with "a window on their own antiquity." Grinde and Johansen write that this belief was shared by Benjamin Franklin, Thomas Jefferson, and Thomas Paine in America, and by Karl Marx and Frederick Engels in Europe. "For two centuries of revolutionaries and reformers, this belief provided a crucial link between Indian societies and their own as well as a counterpoint by which to judge society's contemporary ills."[84] So why do modern theorists of republicanism tend to forget the republican model of the Iroquois and turn for their models to Rome? In this they follow Kant, who, as Tully notes, defined a republican constitution in explicit contrast to the lawless freedom of Indigenous peoples. "In their pre-constitutional state of nature they have a lawless freedom . . . which of all forms of life is without doubt most contrary to a civilized constitution."[85]

---

[82] Brown, "Where the Fires Are."
[83] Tully, *Strange Multiplicity*, 82.
[84] Grinde and Johansen, *Exemplar of Liberty*, 21.
[85] Tully, *Strange Multiplicity*, 80; quoting Kant.

Modern and contemporary Western political theorists typically assume that freedom is a specifically modern Western ideal, and they repudiate any claims that ideals of freedom can be found in non-Western or premodern philosophies, outside the bounds of Greece and Rome. The attempt by Engels and others to look to Indigenous societies for models of equality and freedom is typically framed as a prelapsarian fantasy of a time before civilization. A common thread runs through all the moderns, not just the contract theories and liberals but also Hegel and contemporary critical theorists: the conviction that civilization requires progress beyond the primitive past represented by Indigenous peoples and non-Western others. For Hegel, individual freedom is an historical achievement of the modern West. As Amy Allen writes, Habermas and Honneth continue to ground their normative models of individual freedom and autonomy on Hegel's narrative of historical progress, ignoring the deep connections between this narrative and the theory and practice of Eurocentric imperialism, and rejecting any criticism of this model as mere relativism.[86]

But the ideal of individual freedom invoked by all of these theorists is an ideal that can be found in Indigenous philosophies and practices. Contrary to the fear that taking up Indigenous thought involves a regression to a state of nondifferentiation, of submergence of the individual within the group, Indigenous models of freedom in relationship offer a robust conception of individual freedom that supports democratic freedoms, because it is deeply rooted in the acknowledgment of constitutive relations of interdependence and sociality.

Modern Western theorists—and here I would include a wide range of critical theorists and continental philosophers, liberal theorists and poststructuralists— too often resist recognizing the distinctive practices and models of freedom in ancient and modern Indigenous societies. Can this resistance be attributed to a fear of regression to a primitive past? Are the critiques of essentialism and origin stories leveled against Indigenous claims to distinctive traditions and histories partly effects of this fear? And does the continued grip of the ideal of freedom as noninterference, even among those who explicitly reject it, follow from the logic of colonization: the disavowal of another form of freedom?

The perception of Indigenous existence in a state of nature characterized by a lack of constraint is a foundational constitutive misrecognition that has shaped the colonial legacy and limited our capacity to imagine what freedom might be. Thus the colonizers themselves have been colonized by this foundational image of freedom. To counter this image, I now turn to Indigenous philosophies and political theories of relational freedom.

---

[86] Allen, *The End of Progress*, xv.

Indigenous Traditions of Relational Freedom: Individual Autonomy, Law and Governance, and Sovereignty

A Relational Ethic of Individual Freedom and Autonomy

Many Indigenous societies on Turtle Island (North America) have traditionally valued independence and autonomy in the context of a strong ethic of interdependence, which involves respect not only for human beings but for animals, plants, rivers, rocks, ancestors, spirits, and all other beings, all of whom are regarded as persons in a complex web of interdependent relations. This web of relations is grounded in a profound relation to land and in relations to the ancestors who remain strong presences, rooting individuals in a present that extends back tens of thousands of years. According to many scholars, this worldview has supported a practice of childrearing in which children have a great deal of independence and autonomy.[87] In contrast to European and settler societies in which childrearing and education require the imposition of rules and structure, and many years of direct instruction, Indigenous childrearing has traditionally avoided any kind of coercion or punishment. Dennis McPherson and Douglas Rabb draw a striking contrast between Kantian and Indigenous understandings of the development of autonomy. While both Kantian and Indigenous models value autonomy, for Kant, children learn to be autonomous only by undergoing a long period of heteronomy: children learn to impose laws upon themselves only by learning to obey the laws imposed by parents and teachers. In contrast, Indigenous children are considered to be autonomous persons from a very young age. They are not constantly watched and controlled; they are free to explore their environments, and they are expected to be independent and to take responsibility for their actions and choices. From the Indigenous perspective, the Kantian model is contradictory: what kind of strange society expects people to learn to be autonomous by being controlled?

Some have argued that Indigenous childrearing practices reflect an "ethic of noninterference."[88] This concept, first proposed by Clare Brant in 1990, does appear to describe the noncoercive practices of childrearing in Indigenous societies. As McPherson and Rabb write, "One point on which all researchers seem to agree is that Native children are given much more freedom than their non-Native counterparts."[89] But this freedom is not a lack of intervention.

---

[87] For a discussion of these ideas in relation to feminist relational theory, see Welch, "Radical cum Relational." I am very grateful to Shay for the inspiration and instruction of her paper, an early version of which was presented at a panel we organized together at the 2013 FEAST conference.

[88] Brant, "Native Ethics and Rules of Behavior"; Brundige, "Ungrateful Indian"; McPherson and Rabb, *Indian from the Inside*.

[89] McPherson and Rabb, *Indian from the Inside*, 98.

According to McPherson and Rabb, Indigenous children are taught, but they are taught not through direct instruction (which is considered a disrespectful imposition) but through narratives and rituals, through examples set by elders, and through the direct experience of a way of life. This childrearing philosophy is described by McPherson and Rabb as a *narrative ethic*: parents and elders teach by telling stories that provide frameworks that help the child consider and decide how to act. V. F. Cordova argues that Indigenous childrearing involves pointing out choices, and letting children make their own decisions and experience consequences, so that they learn to accept responsibility. The full status of human is attained when the child comes to recognize that her actions have consequences for all her relations. Thus, autonomy requires "self-initiative combined with a high degree of self-sufficiency," but it also requires "an enhanced perception of the needs and emotions of others as well as a keen perception of where the child was in the world (a sense of place)."[90]

Indigenous theorists who write about an Indigenous practice of noninterference stress that this is situated in the context of a strong ethic of responsibility for interdependence and a practice of supportive guidance. McPherson and Rabb suggest that this childrearing practice follows an "ethic of interventive-noninterference." Parents and elders avoid direct criticism but provide "unobtrusive and gentle but steady moral guidance" by telling stories that "work on you" and "get under your skin."[91] This childrearing practice is consistent with the ethic that guides interactions among adults: "An Aboriginal person does not tell another Aboriginal what to do. The act of directly interfering in someone's life is considered rude.... This is not to say that people never interfere, but when they do, it is in an indirect way designed not to offend."[92]

McPherson and Rabb argue that Indigenous practices of childrearing were neither authoritarian nor permissive, but nurturant. They contrast these nurturant practices with permissive practices based on a mistaken belief in "letting children do what they please."[93] To understand Indigenous childrearing as permissive, they argue, "would be to ignore the important role of stories, modeling elders, the vision quest, and many other traditional ceremonies, in their child rearing practices."[94] Given the strong ethic of interdependence in Indigenous societies, there is no need for ordering, coercion, or punishment. Childrearing takes the form of supportive guidance and empowerment of individuals recognized as responsible for themselves, recognized as having their own powers

---

[90] Cordova, "Ethics," 173–181.
[91] McPherson and Rabb, *Indian from the Inside*, 105; quoting Basso, *Wisdom Sits in Places*, 59.
[92] Brundige, "Continuity of Native Values," 42–46.
[93] McPherson and Rabb, *Indian from the Inside*, 114.
[94] McPherson and Rabb, *Indian from the Inside*, 114.

and needing to express their powers, which were mediated through the knowledge and guidance of elders.

This model of autonomy reflects an understanding of freedom very different from the conception of noninterference described by Hobbes and Berlin, who imagined an atomistic individual whose freedom was demarcated in the space within which he was unconstrained by others, and very different from the image of the American Indian wild and alone on the empty frontier.[95] This conception of freedom is much deeper, broader, and stronger than a Hobbesian conception of noninterference. This is a freedom sustained by the power of the land and the ancestors, by a vast network of relations that hold and support the individual. Given this view of freedom, children didn't need to be dominated, because they were actively and powerfully supported by their network of relations. So their freedom was not just different from but diametrically opposed to the Hobbesian conception of freedom from interference or constraint. This is a view of freedom not based in fear or defense against authority and constraint, not characterized by lonely atomism, and not expressed in the imaginary of doing whatever you want. This is a freedom and autonomy grounded in the security that you are never alone, and the knowledge that your power comes from all your relations, to whom you are always responsible. This form of freedom is not an end in itself, but is situated within a broader conception of freedom in interdependent relations. This form of freedom is not reducible to freedom as noninterference, and it is not characterized by the maximal pursuit of one's own ends.

The model of childrearing and of intersubjective relations that Indigenous scholars describe is a model of noncoercion and nonviolence in a relational practice of nondomination, within a philosophy and politics of relational freedom. If individuals and collectives are understood to be not antagonistic atoms but individuals in relations of interdependence, the solution to conflict and violence will not be constraint by a strong patriarchal leader. Laws and practices of nonviolence are oriented toward the restoration of relationships that are nonviolent and nondominating. This is a model of nondomination that assumes interdependence, rather than atomism and noninterference.

John Borrows writes that in Anishinaabe tradition, freedom is understood as a way of living in healthy interdependence with all beings. Freedom is relational. Borrows writes that Anishinaabe freedom has many dimensions. It can have "property-like connotations": a citizen is one who "owns" their associations, in the sense that they are responsible for and control how they interact with others. He refers to a "tradition of relational mobility": runners were trained to connect

---

[95] Nor is there any conception of the private/public split which later became central to conceptions of the freedom of the person from interference. In Berlin's words, "a frontier must be drawn between the area of private life and that of public authority" (Berlin, "Two Concepts of Liberty," 171).

communities over long distances, and their travels were supported by relations with people in other communities, and by their extensive knowledge of the land and of the plants that would sustain them.[96] Freedom involves questioning and challenging limits, and capacities for transformation. It also involves recognizing the limits that facilitate wellbeing.

Borrows writes:

> our freedom is at its strongest when it is publicly interactive and aimed at good living. In a respectful relational context, the quest for freedom to live a good life becomes a self-governing activity, a simultaneously individual and collective practice. It embodies self-determination *and* individual self-examination, critique and deliberation. In this respect, freedom is pursued inter-subjectively, meaning that Indigenous peoples' identities are non-binary, and are continuously recreated in the context of their struggles against and alliances with one another, occurring under the influence of competing and complementary traditions. There is no relationship-free place for Indigenous or any other peoples, whether positively, negatively, or "mixedly" construed.[97]

Freedom of movement, Borrows argues, is central to Indigenous traditions. Indigenous peoples have always traveled and have often been nomadic. Grounded in movement through both space and time, Indigenous traditions support both physical and intellectual mobility. Traditions develop through intersubjective practices and experiences that flow through time. So Indigenous traditions are not static; they are "fluid, hybridized, contingent, contested, crosscutting, and ever-changing." Yet travel and migration are always rooted in relation to specific places. This rooted freedom is described by Borrows as a freedom in "states of settled flux. Our perpetual motion coexists with a persistent and enduring near-permanence.... Our journeys generally take their orientation from an older sense of place in the world."[98] This freedom of movement in relation to place reflects the continual movement within the natural world. And it continues today among Indigenous people, who are highly mobile: while a majority live in urban centers, they also continually move back and forth between reserves and cities.

Freedom always involves engagement in interdependent relations. As Borrows writes, there is no relationship-free place. This means that the relational freedom of individuals is foundational to democratic freedom. Democratic freedoms are

---

[96] Borrows, *Freedom and Indigenous Constitutionalism*, 7.
[97] Borrows, *Freedom and Indigenous Constitutionalism*, 10.
[98] Borrows, *Freedom and Indigenous Constitutionalism*, 20–21.

not separate from individual liberty but are grounded in a conception of individual freedom that is itself relational.[99]

Relational Traditions of Law and Democratic Governance

As we've seen, the encounter with Indigenous democracies influenced the development of American democratic institutions. Grinde and Johansen document the democratic councils and confederacies of Indigenous nations all along the Atlantic Seaboard, and the effect on settlers of their encounters with those democracies. As Jerry D. Stubben writes, "The scholarly debate has gone beyond proving that indigenous societies did influence the development of American democratic norms, values, and institutions to defining the degree of such influence."[100] Among the Amerindians, settlers encountered established institutions of community, intranational, and international governance. The effect on American democratic institutions includes the well-known influence of the Haudenosaunee confederacy and the Great Law of Peace as a model in the drafting of the U.S. Constitution. But the scope of the influence was much greater. Settlers arriving from feudal and early-capitalist class systems ruled by kings encountered egalitarian forms of social organization and institutions of decision-making in democratic councils absent of hierarchical rule.

Indigenous institutions of democratic governance involved addressing issues through rational argument. But they also involved an awareness that addressing conflict requires more than argument. Accounts of Indigenous democracy describe an understanding of social and political relations as kin relations among diverse and free agents, and an experience of political decision-making as a sacred ritual, expressive of a sacred relationship of kinship. Robert A. Williams Jr. writes that, like relations within communities, treaties among nations were understood on a kinship model of social and political relations: Sioux elder Black Elk has described treaties as *rites of making relatives*. "The language of diplomacy utilized by tribes in their treaty-making practices was the product of a complex, plural cultural landscape. The sacred rituals and symbols of this language circulated as integrative devices on a multicultural frontier. They were adapted

---

[99] The Indigenous view of freedom in relationship is expressed in arguments that the relation to land is essential to freedom of the person for Indigenous peoples. Invoking Article 3 of the United Nations Declarations on Human Rights supporting the right to "life, liberty, and the security of the person," Jack Stevenson has argued that "disruption of their relationship with the land and their traditional way of life is, or can be, a violation of the personal security right of the aboriginal peoples of Canada" (McPherson and Rabb, *Indian from the Inside*, 85).

[100] Stubben, "The Indigenous Influence Theory of American Democracy," 716.

from the most important aspects of tribal life and shared with different peoples to construct a conscious framework for conducting treaty negotiations."[101]

The ritual of the peace pipe exemplifies this understanding. "As the language of Indian diplomacy suggests, . . . smoking the calumet of peace was a sacred act of commitment that made previously alienated groups regard each other as relatives. . . . The calumet pipe is one of several recurrent symbols and ritual systems dispersed throughout the treaty literature of the Encounter era reflecting the basic understanding of American Indians that a treaty was a sacred undertaking. Indian diplomacy recognized that on a multicultural frontier, the making of peace required an act of commitment between two former enemies. The parties to a treaty had to agree to create and sustain a *nomos*, a normative universe of shared meanings—'a present world constituted by a system of tension between reality and vision.'"[102] The smoking of the calumet of peace sought to resolve this tension by invoking the larger forces at work in the affairs of human beings. A treaty sanctified by the smoking of the pipe of peace became, in essence, a sacred text, a narrative that committed two different peoples to live according to a shared legal tradition—an American Indian tradition of law and peace."[103]

Somehow we have arrived at the conviction that to be modern is to reduce human relations—and relations with other beings—to instrumental relations. The idea that such relations should be infused with a sense of the sacred is considered to represent a less sophisticated worldview. But reference to "the sacred" does not commit us to belief in some mystical realm of flying angels, much less some dogmatic patriarchal and racist version of religion. The sense of the sacred described by Williams is a mindfulness of the connection among us: a belief that we are all related. Kiera Ladner writes: "Within the parameters of Indigenist thought, governance is the way in which a people lives best together, or the way a people has structured their society in relationship to the natural world. In other words, it is an expression of how they see themselves fitting in that world as a part of the circle of life, not as superior beings who claim dominion over other species and other humans."[104] Surely this is an exemplary model of democratic governance.

Indigenous democracies and treaty relations were traditionally modeled on interpretations of systems of relationality in the natural world. Indigenous law is rooted in attending to the agency and relationality in nature. John Borrows writes that he learned Anishinaabe law from elder Dr. Basil Johnston, who taught that legal practice begins with drawing analogies from the earth. This is expressed

---

[101] Williams, Jr., *Linking Arms Together*, 43.
[102] Cover, "*Nomos* and Narrative."
[103] Williams, Jr., *Linking Arms Together*, 47.
[104] Ladner, "Governing within an Ecological Context," 125.

in the term *Akinoomaagewin*, which combines the words *Aki*: earth and *Noomage*: to point toward and take direction from.[105] According to this understanding, standards for judgment and action can be found in the natural world. This form of law requires recognizing the agency of other beings, and it involves the careful work of attending to and interpreting what they are communicating. This work becomes a part of everyday thinking and practice. Borrows has long argued that the recovery and revitalization of Indigenous traditions of law and governance is essential to any genuine reconciliation and decolonization.[106]

Borrows's work has generated a rapidly growing body of research on Indigenous law.[107] This work assumes a capacious understanding of law as a system of democratic governance. Val Napoleon defines law as "an active collaborative and public process" that is formed by and forms social, economic, and political dynamics. "It is law that enables large groups of people to collectively manage themselves 'against a backdrop of deep-seated normative disagreement' and to fashion 'collective positions out of the welter of disagreement.' . . . Law is collaborative problem-solving and decision-making through public institutions with legal processes of reason and deliberation."[108] Research on Indigenous law combines the retrieval of systems of customary law with the rebuilding of Indigenous legal systems. This involves critical interpretations of customary law, in conversation with Canadian and international legal systems, through public community consultation. This research also offers resources for transforming Canadian law, offering alternative modes of democratic governance. As Napoleon points out, in Indigenous societies, law and legal authority were traditionally decentralized. "For example, in Cree society, there are four decision-making groups, and their role and authority depends on the type of legal decision required: the family, medicine people, elders, and the whole community. Another example is Gitksan society where law operates through the matrilineal kinship units of extended families and overarching clans."[109]

---

[105] Borrows, "Earth-Bound," 51, 66.

[106] Borrows, *Recovering Canada*.

[107] The Indigenous Law Research Unit at the University of Victoria, established by Val Napoleon and Hadley Friedland, works in research partnerships with Indigenous communities seeking to revitalize their laws, to address political, economic, social, and environmental issues. Val Napoleon is also co-founder of the world's first degree in Indigenous Law, at the University of Victoria Faculty of Law. Many other universities in Canada are introducing courses and programs in Indigenous law and governance. In Australia, Irene Watson's *Aboriginal Peoples, Colonialism, and International Law: Raw Law* analyzes international law from the perspective of Aboriginal law. Research into Indigenous law draws on diverse sources, including narratives, songs, rituals, and recorded practice, as well as recorded law. John Borrows argues that Indigenous societies have at least five sources of law: sacred, deliberative, custom, positive, and natural.

[108] Napoleon, "What Is Indigenous Law?," citing Webber, "Naturalism and Agency in the Living Law," in Hertogh, ed., *Living Law: Reconsidering Eugen Ehrlich, Oñati International Series in Law and Society* (Portland, OR: Hart, 2009), 201 at 202.

[109] Napoleon, "What Is Indigenous Law?"

Borrows argues that the revitalization and recognition of Indigenous traditions of law and democracy is essential to the development of democratic relations among Indigenous people and settlers. A politics of reconciliation would require combining Indigenous and Canadian law. Borrows also argues that practices of freedom include acts of civil (dis)obedience: resistance to state law grounded in obedience to Indigenous laws. In *Freedom and Indigenous Constitutionalism*, he assesses cases of direct action according to their degree of success in resisting domination and opening up democratic spaces.

Indigenous Relational Sovereignty

Relational freedom is expressed in Indigenous arguments for sovereignty that emphasize relationship rather than noninterference. As Maaka and Fleras write, "Indigenous sovereignty rarely invokes a call for independence or noninterference: preference is in cultivating relationships as a way of working through difference in a non-combative manner."[110]

Sovereignty is a contested concept among Indigenous theorists. Joanne Barker writes: "The erasure of the sovereign is the racialization of the 'Indian.'" Without a conception of political sovereignty, she argues, Indigenous peoples are reduced to minority cultures, or "domestic dependent nations."[111] Others reject the language of sovereignty: Taiaiake Alfred has argued that the concept is incompatible with traditional Indigenous notions of power. Alfred resists the assumption that Indigenous nationhood and governance must conform to the imperialist conception of sovereignty, and he argues for the retrieval and development of alternative concepts and language. Alfred has also argued, however, that Indigenous people "need to create a meaning for 'sovereignty' that respects the understanding of power in indigenous cultures."[112] Other scholars use the term *sovereignty* to develop relational conceptions of sovereignty more consistent with Indigenous ways of life and forms of governance.

While Westphalian state sovereignty assumes the primacy of the sovereign state, corresponding to the liberal primacy of the individual, Indigenous relational sovereignty assumes the primacy of relations of interdependence. Where state sovereignty assumes the right of noninterference against outside powers, and the right to police and defend hard borders, Indigenous relational

---

[110] Maaka and Fleras, "Engaging with Indigeneity," 93.
[111] Barker, *Sovereignty Matters*, 17. "Domestic dependent nations" is the phrase used by the United States Department of Justice to describe "the sovereign status of federally recognized Indian tribes." https://www.justice.gov/otj/native-american-policies
[112] Alfred, *Peace, Power, Righteousness*, 54–55. See also Alfred, "Sovereignty," in Barker, *Sovereignty Matters*.

sovereignty focuses on shared responsibilities for land. Where the sovereign state assumes coercive power over citizens (ideally with their consent and limited by their rights), Indigenous relational sovereignty assumes no powers of coercion or control.

Unlike the Hobbesian/Westphalian model of sovereignty, and unlike Pettit's model of nondomination, relational freedom includes no justification for any kind of "interference." Yet noninterference is not the endpoint or ultimate ideal. The avoidance of interference is a part of a practice of respect for the other within relations of interdependence. The concept of "nonarbitrary interference" is appropriate for a model of hierarchical relations between states and citizens, and between states and "domestic dependent nations." Within this hierarchical model, the state has powers of coercion or control. Within a model of relational freedom, nation-to-nation relations and relations among citizens are understood to be relations of interdependence that balance powers among diverse agents. As Borrows writes, Indigenous legal systems are derived by studying the global family of relationships among all forms of life. Treaty relationships of reconciliation are one form of a diverse family of relationships among all forms of life.[113]

Patricia Monture writes: "Sovereignty... is not about 'ownership' of territory.... We have a Mohawk word that better describes what we mean by sovereignty and the word is *tewatatha:wi*. It best translates to 'we carry ourselves.' . . . What sovereignty is to me is a responsibility."[114] Leanne Simpson argues that Indigenous sovereignty is not the sovereignty of the nation state, characterized by state rule over a defended tract of land, with policed borders. "Indigenous thought, which is as diverse as the land itself, roots sovereignty in good relationships, responsibilities, a deep respect for individual and collective self-determination, and honouring diversity."[115] Thus, as Simpson writes, "Indigenous nationhood is a radical and complete overturning of the nation-state's political formations." It centers on responsibility for creating and maintaining good relationships, with an understanding of nation as a web of connections.[116]

Indigenous governance has always encompassed different political systems existing in shared space. Indigenous law thus provides models for legal pluralism, including coexisting relational sovereignties. Simpson writes:

> Borders for indigenous nations are not rigid lines on a map but areas of increased diplomacy, ceremony, and sharing. Peaceful relations were of the utmost importance in this diplomacy, and there are many examples of indigenous

---

[113] Borrows, "Earth Bound," in Asch, Borrows, and Tully, eds., *Resurgence and Reconciliation*.
[114] Monture-Angus, *Journeying Forward*, 36.
[115] Simpson, "The Place Where We All Live and Work Together," 19.
[116] Simpson, *As We Have Always Done*, 10, 8.

nations exercising separate sovereignties and responsibilities over a shared territory—this was indeed the basis of international trade and travel. These areas of overlap are not seen as a threat to individual nations sovereignties because neither nation "owns" the land in a Western sense of the word, and no one believes they have the right to interfere with the political processes of the other nation. Instead, the focus is on our joint responsibilities for caretaking of the land and ensuring that coming generations inherit healthy and clean lands so that life, all life, may perpetuate itself. Our idea of sovereignty accommodates separate jurisdictions and separate sovereignties over a shared territory as long as everyone is operating in a respectful and responsible manner.[117]

Robert A. Williams Jr. describes the early encounters between Indigenous and settler governments as *multicultural encounters* among diverse groups of equal status. The settlers were acutely aware that they were surrounded by a large number of highly organized confederacies, and they depended upon those groups for their survival. Treaties, then, were made in recognition of that dependency. For the Indigenous people, treaty-making was a means of establishing relationships in a rite of *making relatives*. As this phrase implies, treaties were understood within a kinship model of relationship. The treaty was sealed in a ritual that involved smoking the peace pipe, "a sacred act of commitment that made previously alienated groups regard each other as relatives."[118] As Laurelyn Whitt writes: "Establishing affiliational ties with differing peoples was a way of resolving disputes and making peace; treaty-making enabled peoples who were different from and often strangers to one another to unite and form ties of solidarity."[119]

The history of Indigenous treaty-making supports what Robert Warrior calls a process-centered understanding of sovereignty.[120] As Laurelyn Whitt puts it, according to a process understanding of sovereignty, a sovereign nation is not one that has a status as a state, but one that acts in certain ways: one that actively treats with other nations.[121] Following Warrior and Vine Deloria Jr., Wallace Coffey and Rebecca Tsosie argue for a model of cultural and political sovereignty that involves a process of reclaiming culture and building nations. Against the model of tribal sovereignty established in the United States by the Marshall decisions in 1823–1833, which defined tribal sovereignty as that of a "dependent domestic nation" with jurisdiction over a particular tract of land, and against struggles for Native sovereignty as cultural preservation, Tsosie and Coffey argue for a model

---

[117] Simpson, "The Place Where We All Live and Work Together," 19.
[118] Williams, Jr., *Linking Arms Together*, 53.
[119] Whitt, "Transforming Sovereignties," 191.
[120] Warrior, *Tribal Secrets*, 87.
[121] Whitt, "Transforming Sovereignties," 191.

that "analyzes culture as a living context and foundation for the exercise of group autonomy and the survival of Indian nations."[122] Rather than striving to fit an externally determined model of political sovereignty, they advocate building an understanding of sovereignty as it is exercised and understood within tribal communities. This practice of reclaiming and rebuilding cultural sovereignty should be the basis of any political sovereignty.

Relational Freedom and Indigenous Resurgence

A growing body of Indigenous thought advocates an Indigenous practice of freedom as *resurgence*: rather than waiting for state and settler recognition, and rather than devoting endless time and energy to unending battles for political and legal rights, Indigenous people need to focus on empowerment and self-transformation, by retrieving and revaluing Indigenous practices, philosophies, and forms of governance. Taiaiake Alfred, Glen Coulthard, and Leanne Betasamosake Simpson argue that Indigenous thought and practice must be the foundation of Indigenous freedom. And they stress that Indigenous thought is a living practice: freedom requires not returning to static traditions but continuing the practice of Indigenous relations to a changing world, framed within a worldview of interdependence.

Mohawk scholar Taiaiake Alfred has proposed a conception of freedom as empowerment in relationship as the ground for an Indigenous politics of resurgence. For Alfred, this is a politics of freedom through collective self-transformation, rooted first in re-creating relations of freedom among Indigenous people, in relation to Indigenous land and the ancestors, and second in establishing relations of freedom between Indigenous peoples and settlers. The path to regaining freedom, for Alfred, is through "restoring connections to each other, our cultures, our lands" and through this practice of freedom, to remake the relationship between Onkwehonwe [original peoples] and Settler.[123] Alfred defines freedom as living well in relations of interdependence. Freedom, for Alfred, is "an existence for our people where we can know the liberatory effects of experiencing whole health, personal fulfillment, and the ability to express ourselves and flourish as human beings."[124] Resistance to colonization thus requires a process of personal and collective spiritual transformation.

Alfred argues that, within Indigenous political thought, freedom is not located within a circumscribed area of noninterference. Drawing on Foucault, he finds

---

[122] Coffey and Tsosie, "Rethinking the Tribal Sovereignty Doctrine," 191.
[123] Alfred, *Wasáse*, 20, 34.
[124] Alfred, *Wasáse*, 187.

in Indigenous thought a philosophy and practice of freedom as empowerment. This is an expressivist understanding of power focusing on the free expression of powers that are dispersed among diverse persons.

> On the meaning of power, Indigenous thought has traditionally focused on questions regarding the legitimacy of the nature and use of power, rather than its distribution. Within Indigenous cultures it is recognized that forms and levels of power vary, depending on the spiritual and physical resources available to the individual. There have always been two basic questions: What kinds of power do individuals have? And are they using it appropriately? In other words, the traditional Indigenous view of power and justice has nothing to do with competition, or status vis-à-vis others: it focuses on whether or not power is used in a way that contributes to the creation and maintenance of balance and peaceful coexistence in a web of relationships.[125]

Alfred contrasts the conception of power that he invokes here with state power; he argues that Indigenous peoples can resist the power of the state by focusing "not on opposing external power but instead on actualizing their own power and preserving their intellectual independence. This is an Indigenous approach to empowerment. Unlike the statist version, this conception of power is not predicated on force. It does not involve coercing ... it is not inherently conflictual. Nor does it require a contractual surrender of power."[126]

With Alfred, Dene scholar Glen Coulthard advocates a practice of resurgence through self-transformation, rather than seeking recognition and accommodation within settler states. Coulthard draws on Fanon to argue that the politics of Indigenous resurgence requires a mediating struggle, a transformative praxis, through which the colonized shed their colonized identities, in a practice of self-transformation that presents "a foundational challenge to the background structures of colonial power."[127]

Nishnaabeg scholar Leanne Simpson stresses that the politics of resurgence is a politics of everyday life, rooted in love for land. Simpson defines freedom as living well, or living toward good life, in sustaining relations: *mino bimaadiziwin*. Winona La Duke interprets *mino bimaadiziwin* as "continuous rebirth."[128] For Simpson, "resurgence is dancing on our turtle's back; it is visioning and dancing new realities and worlds into existence."[129]

---

[125] Alfred, *Peace, Power, Righteousness*, 49.
[126] Alfred, *Peace, Power, Righteousness*, 48.
[127] Coulthard, "Subjects of Empire," 450.
[128] Simpson, *Dancing on Our Turtle's Back*, 142; quoting LaDuke, *All Our Relations*.
[129] Simpson, *Dancing on Our Turtle's Back*, 70.

A Politics of Relational Freedom: Transformative Resurgence and Reconciliation

As Alfred, Coulthard, and Simpson argue, Indigenous freedom can be found only through a politics of resurgence: a politics of self-transformation that involves a revaluation of Indigenous values as the basis for rebuilding Indigenous communities and Indigenous forms of self-governance. A politics of resurgence can be oriented toward abolition of the state. As Borrows and Tully argue, the politics of resurgence is also essential to a transformative politics of reconciliation between settler and Indigenous peoples.

Settler societies are bound in relations of colonization. To free ourselves, settlers need to resist a politics of asymmetrical recognition, to acknowledge the priority of Indigenous societies and systems of governance on the land on which we live, to acknowledge the history of genocide and colonization, and to participate in a political process of genuine mutual recognition, which will require self-transformation. Decolonizing freedom will require acknowledging our interdependence and transforming our relationships, to create just relations.

A politics of relational freedom through transformative reconciliation must encompass two models of reconciliation: constitutional and ethical. As Kiera Ladner has said, reconciliation will not be a big hug; it's a political constitutional project.[130] Constitutional reconciliation should involve following Indigenous models of plural governance, with coexisting relational sovereignties. As James Tully affirms, these can include at least three coexisting forms: stateless popular sovereignty on Indigenous territory, settler sovereignties on territories ceded, and shared jurisdictions over remaining overlapping territories. The presumption of exclusive state jurisdiction must be replaced with treaty federalism guided by the Indigenous principles that "free and equal peoples on the same continent can mutually recognize the autonomy or sovereignty of each other in certain spheres and share jurisdictions in others without incorporation or subordination." These models follow the legal assumption of Indigenous prior and continuing sovereignty: "prior and continuing 'sovereignty' does not refer to state sovereignty, but, rather, to a stateless, self-governing and autonomous people, equal in status, but not in form, to the Canadian state, with a willingness to negotiate shared jurisdiction of land and resources."[131] The language of sovereignty is not, of course, necessary. Treaties and other forms of nation-to-nation recognition can involve alternative language and concepts more appropriate to defining independence within shared relations of responsibility and interdependence.

---

[130] Ladner, "Bugs, Building Blocks, and Constitutional Pluralism," seminar presentation, Department of Political Science, University of Toronto, December 13, 2019.
[131] Tully, "The Struggles of Indigenous Peoples for and of Freedom," 279–280.

John Borrows writes: "One device for facilitating harmonization is the recognition and application of First Nations laws to other people in society."[132]

For Indigenous nations, treaty constitutionalism involves a process of rebuilding constitutional practices. This is a demanding process, given the destructive legacies of abuse and genocide, and the diversity and dispersal of Indigenous people, more than half of whom now live in urban centers. For settler governments, the difficulty will involve learning to work with Indigenous peoples as equal nations, to honor treaties and to renegotiate treaties that respect alternative forms of governance, and to combine Indigenous law with Canadian law.

Genuine reconciliation will also require a deeper process of ethical transformation, which is also a political practice: a transformation of who we are. For settlers as for Indigenous people, this will require engagement in relations of interdependence rooted in relations with the living earth. John Borrows and James Tully argue that politics and practices of resurgence and reconciliation should be seen as interdependent. Transformative reconciliation involves "practices of reconciliation between Indigenous and settler nations as well as efforts to strengthen the relationship between Indigenous and settler peoples with the living earth ... using 'earth teachings' to inform social practices."[133] Just as Indigenous politics of resurgence depend on rebuilding nations through remaking relations of interdependence with the living earth, so Indigenous–settler reconciliation needs to follow this practice. This will involve developing relations of gift reciprocity, guided by Indigenous philosophies and practices of relational freedom that combine independence and interdependence.

For settlers, the politics of transformative reconciliation requires that we question our dominant models of freedom. I have argued that we need to question the assumption that noninterference is the basis of freedom and to resist identifying this and other conceptions of freedom in the Western European political tradition as descriptions of or prescriptions for Indigenous freedom. I have suggested that the conception of freedom as noninterference may have been produced through a misrecognition of the freedom of the Indigenous peoples of the Americas.

But if this conception of freedom has been produced through misrecognition, then the challenge to freedom as noninterference is necessary not only for the decolonization of Indigenous peoples but also for the decolonization of the colonizers. All of us need to question the conviction that freedom must lie ultimately in noninterference. If we do not question this conviction, we who are colonizers remain colonized ourselves: imprisoned in a conception of freedom that corrodes our relations with each other, that allows us to destroy the land we

---

[132] Borrows, *Freedom and Indigenous Constitutionalism*, 45.
[133] Asch, Borrows, and Tully, eds., *Resurgence and Reconciliation*, title page.

inhabit and to drain our souls in the name of freedom to act as we please in our private spaces. This kind of freedom will eventually destroy us all. We can escape this destruction if we listen and learn from a different conception of freedom: a conception of freedom that can be found only in mutual attentive relations with each other, with "earth others," and with the parts of ourselves that long for these relationships. "[O]ur cultures have much to teach the Western world about the establishment of relationships within and between peoples and the natural world that are profoundly non-imperialist."[134] Decolonization will happen only when settler nations can learn how to practice relational freedom.

---

[134] Coulthard, "Subjects of Empire," 456.

2
For Love of the World
Relational Political Freedom as Love of Land

Why is it so difficult to love the world?
—Hannah Arendt

I believe that our responsibility as Indigenous peoples is to work alongside our Ancestors and those not yet born to continually give birth to an Indigenous present that generates Indigenous freedom, and this means creating generations that are in love with, attached to and committed to their land.
—Leanne Betasamosake Simpson

What can it mean to love the world in the face of forces of colonization that are apparently bent on destruction? Hannah Arendt knew as well as anyone how difficult it is to love the world in dark times. For Arendt, love of the world—*amor mundi*—was deeply connected with human freedom. Human beings are most free when they act creatively together in public political life. And their free interactions are oriented toward and mediated by a world of shared concern. Freedom, then, is public engagement with the world we love. We might say that freedom is the enactment of love of the world.

In this chapter I consider the relationship between Arendt's *amor mundi* and Leanne Betasamosake Simpson's philosophy of love of land, as the ethos or spirit of freedom. Land, in Indigenous philosophies, is the web of relations that connects all beings. As Simpson writes, love of land, as a practice of active care *for* land, is central to Indigenous freedom and resistance, and it is central to *constellations of co-resistance* to multiple forms of colonization. Love of land is a practice of resurgence that addresses fear and violence with the difficult but exhilarating practice of active care *for* the world. This conception of freedom through active care for land and world expands Arendt's conception, to include engagement in a web of consensual and sustaining relationships, organized through an ethic of gift relations, through loving reciprocity. To mediate between Arendt's conception of love of the world and Simpson's theory of love of land, I draw on Ella Myers's *worldly ethics*. Myers expands Arendt's conception of world to include the web of relations that constitute the conditions of our lives. And she draws on Arendt's *amor mundi* to formulate a worldly ethics as the spirit of care for the world that animates relations of contestation and solidarity oriented toward matters of shared concern. Yet Myers retains Arendt's focus on human agency and Arendt's binary between political care for the world and social practices of care for others.

I argue that political contestations over meanings of land challenge the boundaries between human and nonhuman, between public and private, and between agency and responsiveness. Transformative reconciliation between settlers and Indigenous peoples will require learning from what Simpson calls *land as pedagogy*, to develop a *philoxenic* worldly ethics that involves philoxenic solidarity among diverse collective agents in resistance to diverse forms of colonization, in an expanded conception and active practice of love of the world. Drawing on the understanding of land as governed by a gift economy, I propose a conception of *agency* as participation in gift relations: human agency can be seen as a response to gifts. If agency is not an act of a subject toward an object, but participation in a web of diverse relations, agency is a response to the agency of other beings, and to the agency of world as land. Care for the world is a response to the world's love and care for us—a response that risks connection in situations of hostility and conflict. An expanded understanding of political agency as care for the world as a web of interdependent relations integrates care for particular others and care for selves oriented toward care for worldly conditions.

I consider the contrast between Arendt's rejection of love of nation as a politics of destructive self-interest and Simpson's understanding of love of nation as a series of radiating responsibilities. These two conceptions of love of nation correspond to contrasting conceptions of freedom: propertized freedom as right to destroy and relational freedom as engagement in webs of reciprocal relations.

In a brief *coda*, I respond to Arendt's critique of the connection between love and freedom in James Baldwin's "Letter from a Region in my Mind." Arendt's critique is misplaced. Like Arendt and like Simpson, Baldwin conceives of freedom as a practice of love that can combat hate through engagement in the world.

Arendt and Relational Freedom

For Arendt, the form of freedom that Hobbes and Berlin espoused—freedom in the private sphere, sheltered from political life—was not freedom at all, but a form of imprisonment in fear. And the freedom of mastery—of the master in relation to the slave—was not freedom either. For Arendt, freedom for the Greeks was not a status—not the status of a master in opposition to the slave—but an engagement in public political life. In *On Revolution*, Arendt wrote that political freedom in the Greek city-states originally meant not democracy but *no-rule*.

Hence freedom and equality were originally "almost identical."[1] Arendt stresses that this was not an equality of condition or nature, but an equality that must be *created* through collective participation in the political realm.

> The Greeks held that no one can be free except among his peers, that therefore neither the tyrant nor the despot nor the master of a household—even though he was fully liberated and was not forced by others—was freed. The point of Herodotus's equation of freedom with no-rule was that the ruler himself was not free; by assuming the rule over others, he had deprived himself of those peers in whose company he could have been free. In other words, he had destroyed the political space itself, with the result that there was no freedom extant any longer, either for himself or for those over whom he ruled. . . . The life of a free man needed the presence of others. Freedom itself needed therefore a place where people could come together—the agora, the market-place, or the *polis*, the political space proper.[2]

For Arendt, the understanding of freedom in terms of the master-slave binary fails to grasp what freedom is. Not being a slave is not yet freedom. And mastery is not freedom but a state of isolation. What Arendt doesn't point out here is that the ruler is unfree not only because he lacks the company of others, but because he is bound to the slave in a dependent relationship of domination. This interdependence is central to the formulations of freedom in the work of Hegel and Marx. In the tradition of Western critical theory, we are not free so long as we live in unfree relations of domination. The colonizer, then, cannot be free so long as he is bound in relations of colonization. Like the head of the household, he is dependent for his freedom on the walls that surround him, to protect him from the dangers outside. But this is only an illusion of freedom, and the illusion traps him behind those walls. For Arendt, freedom is found not behind walls, but in the company of others. Freedom then requires a place where people come together. For her that place was the polis—the world of the public political sphere.

Amor Mundi as a Practice of Freedom

The public world of democratic engagement is clearly a site of agonistic politics. To see it as a site of freedom animated by love would seem to be a bit of a stretch. Yet the concept of *amor mundi* is arguably central to Arendt's understanding of public life. We know that *Amor Mundi* was the original title of *The*

---

[1] Arendt, *On Revolution*, 30.
[2] Arendt, *On Revolution*, 31.

Human Condition. Arendt was drawn to the classical conception of an *ethos* of public life, and she was drawn in particular to the classical conception of love as a public bond.[3] *Amor mundi*, then, could be seen as the *ethos* or spirit of a public bond that could animate relations of freedom. But what is love of the world? And in what sense can the public realm be considered a site of freedom animated by love?

In *The Human Condition*, Arendt wrote that *the world* is made up of the environment that we create and that conditions us, along with the deeds and words that endure and outlast us. The common world "is what we have in common not only with those who live with us, but also with those who were here before and with those who will come after us."[4] For Arendt, the reality of the common world is guaranteed by the fact that it is the object of human concern: the world is the shared object of a plurality of perspectives joined by our active participation in that plurality. More expansively, Lawrence Biskowski writes: "For Arendt, the world is the entire pragmatic web of relationships in which human beings are caught up, the total interplay between people, things, and relationships." And care for the world is care for "what the world will be like in the wake of one's acting."[5] If the world is the web of relations that connect us, love of the world is love for the world of plurality that preserves our difference while it unites us. This is the world in which we find ourselves and the world that we make together. If human freedom is action in concert, we could say that love of the world is expressed in active engagement in practices of relational freedom: practices that create and re-create the world in which we live together.

Bonnie Honig has argued that engagement in the public sphere involves shared engagement with *public things* that are "sites of attachment and meaning."[6] Public things are things we care about, and "democracy is rooted in common love for, antipathy to, and contestation of public things."[7] Honig considers public infrastructure—including things like schools and universities, parks, roads, communications systems, pipelines—as material public things without which action in common is impossible. Drawing on Winnicott's object relations theory, Honig understands public things as holding spaces, or holding environments of democratic citizenship. Without shared public things, we cannot properly attach to each other as citizens, or to the land we live on. Honig considers Tocqueville's

---

[3] Arendt was ambivalent about relations between love and freedom, and never worked through this ambivalence. I think this would have required working through the differences among diverse forms of love and their relations to diverse forms of freedom: a project she began with *Love and Saint Augustine*, but abandoned. I discuss Arendt's repudiation of love of nation later in this chapter. In Chapter 3, I discuss Arendt's ambivalence about relations between love and freedom, and contrast her affirmation of *philia politikē* with a more radical *philoxenia*.
[4] Arendt, *The Human Condition*, 55.
[5] Biskowski, "Practical Foundations for Political Judgment," 879–880.
[6] Honig, *Public Things*, 6.
[7] Honig, *Public Things*, 4.

observations of the failures of attachment of settlers to their new land, alongside his description of the forced dispossession of the Choctaw people: "It is as if—in that moment, and for just a moment, historically speaking—the land regurgitated the whites whose leaders had thought *they* could swallow *it*, once it was emptied of its prior inhabitants. It is as if the object of white desire had an agency of its own. Could it be that what looks to Tocqueville like an inexplicable white nomadism is in fact the land's vengeful rejection of those who dispossessed and destroyed its prior denizens?"[8]

While public things are sites of attachment, they are also sites of contestation. While the public infrastructure built by settlers on Indigenous land may be a site of attachment, "one community's public thing is the product of an act of theft and dispossession to another."[9] For Arendt, the contestation was central to the attachment: contestation is public engagement with the world we care about. The shared world is possible only because we are participants in contestation, and this allows us to see the world from multiple perspectives. Colonization involves a refusal to recognize the perspectives of the colonized: a refusal to share the world.

Like Honig, Ella Myers understands love of the world as engagement with things we care about. Myers argues that political care for the world focuses not on the world in general but on *worldly things*. For Myers, worldly things are shared *conditions* that are matters of concern, contested objects. Myers theorizes a *worldly ethics*: a democratic *ethos* of contentious and collaborative care for the world. As she notes, the idea of a collective *ethos* or spirit that supports governance and motivates pursuit of the public good was central to Greek political culture, captured in what Plato called *the politea of the soul*. This sense of a shared ethos continues to motivate civic republican formulations of civic virtue. While she supports the quest for a shared sensibility or spirit, a kind of "moral ambience" that could support democratic life, Myers argues that formulations of democratic ethics that center on care for the self and care for the Other are inadequate as sources of motivation for associative democratic politics. Both Foucaultian therapeutic ethics of the self and Levinasian charitable ethics of care for the Other focus on dyadic relations that "obscure the worldly contexts that are the actual sites and objects of democratic action."[10] Theories that attempt to extend these ethics to support democratic life cannot adequately account for the problem of collaboration among diverse actors motivated by shared concern for a worldly problem. Instead, Myers proposes an ethos that centers on the world of common concern. To illustrate the difference among these three perspectives, Myers offers the example of different ways to address the problem of hunger. A therapeutic

---

[8] Honig, *Public Things*, 9.
[9] Honig, *Public Things*, 3.
[10] Myers, *Worldly Ethics*, 2.

ethics would involve work on oneself to cultivate personal habits such as vegetarianism. A charitable ethics involves attending directly to the hungry, to provide food and sources of sustenance. A worldly ethics would involve tending, together with others, to the conditions that produce hunger.[11]

The world, Myers argues, is the third term, the in-between that mediates among political actors, both as the site or context for action, and as the object of that action. For Arendt, the world is common insofar as it establishes both a bond and distance between people. "The world mediates between people in this double sense: it establishes a connection that preserves distinction; it is the simultaneous antidote to isolation and massification. As Reinhardt notes, this emphasis on the world as in-between is striking in its claim to a form of political commonality that is not subject centered; what is common here is extra-subjective, between us not in us."[12] Myers stresses that the world is also not simply *intersubjective*, not reducible to human beings and their relations. The world is the *interspace* that mediates and separates a plurality of political actors through their orientation to shared and disputed objects of attention and concern.

For Myers, *worldly things* are shared conditions, contested objects that are matters of concern for all of us. As Heidegger noted, the term *thing* originally referred to "a gathering, and specifically a gathering to deliberate a matter under discussion, a contested matter."[13] The meaning of the term shifted to refer to the matter that drew people together. Worldly things, then, unite political actors, as individuals and as collectives: people working together in associative activity that is both collaborative and contentious. And worldly ethics refers to the shared spirit of care for the world that animates relations of contested and solidaristic association concerning common and contested objects or matters of concern.

Myers's conception of care for the world draws on and extends Arendt's *amor mundi*—love of the world. "As I read it, the phrase is meant to describe an emotional investment in and deep affection for something other than human selves, namely, for the complex, extrasubjective 'web' that constitutes the conditions of our lives."[14] But the idea of care for the world refers to more than emotional investment: it refers to an "active tending to and looking after"—not just caring *about*, but actively caring *for* the world. Care for the world as a democratic ethos refers to "a mode of collaborative caretaking that is directed not at a person or even persons but at the conditions of their lives."[15]

---

[11] Myers, *Worldly Ethics*, 109. The theorists she criticizes do of course argue that their ethics engage he world of common concern, and would certainly object to the characterization of their approaches as only self-focused or charitable. This discussion lies beyond the scope of this paper.
[12] Myers, *Worldly Ethics*, 123.
[13] Myers, *Worldly Ethics*, 92.
[14] Myers, *Worldly Ethics*, 87.
[15] Myers, *Worldly Ethics*, 87.

Myers's understanding of care for the world thus incorporates a normative conception of world as an inclusive mediating political space and as "shared human home" that provides hospitable conditions for all. Thus "care for the world is expressed not only by associative action that tends to conditions but also by action that pursues particular substantive ends."[16]

For Arendt, the world was the human and human-made world, which she distinguished from the natural world, or earth. Myers rejects the distinction between world and earth, culture and nature. For Myers, "part of the value of the concept of world . . . lies in its broadly anti-anthropocentric character. World displaces human beings from the center of analysis and brings into view a complex material and immaterial assemblage that is irreducible to human beings themselves."[17] If the world is the site and object of human action, it is not simply what is made by human beings. Drawing on Bruno Latour and Jane Bennett, Myers understands world as involving "a vast array of relations, places, practices, organisms, material goods, and so on that coexist with one another in complex webs, defying any neat nature/culture divide and exceeding the category of human being. *World* refers to the sum total of conditions of life on earth."[18]

Yet she rejects Latour's and Bennett's ascription of agency to nonhuman actants, retaining a "focus on the ways in which human beings collectively affect the world of which they are a part."[19] With Arendt, Myers focuses on world as it appears *for* human beings, and on human responsibility for care for the world as it appears as matters of concern for us.

Care for the World as Care for Land: Agency as Gift

I agree with Myers that human beings need to focus on our own distinctive agency and responsibility in active practices of care for the world. But once we consider the contestation among human beings over the meanings of *land*, it becomes less plausible to reserve the concept of agency for human beings alone. Political contestation between Indigenous people and colonizing states over the meaning of *land* requires a further rethinking and expansion of the concept of *world*, and of Myers's Arendtian conceptions of relations between humans and world. These include conceptions of agency, of the subject-object relation between humans and worldly things, and of the normative ideals of world as a shared human home and as a mediating space among humans.

---

[16] Myers, *Worldly Ethics*, 2.
[17] Myers, *Worldly Ethics*, 92.
[18] Myers, *Worldly Ethics*, 100.
[19] Myers, *Worldly Ethics*, 101.

When the Standing Rock Sioux resist the Dakota Access Pipeline, when the Wet'suwet'en land defenders resist the Coastal Gas Pipeline, when Wangan and Jagalingou activists resist Adani coal mines, when Aboriginal peoples all over the world resist the destruction of sacred sites, the contamination of earth and water, and the devastating effects of colonization on biodiversity and climate, they are engaged in contestation not just over ownership of land but over the *meaning* of land. At the heart of all of these conflicts are struggles over land and its meanings. For the colonizing state, and the gas and mining companies, land is property, and a source of resources that generate wealth. At best, land exists for people to use: for human consumption. For Indigenous people, land does offer food and sustenance for human beings, but land is much more than that. Land is a system of relationships among animate beings, and animate beings include not only animals but other beings within Western categories of nature, including rocks, trees, plants, and rivers, as well as spirit beings and ancestors.

The struggle over land is a struggle among humans over the meaning of what Myers calls a worldly thing, a shared object of attachment and contention: land. Any genuine reconciliation between settlers and Indigenous people will require that settlers recognize the legitimacy of Indigenous conceptions of land. The (re)negotiation of treaties does not necessarily require that colonizing states *adopt* Indigenous conceptions of land, but they must at least recognize the legitimacy of these conceptions, and they must negotiate treaties that recognize their legitimacy. (It should be obvious that this requires the recognition of Indigenous peoples as legitimate participants in dialogue and negotiation.)

Ideally, the struggle over land can open up, for settlers, a different meaning of land: an understanding of land not as property but as a system of belonging. For settler philosophers and political theorists, it's not enough to recognize the Indigenous view of land as legitimate. To respond to the contestation over the meaning of land, we need to attend to this view as one that can contribute to our own understanding of the world, and to consider it as a normative worldview that is potentially better than the one we may presently hold. To do this, we need to understand land not just as a *worldly thing*—an object of contention—but as a more expansive conception of *world*. This is of particular importance if we want to avert environmental catastrophe.

Land, like world, is a complex web of relations. Like Myers's conception of world, land is the sum total of conditions of life on earth. But it's more than this: it includes all beings as agents and recipients in a system of reciprocity that incorporates a normative dimension. As Glen Coulthard writes, land as a system of reciprocal relations and obligations is the source of what he calls *grounded normativity*: "the modalities of Indigenous land-connected practices and longstanding experiential knowledge that inform and structure our ethical engagements with the world and our relationships with human and nonhuman others over time."[20] Care for land is care for this system of relationships, guided by the ethic of grounded normativity.

Indigenous thought includes a much more capacious conception of the *agents* of care and concern—the participants in democratic contestation and association. Within Indigenous conceptions, land is not just a human concern but a shared concern among a much broader and more diverse sphere of agents and stakeholders. "All of our relations"—including rocks, trees, and rivers, as well as ancestors and grandchildren—are active participants in democratic relations and in care and concern for land. Moreover, they themselves are included in the understanding of land. Land is not just object and site of intersubjective human interaction, but a complex web of relations that defies the subject/object binary to include all beings as participants in care and concern. This understanding of land can broaden the scope of possibilities for contention in our struggles over land—but it can also help to resolve them.

As Leanne Betasamosake Simpson writes, the Nishnaabeg conception of land as a web of relationships is based on the idea that Aki, the earth, gives and sustains all life. Central to this understanding is the concept of the gift. Land is understood as a system of deep reciprocity, in which all participants engage in giving and receiving gifts.[21] I think this opens up a unique formulation of agency. Agency is not simply an effect of rational intention, nor is it simply creative action, or action in concert. Neither is it reducible to effective causation, as it is in Bennett's reformulation, which is meant to include nonhuman agents.[22] If we follow Simpson's account of Nishnaabeg thought, agency can be understood as gift giving—as engagement in a vast constellation of reciprocal relations of giving and receiving gifts. Conversely, agency might involve the denial of those gifts.

This doesn't mean that there is *no distinction* between human and nonhuman agency and responsibility. If all beings are recognized in their uniqueness, and have diverse powers and capacities, humans have very distinctive forms of agency and responsibility. It does mean that when humans consider and take responsibility for land, they see themselves as taking part in reciprocal relations within a web of diverse relations, rather than subject-object relations. So when there is contestation among humans over land, that contestation is situated within a larger associative constellation of action in concert. Contestation takes place within a framework that assumes the ethical necessity of reciprocal relations.

For Simpson, love of land is a practice of relationship that grounds knowledge and ethics. But this love doesn't begin with humans: human love for land is a response to the love given by land, in the circle of gift relations. Simpson

---

[20] Coulthard, *Red Skins, White Masks*, 13.
[21] Betasamosake Simpson, *As We Have Always Done*, 8.
[22] See Kompridis, "Nonhuman Agency and Human Normativity."

writes that the gifts of the land can be understood with the Nishnaabeg term *gaa-izhi-zhaawendaagoziyaang*, which is translated by Nishnaabe scholar Wendy Makoons Geniusz as "given lovingly to us by the spirits."[23] Love of land, then, can be understood as active participation in reciprocal relations of gift giving, as recipient, respondent, and agent. Environmental biologist Robin Wall Kimmerer argues that our survival on this planet depends on learning from the teachings of plants, so that we can respond with gratitude for the love given to us by the earth. As she writes, the land nurtures and protects us, and facilitates our flourishing. If we observe such behaviors in a human being, we call it caregiving. We call it love.[24] Is the perception of the gifts of the earth as acts of care and generosity nothing but a romantic metaphor? Or is our tendency to ridicule such a worldview a peculiar trap of thinking that is quickly leading to world destruction? Of course, we can work to prevent environmental catastrophe with a more utilitarian view of the earth as a resource. But that is precisely the worldview that is motivating the earth's destruction.

For Kimmerer we can learn to care for the earth only by attending closely to the teachings of plants, rocks, rivers: earthly agents. Central to human participation in reciprocal relations then is what Simpson calls *land as pedagogy*: human beings learn from attending to land. According to the concept of land as pedagogy, our specific human agency is learned, in part, from attention to land—from attention and response to the agency of other beings.

Patchen Markell reflects something like this conception of agency as a response when he characterizes associative action as a *second step* rather than a first: democratic associations form in response to conditions that "occasion, provoke or summons" a response.[25] The world and worldly things, then, actively call for our attention. For Myers, the response to a worldly thing is the source of solidarity—but also contestation. Care for the world as a response to the world could be described as engagement in a cycle of relations: the world constitutes and is constituted by human concern, care, and love. Myers and Markell do not thematize the world's *love* and *care* for us—but if we can see the world as calling for our attention, it is not so difficult to see the earth's provision of life, of air, food, water, as a form of care for humans and other beings.

Interestingly, Hannah Arendt seems to support this understanding when she suggests, in the prologue to *The Human Condition*, that human existence has been given as a gift from Mother Earth. Arendt expresses amazement that the first launch of a satellite into space was hailed as a "step toward escape from men's

---

[23] Simpson, *As We Have Always Done*, 149.
[24] Wall Kimmerer, *Braiding Sweetgrass*, 123.
[25] Markell, "The Rule of the People," 12 (cited by Myers, *Worldly Ethics*, 105). Annette Baier and Lorraine Code argue that human agents are "second persons": personhood and agency develop in response to others. Baier, *Postures of the Mind*; Code, *What Can She Know?*

imprisonment to the earth." She asks: "Should the emancipation and secularization of the modern age ... end with ... repudiation of an Earth who was the Mother of all living creatures under the sky?" Here Arendt questions the arrogance of "a rebellion against human existence as it has been given, a free gift from nowhere (secularly speaking)"—from the earth as provider of the habitat for human beings. This rebellion, Arendt writes, expresses man's wish to exchange the gift of human existence on earth for something made by man. "There is no reason to doubt our abilities to accomplish such an exchange, just as there is no reason to doubt our present ability to destroy all organic life on earth." The decision as to whether we will do this is, Arendt writes, is "a political question of the first order."[26] Arendt seems to recognize that this would be a decision between disavowing or reciprocating the care offered by the earth. If the purpose of her analysis of the human condition is "to trace back modern world alienation, its twofold flight from the earth into the universe and from the world into the self, to its origins,"[27] this analysis is guided by the idea of *amor mundi*. In her consideration of the meaning of *amor mundi* in Arendt's thought, Lucy Tatman writes: "This Arendtian love of the world is the grateful emotional response to the fact that meaningful life has been given unto us."[28]

Does the understanding of agency as participation in webs of gift relations destroy the role of world as in-between, as separation and mediation among participants in democratic life? On the contrary, it expands the mediating role of world with a recognition of worldly things—of objects of consideration, issues and matters of concern—as involving a wider multiplicity of agents who are also unique beings with their own concerns. Far from a regression to a primordial soup of undifferentiated unity or a multiplicity without individuation, this worldview heightens our awareness of the plurality of agency, and the uniqueness of individuals, and heightens a sense of responsibility for relations both to others and to shared and contentious matters of concern.

While it expands the scope of democratic life, this worldview retains the sense of worldly thing as object in the sense that it is a matter of concern. So the meaning and use of the land is the matter of concern, the contested object. And the health and wellbeing of the whole system is a contested object. But this worldview also retains the original meaning of *thing* as *gathering*. When the matter of concern is understood to be situated within the cycle of gift relations, this shifts us out of subject-object relations to focus on the plurality of agents already engaged in constituting the world.

---

[26] Arendt, *The Human Condition*, 2–3. I thank Ella Myers for calling my attention to this passage.
[27] Arendt, *The Human Condition*, 6.
[28] Tatman, "Arendt and Augustine," 635. I continue the discussion of the role of gratitude in Arendt's thought in Chapter 3.

Care for Land as a Practice of Indigenous Freedom: Decolonization as Risking Connection

For Leanne Simpson, Indigenous freedom is enacted through love of land. "Indigenous freedom," she writes, "is a guiding vision or manifesto" for her work.[29] "What does it mean for me, as an Nishnaabekwe, to live freedom? I want my great-grandchildren to be able to fall in love with every piece of our territory. I want their bodies to carry with them every story, every song, every piece of poetry hidden in our Nishnaabeg language. I want them to be able to dance through their lives with joy."[30] Indigenous freedom, for Simpson, is the freedom to love the land, to live in deep relationship, without fear: to know respect, to be nourished by a clean environment, and to be valued, heard, and cherished. "This is the intense love of land," she writes, "that has always been the spine of Indigenous resistance."[31]

Like Arendt, Simpson argues that freedom is found in relations with others—with our peers. For Simpson, our peers are all of the beings on earth—all our relations.[32] And the public world is everywhere. As Borrows writes, there is no relationship-free place. Simpson understands "freedom as a way of being, as a constellation of relationship, freedom as world making, freedom as a practice."[33] Freedom is found in active engagement: in active care for land, in a practice of world-making. This practice of freedom is the core of resistance to colonization: Indigenous resurgence.

This stress on action and on active caring *for* land is important to counteract romantic images of Indigenous relationality. First of all, care for land—care for the world—is difficult work, and it involves confronting danger, fear, and violence. Secondly, care for land—care for the world—involves contestation: it is central to resistance to colonization. Care for land is not a mysterious otherworldly connectedness. It is not natural, and it is not primitive. Care for land is hard work—physical, intellectual, and spiritual work—requiring attentiveness, patience, listening, openness to learning, and the development of knowledge.[34] It requires skilled action and interaction, adaptability, agility, readiness to run, sometimes to attack. It always requires struggle against fear of the strange other,

---

[29] Simpson, *As We Have Always Done*, 7.
[30] Simpson, *As We Have Always Done*, 7.
[31] Simpson, *As We Have Always Done*, 8–9.
[32] Simpson is writing to and about Indigenous people. I'm suggesting that her words apply—or ought to apply—to all of us.
[33] Simpson, *As We Have Always Done*, 18.
[34] Here I am resisting Arendt's distinction between action and work. And following John Borrows, who writes: "I do not claim Indigenous peoples are natural environmentalists. In fact, this can be a damaging stereotype. Indigenous peoples can be as destructive as other societies on earth—we are part of humanity, not outside of it. Caring for the earth is hard work. It does not always come naturally" (Borrows, "Earth-Bound," 49).

and of the manifest violence and danger of forces of nature and other animals, including humans. Hobbes was right: they can kill you. Yet in response to fear, rather than rational agreement based in self-interest and secured by tyranny, rather than finding freedom in protection of private space, care for land is a practice of relational freedom through fierce love of the world. Again, that love is not natural; it's an active practice. It involves risking connection with and against dangerous others. It involves skills of cooperative action and conflict resolution. Care for land is a practice of reciprocity, of gift exchanges that work to create and maintain sustainable relationships.

As Simpson writes, "love of land" has always been "the spine of Indigenous resistance."[35] Simpson advocates a practice of resurgence, an assertion of sovereignty and a practice of nation-building that centers on engaging with *land as pedagogy*: learning from land as teacher. With Coulthard, Simpson advocates shifting focus from struggles for state recognition to reengaging in relations with land. So she understands freedom as a practice of *biiskabiyang*, which means "returning to ourselves": a "flight out of the structures of settler colonialism and into the processes and relationships of freedom and self-determination encoded and practiced within Nishnaabewin or grounded normativity."[36] She recalls her attempts, as a young woman, to learn from elders about Indigenous governance. "I kept asking them about governance, and they would talk about trapping. I would ask them about treaties, and they would take me fishing. I'd ask them what we should do about the mess of colonialism, and they would tell me stories about how well they used to live on the land. I loved all of it, but I didn't think they were answering my questions. I could see only *practice*. I couldn't see their *theory* until decades later."[37]

For Simpson, care for land is not just about returning to ancient traditions. It involves listening to elders and stories of the old ways, but it also involves learning from land as pedagogy, to create new ways of addressing new situations. Land as pedagogy involves learning through playful and spontaneous engagement with the world: "lovingly coming to know."[38] This includes learning from the diversity of land to embrace gender diversity, and drawing on principles of reciprocity and co-creation to criticize heterosexist claims of tradition and to pursue co-resistance and solidarity between Indigenous and Black struggles. With Arendt, Simpson understands freedom as creative action. Simpson's flight into *biiskabiyang* is a flight into "freedom as a way of being as a constellation of relationship, freedom as world making, freedom as a practice."[39] With Arendt,

---

[35] Simpson, *As We Have Always Done*, 9.
[36] Simpson, *As We Have Always Done*, 17.
[37] Simpson, *As We Have Always Done*, 18.
[38] Simpson, *As We Have Always Done*, 157.
[39] Simpson, *As We Have Always Done*, 18.

she understands freedom as a practice of natality, an active practice of love of the world. "I believe our responsibility as Indigenous peoples is to work alongside our ancestors and those not yet born to continually give birth to an Indigenous present that generates Indigenous freedom, and this means creating generations that are in love with, attached to, and committed to their land."[40] We could say that love and care for land is a much more expansive and radical practice of what Arendt called *amor mundi*. It might be better to say that Arendt's invocation of *amor mundi* is a gesture toward an ancient and continuing practice of love and care for land.

Worldly Ethics and Grounded Normativity

The ideal of worldly ethics proposed by Ella Myers is oriented to two normative ends: the world as shared human home, and as mediating in-between. Care for the world as shared human home orients us to the normative end of meeting basic human needs, of building a world where all humans can be at home. Care for the world as mediating in-between, as the public sphere of solidaristic and contesting association, orients us to building inclusive democratic cultures and institutions, to ensure that all can engage in democratic coordinated action. The normative ideal of worldly ethics brings together the substantive and procedural ends of provision of needs and support of democratic life. These two ends do not entail each other, and they can exist in tension.

From the perspective of Indigenous thought, it's difficult to square Myers's claim that part of the value of the concept of world is its anti-anthropocentrism with the anthropocentrism of her normative ideal of world as a human home and as mediating force among human beings, and with her rejection of the concept of nonhuman agency. Myers anticipates the charge of anthropocentrism, and she argues that a form of enlightened anthropocentrism—an appeal to human self-interest that includes consideration for the insights of coexistentialism—is more pragmatic than attempts to reject anthropocentrism. Myers cites Andrew Light's pragmatist-pluralist approach to motivating people to support environmental policy: in many cases, humans are more likely to be motivated by arguments of human self-interest. As she writes, "philosophical purity matters less than ethico-political resonance."[41] While this may be true, it's not clear why Myers resorts to a pragmatic argument to support the limitation of her normative position. The normative ideal of world as shared human home is important and necessary. But

---

[40] Simpson, *As We Have Always Done*, 25.
[41] Myers, *Worldly Ethics*, 128.

there doesn't appear to be a *normative* reason for *limiting* the normative concept of world as home to humans.

Myers is surely right to address her argument to humans, and to argue that we human beings need to aspire to a normative ideal of care for the world. But our care for the world is strengthened if we understand our agency as a participation in relations *with* nonhuman agents and guided by a normative ideal of world as shared home for all beings. For Indigenous thought, the restriction of world to that which concerns humans is a *contraction* of what the world really is. For settlers, Indigenous conceptions of land can *expand* our conception of the world.

Myers extends the concept of world to include the vast network of relations among beings and things, and supports the insights of coexistentialism: the ecological perspective that assumes the interconnectedness of all worldly entities, and that locates human beings within, rather than above, this worldly web. Caring for the world, she writes, "involves not owning, ruling, or enjoying dominion over but collaboratively tending to the world. . . . Such care should be guided by awareness of the webs of relation that link human beings . . . to other 'vibrant matter.'" This will involve skepticism about human needs claims that will cause damage to the ecosphere. "Such awareness does not, however, require that one attempt (in vain?) to thoroughly equalize one's concern for humans with concern for nonhumans. Genuinely ecologically minded self-interest is enough to aspire to."[42]

But is it enough? Myers is surely right that it is not possible to thoroughly equalize the multiple needs claims of nonhuman beings with those of humans. The needs of worms, mosquitoes, and chickens, oceans, trees, and soil are all very different from each other and from human needs. Balancing all of these needs is not as simple as asserting a principle of universal equal rights.[43] And, of course, these needs claims (like human needs claims) are often competing and conflicting. Attending to the web of needs claims requires the difficult work of attunement to each being or part of the web, and to the interdependence of all of the parts. It requires collaboration among those with expert knowledge of and skilled practices of care for each being, and it involves judgment to consider conflicting needs claims. Attending to and balancing needs claims is a never-ending practice. But this is precisely the practice that is necessary for understanding and caring for the webs of relations that make up the world.

In Indigenous thought, this practice of attunement and balance is guided by grounded normativity: by the norm of reciprocity in a cycle of gift relations. Grounded normativity guides practices of knowledge of what various needs

---

[42] Myers, *Worldly Ethics*, 129.

[43] I'm not suggesting that a normative claim to universal rights makes it simple to balance human needs in practice.

are and how they interact with each other in webs of relationship. This practice guides the development of human expertise—and it involves attending to nonhuman expertise. These practices of knowledge are entwined with practices of care and of judgment: they mutually inform each other. From the perspective of Indigenous thought, a normative ideal of enlightened self-interest that prioritizes human needs cannot guide practices of knowledge that will be adequately attuned to the web of relations that connect us. This attunement requires the knowledge learned through attending to what Simpson calls land as pedagogy. It requires the recognition of all beings as agents with particular forms of expertise and as participants in the collaborative activity of democratic life.

Reliance on a normative philosophy of enlightened human self-interest makes it impossible to fairly adjudicate among the competing claims of settler states and Indigenous peoples over land. Self-interest is in fact the assumption that too often guides the adjudication, by state justices, among competing claims of settler states and Indigenous peoples over land. This assumption makes it difficult to recognize Indigenous claims to land as something *other* than self-interest. Land claims are typically perceived to be claims of rights to property ownership, and Indigenous claimants are compelled to claim property ownership. Conceptions of belonging to land and of responsibility for land are difficult to articulate or to recognize within this framework. If they are recognized at all, they are recognized as secondary: as evidence of rights to property ownership.

Care for Others/Care for the World: Rethinking the Public/Private Split

For political philosophers, care for the world of contested matters—worldly things—seems intuitively more important than ethics of care for specific others, and more important than a therapeutic ethics of care for self. Care for worldly conditions is the form of care that is specific to *political* action. Concern for contested matters ideally trains our focus on the "big picture"—on the web of relations in which we are all enmeshed. This is the ideal. But, of course, in practice political agents are not always concerned with the web of relations. Too often contestatory politics is just a war of self-interests. How can contestation over matters that concern us shift from a politics of self-interest to a politics of genuine care for the world? How do we shift our focus to our interdependence in a complex web of relations, and to the plurality of perspectives that must be taken into account?

While Myers's distinction of worldly ethics from care for others and care for self makes sense conceptually, the categorization of care for others and care for self as (merely?) charitable and therapeutic ethics seems to relegate these forms of care to the prepolitical, privatized, feminized, familial sphere of the social. This is a problem because if the primary task of politics is to deliberate about and care for worldly conditions, political deliberation must focus on matters of human and earthly wellbeing, which include the earthly fleshly matter of human and more-than-human needs. If our contestation over issues that concern us is divorced from practical care for specific earthly beings, then we are missing what actually *matters*. And typically these two forms of care are very much divorced in practice. If public deliberators and policymakers are free to engage in the important activities of politics while others (typically unpaid and poorly paid feminized and racialized care workers) do the work of care for specific others, then we re-entrench the public/private split: the *polis* is separate from, and above, while dependent upon, the world of necessity. Jennifer Nedelsky argues that without active experience of care for specific others, policymakers can't make good policy: they have no real knowledge of what others need—or what carers need.[44] What are the matters that concern us? Education, child care, health care, social services, poverty, parental leave, welfare and unemployment benefits, old age security, the economy, immigration, asylum, policing, borders, the carceral state, human rights, reproductive rights, disability, LGBTQ rights—all of these are matters that involve care for human needs and wellbeing. Following Nedelsky's view, ideally, participants in deliberation about social policies on these issues should include the people with experiential knowledge of these issues: people who care for others who have experiential knowledge of their needs. I would argue that deliberation should also include reflection on our own needs as vulnerable beings who depend on each other.

Similarly, political discourse and policy on climate change, the use and treatment of land and water, animal welfare, farming, resource extraction, and pollution need to focus on the wellbeing of all beings on the planet. This means that those who do the skilled work of care for these beings should be central participants in deliberation and development of policy. For Simpson, this requires learning from *land as pedagogy*. The philosophy of land as pedagogy is that active engagement with and care for specific beings gives us *knowledge*. We can understand what a tree needs through active care for it. But to care properly for the tree, we have to attend to its place in the relational web. We have to see how it interacts with other trees and plants, animals and insects, with soil and water and climate—and with humans. Care for the tree and care for the worldly web, then, are closely linked. We can understand what a tree needs through active care for it. We can understand what the world needs through active care for it. And we need to link those forms of care and knowledge together. Through the

---

[44] Nedelsky, *A Care Manifesto: (Part)Time for All* (Oxford, forthcoming). See also Prattes, "I Don't Clean Up after Myself."

philosophies of care for land and land as pedagogy, practices of attention and care for specific and unique beings are necessarily linked to practices of attention and care for the relational web.

Care for the world is also linked with care for self. As Nancy Fraser has argued, participation in deliberation about needs and the creation of policy should include people with reflective knowledge and interpretation of their own needs.[45] For Indigenous theorists, this means that animals and oceans and trees need to be recognized as stakeholders and participants in the creation of policy. But their participation is not understood simply as a form of self-interest. If each being is seen as a participant in reciprocal relations, each being can be recognized as offering knowledge of what it needs in relation to the web. Land as pedagogy involves attending to land as teacher. This means that the land offers knowledge: Simpson writes that the tree contains a library of stories.[46] The task of interpreting the knowledge offered by nonhuman beings still falls to human beings—but can we learn to listen more attentively to their contributions to dialogue? We also need to learn to care better for ourselves *as* political agents. Indigenous and Black queer and feminist movements are recognizing that care for selves and communities is essential to effective political agency that is oriented toward care for the world.[47]

We still need conceptual and practical distinctions among forms of care: contestation and concerted action addressing matters of concern are political practices, different from the practices of care for others and care for self. But the expert knowledges produced through care for others and care for self, oriented toward care for the world, are, in Indigenous thought, central to democratic culture. These three forms of care are linked together, so that political contestation and deliberation about worldly things are linked closely to care for and hence experiential knowledge of others and self. And all three are linked together with care for the *world*. We can't deliberate intelligently about the conditions that will support the wellbeing of humans and the earth unless we are actively attuned to the world as a complex web of interdependent relations among unique and specific beings.

Attention to others' needs, or to our own, does not *necessarily* orient us to care for worldly conditions, or to care for the world. We can care for others' needs without caring for worldly conditions. But we probably can't do it well. For example, caring well for a child requires a world that supports both carer and child. Care for others will give us knowledge that should be part of deliberations, and it can attune us to what the worldly conditions should be. Care for others

---

[45] Fraser, *Unruly Practices*.
[46] Simpson, *As We Have Always Done*, 184.
[47] I return to this discussion in the Conclusion.

is not *sufficient* to enable us to deliberate about shared issues in a way that is oriented toward care for the world. Our knowledge of others' needs and of our own must be connected to an ability to consider a larger framework of needs and conditions. If we are going to make good policy, ideally, it must be connected to an ethic of care for the *world:* a worldly ethic of care for the world as a web of interdependent relations.

In practice, of course, care for others and for ourselves is not always oriented to care for the world or guided by a worldly ethic. But if this is true of care for the needs of others and self, it is also true of engagement in political deliberation about contested issues. As we've seen, Myers uses the example of how to address world hunger to argue that, unlike a charitable ethic of care for the other or a therapeutic ethics of the self, an ethic of care for the world orients us to tend to the conditions that helped to produce hunger in the first place. "Caring for the world, which is to say, tending to a specific worldly thing together with others, requires a shift in perspective, one which involves decentering both oneself and suffering Other(s) in order to bring into view the collective conditions, including worldly practices, habits, and laws, out of which hunger is born."[48] But care for the world as a web of interdependent relations should not be conflated with care about specific worldly things as contested issues of shared concern. The issue of hunger—or let's say, poverty—is a contested object: is poverty the result of a poor work ethic, lax morals, emasculated matriarchal households, the backwardness of savages, or a political economy oriented toward profit rather than human wellbeing? Those who argue that poverty is only an effect of individual or community failings are oriented toward a contested issue—a worldly thing—but they are not oriented toward care for the world as a complex web of interdependent relationships. They are certainly not guided by a worldly ethic. In fact, they may not see it as a worldly thing—a shared issue—at all: they may see it as a problem for others, not for all of us. Similarly, poverty may be understood as the result of worldly *conditions:* a society that takes in too many immigrants, or that supports welfare bums, or that doesn't maintain law and order. But these arguments are not oriented toward a worldly ethic of care for the world as shared human home.

Myers recognizes that care for the world involves more than the fact of contestation and associative action: it involves a normative ethic of care for the world. But this worldly *ethic* is no more specific to political contestation over worldly *things* than it is to care for others, or for self. Only if we define political contestation in Arendt's idealized normative understanding as action that attunes us to the multiplicity of perspectives and engagement with the world as a web of relations is the worldly ethic of care for the world essential to political life. But similarly, if we understand care for self and others as action that necessarily attunes

[48] Myers, *Worldly Ethics*, 109.

us to engagement with the world as a web of interdependent relations, then a worldly ethic is essential to care for others and for self.

For Myers, worldly ethics are oriented to two normative ends: the world as shared human home and the world as inclusive democratic culture. The ethic of care for land that Simpson describes—care for land as a complex web of interdependent relationships—brings these two ends together and goes beyond them. It involves care for the world as shared home for all—not just humans. It attends not just to needs but to the flourishing of unique beings. It is oriented to the wellbeing of individuals as not just recipients but as agents of care. It assumes that all participate as agents in coordinated action. Discourse and contestation are part of this coordinated action, but by no means all of it. An ethic of care for land redefines the world as a web of collaborative activity, involving both contestation and solidarity.

An ethic of care for land assumes that each participant acts not just out of self-interest but as a giver and receiver of gifts with an orientation to the wellbeing of the world. Democratic participation involves not just offering my perspective but, importantly, attending and listening to all of the other perspectives. Myers argues that the normative ideal of world as mediating force requires "fostering practices and building institutions that provide as many citizens as possible with meaningful opportunities to articulate their innumerable perspective. . . . And to influence the conditions under which they live."[49] For Arendt it was equally important that participants in democratic life learn to *listen* and to hold in mind all of the diverse perspectives that make up the common world. Attunement to the multiplicity of perspectives oriented to matters of common concern was, for Arendt, central to democracy.

A Philoxenic Worldly Ethics: Coalitional Politics of Philoxenic Solidarity

Care for land involves a practice of caring for specific others as unique beings, and as participants within a worldly web of interdependent relations. All beings are understood as collaborative participants in reciprocal gift relations, governed by the ethic of grounded normativity. Care for land, then, integrates care for diverse others, and care for shared matters of concern, as care for the intersubjective web. Care for land is oriented to the substantive ends of world as shared home for all beings, and as radically inclusive and democratic mediating space.

---

[49] Myers, *Worldly Ethics*, 125.

The philosophy of love and care for land can perhaps help us to understand the ancient practice of *philoxenia*. Philoxenia—love for the stranger, the foreigner, the other—is typically understood as hospitality: treating the other as a guest. But in the Greek stories of *philoxenia*, the other is treated as a guest because the other may well be a god. And a god may be a bringer of gifts. Philoxenia is a practice that sustains the circle of gift relations.[50] The practice of love for the stranger, then, could be seen as one form of love and care for a world of diverse others.

Love for land is a practice of philoxenia that involves more than hospitality. It involves attending to an endlessly diverse array of strange others in the ecosphere and attending to them as unique beings. These practices involve not just hospitality but active love for and care for the other. And others are perceived as agents in the cycle of gift relations: as gift givers, as well as recipients of gifts. Love for land can be seen as a form of *philoxenia* that involves not just welcoming others in, but opening out, to locate oneself as a participant in a larger world. Love for land, then, can be seen as a form of love of the world that incorporates an expansive philoxenia: love and care for the wide range of diverse others that share the earth with us. The grounded normativity of love for land can be seen as a *philoxenic worldly ethics* that reintegrates care for specific others with the worldly ethics of care for worldly conditions, for matters of shared concern.

This philoxenic worldly ethics attends to the needs and capacities, the ideals and aspirations, the perspectives and contributions of a plurality of specific and diverse others—strangers—and links this together with a worldly ethics, oriented to matters of shared concern. It does this by linking care for specific others with care for the world: for the web of relations in which we are all enmeshed. Crucially, because others are perceived as agents in the cycle of gift relations, *philoxenia* involves an appreciation for and willingness to attend to their perspectives. The philoxenic worldly ethics of love for land involves attending to the plurality of perspectives about particular issues, linking care for a diversity of specific others, including oneself, while maintaining a focus on the relational web. Attending to the web of relationships of human and earthly wellbeing is an expansive and radical practice of *amor mundi*. Love for land is love of the web of connections among diversity that sustain us. And this is the focus of Indigenous practices of relational freedom.

I want to suggest that a philoxenic worldly ethics attuned to world as land can be the affective ethos animating a coalitional politics of resistance to colonization. This shared resistance can be guided by an ethics and politics of *philoxenic*

---

[50] Similar stories can of course be found in many ancient traditions.

solidarity. I take the term *philoxenic solidarity* from Leela Gandhi, who uses it to describe an anti-communitarian community, and in particular to consider a "politics of friendship" among diffuse "individuals and groups that have renounced the privileges of imperialism and elected affinity with victims of their own expansionist cultures."[51] As Gandhi writes, philoxenic solidarities introduce the disruptive category of *risk*, to disrupt "the opposed poles of sameness (communitarianism, the polis, regimes of security) and difference (hospitality, exile, risk)" in Western political thought.[52] A politics of love and friendship across difference and across relations of power is a risky politics. Philoxenic solidarity, then, could be the affective ethos animating settler support of and alliance with Indigenous resistance to colonization. Practices of philoxenic solidarity involve taking the risk of connection, in alliance with Indigenous people, not just across differences, but across relations of power and privilege, in shared resistance to colonization.[53] They can also involve taking the risk of locating ourselves in a universe of diverse others with whom we can live in relations of care and reciprocity, to fight fear and violence with careful nonviolent love. In this sense, philoxenic solidarity includes political solidarities with all of the diverse beings in the web of interdependent earthly relations. Together, these would be practices of relational freedom that would liberate all of us from the bonds of domination. Practices of philoxenic solidarity are, I think, essential to the transformative reconciliation called for by Borrows and Tully: a reconciliation between Indigenous and settler nations, grounded in a strengthened relationship with the living earth. Transformative reconciliation would transform the relationships between settler and Indigenous peoples and between humans and the diversity of life forms that share the earth with us.[54]

A politics of philoxenic solidarity involves much more than care about contested objects. State governments and corporations care very strongly about the objects they want to acquire, and advocates of rights to carry guns and walls to exclude outsiders care very much about the issues of concern to them. Philoxenic solidarity involves active care *for* the wellbeing of diverse others, and for the worldly web of relations that connect us. Philoxenic solidarity as a normative ethos of resistance to colonization would involve what Leanne Simpson calls *constellations of co-resistance*. Genuine transformation requires philoxenic alliances among multiple resistances to multiple forms of colonization.

---

[51] Gandhi, *Affective Communities*, 1. Gandhi uses the term to describe a politics of friendship among political allies. She does not extend its meaning to include nonhuman beings.
[52] Gandhi, *Affective Communities*, 30.
[53] I discuss the risk of connection across relations of power in Weir (2008) and (2013).
[54] Borrows and Tully, "Introduction," in Asch, Borrows, and Tully, *Resurgence and Reconciliation*.

Love of Nation? Freedom as Right to Destroy or as Radiating Responsibilities

Simpson grounds her politics in a specific political nationalism. But she proposes an understanding of nation very different from the nation state, and different from the forms of nationhood that rely on racial or ethnic or religious identity. Instead, she asserts a *"nationhood based on a series of radiating responsibilities."*[55] "Our nationhood is based on the idea that the earth gives and sustains all life, that "natural resources" are not "natural resources" at all but gifts from Aki, the land. Our nationhood is based on the foundational concept that we should give up what we can to support the integrity of our homelands for the coming generations. We should give more than we take." When she asks Elder Doug Williams for an Anishinaabe definition of nation, he suggests that nation is "the place where we all live and work together." Nation, for Simpson, is "a web of connections to each other, to the plant nations, the animal nations, the rivers and lakes, the cosmos, and our neighbouring Indigenous nations." All are *kobade*: links in a chain.[56]

For Simpson, Indigenous nationhood is essential to Indigenous freedom:

> This is what I understand our diplomats were negotiating when settlers first arrived in our territory. This was the impetus for those very first treaties—Nishnaabeg freedom, protection for the land and the environment, a space—an intellectual, political, spiritual, artistic, creative, and physical space where we could live as Nishnaabeg and where our kobade could do the same. . . . This is what my Ancestors wanted for me, for us. They wanted for our generation to practice Nishnaabeg governance over our homeland, to partner with other governments over shared lands, to have the ability to make decisions about how the gifts of our parent would be used for the benefit of our people and in a manner to promote her sanctity for coming generations. I believe my Ancestors expected the settler state to recognize my nation, our lands, and the political and cultural norms in our territory.[57]

The treaties signed with the settlers carried very different meanings for the parties to agreement. According to Simpson, the Anishinaabe understood the treaties to be partnerships in care for shared land. Precolonial treaties could include territorial borders, but these were understood as "areas of increased diplomacy, ceremony, and sharing."[58] The idea of national sovereignty includes sovereignties

---

[55] Simpson, *As We Have Always Done*, 9.
[56] Simpson, *As We Have Always Done*, 8–9.
[57] Simpson, *As We Have Always Done*, 9.
[58] Simpson, "The Place Where We All Live and Work Together," in Teves, Smith, and Raheja, eds., *Native Studies Keywords*, 19.

over shared territory, and these areas of overlap are not seen as a threat to individual nations' sovereignties because neither nation "owns" the land.

Simpson writes that political transformation is rooted in "the intense love of land, of family, and of our nations that has always been the spine of Indigenous resistance." But for Simpson, "family" is "not the nuclear family that has been normalized in settler society but big, beautiful, diverse, extended multiracial families of relatives and friends that care deeply for each other."[59] And nation is not the nation state or ethnic identity but a nexus of responsibility that connects with others. Nationhood is a form of belonging that is not proprietary, but custodial. And it is not exclusive, but connected to a series of radiating responsibilities. A nation is a polity, not an ethnic group, and polities include plant nations and animal nations. These are kinship groups, but kinship is not about blood and marriage relationships. Simpson affirms Indigenous feminist and queer understandings of nation and family that resist heteropatriarchal conceptions.[60] She argues for a resurgent politics that takes the risk of connection, to include politics of resistance to heteropatriarchy and white supremacy, both within Indigenous nations and in alliances with non-Indigenous peoples. In order to flourish, "we need to join together in a rebellion of love, persistence, commitment, and profound caring, and create constellations of co-resistance, working together toward a radical alternative present based on deep reciprocity and the gorgeous generative refusal of colonial recognition."[61]

Clearly the love of nation that Simpson describes as a series of radiating responsibilities is very different from the love for nation that rightly frightened Arendt. Arendt's analysis of the development of fascism rooted in what she calls "tribal" nationalisms is a cogent analysis of the form of "love" for one's own that is entwined with fear and hatred toward enemies. For Arendt, love for nation is a privatizing sentiment that destroys the world between and among us. And love for one's own group cannot be a path to freedom for oppressed and excluded peoples. Arendt was rightly critical of the form of Zionism that would lead to another exclusive regime. While in early writings she supported the idea of a Jewish nation within a European federation of allied nations, she soon recognized that the establishment of the state of Israel would produce the dispossession of the Palestinians. In *The Origins of Totalitarianism*, she traced this cycle of dispossession to the history of the modern nation state, founded on nationalist sentiments rather than on shared rights protected by law, and bounded by state borders that divide citizens from the stateless. In her letter to Gershom Scholem, Arendt responds to his accusation that she has no "love of the Jewish people":

---

[59] Simpson, *As We Have Always Done*, 9.
[60] I discuss these in Chapter 4.
[61] Simpson, *As We Have Always Done*, 9.

You are quite right—I am not moved by any "love" of this sort, and for two reasons: I have never in my life "loved" any people or collective—neither the German people, nor the French, nor the American, nor the working class or anything of that sort. I indeed love "only" my friends and the only kind of love I know of and believe in is the love of persons. Secondly, this "love of the Jews" would appear to me, since I am myself Jewish, as something rather suspect. I cannot love myself or anything which I know is part and parcel of my own person. . . . the greatness of this people was once that it believed in God. . . . And now this people believes only in itself?[62]

Here, love of the Jews is reduced to love of self, and love of self is not only suspect but impossible.[63] But, of course, it is not true that one cannot—or should not—love oneself. As Aristotle argued, one cannot love a friend if one does not love oneself. If love is not just a feeling or sentiment but an active valuing, caring about and caring for another person, then love of self is a form of valuation of self and care for self that is not at all opposed to but is deeply connected with love of others. Ideally, love respects and cares for the uniqueness of the other—and of the self.

Love of self is "suspect" for Arendt because she equates it with self-interest. And love of the Jews is understood here as only a form of self-interest. A people that loves and believes only in itself has succumbed to the privatizing and antipolitical selfishness that is destructive of a polity. Arendt's critique of self-interest as the basis of a nation or society is central to her analysis of the bourgeois roots of the modern nation state. In *The Origins of Totalitarianism*, she turns to Hobbes for an analysis of the state as commonwealth, organized around protection of property and self-interest rather than constitutional law. The "philosopher of the bourgeoisie" provides a clear analysis of privatization as a destructive force. Hobbes's understanding of human equality as "equality of ability to kill" supports the "the ultimate destructive purpose" of the "Commonwealth based on accumulated and monopolized power."[64] When protection of private property is the sole end of political life, when public life takes on the aspect of a total of private interests, government by tyranny is the inevitable effect. Because the aim of property is consumption, "The most radical and the only secure form of possession is destruction, for only what we have destroyed is safely and forever ours. . . . A social system based essentially on property cannot possibly proceed

---

[62] Arendt, *The Jewish Writings*, 206–207.
[63] In this letter Arendt has forgotten her own belief in *amor mundi*—a love that is not directed only to "persons." As Arendt well knows, there are many forms of love. In *Love and Saint Augustine*, she discusses the Latin *amor*, *dilectio*, and *caritas*, and she distinguishes among appetitive desire, the love between humans and God, and neighborly love. The Greeks differentiated among *eros*, *agape*, *philia*, and *storge*, as well as *ludus*, *pragma*, *philia politikē*, and *philotia*: love of self.
[64] Arendt, *The Origins of Totalitarianism*, 195.

toward anything but the final destruction of all property."⁶⁵ The nation, like the individual, focused on self-interest, lives with all other nations, as Hobbes writes, "in the condition of perpetuell war" that can be resolved only by Victory or Death. "By 'Victory or Death,' the Leviathan can indeed overcome all political limitations that go with the existence of other peoples and can envelop the whole earth in its tyranny."⁶⁶

Hobbes's commitment to tyranny as the form of power that secures protection of self-interest is connected to a particular conception of *freedom* as ownership of private property, which is rooted in the right to destroy and which leads inevitably to tyranny and destruction. Eva von Redecker argues that modern authoritarianism is rooted in an unprecedented ideal of freedom as absolute ownership: only with modern capitalism is freedom understood as an absolute right that includes the right to destroy the object of desire. Von Redecker argues that the modern conception of freedom as absolute ownership of property, which one is free to destroy, underlies the violence of the modern institutions of chattel slavery and marriage under couverture. The "phantom possession" of racialized groups in the form of slavery, and of women's reproductive capacities in marriage, promises an absolute freedom that compensates for the unfreedom of white male workers, and the threats to entitlement to these phantom possessions continues to fuel the *ressentiment* of precarious white manhood. Contemporary authoritarian ideologies, then, are responses to threats to propertized freedom.⁶⁷

This analysis can make sense of a conflation of love with self-interest. The kind of love of the master for members of his household who are his property, and over whom he wields a right to destroy, is a privatized tyranny that is simply externalized as totalitarian rule. What we call modern love can take this form: a purely self-interested desire to possess the other, to consume them. A Hobbesian "love of nation," then, takes the same form as love for the women and slaves in one's household. Love of the same against feared and hated outsiders is rooted in a propertized view of nation as purely self-interested love of one's own property: love of that that which we can assimilate and consume, and destroy as we please, without the interference of outsiders.⁶⁸

---

⁶⁵ Arendt, *The Origins of Totalitarianism*, 194.
⁶⁶ Arendt, *The Origins of Totalitarianism*, 196.
⁶⁷ Von Redecker, "Ownership's Shadow," 33–67. Compare the words of Elder Danny Musqua: "If any man owns a piece of the Earth, then he no more respects Mother Earth. He no more respects the Earth, because he believes he can do what he wants with that Earth and he can destroy it, he can do whatever he wants. That's the reason we don't own the Earth: because it belongs to all the people. . . . We were willing to share it" (quoted by Michael Asch, "Confederation Treaties and Reconciliation: Stepping Back into the Future," in Asch, Borrows, and Tully, eds., *Resurgence and Reconciliation*, 35).
⁶⁸ In the Excursus on Freedom and Love: A Speculative Genealogy (this volume), I discuss the theory that the etymological connection between love and freedom is rooted in the love of the master for members of his household.

The love for nation that Leanne Simpson advocates is not self-interested, not privatizing, and not destructive. Law based on fear, she writes, will produce only more suffering and division. Drawing on Audra Simpson's *Mohawk Interruptus*, Simpson argues that struggles over membership in the wake of the status rules imposed by the Indian Act are rooted in fear of disappearance as Indigenous people. Rather than responding with divisive identity politics, both Audra Simpson and Leanne Simpson shift the frame, to address the fear of disappearance with a politics that re-embeds belonging in a *productive* place of refusal. For Leanne Simpson, a politics of *generative refusal* addresses fear by embodying the alternative. *The opposite of dispossession is not possession, but connection.* Because the dispossession of Indigenous people is not the negation of their ownership of property; it's dispossession from grounded normativities, dispossession from their connections to land and to each other.[69] In place of an internationalism of enlightened self-interest, Simpson offers an internationalism that assumes relationality, exemplified in the Nishnaabeg story of Nanabush's journey around the world, visiting and getting to know each being, learning about themselves by learning from each being. This is an internationalism of genuine reciprocal recognition and grounded normativity. And it is rooted in a philoxenic nationalism that is "place based and local, but also networked and global."[70]

The love for nation that Simpson describes supports love of the world, and freedom as world-making. Simpson does not assume that love for one's own is a privatizing and exclusive love that destroys the world. Love for one's own nation is situated in a larger economy of gift relations and is connected to love of the world. This formulation challenges the dichotomy of private love for one's own versus the public world of plurality and dissent. It challenges the formulation of freedom as right to destroy. It challenges the right of propertized violence within the home and within the nation. It challenges the defense of borders as walls around privatized freedoms. It assumes plurality, difference, and dissent in all spheres of life. With John Borrows, Simpson argues that difference, diversity, and dissent within Nishnaabeg thought are positioned not in terms of opposition but as necessary parts of a larger whole.[71] These practices are not restricted to the public realm in opposition to the private but are central to all spheres of life.

In her rejection of the idea of love of the Jewish people, Arendt wrote, "the greatness of this people was once that it believed in God. . . . And now this people believes only in itself?"[72] The self-interested belief of the Jewish people only in itself is, for Arendt, a belief that has lost its orientation to something larger than itself, to a shared meaning or ideal that could mediate—connect

---

[69] Simpson, *As We Have Always Done*, 25.
[70] Simpson, *As We Have Always Done*, 178.
[71] Simpson, *Dancing on Our Turtle's Back*, 59.
[72] Arendt, The Jewish Writings, 207.

and separate—among a plurality of people. In contrast to the *philia politikē* that connected the early American republicans in a democratic practice of building a new world, with a new constitution, the love of the Jewish people, in Arendt's formulation, is concerned only for itself and its own survival. But we could say that like the new Americans idealized by Arendt, the Jewish people cared about finding a home—a place where they could belong, and could build a new world. Like the Americans, they built their new home—a new world—on the land of the dispossessed. While both were oriented toward a worldly thing, a third term that linked them together, neither was oriented toward what Myers identifies as the normative ideal of love of the world as shared human home. Neither was oriented toward a normative ideal of care for land as shared home for all beings. Both embraced a form of nationalism and a form of freedom that assumed the right to destroy the land and its people.

Politics of Generative Refusal

Indigenous resistance to colonization is not, of course, necessarily or always based in the normative ideal and practice of love. As Audra Simpson writes, resistance can take the form of clear and steadfast refusal—refusal of extinction, and of assimilation. Refusal of the "gifts" of "recognition" and rights offered by the colonizing state. "The Mohawks of Kahnawà:ke are nationals of a precontact Indigenous polity that simply refuse to stop being themselves. In other words, they insist on being and acting as peoples who belong to a nation other than the United States or Canada." The Mohawks of Kahnawà:ke affirm a nationhood and a genealogical kinship with other native peoples in North America, and "they know this. They *refuse to let go of this knowledge*."[73]

In *Wasàse: Indigenous Pathways of Action and Freedom,* Taiaiake Alfred argues for a nonviolent warrior culture of resistance based in a *resurgence* of the Onkwehonwe, or original people. *Wasàse* is an ancient Rotinoshonni war ritual, a ceremony of unity, strength, and commitment to action. Alfred advocates an "anarcho-indigenism" that rejects alliances with "legalized systems of oppression," with the institutions that structure the colonial relationship, and calls for a practice of change through direct action and confrontations with state power.[74] Alfred calls for a politics of contention that rejects machismo but affirms what he calls nonviolent militancy, guided by a pragmatist ethics. As he writes, in contrast to the Judeo-Christian "Thou Shalt Not Kill" (a principle which has not been upheld with complete consistently in practice), the Mohawk philosophy

---

[73] Simpson, *Mohawk Interruptus*, 2.
[74] Alfred, *Wasàse*, 45–46.

of resistance is "Don't Kill, Unless You Have To and the Circumstance Requires It"—a principle that is, as Alfred notes, more cumbersome and constraining, "because it depends on human reason negotiating the complexity of the real world."[75] Alfred cites the Oka standoff in 1990, when the Kanien'kehaka successfully resisted the Canadian army's attempt to occupy Kanien'kehaka territory, the Gustafsen Lake stand-off in British Columbia, the Zapatista movement in Mexico, and Indigenous movements in Ecuador and Bolivia, as examples of this path of resistance, and condemns the conservative nationalist ideologies and the co-optive politics of band councils that trade freedom and self-determination for money and control over resources.

Yet for Alfred the warrior ethic of the politics of refusal draws on Indigenous traditions of political relationality and on other classic literatures and practices of nonviolence, including Buddha and Gandhi. The path to regaining freedom, for Alfred, is through "restoring connections to each other, our cultures, our lands" and through this practice of freedom, to remake the relationship between Onkwehonwe and Settler.[76] Resistance thus requires a process of personal and collective spiritual transformation.

Leanne Simpson argues for a politics of *generative refusal* and *affirmative refusal* that combines refusal of colonization with loving resurgence. With Audra Simpson, she "re-embeds belonging in a *productive* place of refusal" that "generates grounded normativity."[77] With Alfred and Glen Coulthard, she advocates a refusal of the politics of recognition that allows the colonizing state to frame issues, and a relocating of energies toward building Indigenous nations.

The video "How to Stop an Oil and Gas Pipeline: The Unist'ot'en Camp Resistance" documents resistance to the Canadian and B.C. government attempts to lay a gas pipeline through Wet'suwet'un land that has never been ceded. Camp supporter Mel Bazil briefs activists on protocol: "We're going to go through all of the peaceful avenues we can. But the way of the warrior is . . . you go through all peaceful avenues first—and when all those fail, it's war."[78]

Unist'ot'en spokesperson Freda Huson puts it differently: "Our people have had enough and we're not going to just stand here and take the bullying, and take it without a fight. We've had enough of these spoiled brats stealing off our lands and not accepting no for an answer, and we're going to be the stern parents and say No, you're not coming in."[79] For Huson, the protection of land and water from dangerous toxins is an act of what we might call tough love. There are no

---

[75] Alfred, *Wasàse*, 54.
[76] Alfred, *Wasàse*, 20, 34.
[77] Simpson, *As We Have Always Done*, 176.
[78] Unist'ot'en Camp, November 2014, https://unistoten.camp/al-jazeera/. See also the film *Invasion* (https://unistoten.camp/media/invasion/) and extensive information on the website (https://unistoten.camp).
[79] Unist'ot'en Camp, November 2014, https://unistoten.camp/al-jazeera/

weapons allowed in the resistance camp. And when in January of 2019 the RCMP come in with semiautomatic rifles, arresting activists and taking them away, the activists respond by singing.[80]

The conflict between the state governments of Canada and British Columbia and the Unist'ot'en resistance reveals starkly opposed conceptions of *freedom* in relation to land. The state government and the pipeline companies view the land as the object of freedom as absolute right to private property, which we are free to destroy. The Unist'ot'en resistance views land as a system of reciprocal relations, and freedom is enacted through active responsibility for all of those relations. These conceptions correspond to incommensurate conceptions of *nation*. The sovereign nation asserts its freedom to destroy the land; to use it as we will. The Unist'ot'en nation asserts its freedom to protect the land. The Unist'ot'en resistance is asserting a right of refusal and a right of noninterference. But that right is asserted in the context of the state's transgression of shared responsibility to protect the land, and to engage in nation-to-nation negotiations.[81]

This is clearly a conflict over ownership. But it's a conflict between very different conceptions of ownership. As John Borrows writes, the Ojibwe term for freedom (*dibenindizowin*) connotes a form of ownership: "It implies that a free person owns, is responsible for, and controls how they interact with others." The related term for citizen (*dibenjigaaqowin*) describes individual membership in a group: one who owns or controls their associations.[82] This is a conception of ownership very different from the ownership of private property. Ownership

---

[80] The Unist'ot'en resistance is an assertion of sovereignty and a refusal to negotiate on the terms of the state: an insistence that any negotiation must proceed within the terms of nation-to-nation mutual recognition. The Unist'ot'en are a house group of the Wet'suwet'en people. Wet'suwet'en hereditary chiefs won state recognition of their ownership of the land in the 1997 ruling by the Supreme Court of Canada, which was the first to recognize Aboriginal title. The ruling does, however, include the provision that Aboriginal title can justifiably be infringed for the development of agriculture, forestry, mining, and "economic development." The Unist'ot'en resistance does not, of course, represent a unified body of "Indigenous people" who speak with one voice. This case has been characterized by a painful division between the Unist'ot'en resistance of hereditary chiefs of unceded lands and the elected councils of twenty bands established under the terms of the Indian Act which have signed agreements with the government to allow the pipeline through their lands (which are separate from the unceded lands claimed by the Unist'ot'en), in exchange for badly needed economic and social supports. Those agreements are criticized as effects of state force and divisive strategies: the band councils instituted by the Indian Act have given in to desperation and have been bought off. Other elders have argued that the Unist'ot'en resistance is not following protocols of dialogue and decision-making among Indigenous groups. While the Unist'ot'en resistance continues to call for non-Indigenous allies to join and support them, opposed elders argue that the influx of non-Indigenous supporters with their own agendas is obstructing intra-Indigenous dialogue. What's clear is that the state governments, the police, and the gas companies should stop trying to force their way onto this land. For more information, see https://unistoten.camp/about/wetsuweten-people/; https://www.cbc.ca/news/opinion/gaslink-pipeline-1.4973825; and https://www.cbc.ca/news/canada/british-columbia/delgamuukw-court-ruling-significance-1.5461763

[81] As John Borrows writes, "an act of disobedience in one context may, in another context, be considered obedience to either Indigenous peoples' law or the state's own unenforced or unrealized standards" (Borrows, *Freedom and Indigenous Constitutionalism*, 53).

[82] Borrows, *Freedom and Indigenous Constitutionalism*, 6–7.

means taking responsibility for relationships. The Unist'ot'en assertion of ownership does not assert a right to destruction. It asserts ownership of responsibility.

For Leanne Simpson, Indigenous resurgence is about reengaging with a form of freedom found in care for land, in love of the world as a complex system of relations. And the grounded normativity of Indigenous resurgence is an orientation to love of the world as a home shared by more than humans. Taking its lead from the politics of resurgence, a transformative politics of reconciliation will require a politics of relational freedom as care for land, a politics of philoxenic solidarity in which freedom is a shared practice of creating and sustaining a world that will be home for all.

Coda: Arendt and Baldwin on Love and Freedom

Hannah Arendt recognized the dangers of love in political life. She condemned the political form of love for nation that affirms homogeneity and privatizes belonging, and is dependent on exclusion of outsiders. Such love, as she points out, is tightly bound with hate for the other. This is obviously true of the antisemitism and racism at the heart of "love" for the Aryan nation, of national borders that render refugees stateless and rightless, and of love for family that excludes queer and deviant others. For Arendt it was also true of nationalisms of resistance. For Arendt the love of members of an oppressed people for their "nation" is simply derivative of the form of nationalism that oppresses them. And it takes the same form. As she wrote in her letter to James Baldwin, "Hatred and love belong together, and they are both destructive; you can afford them only in the private and, as a people, only so long as you are not free."[83] For Arendt, love of nation, like love of family, and romantic love, collapses distinctions and thus destroys the world—that which separates and unites us. In her letter to Baldwin, she chides him for "preaching the gospel of love." Here is the letter in its entirety:

November 21, 1962

Dear Mr. Baldwin:

Your article in the New Yorker is a political event of a very high order, I think; it certainly is an event in my understanding of what is involved in the Negro question. And since this is a question which concerns us all, I feel I am entitled to raise objections.

---

[83] Hannah Arendt, letter to James Baldwin, http://www.hannaharendt.net/index.php/han/article/view/95/156

What frightened me in your essay was the gospel of love which you begin to preach at the end. In politics, love is a stranger, and when it intrudes upon it nothing is being achieved except hypocrisy. All the characteristics you stress in the Negro people: their beauty, their capacity for joy, their warmth, and their humanity, are well-known characteristics of all oppressed people. They grow out of suffering and they are the proudest possession of all pariahs. Unfortunately, they have never survived the hour of liberation by even five minutes. Hatred and love belong together, and they are both destructive; you can afford them only in the private and, as a people, only so long as you are not free.

In sincere admiration,

cordially (that is, in case you remember that we know each other slightly) yours,

Hannah Arendt[84]

This is Arendt's response to Baldwin's essay, "Letter from a Region in My Mind," right after it was first published in the *New Yorker* in 1962.[85] What is most striking about Arendt's response is its profound misreading of what Baldwin actually wrote. Baldwin's essay is a memoir of his youthful vocation as a preacher in the Black Christian church, and a meditation on the meanings of love and freedom in an America divided by racism. Baldwin's assessment of the role of love in the Christian church, both the white church and the black, is as far from preaching as one could hope. And it offers no illusions about the Christian gospel of love. Here is his description of the way that gospel works in the white church:

> It was absolutely clear that the police would whip you and take you in as long as they could get away with it, and that everyone else—housewives, taxi-drivers, elevator boys, dishwashers, bartenders, lawyers, judges, doctors, and grocers—would never, by the operation of any generous human feeling, cease to use you as an outlet for his frustrations and hostilities. Neither civilized reason nor Christian love would cause any of those people to treat you as they presumably wanted to be treated; only the fear of your power to retaliate would cause them to do that, or to seem to do it, which was (and is) good enough. There appears to be a vast amount of confusion on this point, but I do not know many Negroes who are eager to be "accepted" by white people, still less to be loved by them; they, the blacks, simply don't wish to be beaten over the head by the whites

---

[84] "The Meaning of Love in Politics: A Letter by Hannah Arendt to James Baldwin," HannahArendt.net, Ausgabe 1, Band 2, 2006.
[85] It was published in *The Fire Next Time* in 1963.

every instant of our brief passage on this planet. White people in this country will have quite enough to do in learning how to accept and love themselves and each other, and when they have achieved this—which will not be tomorrow and may very well be never—the Negro problem will no longer exist, for it will no longer be needed.[86]

Here Baldwin agrees with Arendt that there is a kind of love that belongs together with hatred: love of the same, which is coupled with hatred of the other. But he recognizes that this "love of the same" is not actually any kind of love. White racism is a response to self-hate, not self-love. When white people are able to accept and love themselves and each other, the Negro problem will no longer be needed. In other words, once white people are able to accept and love those parts of themselves that they project onto a constructed other, they will no longer need to hate that other.

Arendt is not, though, talking about white racists. When Arendt writes that hatred and love can be afforded, as a people, only so long as you are not free, she is referring to the love of oppressed people for each other. What she doesn't note here, and what Baldwin does, is that white people are not free. Baldwin's point is that white people—colonizers—are not free, because their freedom is tied to domination, to othering, and to hatred of the colonized. And Baldwin is pointing out that white people are not free because of the hatred central to their privatized love. But Baldwin also criticizes the hatred in the name of love that he encountered in black churches:

> I really mean that there was no love in the church. It was a mask for hatred and self-hatred and despair. The transfiguring power of the Holy Ghost ended when the service ended, and salvation stopped at the church door. When we were told to love everybody, I had thought that that meant *every body*. But no. It applied only to those who believed as we did, and it did not apply to white people at all.[87]

Again, Baldwin recognizes that the professed love is a mask for self-hatred, in this case an internalization of the hatred of the white racists, and the "love" of the oppressed for each other is tied to hatred of the oppressor—what Nietzsche diagnosed as *ressentiment*. With Arendt, he recognizes that that kind of love is private, exclusive, and opposed to freedom. "And the passion with which we loved the Lord was a measure of how deeply we feared and distrusted and, in the end, hated almost all strangers, always, and avoided and despised ourselves."[88]

---

[86] Baldwin, "Letter from a Region of My Mind," 32–33.
[87] Baldwin, "Letter from a Region of My Mind," 37.
[88] Baldwin, "Letter from a Region of My Mind," 38.

Yet Baldwin insists on a relationship between love and freedom. Toward the end of his essay, and right after the passage cited earlier, he writes:

> But I cannot leave it at that; there is more to it than that. In spite of everything, there was in the life I fled a zest and a joy and a capacity for facing and surviving disaster that are very moving and very rare. Perhaps we were, all of us—pimps, whores, racketeers, church members, and children—bound together by the nature of our oppression, the specific and peculiar complex of risks we had to run; if so, within these limits we sometimes achieved with each other a freedom that was close to love. I remember, anyway, church suppers and outings, and, later, after I left the church, rent and waistline parties where rage and sorrow sat in the darkness and did not stir, and we ate and drank and talked and laughed and danced and forgot all about "the man." We had the liquor, the chicken, the music, and each other, and had no need to pretend to be what we were not. This is the freedom that one hears in some gospel songs, and in jazz.

This is apparently what Arendt finds objectionable: this invocation of a freedom found in something that was close to love. But this is hardly a celebration of the characteristic beauty, joy, warmth, and humanity of the "Negro people." Baldwin has made it clear that he has no illusions about the essential characteristics of the Negro people, and no faith that those people could ever emerge into a pure freedom of pure love. In the music that embodies freedom—jazz and blues—there is "something tart and ironic, authoritative and double-edged. White Americans seem to feel that happy songs are *happy* and sad songs are *sad*, and that, God help us, is exactly the way most white Americans sing them."[89] Baldwin's image of the freedom found in "the liquor, the chicken, the music, and each other" is obviously not without irony. And a freedom where rage and sorrow are present but do not stir is not a simple freedom. The freedom he is describing is a kind of "ironic tenacity" born, as he certainly knows, of suffering, and experienced within the limits of shared oppression. Baldwin anticipates Arendt's objection when he writes: "White people do not understand the depths out of which such an ironic tenacity comes, but they suspect that the force is sensual, and they are terrified of sensuality and do not any longer understand it."[90] Against the stereotype of black sensuality—of "quivering dusky maidens or priapic black studs"—he writes: "To be sensual, I think, is to respect and rejoice in the force of life, of life itself, and to be *present* in all that one does."[91] This is not "the gospel of love" but a glimpse of what love and freedom might be: joy in the force of life.

---

[89] Baldwin, "Letter from a Region of My Mind," 38.
[90] Baldwin, "Letter from a Region of My Mind," 38.
[91] Baldwin, "Letter from a Region of My Mind," 38.

Baldwin writes that the Christian church has been indispensable to conquest: the church has sanctified, with an "unmitigated arrogance and cruelty," the power of the colonizers, and rejoiced in conquest. And that conquest can be undone only when the force of the subjugated can rise up. "The energy that was buried with the rise of the Christian nations must come back into the world." The return of that energy would be a transformation that "contains the hope of liberation" and that is terrifying to the colonizers.[92]

Is this analysis too simple? Is Baldwin's call for the return of the repressed—the sensuality—that was buried with the Christian church—a call for a return to an original state of freedom? Is it too close to the kind of nationalism of blood and soil that Arendt rightly feared? I don't think so. There is, of course, a danger in calling for resistance rooted in the purity of sensuality of an oppressed people. But that is not what Baldwin is talking about here. Baldwin is pointing out that our fear of the danger of *eros* is central to oppression. Racism, like the fascist nationalism of blood and soil, uses the rhetoric of love and joy as a mask for hatred. Fascist ceremonies glorify marching, not dancing. Killing, not living.

If we need to recognize the danger of love as a privatizing force entwined with hatred of the other, we also need to recognize that when we relegate love—joy, sensuality, *eros*—to the private realm, when we see it only as a danger, we accept a privatized understanding of love as self-interest: love of property, consumption, and destruction. But this is not love, and it should never be the form of "love" that we accept in the private realm. Is the attempt to purge *eros* from the public realm partly responsible for the distortion of love in the private? And for the spilling of that distorted love and hate back into the public?[93] Perhaps one way to address that distorted version of "love" is to reenergize love of the world, as care for land, and as philoxenic solidarity.

Love, then, is essential to freedom. "Love takes off the masks that we fear we cannot live without and know we cannot live within. I use the word 'love' here not merely in the personal sense but as a state of being, or a state of grace—not in the infantile American sense of being made happy but in the tough and universal sense of quest and daring and growth."[94] Should we let our fear of the dangers of eros lead us to accept a public freedom restricted to legal rights, or to discourse and debate? Baldwin offers here a glimpse of what freedom might be: full and embodied engagement in the force of life. Not without irony, not without suffering, rage and sorrow, but a life that is "larger, freer, more loving."[95]

---

[92] Baldwin, "Letter from a Region of My Mind," 39.
[93] Marcuse called this *repressive desublimation*.
[94] Baldwin, "Letter from a Region of My Mind," 39.
[95] Baldwin, "Letter from a Region of My Mind," 39.

3
Dancing Resistance, Re-creating the World
Philoxenic Relational Freedom

In the Indigenous resistance movement that came to be known as *Idle No More* in the winter of 2012–2013, round dances played a central role. From the beginning of the movement in western Canada in the winter of 2012–2013, and as it spread across Turtle Island (North America) and throughout the world, round dances served to bring together Indigenous and non-Indigenous activists with people in the streets. "At almost every event, we collectively embodied our diverse and ancient traditions in the round dance by taking the movement to the streets, malls and highways across Turtle Island."[1] The round dance has a long history in practices of resistance to colonization: the Ghost Dances of the late nineteenth century drew together diverse Indigenous resistance movements. More recently, round dances have been part of solidarity movements in support of the Unist'ot'en resistance to the Coastal Gas Pipeline and the Sioux resistance to the Dakota Access Pipeline. This chapter considers the histories and meanings of the round dance, to ask how the dance works to support political resistance. I bring together a range of theories in a series of encounters, to argue that the round dance is a skilled practice of *philoxenia* that works as a practice of public freedom. This is a practice of love of "all my relations"—a practice of relational freedom that creates the world anew.

I begin by introducing Indigenous accounts of the role of the round dance in the *Idle No More* movement and then turn to Indigenous accounts of circle dances as practices of world-creation. While the round dance is specific to many Indigenous traditions on Turtle Island, it can also be situated within a broad history of circle dancing in communities around the world. Drawing on Victor Turner's concept of *communitas*, Barbara Ehrenreich argues that circle dance rituals are practices of *collective love*. I consider Ehrenreich's analysis in light of Indigenous theories of the dance as a practice of world-creation.

In modern Western political thought, collective forms of love have been feminized and repudiated as dangerous, romantic, and apolitical—even antipolitical. Love, for most modern Western political thinkers, is not connected

---

[1] The Kino-nda-niimi Collective, *The Winter We Danced*, 24.

to political freedom. Against Arendt's argument that *philia* is the only political form of love, I bring together Cree theories of the round dance as a practice of mourning and reconciliation with Kristeva's Kleinian psychoanalytic theory, to theorize the work of the round dance as a highly skilled practice of *philoxenic* public freedom. As performances of relationality, circle dance rituals embody an ethics of exemplarity, bringing together diverse and strange beings to dance new worlds into being.

Idle No More: Dancing Resistance

In the anthology *The Winter We Danced: Notes from the Past, the Future, and the Idle No More Movement,* The Kino-nda-niimi Collective writes that the winter of 2012–2113 will be remembered as "one of the most important moments in our collective history"—one moment in a long chain of resistance to colonization of Indigenous peoples on territory claimed by Canada.[2] The Idle No More movement was initiated with a "teach-in" organized by four women in Saskatchewan, Sylvia McAdam, Jess Gordon, Nina Wilson, and Sheelah McLean, to educate Indigenous and Canadian communities about the impacts of the Canadian federal government's proposed legislation, Bills C-38 and C-45, which introduced drastic changes to the Indian Act, the Fisheries Act, the Canadian Environmental Assessment Act, and the Navigable Water Act. They raised particular concerns about effects on water and environmental protection, the use of First Nations land, and lack of consultation with First Peoples. This event coincided with the hunger strike of Chief Theresa Spence of the Attawapiskat First Nation, which inspired and galvanized the movement. Chief Spence refused solid food for several weeks, to draw attention to the fact that unfulfilled treaties are slowly starving her community. She demanded a meeting with then-Prime Minister Stephen Harper and with the Governor General of Canada, to discuss Canada's treaty relations with First Nations leaders. Over the winter of 2012–2013 the movement spread across Canada and became a global movement of resistance of Indigenous peoples to the continuing legacies of colonization.

Like the Occupy movement, Idle No More was a radically decentralized movement, with no single leader, defying orthodox politics. The movement included many diverse groups and communities organizing around multiple issues, focusing on demands to repeal the proposed Canadian legislation, to stabilize emergency situations in First Nations communities, and to establish nation-to-nation relations of mutual recognition and collaboration among Canada, First Nations, Inuit, and Metis communities but also on diverse projects of Indigenous

---

[2] The Kino-nda-niimi Collective, *The Winter We Danced*, 21.

resurgence, and on central issues, including ownership, stewardship and protection of land and water, and responses to the alarming numbers of missing and murdered Indigenous women in Canada.

Throughout the weeks and months of Idle No More, round dances were the heart of the movement. A few days after Bill C-45 was passed by the Canadian Senate, to become federal law, the first flash mob round dance took place at a shopping mall in Regina, Saskatchewan: Aboriginal activists began beating drums and singing, and were quickly joined by hundreds of other people who joined hands in a circle moving clockwise around the mall's giant Christmas tree. In the next few days, the dance was repeated in hundreds of malls, intersections, highways, and reserves across Turtle Island, and the dancing continued over the next several months, supported by dances and protests around the world on International Days of Action. The round dances were multiethnic and multigenerational: people from diverse communities joined hands and moved in circles in support of Indigenous communities, always to a drumbeat and often with singing.

In *The Winter We Danced*, The Kino-nda-niimi Collective quotes a story of the origin and significance of the round dance, as told by Cree Elder John Cuthand. According to this story, a woman who was grieving her mother's death was visited by her mother, who gave her the dance as a way to help the people grieve in a good way. "Tell the people that when this circle is made we the ancestors will be dancing with you and we will be as one."[3] The round dance, then, is a dance of mourning that transforms grief into a performance of relationship among people and ancestors.

> In the winter of 2012–2013, our Ancestors danced with us. They were there in intersections, in shopping malls, and in front of Parliament buildings. They marched with us in protests, stood with us at blockades, and spoke through us in teach-ins. Joining us were our relatives, long-tenured and newly arrived Canadians, and sometimes, when we were lucky, the elements of creation that inspired action in the first place.[4]

The revival of the round dance is part of a practice of Indigenous resurgence: the round dance, along with many other ceremonies that were part of the "Potlatch," was banned by the Canadian and U.S. governments, and nearly disappeared in many communities. Cree singer Ray "Coco" Stevenson notes that while the round dance was originally a funeral ceremony to send the spirit to the spirit world, like all rituals and all cultures, it has evolved to become more celebratory,

---

[3] The Kino-nda-niimi Collective, *The Winter We Danced*, 24.
[4] The Kino-nda-niimi Collective, *The Winter We Danced*, 24.

and is often a social dance—but "the foundation has not changed in terms of what it represents." "Our people had this great faith that there was great power in the round dance," says David Courchene Jr., an Ojibwe spiritual leader. "The dancing itself was calling the spirit to help in healing whatever the community was in need of healing."[5] In the poem "A Healing Time" by SkyBlue Mary Morin, the dance is referred to as "the Friendship Dance" and "a dance of love."[6] For the Idle No More movement the round dances created and sustained solidarity to support resistance to colonization.

The Indigenous leaders of the dances of Idle No More welcomed non-Indigenous participants of all classes, genders, and ethnicities, who joined in dancing the dance of the other—of the Indigenous peoples who led them. Most were probably not aware of the history of the dance. But many were consciously mourning loss: the devastating effect of colonization on Indigenous peoples, the commodification of land and water, the violence that has diminished all of us—and yet celebrating a possible future that would involve nation-to-nation relations of mutual recognition and collaboration between Canada and Indigenous nations.

Re-creating the World

In *Dancing on Our Turtle's Back*, Leanne Simpson tells a Nishnaabeg story of the creation of Turtle Island. Here is a brief version: After a phase of destruction, violence, and imbalance, a flood was sent, not to punish but to allow the Nishnaabeg to begin again. Waynabozhoo and surviving animals gathered on a log floating in the water and decided to dive down to bring back a handful of earth. Many tried and failed. Finally Zhaashkoonh, the muskrat, surfaced, dead, but with a handful of mud in his paw. "Mikinaag (turtle) volunteered to bear the weight of the earth on her back, and Waynabozhoo placed the earth there. Waynabozhoo began to sing. The animals danced in a clockwise circular fashion and the winds blew, creating a huge and widening circle. Eventually, they created the huge island on which we live, North America."[7]

This is a version of a well-known story of re-creation: beginning again. For Simpson, this is a story of Indigenous resurgence. In the wake of the violence and destruction of colonization, people are responsible for rebuilding the world.

---

[5] CBC Winnipeg, "Round Dance: Why it's the Symbol of Idol No More," January 28, 2013. http://www.cbc.ca/manitoba/scene/homepage-promo/2013/01/28/round-dance-revolution-drums-up-support-for-idle-no-more/
[6] Morin, "A Healing Time," 7–9.
[7] Simpson, *Dancing on our Turtle's Back*, 68–69. The story is told in many different ways in oral and written versions.

This will require individual responsibility and vision—diving down for our own handful of earth and bringing it back— and collective action. For Simpson, "Resurgence is dancing on our turtle's back; it is visioning and dancing new realities and worlds into existence."[8] In this story, the dance is a performance of relationality in the wake of destruction. A diverse group of animals, including a human, join hands in a circle and dance the world back into being. The collective action of participants acting in concert rebuilds the world.

Thomas Norton-Smith points out that origin stories in Indigenous cultures are *performative*: the stories themselves create meaning, to create the world. In contrast to the Christian missionaries' conviction that their own origin stories were descriptions of factual truth, Indigenous storytellers recognize that the role of stories is to help people understand their place in the world, to convey traditional knowledge and values, and to strengthen relationships. Like stories, ceremonies and dances are transformative performances that have the power to "*create* and *recreate*" the world: "the action, procedure, or performance is the principal vehicle of meaning and the way by which the world is made."[9] The ceremony of dance, including drumming and rattling, singing and dancing, is itself "an animated entity with a spirit created by the participants."[10] In a discussion of Shawnee Bread Dances, also danced in a circle, Norton-Smith writes: "The dance is a gift of thankfulness to the Creator and so creates the kinds of relationships and obligations characteristic of gift exchanges in gifting traditions. Perhaps most important, the dance empowers its symbols—the drum, the song, and the bread—and transforms its participants and the world."[11]

Simpson writes that while modern consumer culture looks for meaning to replace absence, Indigenous cultures create meaning through action: "storytelling, ceremony, singing, dancing, doing."[12] As Norton-Smith notes, rituals in all cultures create meaning; many of us are perhaps less conscious of the performative nature of our rituals—such as weddings, elections, and awards ceremonies. But Simpson is calling attention to the experience of lack at the heart of consumer culture: a culture organized around greed produces isolated individuals in lives that feel empty of meaning. And she is contrasting this with a culture that is organized around the conscious and deliberate creation of collective meaning through action in concert.

Indigenous dance, then, is collective action that creates relationships, and empowers and transforms its participants. Shay Welch argues that dance is a

---

[8] Simpson, *Dancing on our Turtle's Back*, 69–70. Simpson draws on Edna Manitowabi's interpretation to relate the story to the politics of resurgence.
[9] Norton-Smith, *The Dance of Person and Place*, 96.
[10] Norton-Smith, *The Dance of Person and Place*, 101.
[11] Norton-Smith, *The Dance of Person and Place*, 101–102.
[12] Simpson, *Dancing on Our Turtle's Back*, 93.

paradigmatic way of *knowing* in the performative knowledge system of Native American epistemology.[13] Dance is also a way of *creating*—of world-building. It's significant that Indigenous dances are generally danced in circles. As Norton-Smith argues, circularity is a "world-ordering principle" in Indigenous cultures: circles are patterns of gift exchange, circles of reciprocity that balance relations among diverse participants. We could say, then, that the collective action of ceremonial dance is a practice of relational freedom. More specifically, it's a collective practice of public freedom that creates and re-creates the world by enacting circles of relationality among earthly and spirit beings. Dance creates, empowers, and transforms the world, through the collective creation of a collective *spirit*.

The generalized term "Indigenous dance" encompasses many different dances with different meanings and transformative powers, within and among different communities. Ritual dance can be distinguished from social dances insofar as a ritual is a structured and meaningful ceremony that connects the human participants with the spirit world, whereas social dance simply brings people together. But the distinction between ritual and social dance is often blurred: a dance that brings people together can be a performance of ceremony, an enactment of collective spirit. Ritual dance often includes masking, and masks can represent specific animals or spirits. Through the mimetic performance, the performer embodies and *becomes* the animal by wearing its mask and dancing its dance, in minutely detailed and precise repetitions of the animal's ways of moving. These performances rely on very close attention to the embodiment of the other—the animal or being included in the circle of relationality. By embodying powerful spirits, dancers can be "both empowered by and protected from them" because they include the spirit within the circle of the dancers.[14]

"Indigenous dance" also includes contemporary choreography, which often continues the practice of storytelling. New dances create new ways of telling old stories, and they create new stories. As Jacqueline Shea Murphy writes, contemporary Indigenous dance can be "not the replication of some past dance, but the activation and expression and embodiment, today, in various movements and formats and skills, of Indigenous understandings that remap the future."[15] Like the traditional dances, contemporary dance creates and re-creates the world. Karyn Recollet emphasizes the creation of Indigenous futurities through *decolonial gesture*, focusing on the remix video *Ay I Oh Stomp*, which layers traditional and contemporary dance to "imagine and manifest alternative worlds into

---

[13] Welch, *The Phenomenology of a Performative Knowledge System*, 2019.
[14] Bryant-Bertail, "Old Spirits in a New World," 47.
[15] Murphy, "Editor's Note: Doing Indigenous Dance Today," 5. Dance companies can also play a role in empowering new generations through training and connection with their traditions. For example, the Bangarra Dance Theatre and the NAISDA Dance College in Australia were founded together to strengthen cultural connection. They also, of course, play a role in the education of settlers.

being."[16] Recollet analyzes the remix of documentary footage of Kwakwaka'wakw Thunderbird dance and canoe paddlers with iGlide's contemporary "popping" as a "choreopolitical tactic of defiance through Indigenous motion" that "jumps scale" to remap the future.[17] The remix is an expression of what André Lepecki calls the choreography of protest, emphasizing the resistant role of embodied freedom of movement: for Lepecki, dance is the ultimate expression of political freedom as the ability to move freely.[18] "Indigenous motion, through glyphing," Recollet writes, "produces maps to tomorrow as a result of mobilizing multiple geographical/territorial scales. By glyphing I am referring to the ways that music, dances, and other forms of persistent Indigenous motion activate spatial/temporal cartographies. . . . This work is rooted in the premise that we build a relationship with the land through activating it."[19] These practices of *decolonial gesture* are "generative in the sense of propelling new world(s) and relationalities into being."[20]

The round dance is a traditional dance, but it is continually renewed as a form of decolonial gesture: a practice that propels new worlds and new relationalities into being. In Indigenous communities, the round dance is often a social dance. But it also blurs the lines between social dance and ritual. As the Cree story indicates, the dance originated as a ceremony of grieving for the lost mother, and it was a way to include her and the ancestors in the circle of relations. The round dance, then, has a history as a mourning ritual, creating a bridge between the earthly world and the spirit world, connecting people with the spirits of the ancestors. But it has become a social dance of celebration. It is also a dance of resistance and resurgence: in defiance of colonization, the round dance performs the circle of reciprocity, dancing a new world into being. Sheelah McLean writes that the Idle No More movement has been "re-storying Canada." Decolonization requires re-storying our shared history and reimagining our relationships. "If we change the stories we live by, . . . we change our lives."[21]

The role of the round dance in contemporary political protests has a long history. In the late nineteenth century, Northern Paiute spiritual leaders organized ritual ceremonies to ignite Indigenous solidarity in resistance to colonization. The ceremonies became known as the Spirit Dance, or Ghost Dance. First organized by Wodziwob (Northern Paiute) in 1870, and then revived by Wovoka

---

[16] Recollet, "Gesturing Indigenous Futurities through the Remix," *Dance Research Journal* 48(1): 99. Recollet draws on Laura Harjo's "jumping scale," on Ashon Crawley's "Otherwise Movements," and on Mishuana Goeman's decolonial remapping to analyze the Vancouver-based multimedia art collective Skookum Sound System's digital remixed video *Ay I Oh Stomp* (2012).
[17] Recollet, "Gesturing Indigenous Futurities through the Remix," 93.
[18] Lepecki, "Performance and Corporeality" (lecture).
[19] Recollet, "Gesturing Indigenous Futurities through the Remix," 91.
[20] Recollet, "Gesturing Indigenous Futurities through the Remix," 95.
[21] McLean, "Idle No More," 95.

(Jack Wilson, Northern Paiute) in 1889, the Ghost Dance took the form of round dances, bringing together the round dance traditions of diverse communities, with people joining hands and dancing in a circle, and singing their spiritual visions. The purpose of the dance was to bring together Indigenous communities with the spirits of the ancestors, to resist colonization and to re-create the life of prosperity and abundance before colonization. The Ghost Dance spread through western North America and, like other Indigenous ceremonies, was regarded by the colonizers as dangerous and was repressed. In 1890 the U.S. government broke the 1868 Fort Laramie Treaty with the Lakota, unilaterally dissolving the Great Sioux Reservation of South Dakota into several smaller reserves, in an attempt to break the power of the Lakota Sioux nation. This was followed by the withdrawal of food rations, effectively starving the nation. The revival of the Ghost Dance played an important role in the Lakota resistance, and the dance was outlawed by the U.S. government. In December 1890, the U.S. Army invaded Lakota land to stop the Ghost Dance. The army arrested and shot Sitting Bull, and massacred hundreds of people, mostly women and children. The Massacre at Wounded Knee provoked widespread public criticism and was commemorated in the occupation of Wounded Knee by members of the American Indian Movement (AIM) in 1973. The Standing Rock Sioux resistance to the Dakota Access Pipeline has continued the resistance to the occupation of the land that continues to violate the Fort Laramie Treaty. The resistance has been called "our Ghost Dance" by Sioux lawyer and activist Chase Iron Eyes.[22]

In the politics of resistance the round dance is an assertion of claims to land and an assertion of freedom of movement. The round dances performed on highways and at intersections during *Idle No More*, and the round dances at railway blockades and on contested land, disrupt the freedom of movement that is taken for granted by the occupiers and that is denied to the occupied. As John Borrows points out, critiques of these actions on the grounds that they block movement is ironic: "Non-Aboriginal occupation of Indigenous lands has long overshadowed fleeting Indigenous uses of direct action throughout Canadian history. Nonindigenous civil (dis)obedience has been astonishingly successful in transferring Indigenous land to non-Indigenous people."[23] Colonization has

---

[22] For a contemporaneous settler account of the history of the Ghost Dance, see Mooney, *The Ghost Dance*. For a critique of Mooney's account, see Estes, *Our History Is the Future*.

[23] Borrows, *Freedom and Indigenous Constitutionalism*, 68. For Borrows, intellectual and physical *mobility* is central to Indigenous freedom. "In many systems of legal thought, Indigenous peoples are characterized as being either too nomadic or too static to protect their most significant relationships." In fact, he argues, "Indigenous peoples are constantly in states of settled flux. Our perpetual motion coexists with a persistent and enduring near-permanence." Rootedness coexists with movement across land, and through time, in engagement with diverse peoples and communities. These forms of spatial, temporal, and philosophical mobility mark Indigenous traditions as "fluid, hybridized, contingent, contested, cross-cutting, ever-changing" (Borrows, *Freedom and Indigenous Constitutionalism*, 20–21).

involved severe restrictions of movement: containment of people on reservations and in residential schools, property laws and borders that exclude people from their own lands, prohibition of hunting and fishing, chronic incarceration. The movement of the dance enacts and asserts the freedom of people to move across their lands. It also signifies the freedom of movement of water and wildlife.

The round dances of contemporary political protests can be traced, then, through varied histories as dances of mourning and celebration, of connection with the spirit world, and of resistance and resurgence. They are political performances of relationality that seek to re-create the world. While the form is old, and easily accessible, it is an assertion of freedom, of freedom of movement in rootedness and belonging to land. It is a practice of *decolonial gesture*—"a collective form of futurity-building through inviting others into the frame."[24] As Recollet writes: "Gesturing futurity calls upon us all to engage these multiple scales of desire within which we have the freedom of motion to create choreographies of possibility, hope, and ... yes ... radical love."[25]

Circle Dances as Practices of Collective Love

While the round dances of Turtle Island have specific meanings, roles, and histories, they can also be situated within a broad history of circle dancing common to ancient communities around the world. In virtually all small-scale societies studied by anthropologists, circle dances as part of rituals involving dance, drumming, chanting and singing, masks, costumes, and feasts, and often trance, have been recorded. Emile Durkheim argued that the *collective effervescence* of ecstatic rituals was an expression of the experience of the sacred and at the root of religious life; he argued that the rituals served to solidify social bonds. The anthropologist Victor Turner believed that ecstatic rituals are expressions of what he called *communitas*: "an essential and generic human bond, without which there could be *no* society."[26] The term *communitas* is taken from the Latin, meaning an unstructured community of equals, or the very spirit of community.

In *Dancing in the Streets: A History of Collective Joy*, Barbara Ehrenreich argues that these danced rituals, and the experience of *communitas* they enact, are expressions of a particular form of *love*: "the spontaneous love and solidarity that can arise within a community of equals."[27] We have, Ehrenreich notes, no word for this kind of collective love, which she distinguishes from erotic love. "What we lack is any way of describing and understanding the "love" that may

---

[24] Recollet, "Gesturing Indigenous Futurities through the Remix," 92.
[25] Recollet, "Gesturing Indigenous Futurities through the Remix," 101.
[26] Turner, *The Ritual Process*, 97.
[27] Ehrenreich, *Dancing in the Streets*, 10.

exist among dozens of people at a time; and it is this kind of love that is expressed in ecstatic ritual."[28] This absence is interesting, given that this form of love, performed in ecstatic rituals and festive dance, in particular circle dances, seems to be foundational to virtually all societies. Rock drawings depicting dancing figures have been found in Africa, India, and Australia, as well as southern Europe and the Middle East. The archaeologist Yosef Garfinkel argues that dancing scenes "were a most popular, indeed almost the only, subject used to describe interaction between people in the Neolithic and Chalcolithic periods."[29] In other words, as Ehrenreich notes, "well before people had a written language, and possibly before they took up a settled lifestyle, they danced and understood dancing as an activity important enough to record on stone."[30] Evolutionary biologists and psychologists argue that dance preceded speech in human development. Ehrenreich notes that anthropologists tend to agree that dance served an evolutionary function: to hold humans together in groups. And she points out that it holds people together—and works much better than talking—because it is a source of a deep collective joy, a pleasure in being together that could be called love.

With her characteristic exuberance and creativity, Ehrenreich traces practices of collective joy and love through ancient Greek and Roman cultures, focusing on the cult of Dionysus and its continuation in early Christianity. Women and the poor and marginalized played leading roles in these cults, and the danced rituals overturned hierarchies: Turner argues that in rituals of *communitas*, the lowly and marginal often attain a sacred status, with magical powers, which he describes as "the mystical powers of the weak."[31] Ehrenreich notes that these rituals maintained the worship of a variety of deities, including the earth goddesses, through the emergence of patriarchal Greek and Roman cultures, and through the development of Christianity: the Jesus cults often preserved the Dionysian, which in turn continued the worship of the older agrarian earth goddesses. The danced rituals that held groups together thousands of years ago are repeated in the circle dances of European festivals and continue to be performed in many communities around the world today.

Collective Love as Freedom?

For Victor Turner, *communitas* is complementary to social structures: rituals of *communitas* suspend the rules, roles, and temporality of society, elevating those

---

[28] Ehrenreich, *Dancing in the Streets*, 14.
[29] Quoted in Ehrenreich, *Dancing in the Streets*, 22.
[30] Ehrenreich, *Dancing in the Streets*, 22.
[31] Turner, *The Ritual Process*, 109.

of low or marginal status and debasing the powerful, providing an experience of an egalitarian "we" and of the uniqueness of the individual. Turner argued that rituals of *communitas* are forms of *anti-structure*: inventive and experimental inversions that suggest the instability of hierarchical social orders. Rituals can allow for a freedom from social structures, while ensuring that those structures are renewed. The *communitas* created by rituals serves to strengthen social bonds and facilitates reintegration. Ehrenreich emphasizes instead the potential for *resistance* to and *liberation* from social structures. The "rituals of inversion" that characterize carnivalesque rituals and festivals are forms of resistance to social hierarchies, and while this resistance is often temporary and contained, it also often overflows the boundaries of containment to support sustained struggles for political freedom. This would mean that while the idea of freedom in ancient Rome referred to a status—not being a slave—it also invoked a subversion of the binary slave/not slave—a subversion that was commonly performed in rituals that the Roman government perceived as a threat and attempted to suppress. These rituals performed freedom in collective love, a dangerous freedom that threatened to overturn hierarchies of slave and master, plebeian and patrician.

Rituals of collective love, then, are performances that enact solidarity and resistance. They are also practices of a unique form of freedom. It's important to emphasize the distinctiveness of the *experience* of freedom in the practice of rituals of collective love. This is an embodied and playful freedom, expressed in movement and song, costume and feasting, a celebration of being-with. So collective love is a form of freedom with its own organizing principles and with its own substantive experiential content. It involves the overturning of hierarchies and the practice of equality among heterogeneous participants, inclusive of all in the solidarity of a "we" that supports the expression of individuality and diversity. And it is an embodied freedom, a freedom of bodies and pleasures that resists the patriarchal social order. It is this experience of freedom in love that underlies solidarity and resistance. And it has its own history.

Pleasure and Danger: Love and Freedom in Resistance

Western political theorists have typically not regarded practices of what Ehrenreich calls collective love as practices of public freedom. While dance and ritual are taken up by political movements—including most recently the Idle No More and Black Lives Matter movements, Inust'ot'en and Sioux resistances to gas pipelines, the queer politics of ACT Up and pride parades, and the antiglobalization and Occupy movements—political commentators typically dismiss these practices as romantic and apolitical: as distractions from the serious work of politics. Theorists of political solidarity also tend to prioritize political commitment and rational moral responsibility over affective relations. As Rosemary Hennessey argues, the circulation of *love* through "affective attachments of organizing" in social movements is not well theorized.[32] Thus the importance of alternative "affective economies" for political movements is too often ignored.[33]

The perception of collective love as apolitical is closely linked to a fear that it is dangerous. Ehrenreich notes that the deep pleasure experienced in collective ecstatic rituals has often been treated with suspicion by Western anthropologists (including Turner), who have seen it as a form of savagery, or have stressed its role as a temporary suspension of rules that must be reinstated, to prevent degeneration into wildness and anarchy. This suspicion mirrors the attitude of the Greek and Roman governments, which outlawed the Dionysian cults. But it also mirrors the sense of danger in the sacred often experienced in the cults themselves. In the past century, collective joy has been linked to the fascist romanticism of blood and soil, and to the mindless crowds of fascist festivals, celebrations of the triumph of totalitarianism over the individual. But Ehrenreich points out that Nazi rallies were not festivals of collective joy but spectacles of military might, involving not dancing and feasting but marching. They did not overturn hierarchies but were organized and rigidly controlled by the Party. Ehrenreich argues that the modern horror of crowds and festivals can be traced back to the French Revolution, when the revolutionaries feared that the peasant uprisings that supported the revolution were also sources of resistance to the new order. And the late nineteenth-century Gustave Le Bon's descriptions of the crowd as a form of insanity were uncritically taken up by Freud and by political theorists.

For modern Westerners, a primary danger of Dionysian ritual and festival is the danger of self-loss: the dissolution of self in the unity of the group. The term *Dionysian* conjures images of wild abandon, drunkenness, and self-loss, which can veer toward madness. Thus the freedom it evokes is not political freedom but the freedom of self-loss, a brief return to what Nietzsche referred to as "primal being." As many feminist theorists have argued, this fear of self-loss is connected to a fear of regression to the womb, to a dependence on a phantasied all-powerful mother.[34] So it is important to emphasize that for Turner rituals of *communitas* actually involve an enhancement of individual uniqueness, and an experience and recognition of self and other as unique and independent beings. Turner explicates this experience of equal individuals in community who recognize each other's individuality in terms of Martin Buber's encounter between "I and

---

[32] Hennessey, "Bread and Roses in the Common," 270.
[33] Ferguson, "Feminist Love Politics."
[34] See Irigaray, *Speculum*.

thou" in an "essential We": "a community of several independent persons, who have a self and self-responsibility."[35]

But the perception of rituals of collective love as dangerous is also quite accurate: in Ehrenreich's account, these are rituals that overturn hierarchies, that include and are often led by women and the poor and marginalized. They invoke the possibility of rebellion against patriarchal power and colonization, and the continued power of the cults of matrilineal earth goddesses as sources of subversion, rooted in a powerful experience of embodied and collective freedom. So the association of collective love with the devouring mother is connected with the threat of feminist rebellion. The rituals are indeed dangerous—but they are certainly not apolitical!

Ehrenreich distinguishes between rituals of collective love that are open and inclusive, and rituals of racist nationalisms, defining such rituals as something other than collective love. Yet the danger of nationalist and racist rituals still haunts any invocation of collective love as a practice of freedom. In his early descriptions of rituals of *communitas*, Turner argued that they involved obedience to a leader and only served to reaffirm hierarchies. He later broadened his understanding of *communitas* to include practices of carnival and group experiences of "flow" that were more egalitarian and open-ended. But it is important to theorize how practices of collective love can be open and inclusive, and how they can perform public freedom.

Encounter: Ehrenreich's Theory of Collective Love and Indigenous Theories of the Round Dance

Ehrenreich's interpretation of the history of the circle dance offers a novel understanding of a cross-cultural practice of a specific kind of collective love as collective freedom. The idea of collective love blurs differences among dances within and across cultures, and blurs distinctions between ritual and festive dance. Ehrenreich focuses on the Dionysian cults and their connection with the Jesus cults in ancient Greece and Rome, and she grounds this account in some anthropological interpretations of the circle dance as a formative practice that is common to cultures around the world. This is a creative universalizing account, and it does not attend to debates among anthropologists and theorists of ritual. It does not consider Indigenous theorists' accounts of their own dances and rituals.

Ehrenreich follows Victor Turner's argument that rituals of *communitas* served an evolutionary function: to forge and maintain social bonds. While Turner saw these rituals as forms of anti-structure that could serve to defuse resistance

---

[35] Turner, *The Ritual Process*, 137; quoting Buber.

by temporarily suspending hierarchy, Ehrenreich sees them as celebrations of collective love: subversive practices that could potentially resist hierarchy. But this functionalist account misses what is central in Indigenous theorists' accounts: the performative role of the dance as a practice of world-creation. As Thomas Norton-Smith and Leanne Simpson argue, the dance *performs* the creation and re-creation of a world. And the world it creates and re-creates—the meaning it performs—is the world of relationality. Each round dance, each ritual and each social dance, is a ceremony that performs and enacts the balancing of relations among beings—human, nonhuman, and spirit beings—in a system of relationality guided by the practice of the gift.

What kind of love do the dances enact? Ehrenreich's account describes the circle dances as expressions of a collective love which is a particular form of pleasure: joy. Collective love is an "ecstatic merger with the group" which nevertheless enhances individual uniqueness. Collective love is primarily the joy of being together. Indigenous accounts of the round dance do emphasize the pleasure in being together: the round dance is a social dance of celebration. But insofar as the round dance is also a ritual, it is a manifestation of relationality that bridges the realms of the earthly and the spiritual. The love it expresses is love of "all my relations"—all beings in relation with each other. Ritual dance that enacts relationality is not simply an ecstatic merger with the group. And while it does celebrate communal bonds, the love that motivates and sustains the circle is not just the love of community, nor is it the love of all of nature as familial oneness. It is not the love of one's own, a love that reduces all in the circle to a homogeneous unity. The love that builds the world of relationality is a *philoxenic* love that risks the inclusion of the radically other.

What kind of freedom do the dances enact? Ehrenreich's account emphasizes the subversive and liberatory freedom of resistance to the social order. Indigenous theory emphasizes the role of ceremony as a practice of freedom as *world-creation*. The dance is a practice of freedom in Arendt's sense: creating a world, making meaning. This interpretation resists the binary of structure and anti-structure. The form of freedom enacted in ritual dance is not freedom from social order. Freedom is creation of the world of relationality that *is* a social order. When it is performed as resistance, the round dance is a call for freedom from colonization, but the freedom it performs is the freedom of resurgence: freedom as creation and re-creation of the world of relationality.

In the Nishnaabeg story of the creation of Turtle Island and the re-creation of the world, the animals join together in a circle to dance the world into being. The dance is a performance of relationality in the wake of destruction, an act of collective love and freedom that defies the violence that had thrown their relations out of balance. Just as the dance in the story performs the re-creation of the world, each ritual dance creates and re-creates the world again. It does this by creating the meaning that holds the world together, creating new meaning through an embodied transformative performance. The round dance does this as well. As the Cree story indicates, the round dance was a dance of mourning that brought the spirit of the lost mother back into the circle of the living, including the ancestors within the community. It has become a dance of celebration of relationship, and a dance of resistance to colonization that reaffirms relationality.

James (Sákéj) Youngblood Henderson writes that the Ghost Dance has been misinterpreted by Eurocentric theorists:

> Eurocentric writings about the ghost dance misunderstood the visions. The normative visions and the dances were not part of a messianic movement but a sustained vision of how to resist colonization. It was a vision of how to release all the spirits contained in the old ceremonies and rites. The dance released these contained spirits or forces back into the deep caves of mother Earth, where they would be immune from colonizers' strategies and techniques. Their efforts were a noble sacrifice for future generations. What is more important, the dance would allow the spiritual teachings to renew the ecology, and eventually the forces of the ecology would forge a traditional consciousness of the following generations. In time, through postcolonial ghost dancing, these forces would foster a new vision of Aboriginal renewal, thus restoring the traditional consciousness and order. Part of the renewal is understanding the colonizer's strategy of Eurocentrism, epistemological diffusionism, universality, and enforcement of differences.[36]

Philia and Philoxenia: Arendt and Rituals of World-Creation

Dance is not typically understood as a political practice by Eurocentric political theorists. Yet I've suggested that the dance is a practice of freedom in Arendt's sense: it's a practice of world-creation. For Arendt, practices of world-creation are rooted in *amor mundi*: love of the world. For Leanne Betasamosake Simpson and Thomas Norton-Smith, Indigenous practices of world-creation are rooted in love of land, in gratitude for the gifts of the earth. Ceremonies, like stories, are transformative performances that create the world by creating new meaning.

In her analysis of the meaning of *amor mundi* in Arendt's thought, Lucy Tatman writes: "This Arendtian love of the world is the grateful emotional response to the fact that meaningful life has been given unto us."[37] For Arendt, as for Augustine, meaningfulness requires memory. "[W]e have entered the

---

[36] Henderson, "Postcolonial Ghost Dancing," 88–89.
[37] Tatman, "Arendt and Augustine," 635.

world through birth . . . Fear of death and inadequacy of life are the springs of desire. In contrast, gratitude for life having been given at all is the spring of remembrance."[38]

We are born into a world that has been made meaningful through the telling together of stories. And we continue to create meaning by telling stories, to re-create the world we love. "The story," Arendt remarked, "reveals the meaning of what would otherwise remain an unbearable sequence of sheer happenings."[39] The problem of Arendt's essay *Willing* is how to begin again: how to restart time, given a past in fragments, no longer told together by narrative and tradition. The role of judgment, Tatman argues, is to decide what to save from the past and what to will for the future. But "unless our judgments are accompanied by stories in which they are explained and related to the world, then our judgments are just more fragments, bits and pieces unconnected to our lives."[40]

Hannah Arendt argued that freedom is a practice, connected to natality, to birth: the capacity to begin. For Arendt this meant the capacity for spontaneity, the capacity to create, to act; but most importantly the capacity of citizens to act and interact together in the public realm, to participate in the public realm of the *polis*, and in the political creation of a new republic. Arendt locates the roots of the practice of public participation in the Greek *polis*.

Arendt was engaged throughout her work with the exploration of various concepts of love as the source of the public bonds or connections that could hold human actors together in the public realm. We could say that Arendt actively sought the sources of her conception of freedom as political participation in the public realm in forms of collective love. In this she drew on a long tradition in Greek and Latin philosophy in which love was seen as the source of relatively durable relationships, or *vinculum*. In this tradition love was regarded as "the inner organ for freedom" and as "the spring of action."[41] As Shin Chiba writes, in his analysis of the concept of love in Arendt's work, "Arendt's vision of a politics of freedom reveals its fundamental structure as a political theory of *amor mundi*, love of the world."[42] But Arendt was ambivalent about the possibility of love as a source of public freedom.

Arendt's doctoral dissertation, *Der Liebesbegriffe bei Augustin*, distinguished among forms of love in Augustine, focusing on *agape* or *caritas*, and the working title for her major work, *The Human Condition*, was *Amor Mundi*. Yet, as I've discussed in Chapter 2, Arendt frequently argued that love was opposed to politics: "Love, by its very nature, is unworldly, and it is for this reason rather than

---

[38] Arendt, *Love and Saint Augustine*, 51–52; quoted by Tatman, "Arendt and Augustine," 630.
[39] Arendt, *Men in Dark Times*, 104; quoted by Tatman, "Arendt and Augustine," 633.
[40] Tatman, "Arendt and Augustine," 633.
[41] Arendt, *The Life of the Mind*, vol. 2: *Willing*.
[42] Chiba, "Hannah Arendt on Love and the Political," 506.

its rarity that it is not only apolitical but antipolitical, perhaps the most powerful of all antipolitical human forces."[43] Love for Arendt was "unworldly" because it collapses the distance between individuals, dissolving human plurality and difference into an undifferentiated unity. For Arendt political freedom requires that participants engage with a common world; in love people focus only on each other. "Love, by reason of its passion, destroys the in-between which relates us to and separates us from others."[44] Here she is clearly referring to romantic love, but she also extends this critique to *agape*, arguing against the Christian belief that forgiveness (which she sees as essential to freedom from vengeance) is possible only through love. Instead, respect, which is a kind of friendship "without intimacy and without closeness" is the basis of political life.[45] Thus Arendt distinguishes friendship, Aristotle's *philia politikē*, along with *amor mundi*, from other forms of love, including not only romantic love but fraternity, as well as pity and compassion. Chiba argues that there is a tension in Arendt's work between the classical objective conception of love as "the universal quest for a public bond immanent in the human condition" and the modern subjective understanding of love as "mere sentiment or emotion."[46]

Arendt's conception of freedom as political participation draws on Aristotle's association of *philia*—the form of love that is friendship—with the polis. The friendship that constitutes political freedom, for Arendt, is focused on discourse, discussion, and debate among equal participants in the public realm. "For the Greeks, the essence of friendship consisted in discourse. They held that only the constant interchange of talk united citizens in a *polis*. In discourse the political importance of friendship, and humanness peculiar to it, were made manifest." In fact, she writes, for the Greeks, "the common world . . . remains 'inhuman' in a very literal sense unless it is constantly talked about by human beings."[47] Arendt valued political friendship for its world-building capacity: its capacity to create a community of equals focused on a common world. And she believed that a common world is created through political discourse: through agonistic contest conducted through discourse and debate in the public realm. Thus *amor mundi*, love for the world, involves the creation of the world through political discourse among equal citizens, and this is the essence of political freedom.

The ideal of *philia* does not, however, elude the dangers posed by love. Aristotle's *philia*—the friendship of free men in the polis—still carries with it the assumption of sameness, for it is the glue of an exclusive unity. The citizenship of

---

[43] Arendt, *The Human Condition*, 242.
[44] Arendt, *The Human Condition*, 242.
[45] Arendt, *The Human Condition*, 243.
[46] Chiba, "Hannah Arendt on Love and the Political," 510.
[47] Arendt, *Men in Dark Times*, 24.

free men in the Greek polis was based on the exclusion of strangers and slaves, and women.[48] In contrast to Aristotle's *philia*, which united male citizens in their sameness, and was exclusive of noncitizens, the Epicureans argued for the importance of friendship as *philoxenia*: love for strangers, or foreigners, who are guests. As Leela Gandhi notes, *philoxenia* was posited by the Epicureans explicitly against the exclusive form of friendship that is the basis of the polis, which was seen as an "unfriendly place," "destructive of friendship."[49] *Philoxenia* is a form of love that constitutes community with those who are excluded from the status and power of citizens, with different and heterogeneous others. Thus it is surely a better *affective* basis for political freedom than Aristotle's *philia*.

Arendt would surely agree that *philoxenia* should be essential to public political freedom. A central concern in much of her work was the inclusion of outsiders, in particular Jews and refugees, in the common public world. As Shiba notes, "One's readiness to live together with those who are different, diversified, and heterogeneous, is the essential ingredient of *amor mundi*."[50] Yet Arendt's embrace of *philia* reflects an inattention to some forms of exclusion. In arguing that the public realm is a realm of freedom because it is free from necessity, Arendt perpetuates the exclusiveness of this realm, governed by a *philia* untainted by the relationships that sustain the realms of the household and the economy, the realms of work and labor and the body.[51]

For Arendt, it is "the constant interchange of talk" that unites people in the public realm. Agonistic discourse and argument are the essential components of public freedom. In contrast, if danced rituals are understood as meaningful action in concert, they are embodied and affective practices of world-creation, and the world they create is the fully embodied and affective world of relationality. Indigenous theorists' accounts of round dances and ritual dances do not thematize a binary between freedom and necessity, or between a public and a private realm, or between political discourse and the discourse of ceremony, story, and dance. Ritual dance and other forms of ceremony are also forms of discourse. They do not *replace* agonistic discourse and debate as essential to political freedom. But the danced rituals enact and sustain a practice of relational freedom that creates a better affective context for democratic discourse and debate than agonistic contests. Moreover, these rituals can in themselves practice

---

[48] As Leela Gandhi points out, Derrida argues that *philia* still carries with it the connotation of the filial and familial: "stock, genus or species, sex (*Geschlect*), blood, birth, nature, nation" (Gandhi, *Affective Communities*, 27).

[49] Gandhi, *Affective Communities*, 29; quoting Philodemus.

[50] Chiba, "Hannah Arendt on Love and the Political," 534.

[51] In Ehrenreich's account of ritual dance, practices of collective love are practices of freedom in part because they are free from those realms of necessity; the difference is that they include those who are normally relegated to these realms, and who resist this relegation.

an alternative form of politics that resists nationalism and exclusiveness, and resists hierarchy, by creating better relations.⁵²

Would Arendt be able to see danced rituals as practices of public freedom? Arendt might concede that collective dance and song are sources of sociality and community. Certainly they are expressions of the creativity and spontaneity, and the creation of meaning, that Arendt associated with natality and with freedom. But as embodied and nondiscursive practices they would be seen by Arendt as unworldly, as fraternal and social rather than political.⁵³ In *On Revolution*, Arendt wrote that in contrast to the American Revolution, the French Revolution manifested not as deliberative discussion and decision, but as the "intoxication" of "the crowd."⁵⁴ The French Revolution devolved into the Terror because it lost its focus on freedom and sank to the realm of necessity, driven by the claims of poor. Thus it shifted from a political practice of freedom to a social practice rooted in claims of necessity. Hanna Pitkin has argued that Arendt's repudiation of the social as opposed to the political can be read as an expression of a fear of the social as *the Blob*: "the Blob is a fantasy of regression of losing one's separate self and being once more dissolved in—swallowed up by—an engulfing mother."⁵⁵ The social is feminized and feared as antipolitical and dangerous. Probably the embodied freedom of ritual dance would appear to Arendt as an instantiation of the Blob.

Arendt did embrace an ideal of "public happiness" which was synonymous with political freedom. In *On Revolution*, she argues that the American Revolution was successful because it was a practice of freedom of those who were experienced in the art of public freedom, which they experienced as public happiness. Arendt writes: "the Americans knew that public freedom consisted in having a share in public business, and that the activities connected with this business by no means constituted a burden but gave those who discharged them in public a feeling of happiness they could acquire nowhere else." They understood

---

⁵² As we have seen, anthropologists argue that communities are held together primarily not through deliberative discourse but through rituals of *communitas*, and the earliest social bonds were created through dance. These rituals are not performed in a political realm distinguished from the social, and they do not involve discourse on common issues or problems. But they are certainly public, and they are very much focused on a common world: the participants consciously affirm equality among heterogeneous individuals and groups, and consciously overturn hierarchies of status and power, to create a community of equal individuals. In other words, power and difference are thematized, not discursively, but in a playful practice of transformation that temporarily actualizes an imagined equality.

⁵³ I'm using *nondiscursive* in reference to Arendt's sense of discourse as the "interchange of talk." In the broader sense of communicative action, dance and rituals are forms of discourse.

⁵⁴ Arendt, *On Revolution*, 120. In *The Origins of Totalitarianism*, Arendt argues that the nineteenth-century mob could not be identified with the working class or with "the people as a whole," but was composed actually of "the refuse of all classes," the by-product of a bourgeois society, and "essentially irresponsible" (Arendt, *The Origins of Totalitarianism*, 145).

⁵⁵ Pitkin, "Conformism, Housekeeping, and the Attack of the Blob," 79. See also Pitkin, *The Attack of the Blob*.

their participation in democratic governance not simply as a duty, nor as a means to serve their self-interest, but "most of all because they enjoyed the discussions, the deliberations, and the making of decisions."[56] Arendt argues that this happiness and enjoyment are part of the practice of freedom. But what exactly was it that the Americans enjoyed?

"What brought them together was 'the world and the public interest of liberty' (Harrington), and what moved them was 'the passion for distinction' which John Adams held to be 'more essential and remarkable' than any other human faculty." Arendt quotes Adams, who writes: "every individual is seen to be strongly actuated by a desire to be seen, heard, talked of, approved and respected by the people about him, and within his knowledge." Arendt concurs with Adams that the chief virtue of political man is this desire to be seen and "to excel another." Thus the motivation for public freedom, and public happiness, for Arendt, is the passion to be seen, to be of significance, to "excel another." "It is the desire to excel which makes men love the world and enjoy the company of their peers, and drives them into public business."[57]

Arendt is surely right that the experience and practice of public happiness is essential to democracy. But perhaps the desires to appear and to excel another are not its definitive or most useful motivations. Certainly those desires are strong motivations for public life. But we have seen where they can lead: to a culture in which the pursuit of fame is the most pressing pursuit, and where the desire to excel degenerates into the kind of agonistic contest that produces only winners and losers. Of course, for Arendt, the desire for appearance is not simply a desire for fame and recognition. She distinguishes between the will to appear and the desire for fame. Arendt is invoking the concept of appearance in Heidegger, and in Aristotle, as the disclosure of being in a social world. So appearance is essentially related to *Mitsein*—being with. For Arendt the desire to appear is essential to freedom rooted in natality. And for Arendt it is crucially important that the individual appear in his uniqueness and not dissolve into the "we." But I would argue that the experience of pleasure in democratic freedom that should be emphasized is not so much the pleasure of being seen to excel, and not so much the pleasure in excelling others, but the pleasure of *being with* others, and the pleasure of acting together to re-create the world. This is a risky pleasure—the pleasure of engaging with strange others, and risking the exposure of our own strange otherness, as we act together to re-create the world we hold in common. Surely it is this pleasure that is more likely to support working together

---

[56] Arendt, *On Revolution*, 119.
[57] Arendt, *On Revolution*, 119–120. Adams called the passion to excel another "emulation." Though I do not have the space to develop this argument here, I think that when Adams uses the term *emulation*, he is consciously or unconsciously referring back to the concept of the exemplar, which I discuss later. This association is displaced in Adams's odd use of the term to denote not resembling but "excelling another."

in the pursuit of collective wellbeing. This work is more difficult than appearing and excelling, more difficult than engaging in struggles for power. The difficult work of democracy—politics by and for the people—needs to be supported by its own specific form of happiness.

In her discussion of public happiness, Arendt recognizes that the chief vice of political life is ambition, which "aims at power as a means of distinction."[58] Thus ambition must be met with and checked by the ambition of others.[59] But the battle of ambitions for power does not in fact produce an egalitarian public world. It just feeds the will to power. Arendt does not seriously consider the *violence* that the desire to excel another—agonistic contest—can produce if it is not played out in the context of an affective ethos in which we prioritize the pleasure of being together, and in which we accept and embrace the otherness of the other, motivated by our love for the world we share in common. I would argue that the primary source of public happiness, of pleasure in democratic participation, would be the experience of re-creating a world, the experience of *amor mundi*—love of the world, in combination with the pleasure of *philoxenia*—love of the other. This is not an experience that is simple or spontaneous. It has to be created.

Theorizing the Round Dance: Kristeva and Klein on Mourning and Gratitude

Julia Kristeva argues that in her discussions of public happiness, Arendt failed to give serious consideration to the characteristic vice of political life: the tendency to domination.[60] Kristeva argues that if we attend to the role of the body and the psyche in the event of natality, we can better understand the tendency to violence and domination as an effect of the inability to mourn the loss of the original object—the original other—the mother. Drawing on Melanie Klein, Kristeva writes that the separation of self from the mother or primary caregiver is experienced as pain and anxiety, fear of destruction, which is abjected and projected onto the mother, who is blamed and attacked. Only through the capacity to mourn the loss of the good object—the loved mother or primary other—is the child able to move from destructiveness into gratitude and love, to hold together the good and bad object, the loved and hated other, to experience both the pain of loss and the pleasure of gratitude together. The acceptance of the separateness or otherness of the mother allows us both to mourn her loss and to love her as another person, separate from ourselves. As Peg Birmingham writes, "The fragmentation and splitting characteristic of the paranoid-schizoid position is transformed into gratitude

---

[58] Arendt, *On Revolution*, 119.
[59] Arendt, *On Revolution*, 135.
[60] Kristeva, *Hannah Arendt*.

for the 'whole object' whose ineradicable loss is now mourned. The transformation of the violence of the death drive into gratitude occurs through the mourning of the object which remains forever foreign and alien in a primordial and irrecoverable separation."[61] Kristeva's analysis of Melanie Klein shows that this violence can give way to pleasure through gratitude for the other, replacing destructiveness with reparation and love. "Kristeva, following Klein, shows how both anxiety (associated with the death drive) and gratitude (which, like Arendt, she locates in memory and mourning) are part of the event of natality."[62] This gratitude for the other, rooted in the event of natality, which is the source of both destructiveness and love, is the missing piece in Arendt's understanding of our pleasure in the company of others. "The *affective ethos* that underlies public happiness, therefore, is gratitude for what remains ineradicably alien and foreign. It alone makes possible pleasure rather than grief in the company of others."[63]

Klein's argument that aggression is diminished through a process of mourning the lost mother offers a novel interpretation of the work of the round dance. In the Cree story of the round dance, the dance was originally given by a mother to her daughter, to help the daughter mourn her mother's loss. The Kleinian argument that mourning the mother allows us to replace aggression with gratitude and reparative love supports the understanding of the round dance as a practice of mourning that becomes a practice of celebration, and a ceremony of relationality that performs reciprocity in circles of gratitude. The dance can be seen as a skilled ritual practice of the capacity to hold together the pain of loss and the pleasure of gratitude.

We could say that this is a practice that includes the relation to the mother in public political life, addressing the fear of the devouring mother, and the hatred of the one who has hurt or abandoned us, the separate other, in a way that avoids defensive and violent repudiation, in a practice of reparative love. Is it an accident that the tradition of the round dance sustained matrilineal communities in which women had political power? The round dance ritually enacts the mourning of the lost mother, who is included, still separate but among us, in a collective practice of holding together. Just as it bridges the splitting between loved and hated object, it bridges the splitting between earthly and spirit world. That dance has evolved into a dance of celebration, and of nonviolent resistance to colonization.[64]

---

[61] Birmingham, "The Pleasure of Your Company," 70.
[62] Birmingham, "The Pleasure of Your Company," 69.
[63] Birmingham, "The Pleasure of Your Company," 73.
[64] It is significant that Idle No More was inspired and led by women—by Chief Spence and the four women leaders in Saskatchewan. Dory Nason argues that the Idle No More movement is evidence of "the boundless love that Indigenous women have for their families, their lands, their nations, and themselves as Indigenous people. These profound forms of love motivate Indigenous women everywhere to resist and protest, to teach and inspire, and to hold accountable both Indigenous and

As Ryan McMahon wrote at the beginning of the *Idle No More* movement, "The round dance revolution. It's happening. . . . As kids we were told that the drum beat represents the heartbeat of Mother Earth. We were told our songs come from Mother Earth. We were told that our communities are only as strong as the sound of our drums. . . . Our songs were banned. . . . Then slowly, the sound of our drums re-emerged. . . . And we began to gather again. We danced again. And our communities are slowly regaining their strength."[65] Stories of the drum as the heartbeat of Mother Earth and of ritual dance as celebration of the relation to Mother Earth are often dismissed by modern Westerners as stories and rituals of primitive earth-goddess worship. But there is nothing "primitive" about these stories and rituals. They are skilled techniques of ritual inclusion of the other in our midst. Such techniques address the risk and forestall the violence of acting together, facilitating the shared action of re-creating the world of relationality.

Being the Other; Being the Change

In *Strangers to Ourselves*, Kristeva argues that the capacity to live with and love the other requires the capacity to *be the other*. For Kristeva this requires accepting the otherness within ourselves, and the strangeness of ourselves—"to make oneself other for oneself." Kristeva argues that this capacity is central to a political practice of *philoxenia*, of welcoming others, foreigners, into our midst. "Living with the other, the foreigner, confronts us with the possibility or not of *being an other*. It is not simply—humanistically—a matter of our being able to accept the other, but of *being in his place*, and this means to imagine and make oneself other for oneself."[66]

What Kristeva has in mind is not the Kantian categorical imperative that calls on us to recognize our shared humanity, and not simply putting oneself in the place of the other to imagine their experience. It is "the courage to call ourselves disintegrated in order not to integrate foreigners and even less so to hunt them down, but rather to welcome them to that uncanny strangeness, which is as much

---

non-Indigenous allies to their responsibilities to protect the values and traditions that serve as the foundation for the survival of the land and Indigenous peoples." The movement shows us, Nason writes, that "Indigenous women's love is powerful. It is a love that can inspire a whole world to sing and dance and be in ceremony for the people. This has always been so" (Nason, "We Hold Our Hands Up," 186–187). Nason points out that this love also makes Indigenous women vulnerable to hate. Yet Indigenous women continue to risk practices of love in the face of colonization, misogyny, and abuse.

[65] McMahon, "The Round Dance Revolution, 100–101. Nina Wilson (Nakota/Dakota/Plains Cree) tells a story of a woman who was excluded from the community and who is given the drum by a spirit, to bring back to the people as a source of healing and freedom. Wilson, "Kisikew Iskwew, the Woman Spirit."

[66] Kristeva, *Strangers to Ourselves*, 13.

theirs as it is ours."⁶⁷ *Being the other* requires that we experience ourselves as the stranger, and make friends with our own strangeness: accept the hated parts of ourselves that we repress, deny, and project onto others. And this is possible only if we are able to move from splitting to mourning, to integrate loss into a capacity to hold ourselves together. Following Klein, we have to incorporate those parts of ourselves into a more complex self that we can love. James Baldwin makes the same argument when he points out that white racism will not end until whites stop projecting the hated parts of themselves onto the other, and learn to love themselves.⁶⁸

Being the other is facilitated by the capacity to see ourselves from the perspective of the other. This capacity to experience oneself as the strange other is essential to the practice of *philoxenic solidarity* that I discussed in Chapter 2: a practice that involves not just welcoming others in—not just hospitality—but opening out, to displace oneself, to locate oneself in a larger world.

In his essay "Reconciliation Here on Earth," James Tully argues that the alienation of colonizing societies from Indigenous peoples and from the earth can only be overcome by recovering the reciprocal practices of reconciliation that governed Indigenous societies:

> So, to respond to this crisis we need to free ourselves from the one-eyed perspective our unsustainable system gives us. We need to move around and see the crisis from other eyes: from the perspectives of other members of the underlying interdependent commonwealth of all forms of life. The Haida have a wonderful way of doing this. They put on a mask of the other living being whose perspective they wish to inhabit. Wearing the mask *and* performing the appropriate dance enables the person to see and experience the mode of being-with-others of the animal the mask represents. As Levi-Strauss noted, "the essential function of the mask is the *transformation* of the individual wearer into another being."
>
> The crucial feature of this *transformation* is that the wearer not only wears the mask, but dances in a *way* that participates in the way of life of the other being. That is, we can get ourselves out of our one-eyed view of the world only by moving around and participating in another way of being in the pluriverse. This is the central feature of the practices of reconciliation. . . . We have to begin to "be the change" by exercising and enacting our shared responsibilities if we wish to disclose and bring to self-awareness the underlying sustainable world we wish to re-inhabit.⁶⁹

---

⁶⁷ Kristeva, *Strangers to Ourselves*, 191–192.
⁶⁸ See Chapter 2, Coda.
⁶⁹ Tully, "Reconciliation Here on Earth," Dalhousie University Sustainability Lecture, 2014. A different version of this paragraph is in Tully, "Reconciliation Here on Earth," in Asch, Borrows, and Tully, eds., *Resurgence and Reconciliation*.

Here Tully is recognizing the practice of mimesis as a practice of *being the change*: a practice of freedom and transformation. Danced rituals that involve masking and dancing the dance of the other are not just celebrations of belonging; they are mimetic rituals that reconcile conflict not through argument and debate, and not just through listening to others' perspectives, but through, for that moment, *becoming the others*: wearing their faces, dancing their dances. Through this practice participants transform themselves and thereby transform the collective. Against the perception of mimetic rituals as "primitive" practices, we can see these rituals as sophisticated techniques of inclusion of the strange and potentially dangerous other within the circle of relationality. Participants in the ritual take the risk not only of being with the other, but of embodying and acting from the perspective of the other, experiencing the world and seeing oneself from that strange body and perspective.[70]

Following Kristeva, we can say that seeing oneself through the eyes of the other allows the participant to "make oneself other for oneself," to accept the strangeness of oneself. The masked dance can be seen as a performance of *philoxenia*, of inclusion of the other, the stranger, that is made possible by a capacity to make oneself other for oneself. The masked dance acts simultaneously to bring the other in and to move outside oneself. The dance takes the risk of decentering and displacing oneself, to locate oneself in a larger world: to become a participant in the world of plurality. These are the skills of philoxenia: including the other, the stranger in our midst. These are the skills of holding together, which is essential to social and political solidarity.

Dances of Relationality: *Philoxenia, Amor Mundi,* and *Love of Land*

The stories and interpretations of the round dance and masked ritual dance offer two ways of enacting relationality. The round dance performs the mourning of the lost mother, healing splitting and defusing aggression, to include the other in celebration of relationship. It works to address the fear, pain, and hostility provoked by our dependence on the other, and to transform that dependence into relations of interdependence. The masked ritual performs being the other, dancing the dance of the other, to decenter and include all participants in their strangeness

---

[70] This analysis is confirmed by Sarah Bryant-Bertail, who writes that masked dances are embodied mimetic relations: "Mimesis also involves embodiment, not just the replication of surface, and by embodying powerful spirits, one is both empowered by and protected from them." Because this "multidimensional mimesis" draws boundaries between animal, human, and spirit, "it is able to encompass and embody the cosmic system of life itself." Bryant-Bertail, "Old Spirits in a New World," 47.

and complexity in circles of relationality. Similarly, the story of the dance on the turtle's back includes all of the animals, including but not prioritizing humans, in the re-creation of the world. All of the circle dances are skilled techniques that re-create the world of relationality by enacting relationality: including the plurality of all beings in the world, including those who might be feared or hated. They are dances of *love of land*—dances of radical relationality that combine *philoxenia* and *amor mundi*: love of the other and love of the world. The skill of *philoxenia* is not a denial of conflict but an acceptance of fear, hate, strangeness, aggression, and conflict *within* relations of love. Within those relations we are not us and them, good and evil, but mixed, complex. The philoxenic love for all our relations, in all of their strangeness and diversity, grounds intelligent responses to the fear and hatred of the strange other, and works to accept and include that otherness within us. The skill of philoxenia is essential to the skill of re-creation of the world, through loving the world that unites and divides us. These are the practices of public freedom.

The round dance works as a dance of resistance by performing relationality, in defiance of domination—by inviting others to participate in relations of reciprocity and reconciliation. As a practice of resurgence, it works through both negation and affirmation. Glen Coulthard has argued that direct actions such as blockades and reclamations of land work both as negation of colonization and affirmation of Indigenous law. They are not simply reactive, acts of *ressentiment*. But they are not simply affirmative returns to a romanticized, *ressentiment*-inflected past. They "embody an enactment of Indigenous law and the obligations such laws place on Indigenous peoples to uphold the relations of reciprocity that shape our engagements with the human and nonhuman world—the land."[71]

Oneself as the Stranger

For those who are already habituated to being othered, the practice of *being the other* may seem like just more of the same. For the subaltern who is already forced to see oneself from the perspective of the dominant other, the challenge is *not* to take the perspective of that other. The challenge is to experience oneself not as the other's projection—the reviled strange other. But also not as the pure authentic good other. The challenge is to experience and love oneself as the unique complex mix of strangeness that each of us is, and to accept all of that strangeness as part of our plurality. With Fanon, Glen Coulthard argues that a central challenge for colonized subjects is to resist internalized forms of domination: to resist the capacity of the colonial system of governance to "transform the

---

[71] Coulthard, *Red Skin, White Masks* 170. Coulthard resists Fanon's rejection of *negritude* as oriented to an idealized past, and argues for a practice of resurgence that reclaims Indigenous tradition in a transformative present.

colonized population into *subjects* of imperial rule."[72] The politics of resurgence are a politics of loosening the psycho-affective attachment to colonial structure, not through nostalgic returns to a lost past, but through enactments of "critically revitalized traditions" that can ground transformation.[73]

As Coulthard recognizes, resistance to colonization also requires coalition politics and critical assessments of othering within Indigenous communities. This means that everyone, however othered, has to practice being the other with a plurality of others. Coalition politics requires accepting the strange mix of complexities within and among ourselves and each other. Billy-Ray Belcourt's poem "sacred" describes the experience of being rejected as too queer for the round dance. The poem begins: "a native man looks me in the eyes as he refuses to hold my hand during a round dance." And ends: "Even though i know i am too queer to be sacred anymore, i dance that broken circle dance because i am still waiting for hands who want to hold mine too."[74] Leanne Simpson includes Belcourt's poem, along with a critique of the demand that women wear skirts in ceremony, in a critique of contemporary attempts to reconnect with Indigenous tradition in ways that are exclusive. "Breaking Indigenous peoples' spiritual connection to each other and to land is a critical part of dispossession.... As we re-embed ourselves in this system [of relationality] we have to confront fear, shame, and anxiety and the idea that we are not good enough to be here among our ceremonial leaders.... we have to stop practicing interpretations of Nishnaabewin that cast people out. We don't exist unless we all belong. We all belong."[75] Simpson argues for a centering of queerness in resurgence. She doesn't mean that queer people need to be included. She means that "Nishnaabeg thought is queer."[76] For settler allies and supporters who join the dance, the task is not just to join in a colorful tradition. It is also not to become mired in guilt and shame, or to deny guilt and shame by identifying with the colonized other. The task is decolonization. This involves accepting responsibility for colonization and accepting ourselves as foreigners, as we acknowledge the multiple forms of otherness, the queerness of ourselves and each other. The task is to find a way of being that can affirm queerness at the center.

Exemplarity as a Politics of Freedom

All of the ritual dances in circles enact the re-creation of the world by performing relationality. These performances reflect the ethics of *exemplarity* in many

---

[72] Coulthard, *Red Skin, White Masks*, 31.
[73] Coulthard, 148.
[74] Belcourt, "sacred," in *This Wound Is a World*.
[75] Simpson, *As We Have Always Done*, 143.
[76] Simpson, *As We Have Always Done*, 138.

Indigenous philosophies. The ethics of *being the change* is an ethics of transformation. Dances of relationality are misconstrued as simply celebrations of togetherness and belonging. They are misconstrued as practices that deny conflict, difference, fear, and domination, to assert a simple unity and harmony. And while dances can perform *communitas*—joy in being together, collective love— they do more than that. They do some of the work of public freedom by actively addressing and working through the limits of relationality. They are skillful techniques that actively address and work through not only difference and conflict but fear and hatred, violence and domination. These rituals are repeated over and over, in recognition that good relations are never permanent. Hatred, fear, and violence are never permanently banished. They have to be addressed and worked on again and again.

The dances of relationality can be seen as practices of *exemplarity as political action*. They are embodied enactments of the kind of power—*power-with*— that is essential to a politics of nonviolence: to what Mohandas Gandhi called Satyagraha.[77] Akeel Bilgrami has argued the idea of exemplary action is the integrating theme in Gandhi's political philosophy. The originality of Gandhi's thought lies in the fact that "the concept of the exemplar is intended to provide a wholesale alternative to the concept of principle in moral philosophy."[78] One can be confident in one's actions and the example they set without arrogance, and without generating a principle by which we judge others. Rather, the example is a form of action that will itself create a transformation in the world. Thus Gandhi believed that the practice of nonviolence requires exemplary action, rather than criticism: "there is no true non-violence until criticism is removed from the scope of morals."[79] While he admires the romanticism of Gandhi's thought, Bilgrami argues that this position is based in fear, in a religious pessimism about human nature: a fear that if we criticize and argue, we won't be able to get beyond conflict, and will descend into violence. Modernity's great achievement, for Bilgrami, is the commitment to political means of dealing with conflict, through institutions of democratic deliberation, to allow democratic contestation without destruction.

I would suggest that the ethics of exemplarity is rooted not so much in the fear that critique and argument will lead to violence as in the recognition that the potential for violence needs to be addressed directly. And the best way to do this is through exemplary action. Fear and aggression need to be accepted and confronted through therapeutic strategies: stories, rituals, performances that actively work through these emotions, and that serve as models for how to do this

---

[77] Tully describes the power of nonviolence (*ahimsa*) as *power-with*, in his Introduction to Gregg, *The Power of Nonviolence*.
[78] Bilgrami, "Gandhi, the Philosopher," 112.
[79] Bilgrami, "Gandhi, the Philosopher," 114–115.

in situations of conflict and danger. The philosophy of exemplarity supports a powerful politics of nonviolent resistance: a political strategy based not in fear but in a recognition of the power of exemplary action, and the courage to risk being the exemplar.

Exemplarity and Democracy

Contrary to the common assumption that democracy is an achievement of the modern Western world, trialed only among an exclusive citizenship in ancient Greece, we know that many Indigenous societies have had highly developed systems of democratic governance both within and between nations for hundreds and perhaps thousands of years. The ethics of exemplarity have been central to these democratic systems. Rather than assuming that participants are fundamentally enemies, and that debate is battle through other means—through discourse and debate—democracies that emphasize exemplarity prioritize creating relationships. Discourse is a practice of decentering, of listening to the perspective of the others, and building on those perspectives to attempt to come to decisions that will take into account not only the plurality of perspectives but the plurality of powers in relationship. Power differentials are not ignored but thematized in a democratic practice that recognizes diverse powers. Affirmations of relationality, including dance and ritual that address the potential for violence, actively support and enable democratic discourse and debate.

Indigenous democratic systems are often oriented toward consensus. Again, the idea of consensus is often misconstrued as a belief in the possibility of simple unity and agreement, stasis, or end of conflict. In fact, the orientation to consensus includes direct recognition of difference and power relations, and the inevitability of ongoing conflict. Consensus is not an end; it's an agreement that all can endorse on a particular issue in the present. Agreement has to be continually renewed or revised. Rituals of relationality facilitate both the renewal and the revision by enacting relationship and recognition of the other's perspective. The orientation to consensus makes sense within an ethics of exemplarity grounded in an acceptance of conflict. Conflict does not have to end in destruction. Conflict is eternal, and democracy requires the patience to engage in the ongoing work *with* conflict, to affirm balanced relations in the tension of harmony. This practice of democracy assumes an understanding and affirmation of power *with* diverse and strange others. This affirmation of *power with* is grounded in the philosophy of relationality and relational freedom: a belief that if I criticize and attack my relations, I diminish my own freedom and the freedom of all.

In many Indigenous democratic systems, power is dispersed. Different groups and individuals have different powers and responsibilities. The image of the

Indian chief as supreme leader is an image created by Western popular culture and assumed by colonizing governments. In communities where powers are dispersed, leadership involves the sharing of power. And this power-sharing is facilitated through rituals of power-with. This kind of democratic system is arguably more sophisticated, and more democratic, than the battles among opposed teams and the elections of charismatic leaders that characterize contemporary Western "democracies." Could this form of power-sharing be an exemplary model that could guide the transformation of contemporary world democracies? Could we imagine democracies in which power is shared by elected groups of people with distinct powers, who are required to work together, and who would be removed from office if their political behavior is not exemplary?[80]

Exemplarity and Political Action: Resistance, Resurgence, and Reconciliation

The philosophy of exemplarity lies at the heart of nonviolent resistance to colonization. The power of nonviolent action comes from this: it does not seek to overpower, to trade one form of domination for another. It seeks to disarm the oppressor, by exemplifying another way of being. When the round dance is performed by resistance movements, the goal is to displace systematic oppression, to enact the reciprocal relations performed and modeled in the dance. The goal is to transform relations, to create relations of reciprocity.

The politics of resurgence is a politics of exemplarity that shifts the focus from the colonizer, and shifts energies from endless legal and political battles. This politics of exemplarity turns toward the tasks of rebuilding Indigenous selves and communities through rebuilding what Coulthard calls "critically revitalized traditions" of relations with land. Yet resurgence is also part of a politics of reconciliation: the rebuilding of traditions of relations exemplifies the work that must be done by settlers and by settler governments, to re-create the world.

The public round dances of resistance and resurgence invite others in, risking relation with the other to enact another way of being. The movement of the dance, "a complicated movement filled with the task of finding unity,"[81] inspires and sustains a movement of resistance and a movement of reconciliation. This is a practice of freedom as exemplary action: freedom in relationship. It is a transformative practice of public freedom oriented toward the inclusion of all in the world we love.

---

[80] In the Iroquois confederacy women elders had the power to remove from office male leaders whose behavior was not exemplary.
[81] Bird, [Untitled], 440.

EXCURSUS
Freedom and Love: A Speculative Genealogy

Free:
not in bondage or subject to control from outside. OE. *frēo* = OFris., OS., OHG. *frī* (Du. *vrij*, G. *frei*), ON. **frīr* as in *frjáls* free :- **frīhals* 'free-necked'), Goth. *freis* :- Gmc. **frijaz* :- IE. **prijos*, the stem of which is repr. also by Skr. *priyá-* dear, W. *rhydd* free, OSl. *prijatelī* friend, OE. *frēoġan* love, set free, Goth. *frijōn* love; cf. FRIEND. The primary sense is 'dear'.
—Concise Oxford Dictionary of Etymology

Most contemporary discussions of the concept of freedom trace its origin to the ancient Greek and Roman institutions of slavery: to be free was not to be enslaved. And that is the most commonly accepted use of the term today. But the etymology of *freedom* is more interesting. The term *free* can be traced to an Indo-European root meaning "to love." And this root is shared by the word *friend*. The primary sense of the original term was "dear": in Sanskrit, *priya*. This usage (referring also to devotion, love, and one's own) is found in the Rig Veda, one of the oldest ancient Vedic Sanskrit texts, dated to 1500–1200 BCE. How is it that the term which now most typically means "absence of constraint" is derived from a term meaning "to hold dear" and "to love"?

Another puzzle: while Western secular conceptions of freedom focus on the individual's capacity to act without constraint or to follow one's own will or desire, the concept of freedom in Eastern teaching traditions and in monotheistic mystic traditions appears to be diametrically opposed to this. In these traditions, freedom is found precisely in *not* following the self's will or desire: freedom is found in a practice of nonattachment to the self and its objects, and in union with the universal. These two puzzles might be connected. Here I shall draw a possible connection through traces of a distinctive historical tradition of an experience and practice of freedom in relationship.

The study of etymologies is a speculative science. While etymologists are able to find recorded usages of particular words, the links between them often require a good deal of theorization. Etymologists agree that the word *free* can be traced to words meaning "love" and "dear," but the link between these two very different concepts is not at all clear, and numerous theories have been proposed to account for the connection. The most widely accepted theory, first proposed by the philologist Otto Schrader in 1898, and still proposed by the *Oxford English Dictionary*, is that the term came to refer to the members of a household who were connected by ties of kindred with the head, as opposed to the slaves, and who formed a social class. So the beloved or dear ones came to be identified with the status classification *free*: not a slave. This is a plausible hypothesis, but even if it is correct, it leaves a lot out.

All of the etymologists agree that the term *priyos/priya* originally was used to express affection or closeness or sentimental attachment—sometimes to one's own body and possessions (one's own), but more often to people with whom one had a close emotional connection (dear, beloved). Emile Benveniste notes that this term is also used to refer to relations between humans and gods, "thus expressing a sort of 'mutual belonging,'" and this latter meaning is developed in European religious discourses.[1] Benveniste notes that the term *free* is clearly derived from *priyos* and hypothesizes that this evolution "may be explained by the exclusiveness of a social class. What was a personal qualification of a sentimental kind became a sign of mutual recognition which was exchanged between members of the class of the 'well-born.'"[2] But there seems to be no evidence whatsoever for this claim, which is purely speculative. The argument depends on a background of claims for the parallel development of the concept of *liberty*. The Latin *liber* and Greek *eleutheros* are traced to the Venetic *leudheros*. Benveniste notes that there is a Venetic goddess *Louzera*, the Latin equivalent of which would be *Libera*, the feminine consort of the god *Liber*, who is identified with Bacchus (the Roman form of Dionysius). The root *leudh* "to grow, develop" becomes a collective term for "the people" (e.g., the German *Leute*), the name of a divinity, *Liber*, and the name for children (*liberi*). "The relationship between these forms is easy to establish," writes Benveniste, "but what are we to make of the variety of meanings? These are so peculiar that at first sight they seem irreconcilable."[3] But the problem is solved with the claim that the idea of *liberty* was "constituted from a socialized notion of 'growth', the grown of a social category, the development of a community. All those who issued from that 'stock' are endowed with the quality of *(e)leudheros*."[4] Thus, he writes, "We grasp the social

---

[1] Benveniste, *Indo-European Language and Society*, 266.
[2] Benveniste, *Indo-European Language and Society*, 267.
[3] Benveniste, *Indo-European Language and Society*, 263.
[4] Benveniste, *Indo-European Language and Society*, 264.

origins of the concept of 'free'. The first sense is not, as one would be tempted to imagine, 'to be free of, rid of something'; it is that of belonging to an ethnic stock designated by a metaphor taken from vegetable growth. Such membership confers a privilege which a stranger and a slave will never possess."[5] Benveniste summarizes: "In Latin and Greek the free man, *(e)leuderos*, is positively defined by his membership of a 'breed', of a 'stock': proof of this in Latin is the designation of (well-born) children as *liberi*; to be born of good stock is to be free; it comes to the same thing. In Germanic, the connexion which is still felt, for instance, between German frei *'free'* and Freund allows us to reconstitute a primitive notion of liberty as the belonging to a closed group of those who call one another 'friends.'"[6]

There is one other theory about the relationship between the terms *freedom* and *love*: several etymologists, including T. G. Tucker, Richard Broxton Onians, and Theodore Thass-Thienemann, argue that all of these terms can be traced to terms referring to the pouring of liquids and to pleasure, desire, sexuality, fertility, procreation, and love. Thus, slavery is defined by its constraint on eros: on pleasure and sexuality, and on procreation. In *The Origins of European Thought*, Richard Broxton Onians, an editor of the *Oxford English Dictionary*, argues that both *liberty* and *freedom* developed from terms which originally meant erotic desire and joy. For the early Romans, freedom was connected to sexuality and procreation, and the essence of slavery was the denial of sexual and procreative freedom. There is a clear connection between the Roman term *liber*, the term applied to a man or to his head when the "procreative spirit was naturally active" in him, and *Liber*, the name of the god of sexuality and fertility. Onians suggests that the term *liber* originally expressed "a natural state, a distinctive activity or attribute of the procreative spirit or deity."[7] Hence the connections between the Latin *libido* and the later Germanic *lieben* and English *lief* or love, and liberty. He suggests that the root can be found in a single Greek term λιψ, which meant both "to pour liquid" and "to desire." Liber, like Dionysius, is associated with the drinking of wine, as well as feasting, dance, and revelry. And he notes that there is a parallel development of the English term *freedom*. The Anglo-Saxon and Germanic and English terms *freo, frei, free* mean not only "free, noble" but also "and must mean in the first place 'having desire, joy' "—for they are clearly related to *fréon* (to love) and *Freund* and *friend*. The variants *fri* and *frig* (free, noble) and *fria* (lord, master) are related to *fria* and *frig* (love, affection) and *Frig* (*Freya*), the goddess of sexual desire, love, and fertility. In other words, if

---

[5] Benveniste, *Indo-European Language and Society*, 264.
[6] Benveniste, *Indo-European Language and Society*, 262.
[7] Onians, *The Origins of European Thought*, 473.

freedom has come to refer to the status of mastery, that meaning is secondary to an experience of freedom as erotic pleasure, love, and joy.

We have, then, two theories of the genealogy of freedom in relation to love. One is negative: the concept of freedom originated with class hierarchy and with the institution of slavery. To be free is not to be enslaved. The other theory is positive: freedom is primarily an erotic experience of pleasure, joy, love, in the company of others. The status of mastery in contrast to enslavement is secondary.

Benveniste argues that the etymology of the concept of freedom clearly indicates that the primary sense is not negative—not freedom from constraint. He claims that the "primary sense" is the status of mastery: the closed group of friends in a social class. But if the status of mastery is sometimes understood to be a positive conception of freedom, it is in fact defined negatively, in contrast with slavery. And the distance between "not enslaved" and "not constrained" is pretty short. The concept of mastery defines a relation of ownership that denies constraint. If the ideas of freedom and love are united in a relation of belonging to a closed group of free men, that group is also defined negatively, in contrast with slavery. And while the *Oxford English Dictionary* suggests that the free dear ones were the members of a household, that suggestion is misleading. In most societies the free dear ones would include only the master's legitimate sons and his brothers: the masters of other households. So freedom would refer to membership in a social class of brothers and sons. This genealogy skips over any possible histories of connection between freedom and love prior to and outside of the heteropatriarchal family, and the systems of class and slavery. In fact, the connection between *beloved* and the sense of *free* as "not enslaved" emerges only in the Germanic and Celtic. Benveniste reads this connotation back into the Latin *liberi*, which he claims is proof that the term originally referred to membership in an ethnic stock, closed group, or class. He assumes, then, that the connection between the free and the beloved is defined by the exclusion slaves—and of strangers. Membership in a social class distinguishes the members of a closed group from "strangers, slaves, and, in general, from those who are not 'well-born.'"[8] This explains, he argues, the social origins of the concept of "free." The etymology of the concept of freedom requires an explanation for the convergence of a number of apparently irreconcilable terms that refer to affective relations, relations of mutual belonging, growth and development, children, the people, and conceptions of freedom. The explanation offered by Benveniste might account for the understanding of freedom as mastery, in contrast to slavery. But it cannot explain the wide variety of meanings of the concept of freedom, which are not reducible to the concept of membership in a social class.

---

[8] Benveniste, *Indo-European Language and Society*, 267.

A more plausible and less convoluted understanding of the convergence among the diverse terms that are linked to the term *freedom* can be found in Indigenous concepts of relational freedom: a conception of freedom that expresses the affective relations among all beings that grow and develop interdependently, in an animist worldview. This understanding brings together the birth and growth of children, plants, and animals, including humans, who understand themselves to be in relations of mutual belonging with each other and with spirits, ancestors, and gods. This understanding encompasses the second theory of the relation between freedom and love: the understanding of freedom as connected to eros. And it provides a better explanation of the connection to the growth and development of plants, and the birth of children. The combination of movement, pleasure, eros, joy, sexuality and fertility, the growth and development of plants and of people, the birth of children and the flow of liquids, drinking, feasting, dance, and revelry is found in an experience of freedom in mutual belonging with others that could be called freedom in love. This is the form of freedom that Ehrenreich identifies in her understanding of Dionysian rituals as celebratory enactments of collective joy, love, and freedom.⁹ The etymological connection can be seen in the lineage of the Germanic goddess *Freya* (*Frig*), who is seen as an incarnation of the proto-Indo-European goddess *Priya*. Both are goddesses of springtime and fecundity, love, sexuality, and fertility. Freya is associated with the May Day festivals that continue to be celebrated in many parts of Europe today. In Germany, the festival marks the night of the witches' celebrations, Witches Night or Walpurgis Night, on the summit of a mountain. May Day festivities have traditionally involved the lighting of bonfires and wild dancing around maypoles; it's unclear whether the dancing is meant to repel the witches or to join in their celebrations—or both. In any case, the goddess Freya, whose name connects freedom with love and friendship, and is traced to Priya, meaning "dear or beloved," is also connected to the festival of witches and springtime, love, and revelry, where dances around the maypole continue the tradition of the ancient circle dances.¹⁰

The *Oxford English Dictionary* suggests that the connection between terms referring to freedom and love can be found in the Greek term *peri*, meaning "round, around, and round-about." This would support the theory that the

---

⁹ Ehrenreich argues that the ecstatic rituals of collective love were not celebrations of erotic or romantic love. But that distinction is difficult to make. It's pretty clear that Dionysus and Liber represented sexuality and fertility. Ehrenreich is at pains to discredit Freud's assumption that collective forms of love can only be sublimations of erotic desire. She also wants to make it clear that ecstatic rituals were not orgies—though she admits that sex could sometimes be involved. But it is not necessary to dissociate collective love from erotic love. Probably in the earliest matrifocal societies they were unproblematically connected. The classical Greek conception of eros as dangerous mad passion aimed at possession was already a reaction against the Dionysian cults.

¹⁰ Freya is also associated with death and the afterlife. It's not clear whether this is an effect of the repudiation of the cults of freedom and love.

round dances Ehrenreich describes as rituals of collective love and collective joy, and that Indigenous theorists describe as rituals of relationality, are central to an ancient and continuing understanding of freedom. For Leanne Simpson and Thomas Norton-Smith, Indigenous round dances are rituals of mutual belonging: rituals of relationality that perform the creation and re-creation of the world. They perform the circulation of love of relations, love of land, that constitutes relational freedom.

Ehrenreich argues that rituals of collective joy expressed "a *hedonic* vision of community, based on egalitarianism and the joyous immediacy of human experience—as against the *agonic* reality of the cruelly unequal and warlike societies" in which they erupted, and which attempted to suppress them.[11] We could say that they expressed a form of *hedonic* freedom: a freedom in mutual belonging. As I've suggested in Chapter 3, this would mean that if freedom in the Greek polis and in ancient Rome referred to the status of the master—the status of not being a slave—it also invoked a *subversion* of the binary slave/not slave, a subversion that was commonly performed in the Dionysian rituals that the Greek and Roman governments perceived as a threat and attempted to suppress. These rituals performed freedom in what Ehrenreich calls collective love, a dangerous freedom that threatened to overturn hierarchies of slave and master, plebeian and patrician. If the concept of freedom referred to a status, in opposition to slavery, it also refers to a practice of dissolving hierarchies, in a memory and experience of a more inclusive freedom: an encounter with each other in a celebration of freedom in love. Thus, the freedoms of individual rights of citizenship, and the republican rights to participation in self-government, sought by the Roman plebeians and French and American revolutionaries, were compensatory freedoms, shadowed by the loss of a much more expansive and dangerous form of freedom. The Dionysian rituals were banned by the Greek and Roman governments, just as Indigenous round dance rituals were banned by the colonists in the Americas. These rituals were recognized as powerful performances of freedom in love, freedom in relationality. Any understanding of freedom as belonging to the class of the master, and the master's household, would have to compete against—and suppress—these much more exhilarating experiences of freedom.

Political Freedom and Love: Arendt Again

The etymological link between *freedom* and *love* can be explained, then, by two kinds of theories which correspond to two broad traditions of political freedom

[11] Ehrenreich, *Dancing in the Streets*, 60.

in the Western world. One represents the tradition of freedom as a status of mastery, in contrast to slavery, which connects to the understanding of freedom as absence of constraint, and individual liberty. The other corresponds to the understanding of freedom in relationship. The experience of freedom that is found in relations of interdependence, including erotic relations and celebratory rituals of collective social life, corresponds to the understanding of political freedom in participation in public life.

In contrast to the etymologists who claim a close relationship between the concepts of freedom and liberty, Hannah Arendt argued that the term *liberty* refers to negative freedom, while the idea of *freedom* is essentially positive. Liberation can mean freedom from constraint, and freedom from oppression, but true freedom is more than this: true freedom is participation in the public realm of the *polis*. As Arendt wrote, the Greeks understood that the master was not free. "The Greeks held that no one can be free except among his peers, that therefore neither the tyrant nor the despot nor the master of a household—even though he was fully liberated and was not forced by others—was freed."[12] Freedom for the Greeks was not a status—not the status of a master in opposition to the slave—but an engagement in public political life.

In fact, Greek democracy seems to have combined both understandings of the relation between love and freedom, and both traditions of political freedom. The political friendship—*philia politikē*—that defined the Greek *polis* was an exclusive relationship among citizens, members of a social class who were masters of their households. So this model of political participation does seem to have been rooted in the understanding of freedom as being a form of mutual belonging among the master's friends. Yet the idea of democratic freedom seems to be rooted in a competing conception of freedom as mutual belonging in *philoxenic* relations. Like the Greek polis, our modern democracies combine freedom as exclusive citizenship, and struggles over who belongs, with an ideal and practice of freedom as genuinely democratic political participation.

Arendt argued that freedom is connected to natality, to birth: the capacity to begin. For Arendt this meant the capacity for spontaneity, the capacity to create, to act; and the capacity of citizens to act and interact together in the public realm, to participate in the political creation of a new republic.[13] All of these meanings

---

[12] Arendt, *On Revolution*, 31.
[13] Arendt, "What Is Freedom?" Arendt may be right that true freedom is found in political participation, but as Hannah Pitkin points out, none of the etymologists agrees that this is the root meaning of *freedom*. Pitkin notes that Arendt, along with a number of etymologists, argued that the terms *liber* and *eleutheros* referred originally to unimpeded movement. This would be consistent with Arendt's understanding of freedom as the capacity to act. For Arendt this capacity leads directly to active participation in political life. But for Pitkin the focus on movement only confuses Arendt's claim that freedom essentially means political participation; unimpeded movement implies absence of constraint. In her summary of the etymological theories, Pitkin writes, "The etymological origins of 'freedom' and 'liberty' remain disputed, then, and thus cannot authoritatively settle anything about

are included in a conception of democratic freedom that is rooted in an experience of mutual belonging that combines freedom of movement, pleasure, eros, joy, sexuality and fertility, the growth and development of plants and of people, the birth of children, and the flow of liquids: an experience of freedom in mutual belonging with others that could be called freedom in love. We don't find all of these elements in Arendt. Erotic love and natural development had no place in her understanding of political freedom. We do find all of these elements in an Indigenous understanding of relational freedom, which, as I've argued, can be seen as a radically democratic conception of political freedom. The love of land that circulates through social and political practices of relational freedom is echoed in the love of the world that motivates, for Arendt, social and political life.

We know that, in her early work, Arendt was interested in the relationship between political freedom and the forms of love in Augustine's philosophy. Arendt did not pursue this connection. Yet there are clear parallels between an understanding of freedom in social and political relations and conceptions of freedom in love in religious mysticisms. In Eastern teaching traditions and in monotheistic mysticisms, freedom is defined not as the pursuit of will or desire, but as its opposite. Freedom is found in a practice of nonattachment to the desiring self. A central theme is freedom from suffering. This can be seen as a form of negative freedom: not the freedom of the self from constraints, but freedom *from* the self and from the constraints of the body, desire, and the material world. This form of freedom can also be interpreted as the capacity to rise above desires to a higher-order will: thus, freedom is found in self-realization through self-mastery. This was the view of Isaiah Berlin, who argued that this was one form of positive freedom. But the freedom to which mystic philosophies aspire is not reducible to either negative freedom or self-mastery. It involves moving from a focus on the self to a union with the universal, or with God.

The Christian concepts of *agape* and *caritas* refer to union with God: the love of God for humans, and humans for God. But they can also refer to very direct communion with Jesus, in relations of the body with the body of Christ. To take communion still means to eat the body and drink the blood of Jesus, within a community. *Agape* referred to and may have originally meant the "love feast." And it expresses the idea of perfect freedom found in union with God, with Jesus, and with the body. This history of freedom in an embodied loving relationship with the divine coexists with the history of liberation through ascetic disciplines that facilitate mastery of desire and escape from the world into the kingdom of the heavenly father.

The tension between a conception of freedom in mutual and embodied relationship and a conception of freedom as a relation of mastery has a very long

---

the essence of these concepts" (Pitkin, "Are Freedom and Liberty Twins?" 531). Pitkin does note, however, that the Greek *eleuthera* refers to democratic freedom, whereas the Roman *libertas* refers to rights in the context of inequality.

history in religious mysticisms. These are two opposed interpretations of an understanding of freedom in relation or union with God, or with the universal. The ancient philosophy of yoga, which developed out of diverse Indigenous animistic traditions in combination with later Vedic, Buddhist, and Jain traditions, is the spiritual practice of freedom through union, or yoking. "At the heart of all meditative practice in Asia is what Indians call *yoga*, the system that 'yokes' one's consciousness to a spiritually liberating discipline."[14] "Yoga means 'yoking' in the sense of spiritual discipline that requires preparatory exercises to gain control of the body, sense, and mind. It also refers to 'integration' within the spiritual integrity of the individual and the cosmos. In the *Yoga Sutra*, yoga refers both to a process of discipline and its goal. It is the entire process that enables one to realize a state of absolute spiritual integration, which is freedom."[15] In the *Yoga Sutra*, attributed to Patanjali, and dated to around the third century CE, spiritual freedom is found in an "idealized state of cosmic equilibrium" in which spirit and nature are separate and balanced.[16] But in the Tantric tradition, which revives Indigenous Indian practices and beliefs, freedom is found not in separation from the material world but within it. Freedom is found in and through the body, in and through practices in daily life that celebrate the expression of the divine in the world.[17] In his study of yogic traditions, Mircea Eliade wrote that the Tantric revival of the "autochthonous spiritualities" of "aboriginal India" often manifested in "excesses and aberrations" connected with "rites relegated to the lower levels of spirituality and with the behavior patterns of subordinate groups: tantrism finally incorporates the major and minor magic of the people, erotic Yoga encourages the open emergence of secret orgiastic cults and of licentious maniacs."[18] These excesses and aberrations, he assures us, were renounced by the respected spiritual masters. In fact, however, the embodied freedom in the connections among body, spirit, and world characteristic of the older spiritualities has long been intertwined with the classical tradition.[19]

---

[14] Stoler Miller, *Yoga: Discipline of Freedom*, ix.
[15] Stoler Miller, *Yoga: Discipline of Freedom*, 6.
[16] Stoler Miller, *Yoga: Discipline of Freedom*, 3.
[17] Tantric philosophy is dated to around the fifth century CE. In the *Bhagavad Gita*, dated to somewhere between the second and fifth centuries BCE, freedom is understood as worldly freedom: "In the *Gita* liberation enables one to wage the battle of life, while in the *Yoga Sutra* liberation entails an absolute isolation of the spirit from all worldly concerns" (Stoler Miller, *Yoga: Discipline of Freedom*, 11).
[18] Eliade, *Yoga: Immortality and Freedom*, 295.
[19] The tantric revival of the Great Goddess and the conceptions of union between spirit and body and world have influenced social movements as well.
As Vrinda Dalmiya notes, the feminine principle of *Prakr.ti* is retrieved by theorists like Vandana Shiva in "a powerful ecofeminism that envisages freedom not as an emancipation from the 'realm of necessity' (nature) but as rediscovering our submersion in it." While she is attentive to the critiques of a "feminine principle" as a basis for feminism, Dalmiya notes that this Indigenous conception of *Prakr.ti*, recovered from oral traditions and rural practices, underlies grassroots environmental movements in India (Dalmiya, "The Indian Subcontinent," 120).

While Arendt was rightly wary of any connection between political freedom and a unifying love in a closed relation with a master, the connections between political freedom as collective participation and spiritual freedom in relation with the universal can be traced to an older history of love for the world, or love for land, in which the philoxenic connections of humans with nature, and with each other, were experienced as what we might call the union of love and freedom. Like Western political traditions, religious traditions exemplify the tensions between a conception of freedom in embodied mutual relationship and a conception of freedom as a relation of mastery. These traditions hold the memory, and the possibility, of a more expansive democratic life in freedom and love: relational freedom.

4
Colonial Unknowing and Heterogeneous Relationalities
Alternative Formations of Power, Knowledge, and Freedom

> And why is this not a matter for everyone to care about, to teach, to think with, to act upon?
> —Audra Simpson[1]

> One of the most pressing questions we face is how the challenges of these actual-world heterogeneous ways of living are subdued and redirected, or not; why they have such a hard time becoming expansive alternatives—or why they may not wish to be so.
> —Elizabeth Povinelli[2]

In this chapter I argue that colonial unknowing works to delegitimize Indigenous claims to land in part by disavowing philosophies and political systems of relationality and relation to land as alternative formations of knowledge, power and freedom. Critical theories continue the tradition of colonial unknowing when they misrepresent philosophies of relationality and relation to land as naïve essentialisms and backward traditions opposed to freedom and progress. In fact, theories of relationality are philosophies of freedom through movement, change, heterogeneity, and diversity. These philosophies offer alternative formations of knowledge and power that can guide coalitional politics of decolonization.

This chapter is divided into four parts. Part One draws on Indigenous feminist and queer arguments that the colonization of land has worked through undermining the power of Indigenous women, and undermining alternative forms of kinship. The institution of heteropatriarchal and racialized forms of power and property ownership displaces alternative political orders in which power is dispersed. And colonial unknowing has worked to delegitimize

---

[1] Simpson, "The State Is a Man."
[2] Povinelli, *The Empire of Love*, 19.

knowledge of alternative formations of power. Part Two begins with Indigenous feminist arguments for the importance of Indigenous knowledges in politics of decolonization, and takes up Indigenous relational epistemologies as alternative orders of knowledge in relation to alternative understandings of freedom. A polycentric understanding of knowledge supports an understanding of freedom as participation in democratic governance.

Part Three draws on feminist and queer critical Indigenous theories to criticize the assumption that freedom is necessarily opposed to rootedness, and to address critiques of Indigenous essentialism and Indigenous claims to tradition. Against assumptions that philosophies of relationality and relation to land constitute naïve essentialisms, these philosophies ground critical Indigenous theories of heterogeneous relational selves and identities, and dynamic traditions. Part Four draws on Indigenous critical theorists' arguments for the resurgence and development of Indigenous politics of diversity and inclusion. I argue that Indigenous political traditions of heterogeneous relationalities can guide a coalitional politics of decolonization that can address the entangled politics of colonization, racialized capitalism, and migration.

This chapter argues, then, that Indigenous philosophies of heterogeneous interdependent relationalities inform practices of freedom as participation in relations of interdependence, and support the politics of inclusion and coalition that are essential to decolonization.

Part One

Breaking Relations

In June 2019, the Report of the National Inquiry into Missing and Murdered Indigenous Women and Girls was published by the Government of Canada. The result of a three-year independent inquiry responding to the demands of the Native Women's Association of Canada and many other Indigenous organizations, the report states that "persistent and deliberate human and Indigenous rights violations and abuses are the root causes behind Canada's staggering rates of violence against Indigenous women, girls, and 2SLGBTQQIA people." It attributes these violations in part to "specific colonial and patriarchal policies that displaced women from their traditional roles in community and governance and diminished their status in society, leaving them vulnerable to violence."[3] "The violence the National Inquiry heard about amounts to a race-based genocide of Indigenous peoples, including First Nations, Inuit and Métis, which especially targets women, girls, and 2SLGBTQQIA people. This violence has been

---

[3] National Inquiry into Missing and Murdered Indigenous Women and Girls, *Reclaiming Power and Place*.

empowered by colonial structures, evidenced notably by the Indian Act, the Sixties Scoop, residential schools, and breaches of human and Indigenous rights, leading directly to the current increased rates of violence, death and suicide in Indigenous populations."[4]

Canada has been founded through a long history of undermining the power of Indigenous women. The early British settlers negotiated treaties only with men, undercutting women's political power and responsibility for land and water, and thereby undercutting Indigenous power. The Indian Act, which was established as Canadian law in 1876, and which continues to regulate the relations between Canada and Indigenous people, instituted patrilineal lineage and heteropatriarchal power, establishing band councils led by men, and erasing the status of Indigenous women who "married out," along with the status of their children, while granting status to white women who married Indians.[5] Such policies delegitimate matrilineal lineage and matrifocal forms of governance. Under Iroquois law, women appointed chiefs, counseled them, and had the power to remove them from office. They held property and could divorce their men by placing their belongings outside the communal longhouse. "They were the inverse of the settler colonial woman, they had legally mandated authority and power, and so, they represented an alternative political order. . . . They embodied and signalled something radically different to Euro Canadian governance."[6] The undermining of Indigenous women's power was an attempted erasure of an alternative political order in which women had legally recognized power. Audra Simpson calls this attempted erasure of women's power *legal femicide*. Given that women's leadership roles have been central to Indigenous governance, the undermining of Indigenous women's power has been central to the attempted erasure of Indigenous sovereignty.

Indigenous women's power has been undermined not only through law but through direct attacks on Indigenous women's bodies. There is, as Simpson writes, an historical and political relationship between Indigenous women's death and settler governance. Simpson puts it bluntly: "Canada requires the death and so called 'disappearance' of Indigenous women in order to secure its sovereignty."[7]

They embodied and signalled something radically different to Euro Canadian government and this meant that part of dispossession, and settler possession,

---

[4] National Inquiry into Missing and Murdered Indigenous Women and Girls, *Reclaiming Power and Place*, 50.
[5] The status rules were altered in 1985, in response to UN pressure, following Indigenous women's organizing. I discuss this further in Chapter 5.
[6] Simpson, "The State Is a Man," 4.
[7] Simpson, "The State Is a Man."

meant that coercive and modifying sometimes killing power had to target their bodies. Because as with all bodies, these bodies were more than just "flesh"— these were and are sign systems and symbols that could effect and affect political life. So they had to be killed, or, at the very least subjected because what they were signalling or symbolizing was a direct threat to settlement.[8]

In settler regimes, an Indigenous woman's body is "loaded with meaning," signifying "land itself, the dangerous possibility of reproducing Indian life, and most dangerously, other political orders. *Other* life forms, other sovereignties, other forms of political will."[9] In the Haudenosaunee Confederacy women transmit the clan and represent land and relatedness to land. For settlers, Indigenous women's bodies, like land, are matter to be used, violated, and destroyed. Attacks on Indigenous women's bodies, then, are attacks on the relation between women and land: they are central to the appropriation of land as property.

All of these violations—both legal and physical—work to undermine Indigenous women's power in relation to land. They work, then, to undermine Indigenous sovereignty and resistance to colonization: to delegitimize Indigenous relations to land and to replace these relations with state ownership. Yet, as Simpson points out, the attempts to undermine Indigenous power have not been entirely successful. Indigenous women and Indigenous polities survive, and continue to signal the failure of the settler regime.

If the attempted erasure of Indigenous women's power is part of a process of disavowing an alternative political order, then this strategy works in a number of interrelated ways. It works through subjecting women to heteropatriarchal norms of legal and political legitimacy, denying their leadership roles, their participation in political life. It works through targeting their bodies as objects of violation. It works through gendered and racialized dividing practices, subordinating Indigenous women to men, and dividing savage Indian women from civilized white women who are theoretically protected from attack by virtue of their domestication in the white nuclear household, and who participate in maintaining that division. At the same time, it works by promising assimilation for Indian women into white settler society, as a servant and laboring class, to the extent that they can be domesticated and civilized. These practices are essential to what Anibal Quijano calls the *coloniality of power* and what Maria Lugones calls the *coloniality of gender*.[10] The disavowal of an alternative political order in which women have power disempowers *all* women, subjecting them, in very different ways, to regimes of the protection of privileged pure white womanhood

---

[8] Simpson, "The State Is a Man."
[9] Simpson, "The State Is a Man," 7.
[10] See, e.g., Quijano, "Coloniality of Power" and Lugones, "The Coloniality of Gender."

from racialized barbarians, and measuring and classifying them according to these regimes. All of these techniques work to legitimize state conquest. So the oppression of women is an Indigenous sovereignty issue, and settler colonization is a feminist issue. Struggles for decolonization ought to be central to feminist theory and activism. This is the project of decolonizing feminism.

The heteropatriarchal power of the state works through gendering and racializing governance and knowledge systems. Matrilineal social and political systems that recognize diverse sources of power, including diverse gender, sexuality, and kinship forms, have been undermined by the imposition of heteronormative family values and social norms. As the National Inquiry into Missing and Murdered Women and Girls points out, heteropatriarchal colonization aims at the erasure of power of 2SLGBTQQIA people, and queer, transgender, and two-spirited people are targets of violence. A racialized system of heteronormativity has been central, as Mark Rifkin argues, to "the ongoing imperial project of (re)producing the settler state as against competing indigenous formations."[11] Through the anthropological, legal, and political redescription of Indigenous *polities* as familial kinship relations among "blood relations" organized by marriage and reproduction, indigeneity is understood as a racial category, defined by blood quantum. Racialized colonization works through a heteronormative disciplinary practice of elimination through assimilation: through the promise of inclusion by "becoming straight," by adopting heteropatriarchal nuclear family forms and domestic practices, and by defining status through heteropatriarchal lineage.[12] Teaching Indians to become straight, the civilizing aim of Christian missions and residential schools, served to manage populations and individuals, to dissolve the body politic into manageable nuclear family households. This was part of an eliminative politics of "taking the Indian out of the child," "killing the Indian to save the man"—to breed out the racialized Indian and whiten the population. The industrial schools would provide a working class and servant population.[13] The point, again, is to eliminate Indigenous political power and to delegitimize Indigenous sovereignty. Again, the eliminatory logic of settler colonialism works not only through physical violence but through policies of division and "assimilation": through law, and through ideologies—knowledges—of civilization and savagery.

---

[11] Rifkin, *When Did Indians Become Straight?* 26. See also Scott Morgensen, "Settler Homonationalism"; Driskill, Finley, Gilley, and Morgensen, eds., *Queer Indigenous Studies*.

[12] Rifkin, *When Did Indians Become Straight?* 26.

[13] The first prime minister of Canada, Sir John A. Macdonald, wrote that the solution to the Indian problem was extinction through gradual assimilation. Part of this solution was the residential school system, which would "take the Indian out of the child." If the child remained with his parents, he would continue to be a savage. The point was to rescue the Indians from barbarity, by putting them in industrial schools, "where they will acquire the habits and modes of thought of white men." The policy of "aggressive civilization" was borrowed from the U.S. government, which used the same rationale for the establishment of residential schools (Churchill, *Kill the Indian, Save the Man*).

Queer and nonstraight Indigenous bodies symbolize an alternative formation of power: a formation in which power is dispersed among diverse agents, and which includes ceremonial and leadership roles of diversely gendered and two-spirited people. This power is organized through an alternative form of *kinship*. In critical Indigenous theory, Indigenous kinship is understood not as a system of blood ties and racial identities organized in opposition to outsiders. Kinship is understood as a system of relations among people and land, in which the diversity of life forms is recognized as a diversity of interrelated and interdependent powers. For Rifkin, this is an understanding of kinship as *polity*, not family. This is an understanding of a mode of governance through interdependent agents of power.

While Rifkin posits this conception of polity against the centering of reproductive lineage organized by the centering of the heterosexual couple, Indigenous feminist theory often centers the procreative power of the mother and the importance of matrilineal descent. Matrilineal descent is understood to characterize a system that centers women's power, and a system of cyclical and reciprocal interdependence, against heteropatriarchal power. While Rifkin posits polity against family, Leanne Betasamosake Simpson redeploys an understanding of family *as* polity. But for Simpson, *family* is the extended queer and international family of relations among all beings in an animate universe. Rifkin and Simpson both argue that delegitimizing queer forms of kinship works to disavow an alternative formation of *power*. Both develop critical Indigenous theories of kinship as a system of relations among people and land.

The imposition of the heteropatriarchal family was part of the civilizing mission of the Christian church in collusion with the state. Civilizing the natives was accomplished through the systematic destruction of intimate relations: the forcible removal of children from their communities, the abuse and deaths of children in residential schools, the continued removal of children into foster care, and the continued and increasing incarceration of Indigenous people have ravaged lives and communities through generations.[14] All of these attacks on

---

[14] In 2021, burial grounds containing the bodies of more than 1,000 children have been discovered at residential schools in western Canada. The 2015 Report of the Truth and Reconciliation Commission of Canada found that many thousands of children died at residential schools, and few of their bodies were returned home. In most cases families were not notified. Government documents indicate that it was well known that a large proportion of children were dying and would continue to die in the overcrowded and unsanitary conditions of the schools, as the children had no immunity to the settlers' diseases. Some residential schools continued to operate until 1998.

In his search through the archives of the Canadian Museum of History for the music of his Wolastoq ancestors, musician Jeremy Dutcher came across the words of one man in 1763: "As long as there's a child among my people, they will look after the land." Dutcher's response: "Then it struck me: that's why they went for the little ones" (Jeremy Dutcher, Concert in High Park, Toronto, September 8, 2021).

In Canada and Australia, current rates of removal of children from communities into foster care are higher than the earlier rates of removal of children into residential schools.

relations are forms of what Patrick Wolfe calls the eliminative logic of settler colonialism—attempts to destroy the people on the land to make way for free possession of land.[15] Elimination works through genocide and through policies of division and assimilation: through the delegitimization of Indigenous polities and their translation into racial categories. Indigenous polities are reduced to racialized groups, and assertions of sovereignty and of treaty relationships are reduced to demands for recognition as special cultural identity groups. The settler colonial politics of racialization divides savages from the civilized but also underpins policies of assimilation, treating legal claims as appeals for recognition of difference rather than as claims to sovereignty.

Aileen Moreton-Robinson argues that "the existence of white supremacy as hegemony, ideology, epistemology, and ontology requires the possession of Indigenous lands as its proprietary anchor within capitalist economies" in settler colonial societies. Moreton-Robinson cites Cheryl Harris's argument that whiteness is a form of property in law, and that whiteness was constituted in part through the appropriation of Indigenous lands: white property rights were cemented in law through the appropriation of Native American lands and the enslavement of Africans.[16] Racialized colonial capitalism is established through the possession of Indigenous lands as property.

The continued assumption of the authority of the state over Indigenous polities, the treatment of those polities as racialized groups seeking recognition, the refusal to honor treaties, the denial of land claims, the refusal to engage in nation-to-nation negotiations, all rely on the denial of claims of relation to land. Attempts to break connections through physical attacks on bodies, through political systems and knowledge systems that produce manageable populations and individuals, all rely on the form of epistemic ignorance that is *colonial unknowing*. In this chapter I argue that colonial unknowing works to delegitimize Indigenous claims to land in part by disavowing philosophies of relationality and relation to land as alternative formations of knowledge, power, and freedom. Philosophies of relationality and relation to land are central to alternative political orders organized through relations that are inclusive of diversity and heterogeneity.

As Audra Simpson and Andrea Smith argue, settler colonialism is "not only a material practice of dispossession but a representational practice."[17] Settler colonization works, then, in part through the production of knowledge and the production of colonial unknowing. Colonial unknowing works through transforming relational responsibility for land into property and extraction. It

---

[15] Wolfe, "Settler Colonialism and the Elimination of the Native."
[16] Moreton-Robinson, *The White Possessive*, xix.
[17] Simpson and Smith, "Introduction," in *Theorizing Native Studies*, 5.

works through discrediting Indigenous knowledge: knowledge of treaties as agreements between nations, knowledge of Indigenous law and history, knowledge of colonial histories of genocide, knowledge of relationality as an alternative form of power and freedom that is central to what Joanne Barker calls the *polity of the Indigenous*.[18] It works through disavowing philosophies of relationality and relation to land as primitive worldviews lacking a modern recognition of individual freedom and equality, and through disavowing the existence of alternative political orders of heterogeneous relationality that challenge heteropatriarchal white supremacist colonization. Nonindigenous critical theories participate in colonial unknowing when they dismiss Indigenous knowledges as naïve essentialisms and reject Indigenous claims of relation to land as necessarily oppressive and exclusive forms of identity politics. If colonization is dependent on a disavowal of legitimate claims to land, then it is tied also to dismissal and rejection of the philosophies and politics of rooted relationality that ground those claims.

But are philosophies of rooted relationality necessary for land claims? Can't Indigenous nations just claim prior ownership? And are claims to nationhood necessary? Can't they just claim dispossession and subjugation? Reducing Indigenous claims to prior ownership and translating them into property claims assumes that Euro-American terms of property ownership and sovereignty are the only acceptable terms. This is not decolonization. Rejecting claims of nationhood as necessarily exclusive forms of state sovereignty assumes that the form of the nation state is the only form of nationhood, and that Euro-American analyses of nationalism apply equally across contexts, and to forms of nationhood that precede Euro-American forms. Arguments that Indigenous politics should be limited to critiques of dispossession and subjugation assume that there is no defensible politics of rootedness, and thereby assume a binary between backward rootedness and progressive rootlessness and hybridity. Such arguments ultimately support a politics of assimilation of uprooted and displaced subjects. And they rely on a disavowal of the existence and possibility of an alternative political order: an alternative formation of knowledge and power. This is not decolonization. Decolonization involves a critique of state, colonial, and imperial power *and* a transformative politics of relational freedom. For Indigenous people, decolonization involves a politics of resurgence, drawing on Indigenous philosophies, governance, and practices. For settlers, it involves a transformative politics of reconciliation, learning other ways of being and doing. For both, it involves remaking relations to land and to each other. These are the transformative politics of relational freedom.[19]

---

[18] Barker, "Indigenous Feminisms."
[19] James Tully specifies two interconnected projects of reconciliation: "The first is the reconciliation of Indigenous and non-Indigenous people (Natives and newcomers) with each other in all our

Part Two

Decolonizing Epistemologies: Alternative
Formations of Knowledge and Freedom

In "Decolonizing Feminism: Challenging Connections between Settler Colonialism and Heteropatriarchy," Maile Arvin, Eve Tuck, and Angie Morrill argue that decolonizing feminist theory involves taking up the challenge of Indigenous knowledge and epistemologies. "Engaging Indigenous epistemologies, without appropriating them or viewing them merely as a mystical metaphor, is a method of decolonization that could play a significant role in creating a future for Indigenous peoples and Indigenous ways of knowing."[20]

Aileen Moreton-Robinson argues that decolonizing feminism will involve foregrounding Indigenous women's standpoints as sources of knowledge. She outlines an Indigenous women's standpoint theory that both draws from and extends feminist standpoint theory. An Indigenous women's standpoint is produced through inheritance and social positioning, and achieved through struggle. The concept of an Indigenous women's standpoint "does not deny the diversity of Indigenous women's individual concrete experiences. Rather it is where our shared knowledges and experiences within hierarchical relations of ruling and power converge and are operationalised."[21]

> It is constituted by our sovereignty and constitutive of the interconnectedness of our ontology (our way of being); our epistemology (our way of knowing) and our axiology (our way of doing). It generates its problematics through Indigenous women's knowledges and experiences, acknowledging that intersecting oppressions will situate us in different power relations and affect

diversity. The second is the reconciliation of Indigenous and non-Indigenous people (human beings) with the living earth: that is, reconciliation with more-than-human living beings (plants, animals, ecosystems, and the living earth as a whole)" (Tully, "Reconciliation Here on Earth," 83).

[20] Arvin, Tuck, and Morrill, "Decolonizing Feminism," 25. Arvin, Tuck, and Morrill argue that Native feminisms pose five central challenges to mainstream gender and women's studies: problematize settler colonialism and its intersections, refuse the erasure of Indigenous women but go beyond mere inclusion, craft alliances that directly address differences, recognize Indigenous ways of knowing, and question academic participation in Indigenous dispossession. Decolonizing feminism requires centering Indigenous feminism and centering critiques of settler colonialism and its intersections with other forms of imperialism, including heteropatriarchy and heteropaternalisms. Decolonizing feminism involves thematizing questions of sovereignty. The legitimacy of nation-state sovereignty is rarely questioned by political theorists, who fail to question its history and future: to acknowledge that settler states are founded not just on liberal and democratic principles but on genocide, and to question the assumption that nation states will persist into the future.

[21] Moreton-Robinson, "Towards an Australian Indigenous Women's Standpoint Theory," 342. I discuss Moreton-Robinson's argument and the project of decolonizing feminism at more length in "Decolonizing Feminist Freedom," in McLaren, *Decolonizing Feminism*.

our different individual experiences under social, political, historical and material conditions that we share either consciously or unconsciously. These conditions and the sets of complex relations that discursively shape us in the everyday are also complicated by our respective cultural, sexual, racialised, abled and class differences. Thus our cultural and social positioning informs how, when, where and why we conduct research as well as our disciplinary knowledges and training as Indigenous women academics. Our lives are always shaped by the omnipresence of patriarchal white sovereignty and its continual denial of our sovereignty. In our everyday existence we deploy a '*tactical subjectivity* with the capacity to recentre depending upon the kinds of oppression to be confronted' within and outside our communities.[22]

Moreton-Robinson argues that the constitutive elements of Indigenous knowledge and research paradigms in Australia, Canada, and New Zealand are a specific ontology, epistemology, and axiology "rooted in our embodied connection to our respective countries, all living entities and our ancestors; our sovereignty" conceptualized as *relationality*.[23] "One is connected by descent, country, place and shared experiences where one experiences the self as part of others and others as part of the self; this is learnt through reciprocity, obligation, shared experiences, co-existence, co-operation and social memory."[24]

---

[22] Moreton-Robinson, "Towards an Australian Indigenous Women's Standpoint Theory," 340. Quoting Sandoval (2004). While she draws from feminist standpoint theories, in particular Patricia Hill Collins's theory of subjugated knowledges, Moreton-Robinson argues that feminist standpoint theories are typically predicated on a body/earth split and do not address their privileged relationship to the nation's sovereignty. Addressing their privileged relationship to the nation's sovereignty requires questioning the state and acknowledgment of settler colonial women's privilege and agency in the dispossession of Aboriginal women and their communities. As Larissa Behrendt points out, the white women's movement has failed Aboriginal women. Women's suffrage movements in the early twentieth century won the right to vote for white women only. And "issues high on the political agenda for Aboriginal women are not issues of concern for white women" (Behrendt, "Aboriginal Women and the White Lies of the Feminist Movement," 34). Such issues include sovereignty rights, land claims and remuneration for stolen lands, Indigenous women's participation in governance and economic development, protection and communication of culture, protection of women's sacred sites, maintaining social relations in their communities, housing and social benefits, the high levels of incarceration and abuse of Indigenous adults and children, destructive government intervention into communities and removal of essential infrastructure, and the continuing practice of removal of children from families and communities, as well as the high rates of violence against women and 2SLGBTQ people. Obviously any feminist movement that claims to represent women would have to prioritize these and other issues of priority to Aboriginal women. It would also not assume the right to intervene in Aboriginal communities on behalf of Aboriginal women or to include Aboriginal women in universalizing claims about women's issues. (See Moreton-Robinson on the "Huggins-Bell debate" in Moreton-Robinson, *Talkin' Up to the White Woman*, 111–125.)

[23] Moreton-Robinson, "Towards an Australian Indigenous Women's Standpoint Theory," 337. The term "country" is used by Aboriginals in Australia to refer to the land to which they belong. It refers also to the relations of connection of all beings to that land, and the various practices and knowledges of relation to land and to sacred places, including songs, art, and stories.

[24] Moreton-Robinson, "Towards an Australian Indigenous Women's Standpoint Theory," 341.

Land as Pedagogy: Relational and Polycentric Knowledge

Knowledge, Leanne Betasamosake Simpson writes, "comes *through* the land." Indigenous knowledge is developed through a practice of engagement with land, through observation, listening, and action that is driven by curiosity, not authority. This is what Simpson calls *land as pedagogy*: learning "both *from* the land and *with the land*." Coming to know requires "complex, committed, *consensual* engagement" which is modeled by reciprocal relations among living beings. "Theory" is generated and regenerated continually through embodied practice, discovering and producing layers of meaning, in the context of community, with the support of elders, and through generations. Coming to know is a practice of freedom that is central to Indigenous resurgence: this practice allows Indigenous people to "not just 'dream alternative realities' but create them, on the ground in the physical world, in spite of being occupied."[25]

The understanding of land as pedagogy assumes that ontology, epistemology, and axiology are governed by principles of relationality and circularity. These are ontological principles: all forms of life on earth are understood to be interconnected in gift relations of reciprocity. And they are epistemological principles: coming to know involves engagement in these relations, and knowledge is knowledge of these relations. They are also normative principles. The principles of relationality and reciprocity inform and guide human responsibility and practices of freedom.

Anne Waters writes that a central and powerful concept in some Indigenous metaphysics is the understanding of breath:

> In Diné (Navajo) thought, for example, because the breath of life (air) is constantly being exchanged in the universe, from the cosmos and to the earth, breath plays a central role in complementary metaphysical thought. . . . smoke, as manifesting aspects of breath, operates as the medium for air to reach the sky, the cosmos, as do words when spoken or sung. The exchange of breath is important because all things in the universe are related through air, and all are made of the same basic elements. Just as we take in air to breathe, so also we let out breath, giving back to that from which we take . . . spirit (energy) infuses everything.[26]

Waters argues that the centrality of the breath that passes through skin and connects rather than separates expresses an Indigenous nonbinary metaphysics, focused on connections rather than on separate and opposed entities and individuals. The breath (energy, spirit) circulates among all elements

---

[25] Simpson, *As We Have Always Done*, 150–163.
[26] Waters, "Language Matters," 103.

in the universe.[27] The focus on breath is present in many Indigenous theories of knowledge. As Nauiyu elder Miriam-Rose Ungunmerr-Baumann tells us: "To know me is to breathe with me. To breathe with me is to listen deeply. To listen deeply is to connect."[28] Knowledge, then, is a practice of *being with* and *knowing with*—very different from the subject-object model of knowledge, which involves a distanced subject who learns by testing objects, asking skeptical questions, and manipulating variables. Research is done *with*, not *on*, other beings who are recognized as free and active persons in relationships. Relational knowing involves a practice of attentiveness and attunement, listening, watching and waiting for signs, attending with all the senses over long periods of time, remembering, reflecting. Knowledge is often conveyed through narrative, in the form of stories, rather than through the assertion and defense of truth claims. As Dian Million argues, stories are forms of *felt knowledge* that contain the affective legacy of experience and that inform practice. Stories are *theories*: "We engage in questioning and reformulating those stories that account for the relations of power in our present. That is theorizing."[29] As Thomas King writes: "The truth about stories is that that's all we are."[30]

"Knowing with" means that knowledge is not universal but is dispersed among diverse knowers. McPherson and Rabb argue that Indigenous knowledges are *polycentric*. Knowledges are specific to the location of the knower. Yet this polycentrism is not, they argue, a form of relativism; it's a form of pluralism. "In order to discover the true nature of reality it is necessary to examine as many different descriptions, as many different worldviews, as possible."[31] Cree scholar Michael A. Hart writes that in the "sharing circle" each person has a different perspective on the topic, which is metaphorically located in the center of the circle. "Everyone expresses their views so that a full picture of the topic is developed. Individual views are blended until consensus on the topic is reached."[32] This

---

[27] See Waters, "Language Matters," for the argument that the centrality of breath is indicative of an Indigenous nonbinary metaphysics. This focus on the breath is found also in yoga and the ancient Eastern teaching traditions, which also have their roots in Indigenous knowledges. So it appears that this ontology is common to many Indigenous worldviews. Some Western feminist theorists have drawn on such worldviews to theorize feminist process metaphysics (e.g., Irigaray, Speculum of the Other Woman). And some have theorized the relational human self in ways that echo the Indigenous conception of connecting breath. Against the assumption that the self is essentially separate and bounded, that it is simply self-evident that the body is a container that separates us from others and from the world, Catherine Keller argues that the human skin is a permeable boundary: "Our skin does not separate—it connects us to the world through a wondrous network of sensory awareness ... Through my senses I go into the world, and the world comes into me" (Keller, *From a Broken Web: Separation, Sexism, and Self*, 234).

[28] Ungunmerr-Bauman, Miriam Rose Foundation videos, https://www.youtube.com/watch?v=pkY1dGk-LyE

[29] Million, "There Is a River in Me," 33. See also Million, "Felt Theory," in *Therapeutic Nations*.

[30] King, *The Truth About Stories*, 2.

[31] McPherson and Rabb, *Indian from the Inside*, 20.

[32] Hart, "Sharing Circles," cited by McPherson and Rabb, *Indian from the Inside*, 121.

assumes, of course, that consensus can be reached. Can this model address intractable conflicts? An understanding of knowledge that is dispersed among diverse knowers would mean that each person recognizes the partiality of their own knowledge, understands that knowledge involves a diversity of perspectives, and is therefore more likely to listen to the perspectives of others as contributions to a more comprehensive knowledge. If the polycentric understanding of knowledge is accompanied by what McPherson and Rabb call the *narrative ethic*, according to which knowledge and ethical positions are exemplified through stories that invite addressees to form their own conclusions, rather than through arguments that defend a position by attacking the position of the opponent, then this understanding of knowledge would include the recognition that difference and conflict are inevitable, and it would allow for the existence of conflicting knowledges without always requiring that they be reconciled. Toleration of difference and need for consensus would depend on the situation.

Such an understanding of knowledge has significant implications for political governance. If knowledge is understood to be polycentric, then democracy is much more likely to be successful. In other words, a polycentric understanding of knowledge facilitates a practice of freedom as participation in democratic governance. This may appear to be an idealized description of Indigenous practices of knowledge and democratic discourse—and surely it is. Indigenous peoples were no strangers to violence and war. Yet the European settlers, missionaries, and travelers were impressed by the sophistication and equanimity that characterized democratic discourse among the Indigenous peoples with whom they came to live. Many reports in the *Jesuit Relations* and other sources noted the contrast between the rational and orderly discourse in the frequent public discussions of the Amerindians and the rudeness and vulgarity of the common discourse of the French. Such reports included the perceptions of the Wendat and the Mi'kmaq who saw the quarrels among the French as consistent with their general lack of generosity—or greed.[33] The contrast between modes of discourse does seem to reflect the difference between an understanding of knowledge as property—as something one owns and must defend—and an understanding of knowledge as polycentric—as produced through collective discourse.

Indigenous understandings of knowledge as polycentric, and of freedom as participation in democratic governance, are rooted in understandings of land as a system of relationships among diverse and interdependent beings, and in a grounded ethics of mutuality and reciprocity. This means that the polycentrism

---

[33] Graeber and Wengrow include several quotations from the *Jesuit Relations* and from Sagard's *Le Grand Voyage du Pays des Hurons* to make this point, and to argue that the Age of Reason was influenced by the encounter with the Amerindians (Graeber and Wengrow, *The Dawn of Everything*).

of knowledge supports a politics that is much more radically democratic than settlers could imagine. Given that it is rooted in relations with land, the polycentrism of knowledge extends to what Thomas Norton-Smith calls the *expansive conception of persons* in Indigenous thought.[34] Humans do not assume their knowledge to be primary or superior to the knowledge of rocks, trees, animals, spirits, and ancestors. Relational knowing means not prioritizing human knowledge: listening to the specific knowledges of rivers and trees, recognizing those other beings as co-knowers, collaborators, and sometimes recognizing their knowledge as primary and superior to ours. For some Indigenous thinkers it is self-evident that stones have the most knowledge, because they have been there for the longest time.

That means that any view that assumes that humans take primacy as knowers *fails* to situate the knower in a web of relations with all beings. And any knowledge of the world or any part of it that does not include these relations is incomplete and inadequate knowledge. But it's worse than inadequate. This kind of knowledge is directly linked to the relations of domination that characterize colonization. The arrogance of assuming that humans are the only ones who know, and the failure to listen to the knowledge of animals, and of rivers and trees, is what leads to the understanding of the land as property, to the perception of land and all elements of the earth as raw material to be transformed into commodities. José Medina has argued that blindness to social relationality is an epistemic vice.[35] The implication of Indigenous relational epistemology is that blindness to the radical cosmic relationality of an entirely animate world is an epistemic vice of even greater magnitude.

The idea that knowledge is dispersed among multiple knowers in an entirely animate universe is, of course, difficult for Western secular academics to comprehend, let alone accept. What does it mean to say that a stone or a river has knowledge? The impulse is to see these ideas as primitive and prescientific, or, if we are more generous, romantic and beautiful but not real: not accurate representations of reality. It may be possible to see this as "Indigenous knowledge," but it's much more difficult to accept it as *knowledge*. But this may be changing. For example, in the science of forest ecology, in the past twenty years there has been "a burst of careful scientific research occurring worldwide that is uncovering all manner of ways that trees communicate with each other above and below ground."[36] Forest ecologist Suzanne Simard has found that trees in forests communicate with each other through what she terms the "wood wide web," and she argues that "mother trees recognize and talk with their

---

[34] Norton-Smith, *The Dance of Person and Place*.
[35] Medina, *The Epistemology of Resistance*.
[36] Simard, "Notes from a Forest Ecologist," 249.

kin, shaping future generations." In this research, trees are seen as active and knowing agents. Moreover, they are seen as social beings. Simard writes: "These discoveries have transformed our understanding of trees from competitive crusaders of the self to members of a connected, relating, communicating system."[37] In the popular book, *The Hidden Life of Trees*, Peter Wohlleben describes the ways in which trees know how to interact with each other and with other beings in the natural world. With Wohlleben, Tim Flannery writes that trees are clearly sharing information, and that they appear to be in relations of care for each other and for members of other species.[38] It appears that Western science is just discovering what Indigenous scientists have known for many thousands of years. In the words of Murrumu Walubara Yidindji: "When you look at a tree, you see a tree. When I look at a tree, I see the tree and all of its friends."[39,40]

Some Western scientists are now pursuing connections between Indigenous knowledges and Western science, and processes of sharing knowledge.[41] But the idea that trees are knowers is, of course, controversial. Can communication among trees be recognized as knowledge? Or is this "knowledge" really just an automatic response to stimuli? (Of course, some scientists believe that human knowledge, too, can be explained mechanistically.) As feminist epistemologist Elizabeth Potter has written, empirical facts can be open to diverse and competing interpretations that explain the findings equally well. The choice of explanatory frames is influenced, in part, by our politics.[42] In this case, our understandings of the relationships among trees are influenced by the political and ethical commitments that shape very different worldviews, or systems of knowledge. Is the communication of trees a form of knowledge among sentient beings, or is it just a mechanistic processing of electronic impulses? Are trees

---

[37] Simard, "Notes from a Forest Ecologist," 248–249.
[38] Wohlleben, *The Hidden Life of Trees*; Flannery, "Introduction" to *The Hidden Life of Trees*.
[39] Murrumu Walubara Yidindji, in discussion with Nikolas Kompridis, during a visit to the Institute for Social Justice at ACU, Australia. Murrumu Walubara is Foreign Affairs Minister of the Sovereign Yidindji Government, on land that has never been ceded to the government of Australia.
[40] We can find echoes of this understanding in feminist theories. For example, consider the analysis of the work of Barbara McClintock by Evelyn Fox Keller, which has been hugely influential for feminist epistemology. For McClintock, Keller writes: "In comparison with the ingenuity of nature, our scientific intelligence seems pallid" (Fox Keller, *Reflections on Gender and Science*, 162). McClintock believed that good science required listening with humility and getting to know the plants she was studying. "No two plants are exactly alike. . . . I don't feel I really know the story if I don't watch the plant all the way along. So I know every plant in the field. I know them intimately, and I find it a great pleasure to know them" (164). In her study of chromosomes she wrote that she felt like she was part of them and they were her friends (165).
[41] See the annotated bibliography of *Traditional Indigenous Knowledge in Climate Change Research*, developed by Carson Vile and Kyle Powys Whyte: https://michiganstate.academia.edu/KyleWhyte
[42] Potter, "Gender and Epistemic Negotiation."

competitors in a universe of selfish individuals, or social beings in relations of not only power but also cooperation, knowledge, and care?

As the example of the knowledge of trees indicates, expanding our understanding of *who knows* requires expanding our understanding of *what knowledge is*. Does knowledge require consciousness and reflection? Is knowledge necessarily universal, or are there diverse knowledges? Feminist standpoint theorists do recognize diverse knowledges among human knowers, who are situated in diverse positions and relations of power, producing dominant and subjugated knowledges. Can Western feminist theorists recognize the diverse knowledges of trees and even rocks?

These questions of knowledge raise questions of relativism and universalism. Is the knowledge of trees (and the Indigenous knowledge of that knowledge) something all of us could and should learn? Or should these knowledges be recognized as specific and local knowledges? Indigenous theorists argue that both are true. There are knowledges that are not meant for all of us. And there are specific knowledges that can transform universals. Many Indigenous peoples recognize diverse knowledges, connected to responsibilities for specific areas of land, and to specific roles and kin relations.[43] Recognizing the diversity of knowledge would in itself transform our general knowledge and our understandings of objectivity and universality. A decolonized theory of knowledge would need not only to recognize some Indigenous knowledge as "Indigenous knowledge" but to recognize it as *knowledge*—and, in many cases, as *better* knowledge. As Moreton-Robinson argues, Indigenous knowledge, learned through thousands of years of study, can provide a basis for what Sandra Harding calls "strong objectivity."[44]

A conception of knowledge as dispersed among diverse knowers, both human and nonhuman, is consistent with ancient and modern pragmatist understandings of knowledge as inseparable from practice, knowledge as both conditioned by and guiding ways of life. In Indigenous philosophies, knowledge is specific to place, and different beings in different places have different forms of knowledge emerging from and guiding their interactions with those places. A tree's knowledge of its place and role in relation with other trees and other beings will be substantially different from human knowledge. The tree's knowledge is (probably) not conscious or conceptual; it's the kind of knowledge appropriate to a tree. Why call this knowledge? That's the skeptical Westerner's question. It's a useful question, as long as it is the first step in a genuine attempt to understand. Too often, it is used to dismiss a way of life and form of knowledge without attempting to learn or to know anything about it.

---

[43] This can include knowledges specific to gender groups: women's knowledge and men's knowledge. This is clearly another difficult issue for feminism.
[44] Moreton-Robinson, "Towards an Australian Indigenous Women's Standpoint Theory," 342.

Emergent Normativity

The oppositions between Indigenous and Western sciences are increasingly being challenged by Western ecological theories. Earth science theorists Lynn Margulis and James Lovelock argue that earth systems are basically life-supporting and symbiotic. According to their Gaia Hypothesis, the earth functions as a single self-regulating system. Margulis writes, "Gaia is not an 'organism' but an emergent property of interaction among organisms. Gaia is the series of interacting ecosystems that compose a single huge ecosystem at the earth's surface. Gaia is symbiosis on a planetary scale."[45] As James Tully argues, "If this is correct, then the very norms that could guide humans from a way of life that is destroying the conditions of life toward a way of life that sustains the conditions of life can be found in the self-organizing and self-sustaining patterns of interaction of the living conditions of life themselves."[46] With Akeel Bilgrami, Tully argues for an understanding of what we call nature as a source of meaning and values. Bilgrami writes: "There is a superstition of modernity, which declares that nature contains no properties that are not countenanced by the natural sciences." In fact, he argues, "the world (including nature) contains value properties that make normative demands on us."[47]

As Tully points out, for 95 percent of our history, humans have followed the model of earth systems to live in predominantly sustainable social systems rooted in understandings of ourselves as belonging to land. Of course, there has always been violence and catastrophe, but these were not the central driving forces. If this were not the case, we would have destroyed ourselves long ago. Life in general and humans in particular have evolved through the development of living networks, not through relations of conquest and control. "Humans and nonhumans learn ways to live together and settle their disputes nonviolently or with types of violence—such as predator-prey relations between deer and coyote—that keep species and the ecosystems on which they interdepend in rough equilibrium, punctuated with occasional rapid and drastic change."[48] Tully cites Donald Worster, America's leading ecological historian, who argues that it is doubtful that anyone from any civilization outside the modern West would even understand the view of nature as organized by competition, conquest, and control.

Relational Axiology: Normative Practices and Politics of Knowledge

Anishnaabe scholar Deborah McGregor identifies "the fundamental dichotomy at the heart of current controversy in the field of Traditional Ecological

---

[45] Margulis, *Symbiotic Planet*, 120. Quoted by James Tully, "Life Sustains Life 1," 167.
[46] Tully, "Life Sustains Life 1," 167.
[47] Bilgrami, "Value and Alienation," 68.
[48] Tully, "Life Sustains Life," 192, 172.

Knowledge (TEK) in Canada: namely, the vast and ongoing separation between the academic 'experts' who study TEK and TEK issues, and the Aboriginal people who actually live according to TEK teachings."[49] As McGregor points out, Indigenous knowledge is inseparable from doing. Knowledge is meant to be *lived*. Anishnaabe philosopher Winona LaDuke describes the Aboriginal concept of *Minobimaatisiiwin*, meaning "the good life" or lifeway.[50] "From an Aboriginal perspective, if you are not living the good life, then you are not doing TEK."[51]

Using Indigenous people and knowledge as objects of research is a transgression of the principle of reciprocity that is central to Indigenous knowledges. Linda Tuhiwai Smith writes that "research" is "probably one of the dirtiest words in the indigenous world's vocabulary. . . . It appalls us that the West can desire, extract and claim ownership of our ways of knowing, our imagery, the things we create and produce, and then simultaneously reject the people who created and developed those ideas and seek to deny them further opportunities to be creators of their own culture and own nations."[52] Indigenous people have been "researched to death."[53] For centuries Indigenous peoples have been the research objects of the colonial anthropologist as knowing subject. The knowledge extracted and produced through such research has been central to the maintenance and development of regimes of colonization. Pharmaceutical corporations routinely steal Indigenous knowledge of plants to produce medicines, cosmetics, and "natural" supplements. Vandana Shiva has written and worked extensively against the practice of biopiracy: the corporate theft of seeds, water, and other forms of natural life, and of the Indigenous knowledges of these forms of life.[54] Against the common perception that settlers taught agriculture and other technologies to Indigenous hunter-gatherers, the plants bred and cultivated by Indigenous people have been primary sources of setter and European survival and wealth.

Like most ancient philosophies, Indigenous philosophies have been primarily oriented to questions of how to live. In Indigenous philosophies, this means that living the good life, following the right path, are both the means and ends of knowledge. Normativity, then, is inherent in epistemologies: what is true is inseparable from what is right. Thomas Norton-Smith argues that truth is not just a function of correspondence to objective facts; truth is a property of action or performance. So Indigenous philosophies focus more on procedural than on propositional knowledge. And all action has a moral dimension. The

---

[49] McGregor, "Traditional Ecological Knowledge," 103.
[50] LaDuke, *All Our Relations*.
[51] McGregor, "Traditional Ecological Knowledge," 104.
[52] Tuhiwai Smith, *Decolonizing Methodologies*, 1.
[53] Goodman et al., "We've Been Researched to Death."
[54] See Shiva, *The Vandana Shiva Reader*.

pursuit of knowledge is guided by principles of relationality and circularity as *world-ordering principles*: this means that the pursuit of knowledge is a practice of reciprocity.

Brian Yazzie Burkhart argues that unlike modern Western philosophy and science, which depend on skeptical questioning, testing, and manipulation, Indigenous philosophy is based on patient observation and contemplation. To formulate questions to test the earth, "to see if it conformed best to this pattern or that" is "to not really observe, to not really listen."[55] While it involves contemplation, this knowledge practice is different from the ancient Greek contemplation of an objective world separate from the subject, and different from practices of skeptical questioning. "Unlike Thales and Plato, American Indian philosophers see the act of displacing oneself from the world in order to do philosophy not only as unnecessary but as highly problematic, since in doing so one is only guessing whether what one is striving after is really knowledge at all and whether the questions one has formulated are even really questions."[56] This means, according to Burkhart, that there is *a limit to what should be questioned*. This is a startling and potentially dangerous assertion, which should surely be questioned. And certainly not all Indigenous philosophers agree that this is a principle common to Indigenous philosophies. But Burkhart's point is that questions need to be motivated by a sense of appropriateness, a conscious responsibility to context and relations. Western epistemologies, he argues, have traditionally assumed that knowledge is justified true belief, and that justification requires foundations. So questions are challenges oriented to justification, understood as evidence for objective truths. In contrast, Indigenous philosophies are oriented to the meaning-shaping principle of action that supports responsibility to relations. Burkhart gives the following example. In response to the Indigenous creation story of the earth resting on the back of a turtle, a Western philosopher will ask, what holds the turtle? "One elder storyteller responded to this question by saying simply, 'Well, then there must be turtles all the way down.' The storyteller had no patience with this way of thinking. It seemed to her that asking such a question was like asking for proof that she had a mother or for proof that plants grow in the earth and nourish the people—questions, in her mind, that only someone extremely confused would ask."[57]

The "turtles all the way down" story seems to be common to many Indigenous as well as East Indian cultures (it was encountered by Jesuits in India in the sixteenth century) and has been used in both East Indian and Western philosophy to illustrate the problem of infinite regress. In the Western stories the turtle view

---

[55] Burkhart, "What Coyote and Thales Can Teach Us," 22.
[56] Burkhart, "What Coyote and Thales Can Teach Us," 21.
[57] Burkhart, "What Coyote and Thales Can Teach Us," 20.

of the world is typically attributed to an "Oriental" or an old woman. In response, the Western man of knowledge scoffs, pointing out that such a view is incoherent. But what if it's the Western man of knowledge who doesn't get it? What if the story of the earth resting on the back of a turtle, who perhaps stands on the backs of more turtles, is a different form of knowledge: a story of interdependence and responsibility, in a nonmechanistic animate universe held together not by truth claims but by stories, not by inanimate materials but by active agents? The appropriate response to such a story is not to question its truth claims, but to understand and appreciate the connectedness of all of creation, and the responsibilities entailed by that interdependence. Is it an accurate representation of the mechanics of the universe? No. But it does seem to have guided Indigenous communities to develop very detailed and accurate knowledge of land, water, and weather patterns, and plant and animal life, along with ways of cultivating and sustaining country. If the point of knowledge is to understand our place in the universe and to guide our actions, to guide us in our interactions with each other and with the world, then this kind of knowledge has served very well.

Thomas Norton-Smith interprets Burkhart's principle of a limit to questioning as an expression of the principle that the pursuit of knowledge is oriented to questions of how to live: questions without a practical end are empty questions. Moreover, the act of questioning is an act of world-making that has moral consequences. In a relational moral universe, "the act of questioning and the motives behind it shape a world in which *creativity* is the moving force."[58] Questions, like all human actions and performances, contribute to the creation of a world that is dynamic, animate, and continually unfolding. Burkhart expresses this creative participation in making the world as the *meaning-shaping principle of action*.

The differences between Western and Indigenous modes of knowledge identified by Burkhart and Norton-Smith correspond, then, to different conceptions of freedom. Western models of knowledge derived through skeptical questioning and critique are linked to a particular conception of freedom: the subject is free from ties to the object and is free to test and manipulate the object. Freedom allows, even requires, that we criticize, question, and test; these are the actions of the free thinker. We typically regard the absence of this capacity to engage in skeptical critique as an absence of individual freedom. Indigenous knowledge is linked to a conception of freedom as world-making. Human freedom is a creative practice of participation in the collective creation of a world. In this conception, knowledge is developed in relations with other beings, and freedom is situated in these relations. Human beings are not free to subject others to interrogation or manipulation, because human freedom is relational freedom: human

---

[58] Norton-Smith, *The Dance of Person and Place*, 63.

beings are free only in and through relations with others, including all creatures in an animate universe. So all investigation has a moral dimension: if questions are free practices that contribute to the shaping of a world, they carry the responsibility of attention to the kinds of relations they shape. This is a pragmatist, performative conception of the development of knowledge through free relations in a world in which all share responsibility.

Burkhart's claim that some questions are inappropriate, of course, poses the danger that critique is inappropriate, and this claim can be used to silence feminist, queer, and antiracist critiques of claims to "tradition." Indigenous knowledge and knowledge practices do, of course, include capacities for critique, and they provide a basis for very strong political critiques of colonization, as well as critiques of sexism, homophobia, and racism in contemporary Indigenous communities and organizations. These are not distanced and skeptical critiques: these are critiques of domination from within a relational perspective: critiques of distorted and broken relations, and critiques of contempt for relations.[59]

Indigenous critical theory shares with the Western tradition of critical theory the distinction between the distanced skeptical questioning of the subject confronting an opposed object and the engaged critique of the embedded subject. But the traditions are different. While Western critical theory assumes that the subject is embedded in historical social and political relations, and focuses particularly on relations of power and freedom, Indigenous critical theory assumes that the subject is embedded in normative relations with land. As Vine Deloria Jr. has argued, while Western political thought is oriented to the problem of historical progress, and hence of *time*, Indigenous place-based knowledge is oriented to the philosophical problem of *space*. These orientations provide different bases for normative ethics. While Western critical theory appeals to norms that are immanent in Western social and political histories, Indigenous critical theory appeals to norms that are immanent in place-based relations. Another way of putting this is that normative ethics emerging from place-based relations are oriented to cyclical rather than linear time.

The focus on place-based relations is the basis of what Glen Coulthard calls grounded normativity. As Coulthard writes, land is the ontological framework for understanding relationships. Land is "a field of relationships" and place "is a way of knowing, of experiencing and relating to the world and with others."[60] Grounded normativity, then, is the form of ethics that is immanent to and emerges from the cyclical and reciprocal relations among beings in webs

---

[59] See Cynthia Willett on the philosophy of hubristic contempt for relationship in social domination (Willett, *The Soul of Justice*).
[60] Coulthard, *Red Skin, White Masks*, 61.

of relations. This ethics of reciprocity guides human obligations to each other and to all other beings. The claim is not that relations among all beings are in fact balanced and reciprocal, but that attention to the web of relations guides knowledges and practices oriented to reciprocity: to the normative ideal of reciprocity and cyclicity that is immanent in and emergent from those relations. Following the ethics of reciprocity is not simply "natural," but requires the active agency of receptivity, interpretation, judgment, and care.

This means that in critiques of colonization, Indigenous critical theories negotiate a difficult balance between place-based normative theories and historical critiques of power and conquest. Critiques of colonization challenge histories of colonization in the name of historical progress by invoking place-based knowledge and ethics. For the colonizer, place-based arguments are difficult to recognize: such arguments appear to be located in a particular time, in a past that has been superceded. Land claims are misrecognized as economic claims to land as property; sovereignty claims are misrecognized as claims to statehood, or to "culture" as quaint tradition. For Coulthard, land claims are claims to a *mode of life* that challenges both state sovereignty and the capitalist political economy.[61]

Max Horkheimer wrote that the aim of critical theory is freedom. In the tradition of Western critical theory, freedom as a normative ideal emerges in historical struggles which are also struggles for equality and for relations of reciprocity: shared ownership of the means of production, just distribution, equal recognition, equal rights, and solidarity. Against the classic liberal opposition between individual freedom and equality, critical theory recognizes that these ideals are interrelated and rooted in substantive conceptions of freedom in relationship with others. In Indigenous critical theory, the aim of decolonization is a freedom defined according to the ethics of grounded normativity: as fulfilment of obligations among humans and other beings in relations of reciprocity.

Spirituality and Secular Myths

The practices of knowledge oriented toward stories rather than truth claims, toward deep listening and *being with* rather than distanced observation, testing, and skeptical questioning, are rooted in what some refer to as Indigenous spirituality. As the image of breath as spirit suggests, Indigenous relationality includes more than the natural world. It also includes relations to the ancestors and spirits that animate that world. This means that ancestors and spirits must also be recognized as knowers, and human knowledge will be practiced in relation with these knowers. In this animate and enspirited world, relations to all elements of creation are sacralized, and the spirits of ancestors who have passed on are still present. Leanne Simpson writes: "Nishnaabeg knowledge originates in the

---

[61] Coulthard, *Red Skin, White Masks*, 65.

spiritual realm, coming to individuals through dreams, visions, and ceremony and through the process of gaa-izhi-zhaawendaagoziyaang—that which is given lovingly to us by the spirits."[62]

For secular theorists, this raises the difficult question of the relation between the secular and the spiritual. What is the status of forms of knowledge that McPherson and Rabb describe as "higher states of consciousness" such as the vision quest in North American communities and the dreaming in Australian Aboriginal communities? How can Western secular philosophy respond to the belief that knowledge involves sustaining relations in a sacralized world, without romanticizing and othering? Linda Tuhiwai Smith writes:

> The arguments of different indigenous peoples based on spiritual relationships to the universe, to the landscape and to stones, rocks, insects and other things, seen and unseen, have been difficult arguments for Western systems of knowledge to deal with or accept. . . . Concepts of spirituality which Christianity attempted to destroy, then to appropriate, and then to claim, are critical sites of resistance for indigenous peoples. The values, attitudes, concepts and language embedded in beliefs about spirituality represent, in many cases, the clearest contrast and mark of difference between indigenous peoples and the West. It is one of the few parts of ourselves which the West cannot decipher, cannot understand and cannot control . . . yet.[63]

The spiritualities central to Indigenous ontology and epistemology present a challenge for secular Western feminism. But a practice of decolonizing feminism requires that we ask just how secular Western feminist theory actually is. The modern Western faith in the primacy of the individual is bound up with a Christian heritage: this is a culture organized around the idea that a human individual (and only a human individual) is the incarnation of a transcendent and omniscient God on earth. From this perspective, the Western feminist faith in women's individual rights and autonomy, and in a conception of individual freedom characterized by a capacity for distanced questioning, in a quest for universal truths, appears somewhat less than secular.

For Vine Deloria Jr., Christianity is the foundation of Western secular thought. In *God Is Red: A Native View of Religion*, he argued that the Christian missionaries' belief that the white human being is not a part of nature but a transcendent species has been central to the domination of Indigenous peoples. The Christian faith in the hierarchical ordering of beings justified and organized, through missions in support of settler states, the domination of Indigenous people classed

---

[62] Simpson, *As We Have Always Done*, 155.
[63] Tuhiwai Smith, *Decolonizing Methodologies*, 78.

as lesser beings. Moreover, Deloria argues that Christian proselytizing is rooted in the disconnection of truth from land: whereas Indigenous knowledge is relative to particular land areas and the inhabitants of those lands, the claim to a single universal truth that should be recognized by all, and the attempt to convert all to that truth, has been central to Christian missions and imperialist regimes.[64]

Talal Asad argues that while it is certainly connected to Christianity, liberal secularism has its own distinctive myths—or is in itself a myth—distinct from Christianity.[65] Deloria and Asad agree, however, that the faith in the primacy of the individual and in the individualist model of distanced and skeptical critique without limits is central to this myth. And both argue that from nonsecular perspectives, this kind of critique can be seen and experienced as a transgression of relationship.[66] The Western secular understanding of individual *freedom* involves a very particular myth: that the individual has not only the right but the duty to question and criticize without limits. Ironically, this is a certainty that we tend to accept without question. It is rooted in the secular myth that question-asking will lead us to the Truth, which is in turn linked to a particular conception of progress. While we may believe that we can sever the practice of skeptical questioning from its roots in seeking the Truth, from an Indigenous perspective, this practice becomes not only destructive but irrational: we keep asking questions without knowing why we are doing it, in the name of a freedom that is effectively meaningless.

Thomas Norton-Smith argues that Indigenous origin stories are recognized as stories, not as universal and unquestionable truths. They don't require the mindless credulity of religious dogma. Stories are performances that do things: they strengthen relationships, they put experiences into perspective, and they convey knowledge and values. Most importantly, "the telling of an origin story *centers* the people—it reminds them that 'This is who you are and this is where you belong.'"[67] Origin stories relate people to place. This means that stories, and the truths they tell, are specific to places. There is no single universal truth, but multiple realities corresponding to peoples with different experiences, values, histories, and traditions. This idea can be dismissed as mere relativism, or it can be recognized as a sophisticated perception of the diversity of knowledges, with an ethic of humility. Knowledge, then, is not the discovery of a hidden truth—an essence or abstraction. Norton-Smith argues that Indigenous knowledge does not share the dominant Western distinction between deceptive appearance and true reality. There is no hidden real world distinct from appearance. Dreams and visions are experiences that are valid forms of knowledge, and spirits are as real

---

[64] Deloria Jr., *God Is Red*.
[65] Asad, *Formations of the Secular*.
[66] See Asad's and Saba Mahmood's contributions to *Is Critique Secular?*
[67] Norton-Smith, *The Dance of Person and Place*, 66.

and present in the world as other beings. Indigenous knowledge, he writes, is characterized by "an absence of scepticism about the veracity of any and all experience."[68] Expansive knowledge involves a synthesis of multiple perspectives and experiences.

We could say that the dominant forms of Western knowledge are guided by a conception of freedom as skepticism, and the goal is demystification: the point of knowledge is to discover the hidden truth. Indigenous knowledge is guided by a conception of freedom as relational and creative: the recognition that a more expansive knowing is possible only in and through relations with others, and that our ways of being and of knowing create the world.[69]

Part Three

Colonial Unknowing: Freedom and Essentialism

Part Two argued that the understanding of knowledge as polycentric, as dispersed among a wide and diverse range of knowers in an animate universe, supports an understanding of freedom as participation in relations of interdependence. I have suggested that these understandings of knowledge and freedom facilitate democratic politics: this argument will be developed in Part Four. Part Three argues that these modes of knowledge and freedom are misrecognized in forms of colonial unknowing that construe Indigenous understandings of identity in relation to land as simple essentialisms. Relation to land is equated with fixed characteristics held and constrained by fixed roots: an absence of freedom. Theories of the self in relation to land are perceived as naïvely essentialist claims to authenticity, rooted in mythical origin stories of dubious validity. Claims of collective identity are criticized as essentialist and exclusive forms of identity politics rooted in patriarchal traditions.

Critiques of Indigenous essentialisms rely on conceptions of freedom that are opposed to rootedness. Thus they *misread* Indigenous relationality and Indigenous relational freedom. This misreading leads to misrepresentations of Indigenous political struggles: of identity and status politics, and of Indigenous struggles for sovereignty. As Jodi Byrd writes, "indigenous studies is sometimes erroneously read as a nativist project laced with xenophobia in a world that turns increasingly to the potential liberatory spaces of cosmopolitanism and diasporic movements, where place is relinquished for reinvention."[70] The imagining of

---

[68] Norton-Smith, *The Dance of Person and Place*, 70.
[69] Of course, these are broad and schematic generalizations that do not do justice to the wide range of perspectives and arguments in Western and Indigenous philosophies.
[70] Byrd, *The Transit of Empire*, xxxii.

freedom as opposed to rootedness, tradition, and identity can obscure the existence of what Povinelli refers to as *heterogeneous ways of living*: alternative forms and imaginaries of power and freedom.

Responding to Critiques of Essentialism: Heterogeneous Relational Selves and Freedom

In response to the charge that Indigenous conceptions of the self as rooted in relations to land are essentialist, Aileen Moreton-Robinson turns this critique around: from an Indigenous standpoint, antiessentialist critiques of the idea of an Indigenous relational self rely on an essentialist, falsely universalized ideal of the self as disconnected from relations with the earth, and as essentially "multiple, becoming and unfixed." Insistence on this ideal of self as a universal "can silence and dismiss non-Western constructions, which do not define the self in the same way."[71]

Theories of the subject as unfixed, fluid, hybrid, plural, and in process have been developed by feminist, queer, postcolonial, and poststructuralist theorists as an alternative to the ideal of a true and authentic pregiven self, and against the ideal of a unitary, independent, and self-determining subject bent on mastery and control. But conceptions of fluid and unfixed selves often bear traces of the ideal of the liberal individual and the ideal of negative freedom. Like the cosmopolitan liberal individual, the fluid subject in process who is heterogeneous and mobile, who easily crosses borders, is contrasted to a premodern native subject who is defined by ties of belonging and connection to land, and thus is locked in place and in history. Like the ideal of the autonomous individual, the ideal of the unfixed, border-crossing subject imagines a freedom that is opposed to the rootedness of the native.

Some queer of color theorists have argued that in valorizing a fluid and unfixed self, a "tradition-free subject," a "postidentity" politics, and "subjectless critique," queer theories can retrench white liberal identities and ideals of freedom while disavowing them.[72] As Sara Ahmed writes, "the idealization of movement, or transformation of movement into a fetish, depends on the exclusion of others who are already positioned as *not free in the same way*."[73] Jasbir Puar points to the collusion with paradigms of individual freedom of choice in ideals of queerness as transgression and subversion, and in understandings of freedom as travel, movement, and border-crossing. The commodification of freedom as travel and transgression perpetuates identification with the ideal of the transcendent subject, with what Rey Chow calls the *ascendancy of whiteness*, in opposition to

---

[71] Moreton-Robinson, "Towards an Australian Indigenous Women's Standpoint Theory," 343.
[72] See Smith, "Queer Theory and Native Studies"; Puar, *Terrorist Assemblages*.
[73] Ahmed, *The Cultural Politics of Emotion*, 151.

communities of color that are fixed in place.[74] Yet as Mark Rifkin argues, Puar's imagining of a queer diaspora "beyond or different from sharing a common ancestral homeland" and her argument for a movement away from "the defense of the integrity of identity" and toward "a queer praxis of assemblage" repeats the assumption that freedom must be found in escape from rootedness and tradition. The affirmation of a queer diasporic praxis of assemblage that will turn the imperial logic of assemblage back on itself rests on the assumption of a hermetic relation of the imperial logic with itself. The assumption that imperialism can be subverted only through being turned back on itself erases the histories of social and political formations engaged in struggle with imperial powers, and it denies the reality of already existing alternative power formations. While it is rooted in analyses of the biopolitical production of raced and gendered populations, Puar's model of resistance loses track of "the geopolitical formations that biopolitical techniques work to efface or to translate into more manageable terms. Such an oversight ends up eliding other extant modes of collectivity, place making, and sovereignty, including those of Indigenous peoples."[75] Such arguments fall back on a negative form of critique, disconnected from any relationship to an existing political order or a substantive practice of freedom in relation to land.

While she argues that queer critiques of origin stories are useful for questioning claims of tradition, Andrea Smith criticizes a tendency to represent "queer culture as free-floating, unlike race, which is marked by belonging and not-belonging."[76] These understandings of freedom as cosmopolitan border-crossing, fluidity, and transgression are often posited against the background of the fixed and unchanging Native. "The 'Native' serves as the origin story that generates the autonomous present for the white queer subject."[77] Smith directs this critique also to the figure of the *mestiza*, the border identity described by Gloria Anzaldua and taken up in feminist theory as an alternative to a fixed essential identity. For Smith, Anzaldúa's *Borderlands* "situates Indians and Europeans in a dichotomy that can be healed through mestizaje." Anzaldúa, Smith argues, "positions Indian culture as having 'no tolerance for deviance,' a problem that can be healed by the 'tolerance for ambiguity' that those of mixed race 'necessarily possess.' A rigid, unambiguous Indian is juxtaposed unfavourably with the mestizo who does not 'hold concepts or ideas in rigid boundaries.'" Native identity is "relegated to a primitive past, a premodern precursor to the more modern, sophisticated mestizo identity."[78] Indigenous claims of connection to land are reformulated as expressions of fixed essences locked in place and time, and serve as a contrast or

---

[74] Puar, *Terrorist Assemblages*.
[75] Rifkin, "Making Peoples into Populations," 157–158.
[76] Smith, "Queer Theory and Native Studies," 45.
[77] Smith, "Queer Theory and Native Studies," 48.
[78] Smith, "Queer Theory and Native Studies," 52.

ground for images of mestiza world traveling, boundary-crossing, heterogeneity, fluidity, and multiplicity.

The assumption that the rooted relational self is a fixed unfree self is a form of colonial unknowing that perpetuates the liberal opposition between individual freedom and the constraints of tradition.[79] Denise Ferreira da Silva has argued that the liberal ideal of the self-determining subject reflects an anxiety about control and a defensive opposition to the "affectable" raced or Native other.[80] The assumption that freedom is opposed to rootedness legitimates the propertized freedom of settlers who relate to land only as commodity, while denying the basis of Indigenous claims to land: relational freedom.

Against the dualistic opposition of a heterogeneous, unfixed self and a fixed Native self related to land, the relational self described by many Indigenous theorists is both heterogeneous and rooted in place, connected to land. Against the opposition of movement and fixity, movement is grounded in connection to place, and it is oriented through relations to and knowledge of particular trees, rocks, rivers, birds, and other living beings. "Freedom to roam" is not opposed to rootedness but is essential to rooted relation to land.[81] For example, in Australia, many Aboriginal tribes are able to navigate vast distances following songlines, detailed maps of the land held in songs. Precontact life involved travel and migration, and social, political, and economic interactions with other communities and nations. John Borrows writes that freedom of movement is part of Indigenous living traditions: both physical and intellectual movement are constrained by colonial laws that restrict Indigenous people to reserves and by perceptions of Indigenous peoples as located in the past, as not belonging in contemporary democracies.[82]

The understanding of who someone is, Audra Simpson writes, is a matter of "how she is connected." Knowledge of self and other involves understanding their place in the world, but that place is not fixed: it is shaped and interpreted in changing contexts through material and linguistic relations with others and with land. When people meet for the first time, their introductions include accounts of their histories and relations with others and with places. Relationships are established through language: through mediating narratives and dialogues. Webs of kinship "have to be made material through dialogue and discourse."[83]

Against the assumption that the Native self is fixed and homogeneous, Indigenous groups and peoples *are* heterogeneous, multiple, and diverse. Many can trace their lineages through relations among diverse groups, including

---

[79] In *The Empire of Love*, Elizabeth Povinelli criticizes the liberal binary of individual freedom and social constraint in relation to social dependencies in settler colonies.
[80] Ferreira da Silva, *Toward a Global Idea of Race*.
[81] Watson, "Settled and Unsettled Spaces."
[82] Borrows, *Freedom and Indigenous Constitutionalism*, 19–49.
[83] Simpson, *Mohawk Interruptus*, 9.

diverse groups of settlers. But this heterogeneity is not opposed to a strong affirmation of identity in relation to land. Indigenous struggles against colonization depend on a conception of self that is rooted in belonging to place *and* is heterogeneous and in process.[84] The relational self is rooted in a radical relationality: connection to land includes connection to the living enspirited world, in all of its diversity and processes of change. So this self is not "fixed" but is *radically heterogeneous through its connections*. This radical relationality is connected to a distinctive conception of relational freedom. Individual freedom is not based on an opposition between fixed and unfixed, autonomous versus determined, but is found in relationality, in dynamic rootedness and movement.

Questions of Essentialism and Collective Identities as Heterogeneous Polities

Indigenous claims to collective identities in relation to land and Indigenous politics of self-determination and nationhood are frequently misrecognized as essentialist identity politics. The category of the Indigenous is, of course, a social construction, produced through colonization. The racialized and essentialized category, with the assumption of a binary opposition between white settlers and Indigenous people, has been imposed upon diverse peoples and nations, to identify and discipline populations. Subsumed within this category, Indigenous nations are forced by states to provide evidence of authentic Indigenous identity and continuation of precontact traditions to substantiate land claims and intellectual property claims. The demand that preexisting nations must prove their authenticity in order to qualify for recognition by the colonizing state, to claim land that is rightfully theirs, is, of course, bitterly ironic. Such policies have served to fragment and divide communities and to perpetuate racialized discourses as to who counts as a "real Indian" or "real Aboriginal." Given that evidence of authentic identity is required by states to substantiate claims of belonging to land, it's ironic that these identities are blamed as the sources of essentialist traditions.[85]

---

[84] This affirmation of Indigeneity that includes heterogeneity has been particularly important in combatting the divisive tactics of colonizing states. In Australia, for instance, the Half Caste Act of 1886 and the Aboriginal Protection policies that were in effect until 1969 legislated the removal of children of "mixed" parentage from Aboriginal communities, as a means of assimilating them into white society, in an explicit eugenics policy: the aboriginal would be gradually bred out of those with white blood, who could be civilized, while the "full-blooded" Aboriginals would die out. In response to these tactics, many Aboriginal Australians resist the label "mixed race" as inherently racist, recognize that most people are of "mixed" descent, and affirm that Aboriginal identity includes any line of descent, along with identification and acceptance as part of an Aboriginal community or kin network. Thus Aboriginal identity often explicitly includes heterogeneity. However, divisive state policies and laws have led to internecine battles among status Indigenous people and those who claim Indigenous descent. See Simpson, *Mohawk Interruptus*; Jaimes, "Some Kind of Indian."

[85] Linda Tuhiwai Smith writes that while claiming essential Indigenous characteristics is often strategic, as it is required by states adjudicating claims for rights and land, there are also spiritual conceptions of essence that are important to many Indigenous worldviews. "A human person does

Like other categories constituted through oppression, the category of the Indigenous is reclaimed and deployed in forms of solidarity and resistance. Indigenous peoples are people whose homelands have been colonized. The term "Indigenous" is used to identify vastly different and diverse peoples, and Indigenous scholars and activists certainly do not agree about what kinds of generalizations can be made about Indigenous people. Many argue that no such generalizations can be made.[86] Yet, as is evidenced by the United Nations Declaration of the Rights of Indigenous Peoples, diverse nations and groups are able to unite around shared interests and struggles, and shared philosophies of relation to land. This unity does not preclude conflicts and divisions. As Hayden King writes, "We Natives are deeply divided. There's nothing wrong with that."[87]

Indigenous critical theorists reject the understanding of Indigenous nations as ethnic and racialized cultural groups claiming special status. Indigenous nations are political entities asserting political rights. The politics of Indigenous self-determination are not claims for recognition of special status in a multicultural liberal state. The politics of Indigenous nationhood are political claims of *polities*, and they are assertions of what Joanne Barker calls *the polity of the Indigenous*: "the unique governance, territory and culture of an Indigenous people in a system of (non)human relationships and responsibilities to one another."[88] Indigenous theorists and activists do not, of course, all agree about the terms and aims of the politics of Indigenous nationhood, self-determination, and decolonization. The terms *nation* and *sovereignty* are contested terms. The politics of treaty constitutionalism can conflict with the politics of resurgence and with refusal to recognize the state. Yet these are all assertions of Indigenous *polities*.[89]

Robert Nichols writes that investigations that begin from abstract and naive questions such as "what is indigeneity?" deflect attention from critiques of

---

not stand alone, but shares with other animate and, in the Western sense, 'inanimate' beings, a relationship based on a shared 'essence' of life." These forms of essence are not claims of sameness but spiritual relations (Tuhiwai Smith, *Decolonizing Methodologies*, 77). The essence of a people can be defined in relation to place and land. Many people trace their genealogies through their relation to place and kin groups, sometimes identified with animal clans.

[86] And again, many other generalizing terms are used and debated, including Aboriginal, Native, Indian, First Nations, and NDN.
[87] King, "We Natives Are Deeply Divided."
[88] Barker, "Indigenous Feminisms."
[89] "Aboriginal peoples are not racial groups; they are organic political and cultural entities. Although contemporary Aboriginal peoples stem historically from the original peoples of North America, they often have mixed genetic heritages and include individuals of varied ancestries. As organic political entities, they have the capacity to evolve over time and change in their internal composition.... Only when Aboriginal peoples are viewed, not as 'races' within the boundaries of a legitimate state, but as distinct political communities with recognizable claims for collective rights, will there be a first and meaningful step towards responding to Aboriginal peoples' challenge to achieve self-government" (Report of the Canadian Royal Commission on Aboriginal Peoples, 1996).

colonization, reducing indigeneity to a determinate content of social and cultural difference that can be assimilated within the state. Critical Indigenous studies, he argues, need to focus on the usurpation of political agency.[90] The focus on critique and political agency, however, doesn't entirely obviate questions of identity. Alfred and Corntassel write that indigeneity is an identity constructed in the context of colonization: a contentious oppositional identity.[91] While some critical Indigenous theorists argue for a rejection of questions of identity and identity politics, for a shift from identity to polity, Audra Simpson argues that Indigenous identity *is* political membership. As she points out, the heterogeneous composition of the historical community of Kahnawà:ke was organized by the clan structure, which "made it possible for all those people to become Mohawk." Mohawk identity, then, was not racial but political. "Thus identity was not a problematic, ethical issue, a matter to be confused by. It was not confused with political membership. It was political membership."[92]

As Audra Simpson writes, "the very notion of an *indigenous* nationhood, which demarcates identity and seizes tradition in ways that may be antagonistic to the encompassing frame of the state, may be simply unintelligible to the western and/or imperial ear."[93] Simpson points out that many Indigenous peoples, such as the Iroquois confederacy, have a long and well-documented historical self-consciousness of themselves as *nations*. They have documented and experiential and continuing histories that include treaties, diplomacy, procedure, and political structure. The form and content of a nation, Simpson argues, is specific to its context: the nation defined by Ernest Gellner is the form of nation particular to the material conditions of industrial England, and the form of the contemporary nation state is specific to the conditions of international political economies. Indigenous nationhoods are different entities, specific to their historical contexts. Mohawk nationalism today is a hybrid form, combining Iroquois and colonial forms of governance, focusing on resistance and self-identity, political strategy and lived experience, and historical knowledge.

Against the opposition of political identity to cultural identity, Taiaike Alfred has argued that Indigenous nationhood is a form of *political* identity that is informed by a complex of *cultural* practices and traditions. The aim of Indigenous political struggle for recognition of nationhood is a form of cultural and political sovereignty not through the creation of a nation state but "through the achievement of a cultural sovereignty and a political relationship based on group autonomy reflected in formal self-government arrangements."[94] Glen Coulthard

---

[90] Nichols, "Contract and Usurpation," citing Markell, "The Insufficiency of Non-Domination."
[91] Alfred and Corntassel, "Being Indigenous."
[92] Simpson, *Mohawk Interruptus*, 48.
[93] Simpson, "Paths Toward a Mohawk Nation,"114.
[94] Alfred, *Heeding the Voices of Our Ancestors*, 14.

writes that Indigenous *culture* is a mode of life that encompasses the economic, political, spiritual, and social. Coulthard points out that Karl Marx understood *mode of production* more broadly as a *mode of life*.[95] This means that forms of state recognition of "Indigenous culture" as quaint traditions, and of Indigenous polities as subordinate to the state, both fail to recognize Indigenous nationhood. Genuine recognition would be mutual recognition of political autonomy and recognition of a mode of life organized through an alternative socioeconomic system that challenges the capitalist economy.

Indigenous identity, then, can refer both to a political identity or polity and to a distinctive mode of life and philosophy of relation to land. As Dian Million writes, indigenism as both political identity and as lived ways of life can be understood as "a current articulation that brings a multitude together in our times."[96] This current articulation is formulated through knowledges and interpretations of diverse histories and traditions.

Given the diversity of Indigenous nations and the multiple interpretations of tradition, is the claim of a distinctive Indigenous philosophy of relationality that organizes a distinctive Indigenous mode of life an essentialist claim? That depends on what is meant by *essentialist*. The argument for the existence of a distinctive Indigenous philosophy and mode of life—connection to land, and relationality—does not entail that all Indigenous people embrace this philosophy or follow this mode of life. It is an argument not for *universality* but for *specificity*: this philosophy and mode of life are specific to many Indigenous peoples. The extent to which a particular worldview is generalizable across diverse Indigenous groups and diverse individuals is, of course, open to question. At this point we know that the worldview of relationality has been identified by many Indigenous philosophers, scholars, and activists as a distinctive Indigenous worldview, a specifically Indigenous philosophy, practice, and politics. No one claims that the philosophy and practice of relationality is a *unified* and *homogeneous* tradition, or that all or any modern Indigenous individuals follow this mode of life exclusively. Many Indigenous people identify as Christians, Muslims, or Buddhists, and many embrace liberal modernity and capitalism. To what extent do they subscribe to an "Indigenous worldview"? Like other modern individuals, Indigenous individuals embrace heterogeneous perspectives and worldviews that do not cohere and may be in conflict. Like other modern individuals, Indigenous people are heterogeneous and negotiate multiple, conflicting, and changing perspectives, politics, and practices.[97] Indigenous

---

[95] Coulthard, *Red Skin, White Masks*, 64.

[96] Million, *Therapeutic Nations*, 13.

[97] See, for example, Vera Palmer's analysis of the preservation of Iroquoian worldviews in the seventeenth-century "conversion" to Christianity of Kateri Tekakwitha, who was recently canonized by the Vatican. Palmer, "The Devil in the Details."

practices and traditions are not fixed but change through history, and through various interactions and relations. Indigenous cultures are continuous, not static. The philosophies of relationality formulated by Indigenous critical theorists do not identify fixed essences or characteristics that categorize Indigenous people. They are philosophies of heterogeneous relations and rooted dynamisms. These philosophies inform indigenous polities that are inclusive of difference, heterogeneity, and change.

Critiques of essentialist identity politics do, however, identify genuine dangers in contemporary Indigenous theory and politics. Indigenous leaders, scholars, and activists can romanticize the image of the authentic Indian, and they can make truth claims about origins and history that are open to question. In the context of essentializing status categories imposed by colonizing states, the assertion of a special connection to land can pose real dangers. Indigenous feminist and queer theorists point out that claims of Indigenous tradition often mask patriarchal, homophobic, and racist views and practices that exclude women, queers, and racialized groups from status and participation in Indigenous communities.[98] When they are used to defend essentialist status categories, claims of a special connection to land can support exclusive nationalisms. Claims to sovereignty often do fail to consider the claims of other precarious groups, including Indigenous people without recognized status, nonindigenous migrants, and racialized groups. And the identification of indigeneity with relation to land can be used to exclude urban dwellers.[99] Ideologies of a pure and homogeneous culture and unchanging traditions typically mask not only differences but power relations internal to "cultures," and obscure interpenetrations between and among cultures. In fact, what counts as "culture" is produced through historical change and is subject to interpretation, conflict, and contestation.[100]

Indigenous feminist and queer critical theorists argue that the philosophy of relationality rooted in relation to land is a philosophy of inclusion and affirmation of heterogeneity and diversity. When Indigenous leaders and groups use the language of tradition to exclude and oppress, they are forgetting this philosophy. This means that in such cases, the philosophy of relation to land is falsely conflated with the essentialist status categories imposed by colonizing states.

---

[98] See, for example, Joyce Green, ed., *Making Space for Indigenous Feminism*; Smith and Kauanui, "Native Feminisms Engage American Studies."

[99] Some Indigenous theorists and activists argue, however, that the experience of relation to land is just as strong among urban groups as it is among those living on country. Urban centers have typically been built on Indigenous land, and many urban Indigenous communities continue to cultivate and to sustain the lands on which they live. Renya Ramirez draws on her ethnography of urban Indigenous communities to argue that traveling back and forth between city and country actually strengthens connection to country for urban Indians. She argues that Indigenous people in diverse geographical areas are oriented around "hubs" that organize their relations and roles in community (Ramirez, *Native Hubs*).

[100] Narayan, *Dislocating Cultures*.

John Borrows argues that interpretations of Indigenous traditions as pure and homogeneous are effects of internalized colonialism and racism.[101] In these interpretations, colonial unknowing is internalized, obscuring the knowledges of heterogeneous and dynamic relationalities that can support a radically relational and inclusive politics of decolonization.

Part Four

Politics of Exclusion, Traditions of Inclusion: Heterogeneous Relationalities and Coalitional Politics of Decolonization

Indigenous status in Canada and the United States has been instituted through state laws and policies that define identity on racialized and gendered grounds. In response to state policies that recognize land claims and allocate rights and benefits on the basis of Indigenous identity, many Indigenous communities have established their own racialized and gendered membership rules. As noted earlier, the Indian Act in Canada explicitly excluded women who married nonstatus men from Indian status, until Indigenous women finally succeeded in winning amendments to the Act by appealing to human rights law. Their activism has too often met with hostility from Indigenous leaders, who have responded by instituting their own sexist and racist membership policies that define membership in terms of blood quantum.[102] Métis and Indigenous people without status have long been excluded from rights and benefits from the Canadian state, and by Indigenous bands. Blood quantum membership policies have been instituted by some nations in the United States; the Cherokee Nation of Oklahoma has instituted blood quantum status policies to disenfranchise descendants of African American slaves. Many Native communities support sexist and homophobic Christian Right ideologies in the name of tradition.

Many of these struggles have been taken to federal and international courts, and sexist and racist policies have been overturned on human rights grounds. This has led critics to argue that Indigenous traditions are *essentially* oppressive and exclusive, and that Indigenous self-determination must be subsumed under state governance and human rights law. But are Indigenous traditions necessarily oppressive and exclusive?[103] And do claims of nationhood and sovereignty

---

[101] Borrows, *Freedom and Indigenous Constitutionalism*, 42.

[102] Audra Simpson discusses the continuous discourse and debate on Indigenous identity in Kahnawà:ke in *Mohawk Interruptus*. I discuss Indigenous women's resistance to exclusionary policies and gendered structures of violence in Chapter 5.

[103] See Serene Khader's critique of feminist assumptions that "traditions" are necessarily oppressive. In *Decolonizing Universalism*, Khader argues that claims to tradition should be judged according to whether or not they enforce sexist oppression.

rooted in "relation to land" necessarily produce divisive and destructive identity politics?

Indigenous feminist and queer critical theorists point out that Indigenous identity politics are not "traditional" but are effects of colonization. Oppressions and exclusions based on identity categories of gender and race have been produced by the status rules introduced by the settler state, which uses these categories to distribute Indian rights. When band leaders and members use these categories to determine membership, they are not following Indigenous tradition, but redeploying the heteropatriarchal and racist institutions—and traditions—of the colonial state. As Audra Simpson writes: "Race and sex became meaningful categories for determining membership in the consciousness of Kahnaw'kehró:non when resources were threatened and Mohawks became 'Indians.'"[104]

Against the assumption that Indigenous traditions are necessarily oppressive, Indigenous feminist and queer theorists employ several arguments. First, the source of divisive, oppressive, and exclusive gendered and racialized identities has been the colonizing state, not Indigenous traditions. Many argue that Indigenous traditions were often nonhierarchical and inclusive of gender diversity, heterogeneity, and women's power. Nations were organized by kin relations that were not restricted to "blood" relations and not organized according to racial categories but were alternative forms of *polity*. These political kin relations structured relations to those outside a group and allowed for the inclusion of "outsiders." Second, Indigenous feminist and queer theorists distinguish between traditions that are oppressive and those that are inclusive, to argue that only inclusive traditions ought to be reclaimed. Third, they argue that traditions and cultures are dynamic, not fixed, and are always subject to interpretation. The reclamation of traditions should be oriented not to a fixed and romanticized past but to a decolonizing future. Finally, they employ all of these arguments not to romanticize traditions but to reclaim and to imagine alternative conceptions of nationhood and sovereignty.

In a sharp critique of the imposition of binary gender roles and the elimination of queer bodies from many contemporary Indigenous spaces, Leanne Betasamosake Simpson argues that "2SQ Indigenous peoples flourished in many Indigenous nations and were highly visible to the first European 'explorers'" who condemned and shamed and worked to eliminate what they considered to be deviant practices.[105] "The powerful relationships queer bodies house—consent, diversity, variance, spiritual power, community, respect, reciprocity, love, attachment—were the very first thing colonizers sought to eliminate."[106] Queer

---

[104] Simpson, *Mohawk Interruptus*, 60.
[105] Simpson, *As We Have Always Done*, 123.
[106] Simpson, *As We Have Always Done*, 126.

bodies, she writes, express the diversity of the natural world: "the land... provides endless examples of queerness and diverse sexualities and genders."[107] For Simpson, settler gender norms were imposed in an attempt "to break the network of intelligent relationships housed in Indigenous bodies in order to prevent the replication of Indigenous freedom, in order to get land."[108] Queering resurgence, then, involves both reclaiming queer traditions and creating new ones.

Bonita Lawrence points out that the Métis, diverse communities of people designated as "mixed bloods" or "half-breeds," have historically been excluded from the rights accruing to Indian status. The "mixedness" of the Métis is evidence of the heterogeneity of kin relations, as the economy of the fur trade included marriages between Native women and white men, who were absorbed into Native communities. Reclaiming the category of Métis has involved reclaiming histories of heterogeneity. Lawrence writes: "In Indian communities such as Toronto, Nativeness is alive and well, if one simply adopts a flexibility around the relationship between race and Nativeness."[109]

Mixedness is not peculiar to the Métis. Indigenous nations developed through political alliances and conquests. The Anishnaabe and the Haudenosaunee confederacy included multiple nations, which in turn included multiple tribes and clans. The Huron-Wendat developed as an association of several Iroquoian-speaking groups, including eight matrilineal clans which cut across at least four tribes. As Georges Sioui writes, mixedness and heterogeneity are part of Huron-Wendat "tradition":

> In the middle of the seventeenth century, when we became drastically depopulated through epidemics and wars, often caused by missionary interference, we were saved from complete extinction principally because we had matricentrist socio-political traditions.... Our wars, which we did wage just as cruelly as anyone, had as their primary purpose the replacement of lost members through capture of enemies... and ritually, through adoption, giving them a new life in our Nations.[110]

Against what he terms the patricentrist system of racist exclusion, "our good fortune was that we lived within a matricentrist, circular system where people and other species are not disqualified and destroyed because of not being what they are not."[111] Here Sioui invokes a sociopolitical tradition, a kinship system

---

[107] Simpson, *As We Have Always Done*, 122.
[108] Simpson, *As We Have Always Done*, 127.
[109] Lawrence, *"Real" Indians and Others*, 175.
[110] Sioui, "Why We Should Have Inclusivity and Why We Cannot Have It." Quoted by Lawrence, *"Real" Indians and Others*, 175.
[111] Lawrence, *"Real" Indians and Others*, 175.

that incorporated others as a strategy of survival. This is not an imagined pre-lapsarian state of harmony without conflict or violence. It is, however, a system that includes otherness. Elizabeth Povinelli confirms this: "Generally, indigenous communities absorb strangers into local languages of kinship and moiety relations. This certainly was the case when I first arrived at Belyuen in 1984. There, kinship relations—with specific norms for how various kinds of kin are treated—are the presumed backdrop of every relationship of any longstanding nature."[112]

Taiaiake Alfred and Audra Simpson point out that Kahnawà:ke was originally a heterogeneous colony of Christian Indians, including Mohawks but also Abenaki, Huron, Oneida, and Onondaga people, who, in the seventeenth century, sought refuge in the white settlement of Kentaké, where the Jesuits established a mission. As Simpson argues, this was a heterogeneous community of refugees. The Mohawks of Kahnawà:ke included assimilated whites and other Indians who had been taken captive prior to the move North, and the descendants of captives influenced the politics of the community. For example, to honor the kinship ties of the descendants of the captives taken from the Mohawk raid on Deerfield, Massachusetts, in 1704, the Mohawks of Kahnawà:ke adopted an official position of neutrality during the Revolutionary War. And they continued the adaptive structure of kinship clan relations, incorporating outsiders, long after migration to Kentaké. "The clan structure that was in place made it possible for all those people to become Mohawk."[113]

Audra Simpson does not romanticize the Mohawks but points out that their kin structures allowed for integration of "outsiders," and that Kahnawà:ke was a heterogeneous polity.

> As sovereign political orders, these First Nations took, bartered, naturalized, killed, and loved according to their philosophical and political charters, before biopolitics and race became unambiguous techniques of settler-state sovereignty and governance. Yet, when channeling backward, we can see that outsiders from other communities and polities . . . were integrated into the community. This "difference" was not problematic until the construct of race became important to Kahnawa'kehró:non. Race became an issue at the time when being Mohawk became being Indian and being Indian carried rights.[114]

---

[112] Povinelli, *The Empire of Love*, 20.
[113] Simpson, *Mohawk Interruptus*, 48. Simpson notes that because of this heterogeneous history, Kahnawàke has not been particularly interesting to anthropologists who have seen it as a place of "impure culture" in contrast to "more perfect, more culturally 'intact'" Indigenous communities 65). See also Alfred, *Heeding the Voices of Our Ancestors*.
[114] Simpson, *Mohawk Interruptus*, 59.

For Jodi Byrd, reclaiming inclusive forms of kinship is essential to addressing colonial legacies of enforced settlement. The struggles of the Cherokee, Choctaw, Chickasaw, Creek, and Seminole Nations to address the status of African American Freedmen Indians in their midst reflect the legacies of colonization and slavery: the collision of the struggles of Freedmen for inclusion and the struggles of the Southeastern Nations for rights to sovereignty and land. African Americans were held as slaves by the five Southeastern Nations, which the colonists called the "Five Civilized Tribes." Once freed, the African American descendants gained rights of citizenship within the nations, according to reconstruction treaties with the United States. The Cherokee Nation instituted blood quantum rules to disenfranchise Freedmen in the 1980s, and a popular vote evicted the Freedmen from the Cherokee Nation in 2007. The Freedmen took this decision to the courts of both the Cherokee Nation and the United States; the eviction decision was finally overturned by the U.S. government in 2017.

In response to the eviction of African Americans from the Cherokee Nation, Byrd writes: "The inclusion of the Freedmen . . . does not need to be framed as an issue of competition over scarce resources, an attack on indigenous sovereignty, or a reenactment of the removal from traditional homelands that casts Freedman as intruders threatening the rights and lands of traditional peoples. Rather, it is a unique opportunity for the colonized Southeastern Indian nations to enact the kinship sovereignties that have for so long been part of our governance structures in order to form the kind of relations that will not only reconcile the violences of the past but move us towards a decolonial future."[115] Byrd quotes Robert Warrior, who writes that Cherokee Chief Chad Smith "could save us all the trouble by following some of the best examples of Cherokee history rather than the morally corrupting and exclusionary ones he and his supporters have chosen thus far."[116] Byrd argues that decolonizing resurgence demands a future-oriented practice of interpretation and judgment, to reclaim ethical traditions while rejecting those that are oppressive. For Byrd, this involves reclaiming what she calls *kinship sovereignties*: relational sovereignties, generative kinships that form the alternative roots of decolonizing politics.[117] These are structured networks that define obligations and responsibilities in a wide range of political, economic, and social activities.[118] Unlike the form of state sovereignty that corresponds to the sovereignty of the individual, kinship sovereignty organizes collective responsibility. Kinship sovereignties are "intersubstantiations of sovereignty and relationship that connect community to ancestral place and

---

[115] Byrd, *The Transit of Empire*, 146.
[116] Byrd, *The Transit of Empire*, 146; citing Warrior, "Cherokees Flee the Moral High Ground over Freedmen," *News From Indian Country*, August 7, 2007.
[117] Byrd, *The Transit of Empire*, 183.
[118] Byrd, *The Transit of Empire*, 264, n77.

belonging," arising from ontologies of reciprocal complementarity.[119] These are the traditions, Byrd argues, that need to be renewed to negotiate belonging in the wake of colonization.

As Glen Coulthard writes, Indigenous resurgence requires resisting a retreat into an uncritical essentialism. With Leanne Simpson and Taiaiake Alfred, Coulthard calls for a *critical* resurgence that draws critically on traditions in order to radically transform the colonial power relations that have come to dominate our present.[120] As Jodi Byrd argues, "enforced settler cohabitations demand the best of indigenous government traditions to imagine, innovate, and restructure kinship sovereignties in order to repair the violent breaches of family, history, and tradition that forced people into indigenous lands. And it requires ... a recentering of indigenous authority to adjudicate the past and future on those indigenous lands."[121]

Destabilizing Binaries: Entangled Relations of Dispossession

Decolonizing critical theory requires foregrounding relations to land; it also requires destabilizing the simple binary of Indigenous and settler, colonized and colonizer, which obscures the multiplicity of power relations that structure contemporary settler states. The unity of the category of the Indigenous obscures relations of power along lines of gender and status, and obscures the issues and struggles of widely diverse groups of people. It can obscure centuries of interrelations, mixing, and hybridities. The unity of the category of settlers obscures differential relations to the power and sovereignty of the nation. The histories of settler states include multiple waves of immigration of settlers who are very differently positioned on the land. We need, then, to recognize the very different positions of state governments and imperial regimes, corporations, property owners (and there are obviously various types of property ownership and power), renters, squatters, privileged cosmopolitans, mestizas, refugees, asylum seekers, homeless peoples, slaves and descendants of slaves, racialized groups, groups that identify as white, groups that have struggled to be classified as white, ethnic and linguistic and religious minorities, oppressed and displaced nations within states, peasant farmers, landless workers, formerly colonized peoples, citizens of and migrants from postcolonial and still racialized "Third World" states, along with diverse Indigenous peoples of various and mixed lineages, including migrants and descendants of slaves, on traditional lands and in urban centers, on reserves and in prisons, with and without treaties, land, or recognized governments—all of whom occupy very different positions in systems of

---

[119] Byrd, *The Transit of Empire*, 222.
[120] Coulthard, *Red Skin, White Masks*, 154–159.
[121] Byrd, *The Transit of Empire*, 222.

ownership of and responsibility for land. In Australia, for example, many of the original settlers were convicts: desperately poor people charged with petty crimes in Britain and sent to a prison colony on an island on the other side of the world, as an alternative to execution. Many new prospective settlers are asylum seekers detained in prison camps on a barren island off the coast of Australia. Such an analysis complicates any simple binary of colonizers and colonized, settlers and Indigenous peoples. Yet we need to recognize the *specificity* of the history and continuing colonization of Indigenous peoples, of Indigenous relations to land, and the specificity of Indigenous polities and Indigenous struggles for decolonization.

Mahmood Mamdani distinguishes between settlers and migrants: settlers "are made by conquest, not just by immigration. . . . Settlers are *founders* of political orders and carry their sovereignty with them, [whereas] migrants can be seen as *appellants* facing a political order that is already constituted."[122] Settler-colonial theorist Lorenzo Veracini draws on Mamdani's distinction to make the problematic claim that settlers and refugees can be seen as occupying the opposite ends of a spectrum of possibilities, in that the displacement of refugees is premised on an absolute lack of choice, whereas the movement of settlers is "entirely volitional."[123] If "settlers" are understood to be conquering states, this would be true; but given that settler populations have also been constituted by displaced persons, the unity of the concept of "settler" begins to break down. Jodi Byrd introduces the category of the *arrivant*, to signify "those people forced into the Americas through the violence of European and Anglo-American colonialism and imperialism around the globe."[124] Yet all of the categories used to delineate populations and identity groups are inadequate to contend with the heterogeneities and ambiguities that trouble identities and the boundaries between them. The category of the *arrivant* can be used, as Manu Vimalassery, Juliana Hu Pegues, and Alyosha Goldstein argue, to destabilize the binary of settler/colonized, without the need to strictly categorize all individuals and groups.[125] The task of critical Indigenous theory is to theorize the specificity of Indigeneity and Indigenous politics in relation to multiple and intersecting forms of colonization and imperialism, and to theorize the politics of decolonization.

Addressing politics of racialization and migration along with Indigenous politics requires a critique and analysis of the entangled relations of domination that constitute the nation state, and in particular the borders of the carceral settler

---

[122] Mamdani, "When Does a Settler Become a Native?" See also Mamdani, "Beyond Settler and Native as Political Identities."
[123] Verancini, *Settler Colonialism*, 3.
[124] Byrd, *The Transit of Empire*, xix. Byrd borrows the term *arrivant* from African Caribbean poet Kamau Brathwaite.
[125] Vimalassery, Pegues, and Goldstein, "On Colonial Unknowing."

state, within relations of global racialized capitalism. These entangled relations are the formations of what Byrd et al. call *economies of dispossession*: "those multiple and intertwined genealogies of racialized property, subjection, and expropriation through which capitalism and colonialism take shape historically and change over time."[126] As Harsha Walia points out, state borders are instruments of conquest and control that have served historically to contain and discipline Indigenous and racialized populations, and to exclude the unwanted. This means that Indigenous decolonial and Black abolition struggles are intimately connected with migrant rights movements. "Early US bordering practices were, in fact, conceived of as a method of eliminating Indigenous people and controlling Black people, and US border imperialism is structurally bound up in these genocides."[127] A large proportion of Central American and Mexican migrants to the United States are Indigenous people colonized by the Spanish, captured by Mexico and Central American nation states, subsumed into a pan-Latinx and mestizx identity, and criminalized through the imposition of borders. The borders established following the U.S. invasion of Mexico in the 1840s cut across Indigenous and Mexican lands. Along with the "free trade" agreements authorizing the use of Mexican land and people to produce American and multinational commodities, these borders produce the populations that are now referred to as "illegal." As migrant organizations in the United States point out, "We did not cross the border, the border crossed us." This assertion is echoed in the slogan "No borders on stolen land." The borders between Canada and the United States, like the borders between the United States and Mexico, cross multiple Indigenous territories, and criminalize migrations that were part of precolonial relations of communication and exchange. These borders also served to contain slaves. The Fugitive Slave Act of 1850 enabled border militias and border policing to prevent enslaved people from escaping to Mexico and Canada. As Walia writes, the architecture of contemporary U.S. border controls, policing, and surveillance is rooted in these techniques of regulation and criminalization of Black mobility.[128] The contemporary politics of migration are, then, rooted in systems of racialization. As Rinaldo Walcott and Idil Abdillahi write, "Movements that we now call migration are founded in anti-Blackness, taking their logic from transatlantic slavery."[129] The founding of the United States on stolen lands through violent politics of elimination served, Walia writes, as a model for U.S. imperialism: "eliminationist Indian Wars laid the foundation for

[126] Byrd, Goldstein, Melamed, and Reddy, "Predatory Value," 2.
[127] Walia, *Border and Rule*, 23.
[128] Walia cites Robert Lovato's argument that the U.S. ICE Agreements of Cooperation in Communities to Enhance Safety and Security (ACCESS) program is based on the Fugitive Slave Act (Walia, *Border and Rule*, 29).
[129] Walcott and Abdillahi, *BlackLife: Post-BLM and the Struggle for Freedom* (Winnipeg: ARP Books, 2019), 22; cited by Walia, *Border and Rule*, 28.

conquest abroad, becoming the template for genocidal warfare in Hawaii, Puerto Roco, Guam, and the Philippines."[130] The production of dependent populations through warfare, followed by "fair trade" and structural adjustment programs that regulate the extraction and export of "resources" and "labour"—land and people—are connected, then, to the violent conquest of Indigenous lands and domestication of Indigenous peoples as racialized minorities and "domestic dependent nations." Global capitalism has developed through imperial expansion, colonial dispossession, and racial domination. As theorists of racialized capitalism argue, "the racial expropriation of land, labor, and life is innately constitutive of capitalism."[131] The borders established on stolen lands and policed by settler states continue to work to control and exclude racialized populations. "Border formation through the distinct but interrelated processes of expansion, elimination, and enslavement imposed a white polity, and racial exclusion and migrant expulsion further solidified the white racial state."[132]

Theorizing Coalitions
Given the entanglements of colonization and racialization in the constitution of state borders, and given the mixedness and hybridities among Indigenous, racialized, and migrant groups, struggles for decolonization require coalitional alliances among diverse movements organized around deeper analyses of the interconnections between settler colonization and the system of slavery, and of their legacies in continuing white supremacist regimes tied to ownership of property and border control. Indigenous and Black racialized groups confront shared issues of population management, systemic racism, police violence, and the carceral state, within global and national systems of racialized capitalism.

The connections among white supremacy, colonial property, and the nation state necessitate the theorization of relationships between critical race theory and critical Indigenous theory. This theorization is fraught with tensions: critical Indigenous theorists have argued that critical race theorists and postcolonial theorists tend to ignore the prior and continuing existence of original peoples in histories of slavery and migration, and ignore questions of relation to land and struggles for sovereignty, and can fail to question the inevitability of the state. On the other hand, Indigenous and settler-colonial theories often fail to theorize the roles of differential racializations and subjugations in settler colonization, and the interactions between settler colonialism and other forms of racialized colonization and imperialism. While decolonizing theories engage with postcolonial theories, their geographic focus, historical frames of reference, and

---

[130] Walia, *Border and Rule*, 26.
[131] Walia, *Border and Rule*, 35; citing Cedric J. Robinson.
[132] Walia, *Border and Rule*, 31.

objectives typically diverge. The permanent occupation and project of elimination and replacement of populations characteristic of settler colonialism is very different from the colonization of "distant lands" focused on the extraction of resources and labor. Postcolonial theories oriented toward diaspora and cultural hybridity often dismiss the idea of indigeneity as a naïve or dangerous nativism. With Gayatri Spivak, Jodi Byrd criticizes the tendency in postcolonial theories to normativize the postcolonial migrant, "thus occluding the native once again."[133] However, Indigenous claims to sovereignty can be xenophobic and exclusionary. Constructions of Indigeneity that expel and exclude Black and migrant *arrivants* from land rightly provoke critiques of Indigenous land claims. As Gaurav Desai asks, "in a world that has seen mass migrations across continents over a long period of time, is it reasonable to allow for a strictly regulated indigenous politics, which in its most exclusionary stance can lead to ethnic strife, mass expulsions, civil wars, and genocide?"[134]

As Vimalassery, Pegues, and Goldstein argue, theorizing the interconnections among differential racializations and colonization, and among multiple forms of imperialism, will be essential to theories of decolonization. "Colonial unknowing endeavors to render unintelligible the entanglements of racialization and colonization, occluding the mutable historicity of colonial structures and attributing finality to events of conquest and dispossession."[135] The co-constitution of Indigenous, Black, and migrant groups through border politics can ground a coalitional politics of decolonization. This involves recognizing shared issues while addressing distinctions among specific histories and aims. But can a politics of decolonization rooted in Indigenous relations to land accommodate the claims of racialized and migrant groups to live and be at home on contested land? They can, if coalitional movements for decolonization are grounded in Indigenous politics of heterogeneous relationality.

Politics of Heterogeneous Relationalities

If we follow the guidelines of Indigenous law, the claim of relation to land can both ground land claims and accommodate the claims of *arrivants*. The *kinship sovereignties* described by Jodi Byrd and Audra Simpson, political structures of kinship that have historically allowed for integration of "outsiders," support more expansive conceptions of Indigenous belonging and sovereignty. As Audra Simpson argues, the history of Kahnawà:ke as a heterogeneous community of refugees offers an understanding of *identity as political membership*, rather than a pure and homogeneous identity measured by blood quantum. "Because this

---

[133] Byrd, *The Transit of Empire*, xxxi; quoting Spivak, *A Critique of Postcolonial Reason*, 256–257.
[134] Desai, "Editor's Column"; quoted by Byrd, *The Transit of Empire*, xxxiv.
[135] Vimalassery, Pegues, and Goldstein, "On Colonial Unknowing."

is a space with entries and exits; it is not hermetic. People come and go and come back again." The understanding of who someone is, Simpson writes, is a matter of "how she is connected." The webs of kinship "have to be made material through dialogue and discourse."[136] While degrees of homogeneity and heterogeneity vary among communities (and the majority of Indigenous people now live in urban centers, moving back and forth between cities and ancestral lands), this practice of establishing identity through dialogue and discourse, through narratives that establish relationships, is shared by many Indigenous people and communities. Again, as Jodi Byrd argues, "enforced settler cohabitations demand the best of indigenous government traditions to imagine, innovate, and restructure kinship sovereignties in order to repair the violent breaches of family, history and tradition that forced people into indigenous lands."[137]

Along with kinship sovereignties, Indigenous history and politics provide models of *nested sovereignties:* models of nationhood in which nations share land.[138] As Audra Simpson writes, "There is more than one *political* show in town. . . . Like Indigenous bodies, Indigenous sovereignties and Indigenous political orders prevail within and apart from settler governance."[139] For Simpson, the existence of nested sovereignties supports a politics of *refusal*—an alternative to the politics of recognition, challenging the perception of the nation state as *settled*, in the sense of finished and unchangeable. Nested sovereignties can also provide exemplary models for and ongoing practices of the coexistence of peoples and the inclusion of others in polities. Referencing the histories and presence of the Mississauga Nishnaabeg, Wendat, and Haudenosaunee Confederacy in the city of Toronto, Glen Coulthard and Leanne Simpson write: "These nations negotiated and continue to practice diplomatic relationships with each other to share land while respecting each other's governance, jurisdiction, and sovereignty."[140]

The original treaties negotiated between Indigenous nations and Canada, on behalf of the Crown, were understood by the Indigenous signatories as agreements to *share* land, not to sell it. As Michael Asch argues, there is evidence that at least some of the Canadian signatories shared this understanding.[141] As Gina Starblanket and Heidi Kiiwetinepinesiik Stark write, "Indigenous visions of relationality that were expressed in treaties can help challenge and deconstruct colonial mythologies, including [the myth of] Indigenous acquiescence and land cessation through treaty-making."[142] They ask, "If Indigenous peoples were not

---

[136] Simpson, *Mohawk Interruptus*, 9.
[137] Byrd, *The Transit of Empire*, 222.
[138] Simpson, *Mohawk Interruptus*, 9.
[139] Simpson, *Mohawk Interruptus*, 11.
[140] Coulthard and Simpson, "Grounded Normativity/Place-Based Solidarity," 249.
[141] Asch, "Confederation Treaties and Reconciliation."
[142] Starblanket and Stark, "Towards a Relational Paradigm," 195.

ceding lands, as Indigenous knowledge posits, but instead creating a shared territory that would enable peaceful and mutually beneficial coexistence of separate nations, how must our understandings of treaty rights be transformed to account for these interpretations?"[143]

Treaties, for Starblanket and Stark, are not best understood as agreements about borders and property. As Mishuana Goeman argues, "A consequence of colonialism has meant a translation or too easy collapsing of *land* to *property*, a move that perpetuates the logics of containment." Goeman understands land as a practice of *meaning-making*, rather than an object to be claimed.[144] If treaties were originally agreements about social and political relationships, then we need to consider "the possibilities that treaty relations hold for reimagining social and political relations within Indigenous communities and between Indigenous and non-Indigenous peoples.... Collectively, this renewed attentiveness to relationship represents a resurgence of forms of political organizing that are grounded upon relationships to creation, one another, and future generations."[145]

This does not mean that (re)negotiating and reaffirming treaties does not involve material claims to land. It means that the colonial understanding of land as property is resisted, so that land claims are not based on an acceptance of state law but redeploy understandings of land in Indigenous law. These can include specific forms of property claims. As Goeman writes, "Necessary to decolonization, sovereignty or self-determination is reclaiming land physically and ideologically."[146] It means shifting from a politics of state recognition, or not, of Indigenous appellants, to a politics of nation-to-nation relations, with the understanding that the state has been founded on Native land. Legal scholar John Borrows argues that the right of prior occupancy, as it is understood in Western as well as Indigenous political thought, means that all Indigenous land belongs to First Nations unless it is explicitly given up. If treaties combine the understandings of states and of Indigenous nations, treaties can confer ownership of land to the state—but this grant of land must be conferred by Indigenous nations, as the original inhabitants:

> Treaties are a grant of rights from Indians to the Crown. The Crown is the recipient of land in these arrangements. Land is perpetually vested in the Indians, as first inhabitants, until they give it to other people. The Crown cannot own or govern land in Canada until it receives a grant of such rights from the Indians. Treaties grant the Crown rights to use lands and resources and to set up governing powers. The Crown's rights are limited, because any silence in

---

[143] Starblanket and Stark, "Towards a Relational Paradigm," 180–181.
[144] Goeman, "Land as Life," 73–74.
[145] Starblanket and Stark, "Towards a Relational Paradigm," 176–177.
[146] Goeman, "Land as Life," 77.

treaty agreements should be construed as leaving intact all original Indigenous entitlements.[147]

This interpretation has been supported by Supreme Court rulings in Canada.[148]

Borrows argues that the resistance to state-centric narratives and the shift to nation-to-nation relationships requires a recognition that Indigenous legal traditions have actually been foundational to the development of Canadian law. He advocates a shift toward a multijuridical legal culture, through the recovery of these expansive narratives. This means that in addition to the assertion and recognition of political sovereignties, relational paths to freedom should include the recognition and application of First Nations laws more generally, to settlers.[149]

> I do not believe our legal values should be ghettoized, even as I resist their being universalized. Our ideas about law should be mobilized in practical ways to travel beyond the reserves; they should not be theorized as pure conceptions concerning justice and the good life. Indigenous law should prudently contribute to the formation of finding standards that guide the behaviour of all people on our lands. The point of each innovation is to facilitate non-Indigenous recognition of Indigenous peoples and their political, legal, and cultural participation and representation outside of lands set aside for them within the nation state.[150]

Toward a Coalitional Politics: Addressing Conflicting Imaginaries and Narratives of Freedom

A coalitional politics of decolonization will need to confront and address conflicting imaginaries and narratives of freedom. The politics of sovereignty grounded in claims to political identity and relation to land can put Indigenous critical theory and politics at odds with the ways that freedom is imagined in liberal and left theories and politics, as well as in much of feminist, queer, and postcolonial thought. Progressivist narratives of freedom as a linear future-oriented temporal movement, away from the oppressive roots and constraints of traditions, conflict with spatial conceptions of freedom rooted in traditions of reciprocal gift relations. Spatial imaginings of freedom as diasporic travel conflict with understandings of freedom in relation to grounded normativities.

---

[147] Borrows, "Earth Bound," 63.
[148] Borrows, "Earth Bound," 63.
[149] Borrows, "Indigenous Legal Traditions in Canada," *Washington Journal of Law and Policy* 19 (2006). Cited in *Freedom and Indigenous Constitutionalism*, 45.
[150] Borrows, *Freedom and Indigenous Constitutionalism*, 45–46.

There is a real clash between the narratives of freedom in the liberal and left developmentalist models of history and Indigenous conceptions of freedom in relation to land. As Coulthard and Simpson argue, liberal and left normative assumptions, including the developmentalist ontology that underlies the coloniality of modernity, and the understanding of locatedness as an impediment both to individual freedom and to the formation of larger coalition, produce misrepresentations of Indigenous politics as parochial and particularistic forms of "identity politics" that undermine more egalitarian and universal aspirations. These assumptions underlie the critiques of Indigenous politics in some antiracist and postcolonial views as well.[151]

There is a real clash between postcolonial narratives of freedom in migration and diaspora, in escape from violent and repressive traditions into cosmopolitan hybridities and assemblages, and visions of freedom rooted in claims to traditional knowledge and values of relationality. Queer and feminist politics of freedom involving individual resistance to norms and transgression of tradition clash with understandings of freedom as collective resurgence of traditional values or grounded normativities. Substantive conceptions of freedom in relation with land clash with negative understandings of freedom as critique or subversion, and with models of freedom as an open-ended practice.

Indigenous critical theory challenges narratives that imagine freedom as primarily future-oriented, not rooted in spatial dynamics and cyclical temporalities; as inventive, not rooted in tradition; as escape from past oppressions, not rooted in alternative formations of knowledge and power. Against dichotomies of future-orientation versus backwardness, modernity versus tradition, dynamism versus stasis, diaspora versus fixedness, Indigenous critical theorists invoke "the spirit of relationality and its inherent fluidity, dynamism, and context-dependence."[152] As Starblanket and Stark argue, "By adopting a relational world view, we are better positioned to see the continuity between past, present, and future while also recognizing tradition as dynamic, contingent, and context dependent."[153] The politics of relationality is best understood as rooted in the heterogeneity, diversity, and queerness of a constantly changing animate world.

Conceptions of freedom as groundless capacities for action and progress have justified the economies of dispossession and extraction of resources that we live with today. Our collective survival and flourishing, and our freedom in relations with others and with our world, depends on our capacities of political imagination to consider "the possibilities of relationality as affective and grounded

---

[151] Coulthard and Simpson, "Grounded Normativity/Place-Based Solidarity," 253.
[152] Starblanket and Stark, "Towards a Relational Paradigm," 178.
[153] Starblanket and Stark, "Towards a Relational Paradigm," 196.

alternatives to economies of dispossession and systems of extraction and exploitation."[154] The capacity to see rooted traditions of heterogeneous relationality as exemplary and future-oriented opens, for all of us, an imaginary of freedom that can guide social and political relations among diverse and strange beings in the pluriverse.

---

[154] Byrd et al., "Predatory Value," 11.

5
Indigenous Feminisms and Relational Rights

Indigenous peoples and individuals have the right to belong to an indigenous community or nation, in accordance with the traditions and customs of the community or nation concerned. No discrimination of any kind may arise from the exercise of such a right.
—United Nations Declaration of the Rights of
Indigenous Peoples, Article 9

Heteropatriarchy isn't just about exclusion of certain Indigenous bodies, it is about the destruction of the intimate relationships that make up our nations, and [the destruction of] the fundamental systems of ethics based on values of individual sovereignty and self-determination. The more destruction our intimate relationships carry, the more destruction our political systems carry, and the less we are able to defend and protect our lands, and the easier it is to dispossess.
—Leanne Betasamosake Simpson

Gender must be decolonized and decolonization must be gendered.
—Kiera Ladner

In this chapter, I consider the struggle of Indigenous women against the historic violation of their rights to belong to their communities in Canada, and their rights to participate in Indigenous governance, to argue that Indigenous feminist politics have developed unique formulations of relational rights, rooted in and oriented toward the normative value of relationality. The grounded normative ideal of relationality as a system of reciprocal relations is the motivating force of Indigenous feminist politics of a relational conception of individual and collective rights and freedoms focused on individual and community wellbeing and on resistance to all forms of colonial and heteropatriarchal domination.[1]

[1] While many Indigenous theorists, activists, and organizations embrace the term *feminist*, many do not. I use the term *Indigenous feminist politics* to denote politics and positions that affirm women's rights, equality, inclusion, participation, power, and leadership. I follow the lead of Indigenous

Indigenous women's struggles for inclusion in their communities and for participation in Indigenous governance are struggles for political rights. If political rights are rights to participate in the social and political life of a society, within an understanding of relational freedom, political rights are rights to take responsibility for social and political relations. These rights necessarily entail full rights to protections of individual freedoms.

Indigenous women's struggles for rights to full inclusion in their communities have developed through critique of the discourse of nation and of sovereignty as only the right of noninterference, and through critique of discourses of abstract individual rights and equal gender rights within the colonizing state. Working both with and against these discourses, Indigenous feminist politics have formulated unique understandings of the right to have rights, understood as rights to participate in relations of responsibility for the wellbeing of individuals and communities. These rights are rooted in conceptions of rights to land not as property rights but as rights to responsibility for land. These relational formulations of rights have informed struggles to address multiple forms of violence against Indigenous women and gender-diverse people.

Against the liberal feminist position that individual rights and gender equality rights must supersede Indigenous claims to tradition and to collective self-determination, Indigenous feminists argue that any affirmation of individual rights or women's rights without a critique of state colonization fails to grasp the centrality of racialized gendered colonization in the oppression of Indigenous women.[2] Indigenous feminists affirm the centrality of women's power in Indigenous communities and Indigenous history, and they argue for rights to belong to those communities and to exercise that power in the context of struggles for collective self-determination, resurgence, and decolonization.

Against the Indigenous antifeminist position that individual and gender equality rights undermine collective self-determination, Indigenous feminists argue that this claim denies the history of state-legislated heteropatriarchal dominance and its perpetuation in Indigenous organizations and communities.[3] This ongoing history of the undermining of women's power has violated Indigenous traditions and undermined Indigenous sovereignty. If relationality is the ground for a politics of Indigenous resurgence, the continued violation of relationships

---

feminist theorists and activists who do use the term *feminist*, and I try to avoid using it to refer to individuals who do not.

[2] See, for example, Ervin, Tuck, and Morrill, "Decolonizing Feminism"; Joanne Barker, "Indigenous Feminisms."
[3] See, for example, Joyce Green, ed., *Making Space for Indigenous Women*; Napoleon, "Aboriginal Self Determination"; Barker, "Gender, Sovereignty, and the Discourse of Rights in Native Women's Activism."

between Indigenous women and their communities will continue to thwart Indigenous freedom.

While their positions are opposed, both advocates of women's rights over collective self-determination and critics of women's rights in defense of collective rights of self-determination assume a simple binary opposition between individual and collective rights, assuming that claims to individual rights undermine struggles for collective self-determination.

Similarly, the anti-rights discourses of postcolonial and resurgence critiques assume a binary opposition between rights and decolonial politics. Against arguments that Indigenous feminists who "turn to the state" to claim individual rights are betraying Indigenous sovereignty or resurgence, and that Western rights discourses are necessarily opposed to Indigenous traditions and principles, many Indigenous theorists argue that individual rights and gender equality are in fact central assumptions in Indigenous philosophies.[4] While they recognize the limitations of rights claims, and while no one claims that legal rights—especially in the context of colonization—will end domination, Indigenous feminists have developed hybrid discourses, rejecting the binary of pure traditions. Indigenous feminists seek gender justice in the resurgence of Indigenous law, but they recognize that this involves a *critical* revaluation of Indigenous law. For many, critical resurgence involves a hybrid of traditional and Western law, practices, and solidarities that have long been interwoven. Indigenous feminist theorists and activists have mobilized unique formulations of rights rooted in principles of Indigenous relationality, in struggles for inclusion in Indigenous communities, in struggles against heteropatriarchal violence, and in struggles for Indigenous sovereignty. These formulations have been central to Indigenous resurgence: to the critical revaluation of Indigenous law in struggles for individual and community wellbeing, and for resistance to all forms of domination.

Indigenous feminist and queer theorists argue that because the colonization of land has worked and continues to work *through* the colonization of Indigenous women's bodies, decolonization requires gender justice. And because individual rights and equal rights within a colonizing regime will not secure freedom for Indigenous women and LGBTQ2SL people—or for Indigenous men—gender justice requires decolonization. As Kiera Ladner writes, "colonialism is a gendered enterprise defined by racialized sexual violence perpetuated by the church and state as a means of securing control over a nation and its land—and it is increasingly being perpetuated from within as a result of neo-colonialism, institutionalised sexism and the internalisation of sexual violence." Thus, she

---

[4] See the *Gender Inside Indigenous Law Toolkit* (Indigenous Law Research Unit, Faculty of Law, University of Victoria). For example, Val Napoleon's research indicates that Gitxsan law does include individual and collective human rights. See also Ladner, "Gendering Colonization, Decolonizing Gender."

argues, decolonization must be reframed as a gendered project. "Gender must be decolonized and decolonization must be gendered."[5]

The frame of my analysis is the assumption that practices of freedom must be understood not just in terms of binary agonistic relations of power, but in terms of complex relations of power and solidarity, situated within multiple experiences, discourses, and histories, and oriented toward diverse and shared values, ideals, and futures. Agency is always exercised *in relationship with* all of these constitutive contexts and relations. Agency, then, is always a practice of relations of freedom.[6] Because Indigenous feminist practices of freedom have been rooted in the core value of *relationality*, they have been practices of relational freedom, oriented toward the ideal of reciprocity among diverse beings. This means that they have been grounded in an attunement to the *complexity* of relations among a vast range of strange beings. This attunement to complexity is intrinsic to engagement in relations both local and global, both intimate and cosmic. Indigenous feminist practices of freedom involve engagement in a complexity of agonistic relations with heteropatriarchal and misogynistic institutions and practices, with Indigenous antifeminisms, with the Canadian state, and with non-Indigenous feminisms. They also involve relations of solidarity and coalition with multiple Indigenous, anticolonial, and feminist communities. They involve complex relations with multiple discourses and politics of Indigenous self-determination, antiracist and anticolonial politics, discourses of individual and collective rights and equalities, critiques of discourses of rights and equalities, and philosophies of reciprocity and sovereignty and women's power. They are grounded in histories and experiences of Indigenous women's power, of gendered and racialized colonization, and of physical and structural violence. They are oriented toward ideals of reciprocity in Indigenous philosophy and law. They are hybrid practices of freedom, grounded in and oriented toward multiple traditions and philosophies, understood as dynamic, changing, and interwoven. They are practices of freedom both with and against a multiplicity of forces and relations.

Indigenous feminist activists and theorists have led in reconceiving nationhood and sovereignty in terms of philosophies of relationality, and in relation to the sovereignty of individuals and bodies.[7] They have also led in the formulation of relational rights. While they recognize the limitations and critiques of rights discourses, Indigenous feminists have used the language and legal force of rights strategically and pragmatically in national and international contexts where that language prevails. Yet the recourse to rights has been more than a strategic use of

---

[5] Ladner, "Gendering Colonization, Decolonizing Gender."
[6] See Weir, Identities and Freedom.
[7] See Simpson, *As We Have Always Done*; Barker, ed., *Sovereignty Matters* and *Critically Sovereign*.

the master's tools. Indigenous feminist theorists and activists have reformulated the language of rights. Their reformulations of rights as relational rights have been essential to shifting the central discourses in movements for sovereignty and resurgence.

This chapter begins with a brief history of the gendered politics of settler colonization in Canada, and of the political conflicts between male-dominated Indigenous organizations and Indigenous feminist politics of rights to belong. The chapter then addresses critiques and dilemmas of rights discourses, and considers Indigenous feminist politics of rights to belong as rights to have rights. The remainder of the chapter situates Indigenous feminist rights politics in the politics of decolonization, to develop the argument that Indigenous feminist rights politics have formulated unique conceptions of relational rights.

The Gendered Politics of Settler Colonization in Canada: Breaking Relations

> In Canada a history of gender discrimination in the Indian Act has created an ongoing conflict within Native organizations and reserve communities around notions of individual and collective rights, organized along the lines of gender. It is crucially important, then, to understand the central role that the subordination of Native women has played in the colonization process, in order to begin to see the violation of Native women's rights through loss of Indian status, not as the problems faced by individuals, but as a *collective* sovereignty issue.
>
> —Bonita Lawrence[8]

Settler colonization has historically worked through heteropatriarchal and racist systems of governance, to manage populations deemed primitive and deviant, to secure land as property. In Canada, the "Indian problem" has historically been managed through governance practices that divide populations by racialized identities and by gender. The systematic disempowerment of Indigenous women has been central to the strategy of erosion of Indigenous relations to land and the weakening of capacities for resistance to colonial power. These policies, then, have worked to undermine Indigenous power, in order to expropriate Indigenous land and resources. Societies organized around matrilineality and kin relations, in which women's power was central and diverse genders were included, were systematically undermined by colonization.

---

[8] Lawrence, *"Real" Indians and Others*, 46.

In early treaties the British chose to negotiate only with men, thereby undercutting the stabilizing presence of older women and their traditional authority in major decisions concerning the land. As Bonita Lawrence writes, "To bypass older women in traditional societies effectively removed from the treaty process the people centrally responsible for regulating land access." Clans led by women held the collective land base for all of the nations of the Iroquois confederacy. Removing women, then, was key to privatizing the land base. Thus, "a central aspect of the colonization process in Canada would be to break the power of Indigenous women within their nations."[9] And this would in turn break Indigenous relations to land, facilitating state appropriation of land as property. Thus, "the subordination of Indigenous women has been a central nexus through which colonizers have sought to destroy Indigenous societies."[10] The exclusion of women, then, has been central to the violation of Indigenous laws of relationality, and to the violation of the relations of Indigenous people with the land.

Government policies have worked systematically to undermine women's power and to attempt to break relations between women and men. Legislation in 1869 officially replaced long-standing Indigenous governance with a system of band councils with minimal powers, reporting directly to the superintendent of Indian Affairs, and the 1876 Indian Act restricted leadership and participation in the band councils, and ownership of land and property, to men, officially stripping women of their customary powers of responsibility for land and water, as negotiators and participants in governance. The Indian Act legislated categories of identity and status, dividing populations among those with Indian status and those without. Métis, or "mixed-bloods," are among the populations that have been excluded from status. But as Lawrence points out, the understanding of who is "mixed-blood" and who is not, who is Indian and who is not, is very much shaped by heteropatriarchal gender norms. According to the Act, women who "married out" lost their status as Indians, while men who "married out" retained their status, which was also conferred on their wives. Thus the Indian Act, the body of law that has regulated Indigenous identity and existence for over a century, and which continues to do so, has explicitly enforced male dominance, and the exclusion and disempowerment of women. Indigenous organizations and band councils remain largely male-dominated—like most other Canadian political institutions.

The identities legislated in the Indian Act are effects of colonizer state governance, and these legislated identities have worked in part through the co-optation of male leaders of Indigenous organizations to enforce what Foucault called

---

[9] Lawrence, *"Real" Indians and Others*, 47; citing Jamieson, *Indian Women and the Law in Canada*, 13.
[10] Lawrence, *"Real" Indians and Others*, 62.

dividing practices: dividing not only settlers from Indians but status Indians from nonstatus Indigenous and "mixed-bloods", Indigenous men from Indigenous women. The breaking of relations between men and women, nonstatus and status Indians, has been and continues to be a *sovereignty* issue. The dividing practices have worked to break Indigenous systems of law that are organized around systems of relationality: relations with each other and with land. The strategy of breaking relations has worked to perpetuate heteropatriarchal dominance within Indigenous organizations and band councils, which have resisted women's attempts to battle the provisions of the Indian Act, to be included in their own communities.[11]

Indigenous women have long contested this dominance. Evicted from their communities upon marriage to nonstatus men, denied housing and benefits on reserves even after divorce or the death of their husbands, denied ownership of marital property, and failing in their appeals to band council leaders, Indigenous women began in the 1970s to engage with Canadian and international justice systems to challenge their exclusion from status according to the Indian Act. In 1973, the Supreme Court of Canada ruled against the claims of Jeanette Corbière Lavell and Yvonne Bédard that their rights to status and to live in their communities violated the equality provisions in the Canadian Bill of Rights. The Court ruled that the status provisions in the Indian Act were exempt from the Canadian Bill of Rights.[12] Following this decision, Indigenous women's organizations turned to the United Nations. Sandra Lovelace, a Maliseet woman whose attempt to return to the Tobique reserve had been rejected by the band council, took her claim to the United Nations Human Rights Committee, which in 1981 ruled that because the Indian Act denied equal treatment of women under the law, denying Lovelace the right to live in her community, Canada violated the International Covenant on Civil and Political Rights.[13] Embarrassed by the public humiliation, the Canadian government amended the Indian Act in 1985 to implement gender-neutral status provisions and to allow women who had been excluded to reapply for status, along with their children. However, the amendment instituted new discriminatory status rules, distinguishing between

---

[11] The question as to whether male dominance existed prior to colonization is controversial. Many scholars argue that many Indigenous communities were relatively egalitarian, balancing powers through complementary gender roles along with some allowance for gender fluidity, within matrifocal and matrilineal kinship systems. It should also be acknowledged that a good deal of violence, including male violence against women, predates contact.

[12] Lavell v. Canada 1971; Bédard v. Isaac 1972. Jeannette Corbiere Lavell (Anishinaabe from Wikwemikong) was a founding member of Indian Rights for Indian Women and is former president of the NWAC. Lavell and Bédard (Onondaga, Six Nations) have been recognized, along with Sharon McIvor, Senator Sandra Lovelace, Senator Lynn Gehl, and Dr. Lillian Dyck, as the Indigenous Famous Six, by the Feminist Alliance for International Action.

[13] In 2005, Sandra Lovelace Nicholas (Maliseet) became the first Indigenous woman to be appointed to the Canadian Senate.

levels of status, and cutting off status after two generations of intermarriage. Successive challenges, including another UN ruling won by Sharon McIvor, have finally resulted in the implementation, in 2019, of equal gender rights to status, including recognition of matrilineal lineage back to 1876, under the legal provisions of the Indian Act.[14]

The struggles of Indigenous women for rights to belong to their communities have met with virulent opposition by many male-dominated bands and organizations. Indigenous women's pursuit of equal rights has been framed as the attempt to import Western individual rights, which are fundamentally opposed to collective sovereignty rights, and the attempt to impose Western feminism on traditional cultures. Demonized for espousing an ideology of rights based on selfish individualism and feminism, Indigenous women seeking status and the activist organizations supporting them, in particular Indian Rights for Indian Women and the Native Women's Association of Canada (NWAC), have been attacked and harassed, branded as inauthentic and anti-Indian, and blamed for undermining the "sacred right" of Indigenous sovereignty.

As Joanne Barker points out, the conflict between Indigenous women and the patriarchal Indigenous organizations was played out as a conflict between competing discourses of rights. While Indian women mobilized a specific discourse of rights from the intersections of human and civil rights, feminism, and Native sovereignty politics, the male-dominated Indigenous organizations and band councils drew on international law to defend a discourse of collective rights to sovereignty. The leaders of the band councils and the primary Indigenous organization, the National Indian Brotherhood (which later changed its name to the Assembly of First Nations [AFN]), defended a conception of self-government defined solely as *noninterference* by the Canadian government. Barker writes that this interpretation was initially successful in influencing both the Canadian government and the Supreme Court, which in its 1973 ruling against Lavell and Bédard, accepted the understanding of Indigenous self-government as noninterference, and hence as exempt from individual rights and gender equality rights applicable to Canadian citizens.[15]

The understanding of Indigenous sovereignty as noninterference was developed by the National Indian Brotherhood (NIB) in response to the Canadian government's proposal, in 1969, to abolish the Indian Act: the "White Paper" proposed to abolish discriminatory legislation by terminating all treaties and by abolishing Indian status, which would be replaced with the status of free and equal citizens. This proposal, which ignored consultations with Indigenous

---

[14] Sharon Donna McIvor (Lower Nicola Band), a lawyer and academic, has been a leading Indigenous feminist activist for several decades.

[15] Barker, "Gender, Sovereignty, and the Discourse of Rights in Native Women's Activism."

leaders, was rejected by them, for obvious reasons. The paper was quickly withdrawn in the face of Indigenous protests and public support. In response, the NIB's defense of sovereignty as noninterference was expressed as a defense of the Indian Act, with the demand for the right to self-determination under the provisions of the Indian Act. But, of course, this formulation was self-contradictory: given that the Indian Act was the Canadian government's policy of "interference" in the form of colonization, the defense of the Indian Act was a defense of colonization. And the understanding of sovereignty as noninterference was taken directly from the Westphalian system of state sovereignty—the system that legitimized colonization.

Indigenous Women's Rights and Collective Rights: Constitutional Struggles

> Because the subordination of Indigenous women has been a central nexus through which colonizers have sought to destroy Indigenous societies, contemporary gender divisions created by the colonizer continue to subvert sovereignty struggles in crucial ways. And yet, almost inevitably, when issues of particular concern to Native women arise, they are framed as "individual rights," while in many cases, those who opposed Native women's rights are held to represent "the collective."
>
> —Bonita Lawrence[16]

A significant example of the contesting claims between Indigenous women and the male-dominated Indigenous organizations and band councils was the political challenge of the NWAC to the constitutional negotiations in the 1980s. Following the recognition of "existing aboriginal and treaty rights" under Section 35 of the Constitution Act in 1982, several Indigenous organizations participated in negotiations with the Canadian government, to define the scope of these rights. The NWAC appealed for and was denied a seat at the negotiation table. The AFN initially resisted an amendment to ensure that Aboriginal rights would apply equally to male and female persons, but ultimately accepted the amendment on the condition that the issue of citizenship—that is, the issue of the rights of excluded women and their children to citizenship—be left for further discussions. During the negotiations, which went on for a decade, the AFN and many other Aboriginal leaders argued for rights to self-government that would not be subject to the Charter of Rights and Freedoms. Against this

---

[16] Lawrence, "Real" Indians and Others, 62.

position, and from a position of continued exclusion from the negotiations, the NWAC argued that Aboriginal self-government should be subject to the provisions of the Charter of Rights and Freedoms. This position was taken in response to the continued open resistance of many First Nations band councils to women's rights to citizenship, and the refusal of leaders to address the violence and abuse within Indigenous communities.

While the NWAC has always supported the right to Aboriginal self-government, they argued that the Indian Act had structured status, band membership, and governance according to patriarchal laws, such that Indigenous governance and representation were overwhelmingly controlled by men. Indigenous organizations and bands too often support and continue the sexism of the Indian Act and the violence of patriarchal colonization. Thus they argued that until institutions of Aboriginal self-government recognize the individual rights and equality rights of women, those institutions should be subject to the rights and freedoms guaranteed by the Charter, to ensure that women would have equal rights with men within Aboriginal communities, including rights to status and to live on reserve; participation in Indigenous governance; freedoms of expression, assembly, and dissent; and protection from violence and abuse by the state and by men within and outside of their own communities.[17]

The NWAC challenge was, once again, framed as an assertion of women's individual rights against collective rights. That interpretation has been supported with reference to a statement made by the NWAC: "We recognize that there is a clash between collective rights of sovereign First Nations governments and individual rights of women. Stripped of equality by patriarchal laws which created 'male privilege' as the norm on reserve lands, First Nations women have had a tremendous struggle to regain their social position. We want the Canadian Charter of Rights and Freedoms to apply to Aboriginal governments."[18] Against the assumption that the NWAC is claiming a fundamental clash between collective and individual rights, this statement calls attention to the exclusion of the individual rights of women in the understanding of collective rights espoused by male-dominated First Nations governments.[19]

In fact, the NWAC has always supported Indigenous self-determination, but it has asserted the importance of individual rights as protection from patriarchal oppression masked as collective rights. The passage opposing individual

---

[17] Native Women's Association of Canada, Aboriginal Women, 7–8.
[18] Native Women's Association of Canada, Aboriginal Women, 18.
[19] Glen Coulthard misquotes this statement, rendering it as: "We recognize that there is a clash between collective rights of sovereign First Nations and individual rights of women" (Coulthard, *Red Skin, White Masks*, 91). This makes the claim of individual versus collective rights appear to be quite stark. With the phrase "the collective rights of sovereign First Nations governments," the NWAC is specifying the patriarchal leadership of First Nations organizations.

and collective rights is taken from "Aboriginal Women, Self Government and The Canadian Charter of Rights and Freedoms," a document that opens with an affirmation of the inherent right of Aboriginal peoples to self-government. It argues that Aboriginal governments should establish an Aboriginal Code of Human Rights, to address the gender injustices instituted by the Indian Act and perpetuated by many male-dominated Aboriginal band councils and organizations, and to ensure that Aboriginal governance will uphold the rights and freedoms of dissent. Given the consistent refusal of the dominant First Nations organizations to include and advocate for Indigenous women, the NWAC recommends: "That the Canadian Charter of Rights and Freedoms apply to all Aboriginal governments *once the right to self-government is recognized and affirmed as part of the Canadian constitution until such time as there is developed and constitutionally entrenched and Aboriginal Code of Human Rights."*[20] The NWAC drafted and published *An Aboriginal Charter of Rights and Freedoms* one year later.[21] The NWAC appeals to First Nations organizations to affirm that they will apply the provisions in the Charter of Rights and Freedoms, arguing that "the application of the Charter should not be left to Governments. The federal government has mistreated us as women for 100 years. We want our nations to act within the spirit and intent of the United Nations."[22]

The NWAC has been criticized for engaging with the state rather than with the male leaders of Indigenous organizations. The suggestion that the NWAC was wrong to engage with the state is ironic, given the context in which the NWAC action was taken: the AFN and other Indigenous organizations were engaged in constitutional negotiations *with the state*. As Sharon McIvor points out, in appealing to the courts for the right to sit at the constitutional negotiations table, the NWAC followed the precedent of the Métis National Council and the government of the Northwest Territories, both of whom had appealed to the courts for the same right.[23] And as the NWAC pointed out: "When a Band Council acts,

---

[20] Native Women's Association of Canada, *Aboriginal Women*, 19.

[21] Native Women's Association of Canada, *An Aboriginal Charter of Rights and Freedoms*.

[22] Native Women's Association of Canada, *Aboriginal Women*, 18. The NWAC's position aligns with the conjoining of Aboriginal rights and women's rights in the Declaration of Indigenous Women at the Beijing World Conference on Women in 1995:

> We, the women of the original peoples of the world have struggled actively to defend our rights to self-determination and to our territories which have been invaded and colonized by powerful nations and interests. [We demand] . . . That Indigenous customary laws and justice systems which are supportive of women victims of violence be recognized and reinforced. That Indigenous laws, customs, and traditions which are discriminatory to women be eradicated. . . . That all internally displaced Indigenous peoples be allowed to return to their own communities and the necessary rehabilitation and support services be provided to them. (quoted by Green, Making Space for Indigenous Feminism, 144)

[23] McIvor, "Aboriginal Women Unmasked," 127.

it acts under the authority of federal law, namely the Indian Act. When the Band Council passes a Band Council Resolution, that is a federal law."[24]

Indigenous women are not under any illusion that the state is a neutral body that ensures equality for women; like the male-dominated Indigenous organizations, they are using the limited freedoms that they have within the state to advocate for their rights. If the language of rights is understood to be a Western imposition, it should be recalled that the Assembly of First Nations also invoked the language of rights to make its claims, against Indigenous women: "As Indian people we cannot afford to have individual rights override collective rights."[25]

While the NWAC and other Indigenous women have used the language of individual rights to make their cases, and while it is true that they themselves have sometimes articulated the conflict as a struggle between individual and collective rights, their arguments for inclusion in Indigenous organizations and communities are arguments for Indigenous women's collective rights. They are arguing for the collective right to be included in their communities, and to participate in Indigenous struggles for self-determination, and they have argued for the collective right to participate in negotiations with the state. As the NWAC points out: "Our women want to live within their communities. . . . We have been shut out from our communities because they do not wish to bear the costs of programs and services to which we are entitled as Indians. We are telling you that this situation will not change without our involvement in self-government and in the constitutional discussions. Our men could take the initiative and give us a place at the table. Have they done that? No they have not."[26] The NWAC argues that the enforced separation from their communities, cultures, languages, and people is a denial of fundamental rights. Moreover, the 1985 amendment to the Indian Act, Bill C-31, did not provide substantive equality. "It did not restore us to our former position. It did not give us access to our communities. It did not give us access to land and housing. It did not give us access to programs and services to which we are entitled as Aboriginal peoples. It did not give us access to our culture and languages."[27] In other words, to frame this as a struggle for individual rights in opposition to collective rights clearly misses the point. The NWAC's struggle is for the "fundamental rights" to live in and belong to their communities, to live as Aboriginal peoples with access to their culture and languages, and to participate fully in Indigenous self-governance.

---

[24] Native Women's Association of Canada, *Aboriginal Women*, 18.
[25] Assembly of First Nations, quoted by Coulthard, *Red Skin, White Masks*, 92.
[26] Native Women's Association of Canada, *Aboriginal Women*, 16.
[27] Native Women's Association of Canada, *Aboriginal Women*, 16.

Resurgence versus Rights?

In her analysis of the constitutional debates, Joanne Fiske argues that respectful conversation between men and women was short-circuited by rights arguments.[28] Dian Million argues that the conversations between women and men were "forced into dominant Canadian legal rights discourses." Because of the adversarial nature of Western law, the NWAC had been "forced immediately into the position of defending their 'right' to be at the constitutional talks." For their part, "Male leaders caught in the political games that were Canada's patriation talks consented to the women's exclusion and subordination at the negotiation table."[29] This echoes the statement made by a National Indian Brotherhood/Assembly of First Nations delegate quoted by Joanne Barker: "We would like to make it clear that we agree with the women who spoke so forcefully this morning that they have been treated unjustly. The discrimination they suffered was forced upon us through a system imposed by white colonial government through the Indian Act.... The NIB maintains that 'equality' does already exist within the traditional 'citizenship code' of all First Nations people."[30]

But to claim that the women of the NWAC were "forced" to use the discourse of rights is to discount the agency of those women. Like all people, they were "coerced" to use the languages and participate in the practices of their hybrid societies. To claim that they were forced to use the discourse of rights is to claim that that use was inauthentic, that they were not real Indians, and were misguided by engaging with Western discourses. Similarly, the claim that the men were forced to resist women's equal rights discounts their agency, rendering them passive victims of the colonial system. The reality is that neither the NWAC nor the AFN could draw on pure traditions, in a realm walled off from the rest of the world. Both sides were drawing on the hybrid mixture of cultures, traditions, and systems that have shaped discourses of individual and collective rights. Both the rights claims made by Indigenous feminists and the collective rights discourses used by Indigenous advocates of self-determination are hybrid discourses. Both draw on Indigenous and European/Western discourses, not only to make their claims to the state but to understand their own struggles and identities.[31]

In his analysis of the conflict, Glen Coulthard accepts the framing of the claims of Indigenous women in terms of a destructive opposition between individual and collective rights. Coulthard concludes that while the "concerns" expressed

---

[28] Fiske, "The Womb Is to the Nation as the Heart Is to the Body." Fiske notes, however, that the conflicts between Indigenous women and male leaders long preceded the constitutional negotiations and the use of rights discourses.
[29] Million, *Therapeutic Nations*, 129.
[30] Barker, "Gender, Sovereignty, and the Discourse of Rights in Native Women's Activism," 144.
[31] As Audra Simpson points out in *Mohawk Interruptus*, claims of rights are made continually on all sides in conflicts over identity and belonging on the Kanehsatà:ke reserve.

by the NWAC were "not without merit," "the result, unfortunately, has been a zero-sum contest pitting the individual human right of Indigenous women to sex equality against the collective human right of Indigenous peoples to self-determination."[32] Coulthard praises Patricia Monture's critique of the NWAC's appeal to the Canadian Charter of Rights and Freedoms to protect women's rights, on the grounds that the colonial state is a manifestation of male power, and hence Indigenous feminist appeals to the state as a site of emancipation are misguided. Quoting Monture, he writes: "The Canadian state is the invisible male perpetrator who unlike Aboriginal men does *not* have a victim face."[33] But this claim loses the complexity of Indigenous feminist critiques of the patriarchal nature of settler colonization, which clearly target the patriarchal colonial state as the source of contemporary gender struggles, but which also address the willingness of male-dominated Indigenous organizations and band councils to avail themselves of the (limited) privileges and authority conferred by that state, and to take up violent forms of masculinity deployed and disavowed by the state.

The frame of the zero-sum game assumes that the conflict between Indigenous women's rights and Indigenous patriarchal collective rights is the inevitable result of the politics of rights: both sides have focused their struggles on misguided appeals for state recognition of Western legal rights. Coulthard argues for a redirection of energies from endless political battles for state recognition toward assertions and practices of individual and collective self-recognition and self-determination: toward a politics of resurgence. Addressing conflicts will require that Indigenous people work together to retrieve and critically revalue Indigenous philosophy, practices, and law. This argument for a shift to a politics of resurgence is important. But the reduction of the conflict to a zero-sum game between two sides forced to use the discourses of Western legal rights obscures the differences between the two sides of the struggle. While male-dominated organizations and bands have been oriented to rights of autonomy and control over their own affairs, in a politics of noninterference modeled on state rights, feminist theorists have pointed out that the right to noninterference has historically protected patriarchal rights over women, children, and household chattel, including servants and slaves, in the private sphere of the household. Just as the principle of noninterference has protected the right of the patriarch to ownership of the household and its members as property, the same principle applied to states protects the right of the state to control its own citizens. In line with this history, male-dominated Indigenous organizations and bands have too often argued for their collective rights *over* women and children in their communities. They have defended their arguments with claims to traditional gender roles and authentic

---

[32] Coulthard, *Red Skin, White Masks*, 91.
[33] Coulthard, *Red Skin, White Masks*, 101. Quoting Monture, *Thunder in My Soul*, 175.

Indigenous traditions. Against this understanding of state-like rights to noninterference, the NWAC and Indigenous feminists have used the language of rights to argue for the inclusion of excluded women and their children in Indigenous communities and polities. Against the understanding of Indigenous polities as autonomous states with rights to noninterference, Indigenous feminists conceive of Indigenous nations in terms of relationality. They point out that Indigenous women cannot participate in resurgence if they are excluded from their communities. And the resurgence of communities depends on addressing the heteropatriarchal violence that, along with the violence of colonization, tears them apart.

The discourse of resurgence in opposition to Indigenous women's rights is, then, a false binary. Indigenous feminist politics have been more complicated. Struggles for Indigenous women's rights to inclusion and freedom from violence have been integral to the politics of resurgence. They are struggles for relations of reciprocity and democratic participation, rooted in the grounded normativity of relationality, and oriented to the substantive wellbeing of individuals and communities in relations with land. Indigenous women have been at the forefront of resurgence politics, leading grassroots activism and engaging in daily practices of care and responsibility for communities and land. These practices and politics of grounded normativity have been the foundation of struggles for rights to inclusion and to freedom from violence. And the assertions of these rights have been central to the argument that the retrieval and revaluation of Indigenous philosophy, practices, and law must be a *critical* practice. Indigenous feminists argue that without the full inclusion, safety, and freedom of women and 2SLGBTQQISA people, there is no resurgence.

Dilemmas of Rights

Indigenous feminists recognize that legal rights within the frame of the Indian Act will not in themselves solve the problems of women's exclusion from status, or the violence and poverty that are the effects of patriarchal colonization. Women seeking status under the law are still often treated as outsiders demanding rights and are often blamed for the fact that men are now equally subject to restrictive status rules. The 1985 amendment, Bill C-31, included the provision that bands have the right to establish their own status rules; in some cases this has resulted in new grounds for exclusion. Often, women's claims for gender justice are rejected by band councils, who still argue that such claims invoke Western rights against Indigenous tradition and Indigenous sovereignty.

As the Report on Missing and Murdered Indigenous Women and Girls (MMIWG) notes, 34 percent of First Nations women and girls live in poverty.

Fifty percent of status First Nations children live in poverty. (In Saskatchewan and Manitoba that number rises to over 60 percent.) Indigenous women and girls are five times more likely than any other population to experience violence, including both intimate partner violence and racist violence. Indigenous women make up 16 percent of female homicide victims. (Only 4 percent of the population of Canada is Indigenous.) In the face of all this, the proportion of Indigenous women who are incarcerated has been rising: currently over 44 percent of women in federal prisons are Indigenous. This rate surpasses the incarceration rate of Indigenous men. Women are often incarcerated for fighting back against violence.[34] These grim statistics are the effects of a long history of the gendered and racialized genocidal regime of heteropatriarchal colonization, of the carceral state, of the extraction of children, of the destruction of Indigenous communities and relations to land. And they are the effects of women's exclusion from status, from rights to live in communities, to access housing and benefits, to share in matrimonial property, and to participate in governance. The NWAC argues that violence against Indigenous women includes the structural violence of exclusion from their communities, and marginalization within communities.[35]

Criminalizing violence against women will not solve these problems: many argue that feminist successes in criminalizing violence against women have only increased surveillance, policing, and incarceration.[36] However, "restorative justice" programs have often tended to protect the perpetrator more than the victim.[37] As the MMIWG report argues, addressing the violence suffered by Indigenous women and children, including the structural violence of exclusion from Indigenous communities, requires addressing the legacies of patriarchal colonization. This is a complicated process involving multiple strategies, including socioeconomic support from the state, the development of individual and community wellness programs, the full involvement of Indigenous leaders and Indigenous men working together with Indigenous women and 2SLGBTQQIA people to address heteropatriarchal violence, and the development of Indigenous nationhood to replace the Indian Act with critically revalued Indigenous laws in diverse communities. In response to Indigenous feminist struggles for rights, and despite ongoing tensions, the Assembly of First Nations has instituted a Women's Council, which has increasingly worked together with the NWAC to advocate for Indigenous women and girls and 2SLGBTQQIA

---

[34] See Palmater, "Indigenous Women Warriors are the Heart of Indigenous Resistance," in *Warrior Life*.
[35] Kuokkanen, *Restructuring Relations*, 179.
[36] Million, *Therapeutic Nations*, 39.
[37] See Deer, "Decolonizing Rape Law"; Cameron, "Sentencing Circles and Intimate Violence." Val Napoleon, Angela Cameron, Colette Arcand, and Dahti Scott warn against the conflation of Indigenous law and restorative justice in "Where Is the Law in Restorative Justice?" in *Aboriginal Self-Government in Canada*, ed. Yale D. Belanger (Saskatoon: Purich, 2008).

people. The AFN and NWAC signed a Statement of Partnership in 2011, and they have joined to criticize state failures to consult and to accommodate the views of First Nations and Aboriginal peoples, and to criticize the imposition of legislative solutions. Such legislation, they have argued, often attempts to pit the individual rights of Indigenous women against the sovereignty rights of Indigenous people. Both argue that the Canadian government must address the legacy of violence against women and girls in part by providing the resources to Indigenous nations to address the root causes of violence.[38]

Many Indigenous feminists are critical of rights discourses. Yet many argue that, at least in the short term, given the dominance of rights discourses worldwide, struggles for legal rights are practically necessary, as part of a broad range of strategies for social, economic, and political change. Legal rights structure relations among individuals and between individuals and the state, and structure the relations of Indigenous peoples with and among states. They also structure relations of Indigenous people within Indigenous organizations that have been established through state law. The belief that Indigenous communities can achieve justice by escaping the interference of the state and returning to pure Indigenous traditions relies, as Rauna Kuokkanen argues, on a simplistic binary of state versus nonstate, colonizer versus colonized. This binary reifies the patriarchal Indigenous discourse of noninterference and blames Indigenous women for appealing to the state. In fact, the power of the state has worked through male dominance within Indigenous communities. The power of the state is everywhere within Indigenous communities, in the laws and structure of the Indian Act, in the neoliberal governance of relations among Indigenous people and in relations between Indigenous people and the state, and in internalized ideologies of heteropatriarchal capitalist colonization. Kuokkanen argues that rather than refusing engagement with the state, Indigenous organizations need to hold the state accountable while seeking to transform the conditions in Indigenous communities.[39] This view does not assume the inevitability of the state. It does recognize that Indigenous peoples are currently governed by state laws, and that even if Indigenous nations achieve autonomy, with full implementation of Indigenous legal systems, they will still need to engage with the Canadian state and other states and with international law.

Indigenous feminist critiques of rights can be situated within a history of feminist and anticolonial critiques of Western rights discourses. Liberal feminist theorists have criticized the patriarchal history of legal rights, and feminist critical theorists, including critical race theorists, critical legal theorists, and

---

[38] It should be noted that the exclusion of the NWAC from policy meetings between the Canadian government and Indigenous organizations has continued. See Green, *Making Space for Indigenous Women*, 148.

[39] Kuokkanen, *Restructuring Relations*, 205.

postcolonial theorists, have long criticized the focus on legal rights and state recognition, the individualism of rights discourses, and the abstraction of the equal rights of a universalized category of "women" with "men."[40] But while the critique of rights is important, it should not diminish the importance of Indigenous feminist struggles for rights. Indigenous feminist rights claims are misrecognized as misguided struggles for abstract Western rights. This misperception fails to recognize the significance of Indigenous feminist reformulations of rights as *Indigenous* rights: as rights grounded in Indigenous laws of reciprocity in the context of relationality. Indigenous feminist struggles for rights have been at the forefront of struggles for decolonization.

The Right to Have Rights: Indigenous Feminist Claims for Relational Rights

As Hannah Arendt argued, human beings have individual rights only in the context of a political community. For Arendt, to be human is to exercise the freedom of action, speech, and judgment, as a political being, in political community with others. As Arendt pointed out, the central claim made in the Universal Declaration of Human Rights—that human beings have inalienable and universal rights as individuals—obscures the fact that, since the Peace Treaties of 1919 and 1920, humans have these rights only as citizens of states. As citizens of no state, displaced peoples effectively have no rights. This is the situation of those whose rights to citizenship are not recognized by colonizing states, of those expelled from nation states that define their membership in terms of ethnic homogeneity, of those displaced by war, persecution, and destitution, and of exiled migrants forced to seek asylum in other states where they are placed in internment camps or criminalized as illegal aliens. Arendt argued, then, for the importance of the *right to have rights*: the right to membership in a political community. If the right to have rights is the right to citizenship, politics involves negotiating the boundaries of political community. Arendt recognized that it was the establishment of the nation state in an international community of states that produced the condition of rightlessness. "Before this," she writes, "what we

---

[40] Feminist critiques of Western rights discourses and of the conception of the individual assumed in these discourses have been central to feminist theory since the 1970s: see, for example, early work by Alison Jaggar, Susan Moller Okin, Lorraine Code, Genevieve Lloyd, and Wendy Brown. While some of these theorists affirm reformulated conceptions of women's rights, others are critical of the use of rights discourses for feminism. For critiques of the universalized category of women as the basis for rights claims, see, for example, Patricia Hill Collins, Kimberlé Crenshaw, and Judith Butler. For feminist critiques of the efficacy of feminist rights claims and of the reliance on engagement with the state see, for example, Nividita Menon, Ratna Kapur, Inderpal Grewal, Wendy Brown, Janet Halley, and Kiran Grewal.

must call a 'human right' today would have been thought of as a general characteristic of the human condition which no tyrant could take away."[41] If the human being is, as Aristotle argued, essentially a political being, one who by definition is a member of a political community, expulsion from the modern political community of the state becomes an expulsion from humanity. In fact, of course, the stateless may still participate in political communities, but they lack rights and recognition as citizens because those communities lack rights and recognition as states.

The challenge to the exclusion of Indigenous women from status and band membership has been a long struggle for the right to have rights: the right to be included as citizens in their political communities. At the same time, the challenge to women's exclusion from citizenship has been a challenge to the dependence of individual rights on the state, or on a state-like political entity characterized by sovereignty as the right of noninterference. Defying the opposition between political citizen and nonpolitical human, Indigenous women have insisted that nationhood is a function of individual and community wellbeing in relationship, not sovereign protection from outside interference.[42] Citizenship, then, is a relationship among individuals in social and political community. Individual and collective rights are located within a context of social and political relationships grounded in and oriented toward the support of individual and collective wellbeing. The violation of those rights is a violation of social and political relationships of reciprocity.

It can be argued that the exclusion of Indigenous women from their communities is not a case of the right to have rights: Indigenous women are not rightless because they have rights as Canadian citizens. This has in fact been argued. In the case of Jeanette Corbiere Lavell, the original decision in county court argued that in being exiled from her community Lavell had not been deprived of equality under the law, because the Canadian Bill of Rights afforded her the same protections provided to other nonstatus women in Canada. In other words, Indigenous women did not need rights as citizens of Indian nations because they had individual rights as citizens of Canada. This argument assumes that for Indigenous women the right to have rights is satisfied by their Canadian citizenship. But that, of course, is the challenge of arguments for Indigenous nationhood and for decolonization: that individual rights within a colonizing state amount to the right to be colonized. If citizenship is defined as a relationship among individuals in political community, and rights are defined in terms

---

[41] Arendt, *The Origins of Totalitarianism*, 297.
[42] Jacques Rancière's critique of the opposition between political society and "bare life" is long predated by critiques of the public/private split in feminist political theory.

of relations of reciprocity within that community, the offer of rights within the colonizing settler state does not fulfil the right to have rights.

The rights claims made by the NWAC and Indigenous women excluded from their communities have not been arguments for abstract individual rights. These claims have formulated a unique discourse of rights, and of the right to have rights, in the context of Indigenous relationality. Indigenous women have drawn on the available language of rights to formulate a discourse and politics of *inclusion* and *belonging*. The language of rights has allowed them to engage with the state and the Indian Act, and with band councils established by the state, to challenge the conditions of their exclusion, but that language is grounded in the language and assumption of Indigenous laws of relationality. They have formulated, then, a hybrid discourse of rights and of relationality. They have argued for the rights to inclusion and belonging in Indigenous communities from which they have been expelled, to participate in Indigenous communities and Indigenous governance, and in Indigenous struggles for self-determination. They struggle to be "restored to their former position," invoking traditions of matrilineal descent and women's power, and their responsibilities for traditions of relationality, in particular in relations to land and water. They argue for the realization of Indigenous principles of reciprocity.

As Patricia Monture-Angus argues, Aboriginal peoples are really struggling for the "right to be responsible" for land. "I do not know of anywhere else in history where a group of people have had to fight so hard just to be responsible."[43] Indigenous women have been struggling for the right to be responsible within Indigenous communities and organizations: to be responsible for land, broadly construed, as a system of relations among diverse beings. They insist that that system of relations must include women and girls and 2SLGBTQQISA people.

Situating Indigenous Feminist Struggles for Rights in the Politics of Decolonization: Relational Rights

Indigenous feminist theory and politics involve complex negotiations between discourses of individual and collective rights, between discourses of women's rights and discourses of tradition, and between politics of rights and politics of resurgence. Indigenous feminist struggles for rights can be situated within the politics of decolonization with an understanding of rights as relations, and of struggles for rights as struggles to restructure relations. First, rights structure relations, and relations of colonization are structured through rights. Second, in this context, and in the context of international relations more generally,

---

[43] Monture-Angus, Journeying Forward, 36.

the *denial* of rights has substantive effects on Indigenous women and children, and Indigenous peoples. Third, Indigenous feminist struggles for rights are struggles to restructure relations. Fourth, against the claim that Indigenous feminist struggles for rights are opposed to Indigenous collective rights, Indigenous feminists argue that individual rights and women's rights are essential to collective self-determination. Fifth, against the liberal feminist argument that individual rights and women's equality rights must supersede collective rights, on the grounds that nonliberal traditions and collective identities are necessarily patriarchal and oppressive, Indigenous feminist struggles for rights are grounded in Indigenous traditions, in a critique of the colonizing state and a politics of decolonization. Sixth, against the assumption that rights claims and resurgence are opposed, Indigenous feminist rights claims have been central to the politics of resurgence. Finally, Indigenous feminist struggles for rights have generated unique formulations of relational rights, rooted in and oriented toward principles of relationality. I develop these claims as a series of propositions.

Rights Structure Relations, and Rights Structure Relations of Colonization

Colonization is a relationship.[44] And relations of colonization are structured in part by systems of rights. As Jennifer Nedelsky argues, rights structure relations.[45] My right to own my house in Toronto is dependent on a long history of colonization. My right to my property is dependent on a system of rights of ownership of colonized and stolen lands: property rights. Those rights structure my relationship to the land: according to the law, I own it and can live on it but have no particular responsibility for cultivating it. I can exclude anyone else from living there—including people, animals, and plants of all kinds. If I want to, I can pave over the land. I have the right to destroy it.[46] My property rights also structure my relations to Indigenous women and children who are on the street, first because their land—their home—was expropriated by colonization, and then because the Indian Act (which is the basis of my property ownership) excluded them from status on Indian land. The heteropatriarchal band leadership system

---

[44] Dian Million cites Gloria Bird: "Colonization is a relationship after all." Million, *Therapeutic Nations*, 85.
[45] Nedelsky, *Law's Relations*, 65–77.
[46] As discussed in Chapter 2, the right to property has traditionally included the right to destroy it. Here, I'm referring to the land, not the house. In most cases I have the right to demolish the house, though I'll probably need to apply for a permit. While the destruction of a house is regulated, most regulations do not extend to the destruction of land, though some do cover trees and noxious plants. On legal rights to destroy property, see Sprankling, "The Right to Destroy" and Strahilevitz, "The Right to Destroy."

set up by the Indian Act has facilitated the collusion of many band leaders with the colonizing government, to deny rights of status and belonging to women who "married out," and to continue to exclude those women and their descendants, since 1876. The system of property rights implemented by the Canadian government has facilitated my collusion with the colonizing regime: I get to own my house. My solidarity with other rights holders is also structured through the system of rights, which constructs a *we* of rights holders against a *them* of the rightless. It is true, of course, that rights to property allow Indigenous individuals to own land and houses, too, and to do with them as they please—to destroy them if they want to. Under the law, they have that equal right. That abstract right means nothing if you are impoverished and homeless. It does not allow you to live in and belong to your community. It does not allow you to take responsibility for your land, or any land.

The Denial of Rights Has Substantive Effects on Indigenous Women and Children, and Indigenous Peoples

As Sharon McIvor argued in 2004,

> Aboriginal women in Canada do not enjoy rights equal to those shared by other Canadians. Since 1869, colonialist and patriarchal federal laws—most notably the Indian Act—have fostered patriarchy in Aboriginal communities and subjected Aboriginal women to loss of Indian status and the benefits of band membership, eviction from reserve homes, and denial of an equal share of matrimonial property. Colonialism and patriarchy have also enabled cooperation between male Aboriginal leadership and Canadian governments to resist the inclusion of Aboriginal women in Aboriginal governance. These denials and exclusions perpetuate the exposure of Aboriginal women and their children to violence and consign many to extreme poverty.[47]

As McIvor points out, the denial of rights within the framework of rights in the Indian Act has had substantive effects, producing homelessness, poverty, and high levels of violence for Aboriginal women and children. The history of sex discrimination in the Indian Act is cited as one of the root causes of missing and murdered women and girls in Canada.[48] McIvor argues that "Litigation for equal rights is not a last resort but an empowering element of the broad political,

---

[47] McIvor, "Aboriginal Women Unmasked," 106–107.
[48] See the *Report on Missing and Murdered Indigenous Women and Girls*; see also Palmater, *Warrior Life*, 215.

social, and legal struggle to eradicate sex discrimination against Aboriginal women."[49]

Indigenous Feminist Struggles for Rights Are Struggles to Restructure Relations

Rauna Kuokkanen argues that the project of Indigenous self-determination is to *restructure relations* of domination. Drawing on Jennifer Nedelsky's argument that addressing issues of violence and injustice requires restructuring relations, including personal, institutional, and systemic structural relations, Kuokkanen argues for an understanding of Indigenous self-determination in terms of what Nedelsky calls a core value: a widely shared understanding of what a group considers indispensable for their wellbeing as individuals and as a collectivity.

Kuokkanen formulates this understanding of self-determination in contrast to the understanding of Indigenous self-determination as a right to noninterference. For Kuokkanen, "Indigenous self-determination is fundamentally a struggle to restructure relations. It is a vision for freedom from domination, for justice and dignity in all relations."[50] Drawing on her interviews with Indigenous women, Kuokkanen sees self-determination as a guiding vision that fosters the norm of integrity: both individual integrity and the integrity of the land. These two dimensions are relational and interdependent: they gain meaning and are constituted through one another and are embedded in social relations. Both are constituted in relation to the collective.

Following Kuokkanen's understanding of self-determination as a practice of restructuring relations, I want to suggest that Indigenous feminist struggles for *rights* can best be understood as struggles to restructure relations. While Kuokkanen tends to posit the understanding of struggles to restructure relations in opposition to rights claims, Nedelsky argues that rights are best understood not as individual entitlements but as instruments that structure relationships. "Questions of rights (and law more generally) are best analyzed in terms of how they structure relations. . . . What rights and law actually *do*, right now, is structure relations, which, in turn, promote or undermine core values, such as autonomy."[51] For Nedelsky, a relational approach to rights issues will consider how law is structuring the relations, what are the values at stake, what kinds of relations would foster those values, and how competing versions of a right would structure relations differently. Rights can be seen as collective decisions

---

[49] McIvor, "Aboriginal Women Unmasked," 107.
[50] Kuokkanen, *Restructuring Relations*, 59.
[51] Nedelsky, *Law's Relations*, 65.

about the implementation of core values; rights, then, can be analyzed by asking whether they promote or undermine core values. As Kuokkanen acknowledges, "rights are instruments (though not necessarily the only ones) through which the value of Indigenous self-determination is put into practice and exercised on the ground."[52]

Following this relational analysis, Indigenous feminist struggles for rights can be seen as struggles to restructure relations to realize the core values of grounded normativity and reciprocity in Indigenous philosophies.[53] The NWAC and Indigenous feminists have appealed not for increased state involvement but for changes to a system of rights laws under the Indian Act that have discriminated against women. Recognizing that the existing framework of rights laws upholds a hierarchical relationship between the state and Indigenous peoples, and between Indigenous men and women (and others), Indigenous feminists have fought for a framework of laws that uphold relations of reciprocity and that support individual and collective wellbeing. While the focus of many of these claims has been on changing the laws within the Indian Act, at the same time they challenge the legitimacy of the Indian Act. The NWAC argues that restructuring relations requires abolishing the Indian Act and instituting critically revalued Indigenous systems of laws.

Individual Rights and Women's Rights Are Essential to Collective Self-Determination

Against the view that Indigenous women's struggles for rights have undermined Indigenous sovereignty, Indigenous feminists argue that it's the denial of women's rights, in the context of the Indian Act, that has done this. As Fay Blaney notes, the NWAC acknowledges that "patriarchy is so ingrained in our communities that it is now seen as a 'traditional trait.' "[54] When women's claims to rights are blamed for undermining collective rights and Indigenous sovereignty, the assumption

---

[52] Kuokkanen, *Restructuring Relations*, 35.

[53] In Kuokkanen's terms, they can be seen as struggles to restructure relations to realize the core values of individual integrity and integrity of land. The Indigenous women Kuokkanen interviewed "unequivocally expressed that attainment of self-determination necessitates the restructuring of relations of domination of the settler state as well as other forms of oppression including gender relations, heteropatriarchy, access to meaningful decision-making and participation, and unequal material relations disproportionately affecting Indigenous women, including resources and support for teaching Indigenous children their language, culture and heritage. . . . A robust conception of Indigenous self-determination seeks to restructure all relations of domination, which in turn necessitates an examination of which relations foster the norm of integrity and which relations suppress it" (Kuokkanen, *Restructuring Relations*, 59).

[54] Blaney, in Anderson and Lawrence, Strong Women Stories, 158.

is that multiple forms of violence against women are private matters to be dealt with within the patriarchal household of the Indigenous community. Women are blamed for the breaking of connections. The reality is that those connections are broken by the colonizing state and the patriarchal governance that perpetuates colonization, in part through the system of rights in the Indian Act.

Indigenous feminists argue that individual rights and women's equality rights are central to strengthening the collective. Indigenous feminists stress the *connection* between individual and collective rights, arguing that the strength of the community depends on the strength of everyone. As Val Napoleon has argued, "The aboriginal political discourse regarding self-determination would be more useful to communities if it incorporated an understanding of the individual as relational, autonomous, and self-determining. That is, a developed perspective of individual self-determination is necessary to move collective self-determination beyond rhetoric to a meaningful and practical political project that engages aboriginal peoples and is deliberately inclusive of aboriginal women."[55] As Joyce Green writes, "Aboriginal feminism seeks an Aboriginal liberation that includes women, and not just the conforming woman, but also the marginal and excluded, and especially the woman who has been excluded from her community by virtue of colonial legislation and socio-historical forces. Thus, Aboriginal feminism is a theoretical engagement with history and politics, as well as a practical engagement with contemporary social, economic, cultural and political issues."[56]

As Rauna Kuokkanen writes, "In the end, the success of Indigenous self-determination is measured by eliminating violence against Indigenous women, children, and 2SQ individuals."[57] Conversely, the failure to address this violence will result in the failure of collective self-determination. Indigenous women point out that communities traumatized by cycles of violence cannot successfully govern themselves. Indigenous feminists in Canada have argued for decades that individual and collective self-determination are linked. As Kuokkanen points out, the NWAC has long argued that "violence against women (including structural violence of marginalizing Indigenous women in their communities and their exclusion from their communities) ought to be at the centre of self-government agenda."[58] This link has long been resisted by Indigenous male leaders. Male violence is too often blamed on colonization and on the victimization of men by the violence of colonization.

---

[55] Napoleon, "Aboriginal Self Determination," 31.
[56] Green, "Taking Account of Aboriginal Feminism," in Green, ed., *Making Space for Indigenous Feminism*, 25.
[57] Kuokkanen, *Restructuring Relations*, 179.
[58] Kuokkanen, *Restructuring Relations*, 179.

Indigenous Feminist Struggles for Rights Are Grounded in Indigenous Traditions and Struggles for Decolonization

Against the liberal feminist position that individual rights and gender equality rights must supersede Indigenous claims to tradition and to collective self-determination, Indigenous feminists argue that any affirmation of individual rights or women's rights without a critique of state colonization fails to grasp the centrality of racialized gendered colonization in the oppression of Indigenous women. Indigenous feminists affirm the centrality of women's power in Indigenous communities and Indigenous history, and they argue for rights to belong to those communities and to exercise that power in the context of struggles for collective self-determination, resurgence, and decolonization.[59]

An affirmation of Indigenous women's rights that is not grounded in a critique of racialized and gendered systems of colonization misses the specificity of the interlocking systems of domination that produce specific forms of violence against Indigenous women and gender-diverse people, including physical abuse, exclusion and marginalization from communities, poverty and homelessness, incarceration, the removal of children, and other forms of racialized abuse and discrimination. The MMIWG report lists four pathways to violence: historical, multigenerational, and intergenerational trauma; social and economic marginalization; government maintenance of the status quo and institutional lack of will; and ignoring the agency and expertise of Indigenous women, girls, and 2SLGBTQQIA people. The NWAC Action Plan to end the Attack Against Indigenous Women, Girls, and Gender-Diverse People (2021) stresses that ending the genocide requires a framework of substantive equality and human and Indigenous rights rooted in a politics of decolonization, led by self-determining Indigenous women and gender-diverse people. Any affirmation of Indigenous women's individual rights must be grounded in a politics of decolonization.

Arguments for the precedence of legal rights not grounded in a critique of colonization fail to recognize the history of the formation of liberal Western rights through constitutive exclusions of Indigenous people in general and Indigenous women in particular. The colonization of Indigenous people by the "liberal" heteropatriarchal state has worked through undermining Indigenous women's power. As we've seen in Chapter 4, Audra Simpson argues that Indigenous women have long represented an alternative political order in which women

---

[59] In *Decolonizing Universalism*, Serene Khader criticizes Western feminist assumptions that traditions are necessarily patriarchal and argues that claims to tradition should be assessed according to their normative content, to determine whether they support or resist sexist oppression. This argument is central to the critical assessments of Indigenous customary law advocated by Indigenous feminists.

had power. In contrast to the Western liberal tradition, in which women were the legal dependents of fathers and husbands, barred from property ownership and from participation in political institutions, and subject to an ideology (if seldom a reality) of protection in the private household (which is where most abuse takes place), many Indigenous traditions recognized women's inherent rights and powers as women and as individuals. In the Western liberal tradition, rights were traditionally vested in male individuals—in white male property owners who were heads of households. Rights were extended to white women only in response to a long feminist struggle—and that struggle was influenced by encounters with Indigenous women.

In "Who Is Your Mother? Red Roots of White Feminism," Paula Gunn Allen points out that the power and agency of Indigenous women, and the egalitarianism in Indigenous communities, served as a model for the white feminist suffragist movement in America and influenced American and European ideals of freedom and egalitarianism.[60] As Sally Roesch Wagner has documented, the white women suffragists of late nineteenth-century America were directly influenced by their encounters with the nations of the Haudenosaunee Confederacy, where they were able to observe women's civil and political *rights*: women had rights to own property, to initiate divorce, and to participate in governance. Matilda Joslyn Gage, an honorary member of the Wolf Clan of the Mohawk nation, discussed that influence in an 1875 article in the New York *Evening Post*, "The Remnants of the Five Nations." Elizabeth Cady Stanton argued that Western nations were indebted to what she called the Matriarchate of the Haudenosaunee "for its first conception of inherent rights, natural equality of condition, and the establishment of a civilized government upon this basis."[61] Paula Gunn Allen notes that the constitution of the Iroquois (the Haudenosaunee Confederacy) codified the executive decision-making power of the clan mothers, as well as their economic power. Kiera Ladner points out that Indigenous constitutional traditions provide citizens with rights and responsibilities, and these include rights and responsibilities of women and children. For example, the Haudenosaunee constitutional order can be interpreted to recognize the property rights of women and the rights of those raising the children, and "the Blackfoot constitutional order is quite definitive that property is almost exclusively 'owned' by the women."[62] Ladner argues that the practice of

[60] Allen, "Who Is Your Mother?"
[61] See Wagner, ed., The Women's Suffrage Movement.
[62] Ladner, "Gendering Decolonization, Decolonizing Gender," 74. Ladner defines Indigenous constitutional orders as "the mainly unwritten constitutional traditions in Indigenous North America with each nation typically having its own unwritten constitutional order. Like the British Constitution, Indigenous constitutions consist of a myriad of written and unwritten documents and traditions (which in the case of some nations consist of orations of constitutional documents while in others the constitution is outlined by bundles, ceremony, song and story). As with other constitutional orders, Indigenous orders establish and maintain political systems, provide citizens with

decolonization through treaty constitutionalism must look to Indigenous constitutional orders for traditions of women's equality and rights. Sharon McIvor has argued that contemporary Indigenous women's rights claims are rooted in Aboriginal customary law.[63] Traditions of women's rights and freedoms, then, do not originate in the liberal West. Claims that Western liberal values must supercede nonliberal traditions are based in both ignorance of traditions and denial of the history of colonization.

Indigenous women's rights are often framed as claims to recognition of women's traditional powers, responsibilities, and relations to land, water, and communities. As Dian Million writes, in their struggles for rights to inclusion, the NWAC and Indigenous women in Canada have "argued from their historical position as mothers of nations rejecting the intense inequalities that had stemmed from the Canadian Indian Act's gendered evisceration of Indian family and community. They argued from positions of shared gender power instituted in their roles as clan mothers and as once primary and honoured negotiators for their historical Indigenous nations. Indigenous women argued for Aboriginal nations that foregrounded forms of customary law, laws that would inform governances that respected, honoured, and afforded Indigenous women their rightful place."[64] The grounding of rights in assertions of women's traditional powers, and particularly in their power as clan mothers, is, of course, controversial. As Emma LaRocque argues, claims about women's traditional roles are often unsubstantiated and often repeat the claims of gender complementarity that feminists have long criticized. "It is simply not true that there was any universalized Aboriginal understanding about 'womanhood,' especially one that made much of masculinity or femininity in the western sense."[65] As discussed in Chapter 4, many argue that precontact societies allowed for a great deal of gender fluidity, and that rigid binary gender roles were imposed by heteropatriarchal colonization. Claims that women are defined by maternal roles, and the ideal of woman as the mother of the nation, have long been used to justify women's subordination. As Jo-Anne Fiske notes, when Aboriginal women have drawn on discourses of native womanhood to argue for their empowerment as mothers of the nation, and to affirm a vision of gender harmony and complementarity, this vision has not been taken up by the Indigenous male leadership, which is more concerned with challenging while emulating the power of the state.[66] Claims to

rights, responsibilities, legal systems and traditions, and outline the interrelationship of society, politics and religion."

[63] McIvor, "Aboriginal Women's Rights as 'Existing Rights.' "
[64] Million, *Therapeutic Nations*, 127.
[65] LaRocque, "Métis and Feminist," 64.
[66] Fiske, "The Womb Is to the Nation as the Heart Is to the Body," 74.

tradition are typically used by patriarchal leaders to protect "traditions" of rigid gender roles enforcing women's subordination and the exclusion of deviant genders. As Gina Starblanket and Heidi Kiiwetinepinesiik Stark point out, the discourse of relationality can be used against Indigenous women, to enforce their responsibilities as keepers of relationship while denying their political agency. While the project of reconceptualizing systems of law and governance upon relational grounds can facilitate an appreciation of the political significance of women's everyday relations and interactions, calling into question public/private and individual/collective rights dichotomies, it is also important to critically examine discourses of relationality as gendered discourses.[67]

Others argue that complementary gender roles in Indigenous traditions are not reducible to the traditionally feminine and devalued roles criticized by feminists. Many Indigenous women argue that Indigenous traditions have sustained balanced and equitable forms of gender complementarity that also allowed for gender fluidity. As Audra Simpson writes: "Iroquois women are too often and too easily imagined simply as 'caretakers of the land' and 'mothers of the nation' in a way that is stripped of its contemporary valences, instantiations, and meaning."[68] For Simpson, the Kanehsatà:ke/Oka standoff in Canada in 1990 is an example of "the empirical face of that caretaking." It was women who called the peaceful protest against the latest move in a history of state expropriation of Mohawk land in Kanehsatà:ke, this time to extend a golf course on sacred burial lands. When months of peaceful protest proved ineffective, it was women who called the men of the Warrior society to armed resistance. And it was women who were the prime negotiators with the Quebec police force and the Canadian armed forces. Along with the armed resistance at Kanehsatà:ke/Oka, the movement *Idle No More*, the Standing Rock resistance to the Dakota Access Pipeline, the Unist'ot'en resistance to the Coastal Gaslink pipeline, and many other actions have been inaugurated and sustained by women who act in their roles as caretakers of land and water. As Pamela Palmater argues, "Indigenous Women Warriors are the Heart of Indigenous Resistance."[69]

But does responsibility for the collective extend to individual rights? It is important that the recognition of traditions of Indigenous women's power and responsibility for land does *not* entail that Indigenous women's rights should be *limited* to rights to responsibility. Traditions of Indigenous women's power, along with traditions of Indigenous women's individual rights, serve as precedents for contemporary Indigenous women's rights claims. Indigenous women have long histories of political power rooted in responsibility for relations, and they have

---

[67] Starblanket and Stark, "Towards a Relational Paradigm."
[68] Simpson, *Mohawk Interruptus*, 148.
[69] Palmater, *Warrior Life*.

been able to draw on these histories to formulate their claims to civil and political rights. When these rights are formulated as rights to take responsibility for relations, this does not mean that rights are *only* responsibilities. Rights as responsibilities for relations must be protected with full individual rights and freedoms. As noted, there are plenty of precedents in Indigenous customary law for women's individual rights. But those rights are situated in an understanding of relationality: reciprocal relations of freedom.

The recognition of traditions of Indigenous women's power and responsibility for land does not entail that Indigenous women's rights must be rooted in traditional gender roles, whatever they may be. Arguments for traditions of women's power are one of many sources cited in Indigenous women's rights claims. Responsibilities for relations are not exclusive to women in Indigenous communities. The ethic of grounded normativity rooted in an understanding of land as a system of reciprocal relations and obligations is claimed as an Indigenous ethic that is common to all.

The history of Indigenous women's power and agency both as individuals and as caretakers of land and water does inform contemporary movements for Indigenous women's rights: struggles for inclusion in their communities and for participation in governance, and struggles against all forms of gendered violence, draw on long histories of Indigenous women's power. At the same time, it is important to resist the romanticization of precontact traditions as ideal models of gender harmony. Against the claim that gendered violence is only an effect of colonization, Snyder, Napoleon, and Borrows assert that there was gendered violence in precontact Indigenous societies. They argue, moreover, that historic accounts of gender violence and responses to it can provide legal resources for dealing with gendered violence today.[70]

Indigenous feminist theory and politics, then, involve the negotiation of complex relations of power and solidarity: both the critique of patriarchal defenses of tradition and the critique of liberal arguments that individual rights must supersede collective rights and claims to tradition. This involves problematizing the false opposition between individual rights and collective self-determination, and the opposition between Western rights and Indigenous traditions. These oppositions are assumed both by Indigenous leaders who criticize and dismiss Indigenous feminist rights claims and by liberal pluralists who criticize and dismiss Indigenous claims to self-determination. When liberal pluralists assume that collective identities are necessarily oppressive and must be supplemented by Western rights, and when Indigenous leaders argue that individual rights claims are not authentically Indigenous, both are claiming cultural incommensurability: both are accepting that individual rights are

---

[70] Snyder, Napoleon, and Borrows, "Gender and Violence," 597.

definitively Western, and collective self-determination is incompatible with individual rights claims. Both see traditions as necessarily patriarchal and individual and equality rights as definitively Western. Indigenous feminist theory and activism thus involves a complex negotiation between discourses of rights and discourses of tradition, and a complex negotiation of relations of power and solidarity with and against nonindigenous feminisms and Indigenous claims to tradition.

The opposition between women's individual rights and collective self-determination can be broken once Indigenous feminist rights claims are recognized as appeals to Indigenous relational ethics, in support of struggles for self-determination. Indigenous feminists criticize the violation of relationships between Indigenous women and their communities and their lands, and point out that this violation of relationships has been a key strategy of colonization. Indigenous feminists argue that struggles for Indigenous self-governance would be strengthened with the inclusion of Indigenous women, and that their exclusion has undermined those struggles. Once it is acknowledged that Indigenous feminist rights claims draw on and appeal for the realization of traditions and principles of Indigenous relationality, the perception of a deadlock between Indigenous women's claims to individual rights and Indigenous claims to collective rights of self-determination cannot be sustained.

Indigenous Feminist Rights Claims Have Been Central to the Politics of Resurgence

Indigenous feminist rights claims have been central to refocusing Indigenous conceptions of nationhood, to prioritize individual and collective wellbeing through the revaluing of traditions of reciprocity rooted in relationality: in sustainable relations with land, understood as "all my relations." In other words, Indigenous feminist rights claims have been central to the development of the philosophy and politics of resurgence. This claim contradicts much of the thinking on the politics of resurgence. Typically, resurgence politics are assumed to be opposed to rights politics. As Glen Coulthard argues, resurgence politics involves turning away from struggles for rights and recognition from the state, toward revaluations of Indigenous traditions of relationality and grounded normativity. Leanne Simpson claims that the Idle No More movement was composed of distinct political approaches: struggles for rights through policy, bills, and electoral politics, and struggles for treaty rights, both aimed toward changing the relationship between Indigenous peoples and the state, were distinct from "a nationhood approach that involved the rejection of recognition and rights-based politics and a turn toward Indigenous resurgence and that was anticapitalist in nature."[71] Yet Indigenous feminist struggles for *rights* have consistently focused on the issues central to *resurgence*: the development of individual and collective wellbeing, rooted in relations to land and oriented toward the grounded normativity of reciprocity.

Against the understanding of nation on the model of the state, Indigenous women have argued for radically different understandings of nation.[72] Kiera Ladner argues that "the idea of community well-being and its relationship to governance has largely been overlooked in the indigenous governance literature, and no attention has been paid to the relationship between self-determination and communities in crisis."[73] Rauna Kuokkanen identifies a distance between "hard" and "soft" understandings of nation and governance: between a focus on land rights, resources, and band governance and a focus on the "social issues" of welfare and wellbeing of individuals and communities.[74] Against a focus on state-like legal rights of control and resistance to interference, Indigenous women have been oriented to a politics of self-determination through collective responsibility for individual and community wellness, through restoring relations of reciprocity with land and with each other.[75]

Rauna Kuokkanen argues that Indigenous women activists often confront a "gender fault line" in interpretations of self-determination. While Indigenous leaders (typically men) have focused on negotiations with the state and corporations for control over territory and resources, Indigenous women have typically engaged in grassroots activism to address individual and community wellbeing and sustaining relations to land and water.[76] As an example, she

---

[71] Simpson, *As We Have Always Done*, 219.The opposition between the politics of rights claims and the politics of resurgence is sometimes framed as an opposition between a philosophy focused on lack and a philosophy that assumes an inclusive circle of life (e.g., Million, *Therapeutic Nations*, 136). As Lee Maracle puts it, "I think we have rights to national self-determination. . . . But it's not something that I would advocate. For me, I'm always talking about self-determination in the context of all our relations and the continuance of those relations and the laws that govern those relations" (interview quoted in Kuokkanen, *Restructuring Relations*, 23). Yet others argue that rights are inherent in Indigenous philosophies. As Kiera Ladner writes, "Self-determination is an inherent right that was given to each nation by Creator. While it is recognised and affirmed in the Canadian Constitution, it is sui generis, meaning that it originates outside of Canadian and British legal and constitutional traditions, and is instead vested in Indigenous legal traditions, which can be said to comprise Indigenous constitutional orders" (Ladner, "Gendering Decolonisation, Decolonising Gender," 62). Ladner argues that Indigenous constitutional orders include women's and children's rights.

[72] See Chapter 2 for Leanne Betasamosake Simpson's conception of nation. See Chapter 4 for Audra Simpson's.

[73] Ladner, "Understanding the Impact of Self-Determination on Communities in Crisis," 89.

[74] Kuokkanen, *Restructuring Relations*, 17.

[75] Jo-Anne Fiske has argued that Indigenous women's discourses of nation are "maternal discourses" that invoke the stereotypical trope of the mother of the nation and emphasize the feminine virtues of nurturance and care. While such discourses are common, discourses of Indigenous relationality are not reducible to maternal discourses.

[76] As Kim Anderson has written, "Women tend not to lose sight of the social issues in our community, where the male leaders are more focused on logging and fishing, not realizing that the health of our young people is important."

cites the resistance of a small group of women to the fracking agreement signed by the male-dominated band council of the Kainai First Nation (the Blood reserve) with Murphy Oil and Bowood Energy in 2010, without consulting the 11,000 members of the community.⁷⁷ Elle-Máijá Apiniskim Tailfeathers and two other Kainai women, one of whom was an elder, were arrested by Blood Tribe Police and charged under the Canadian criminal code with intimidation.⁷⁸ "A prime example of gender fault line, the two sides of the barricade consisted of female protectors of the land on the one side, and male tribal police on the other."⁷⁹ Kuokkanen argues that the standoff reflected opposed and often gendered interpretations of self-determination: "For Tailfeathers and the other women participating in the peaceful blockade, self-determination is seen as a foundational value inseparable from the norm of integrity. Fundamentally, self-determination in their interpretation is about the health and well-being of people and the land alike. For her band council, self-determination is seen as being in charge of the band's own affairs."⁸⁰ The "gender fault line" is not, I think, simply a generalization about what men do and what women do: there are many men who support the interpretation of self-determination as a revaluation of Indigenous traditions of relationality in support of individual and collective wellbeing, and women who support contracts for pipelines that will bring much-needed resources to desperate communities. The gender fault line is the division between a patriarchal politics of control and noninterference, and an Indigenous feminist politics of sustaining relations with land and each other.

But it is not typically acknowledged that feminist claims to rights to belong to their communities have led in the push to shift the focus of Indigenous politics from the assertion of rights of noninterference to a politics of attention to wellbeing, inclusion, and participation, through the resurgence of Indigenous traditions of relationality. The critique of the patriarchal politics of control and noninterference in Indigenous governance, and the insistence on an alternative politics focused on the wellbeing of individuals and communities in relations with land, has been central to Indigenous feminist rights claims. Against the politics of control and noninterference, Indigenous feminist rights politics focus on land not as a right to property that serves as a basis of exclusion, but as the basis of a right to a relation of belonging and inclusion, and a right to participate in relations of responsibility. These relational rights are obscured by discourses of tradition and relationality that protect relations of violence, abuse, and exclusion. Those relations destroy communities and block resurgence. Indigenous

---

⁷⁷ The Blood reserve, part of the Blackfoot Confederacy, is the largest reserve in Canada, located in southern Alberta.
⁷⁸ Tailfeathers, "Fractured Land."
⁷⁹ Kuokkanen, *Restructuring Relations*, 45.
⁸⁰ Kuokkanen, *Restructuring Relations*, 46.

women's claims for political rights to belong to their communities and to be full participants in Indigenous governance, and their claims for rights to be free of violence and abuse, have long been central to the politics of resurgence: to a politics of decolonization that asserts Indigenous self-governance through the restoration and revitalization of Indigenous values, practices, and laws.

Sharon McIvor has argued that the civil and political rights of Aboriginal women are not only fundamental human rights but Aboriginal rights that predate contact. Aboriginal women's rights form part of the inherent right to Aboriginal self-government, which is now recognized and protected under section 35(1) of the Canadian Constitution Act of 1982. "Aboriginal women's civil and political rights are foundational and do not derive their existence from documents or treaties. The right of women to establish and maintain their civic and political role has existed since time immemorial. . . . These rights are part of customary laws of Aboriginal people and part of the rights of Aboriginal self-government." Quoting the *Sparrow* decision of the Canadian Supreme Court, McIvor argues that such rights "do not require the imprimatur of state action to qualify as rights."[81] Aboriginal women's rights, then, are rooted in multiple traditions: they are fundamental and inherent individual rights, they are rights under customary Aboriginal laws, and they are recognized by the government of Canada and by international law.[82] These multiple sources of rights are reiterated in The *Final Report of the National Inquiry into Missing and Murdered Indigenous Women and Girls:* the report's *Calls for Justice* affirms "substantive equality and human and Indigenous rights" and asserts that Indigenous women and girls and 2SLGBTQQISA people are "holders of inherent Indigenous rights, constitutional rights, and international and domestic human rights."[83]

Indigenous feminist rights politics have been central to the distinction between critical and uncritical resurgence politics: between feminist and queer conceptions of resurgence, and conceptions of resurgence that merely continue heteropatriarchal domination. In arguing for a turn away from relations with the state, resurgence theorists sometimes continue the emphasis on control and noninterference. A noncritical heteropatriarchal conception of resurgence can perceive nation-building as predicated on the right to control membership, or to return to original traditions that reify sexist binary gender roles. Indigenous feminist rights politics have shifted the discourse of resurgence

---

[81] McIvor, "Aboriginal Women's Rights as 'Existing Rights.'" The Sparrow decision of 1990 set out criteria to determine whether government infringement of Aboriginal rights could be justified.

[82] McIvor notes that they are recognized under the International Covenant on Civil and Political Rights, the Convention on the Elimination of All Forms of Discrimination Against Women, and the Universal Declaration of Human Rights. This article was published prior to the Universal Declaration on the Rights of Indigenous Peoples.

[83] National Inquiry into Missing and Murdered Indigenous Women and Girls, *Reclaiming Power and Place*, 2.

to focus on *critical* revaluations of Indigenous traditions, to attend to feminist and queer interpretations of traditions and formulations of nationhood and self-determination. For example, *Violence on the Land, Violence on Our Bodies*, a report authored by the Women's Earth Alliance and the Native Youth Sexual Health Network, focuses on the connections between Indigenous land and Indigenous bodies, and draws an explicit connection between the destruction of land and the violation of Indigenous bodies, in particular the bodies of women, children, and gender-diverse people. The report traces connections between attacks on the earth and attacks on women, and between the effects of environmental destruction of extractive industries on health and the high rates of sexual violence by workers in "man camps."[84] Extractive industries are seen as patriarchal practices of domination that produce forms of *gender-based environmental violence*. In response to gendered environmental violence, Indigenous women and queer youth draw on Indigenous traditions. As Vanessa Gray says, "Some of us who listen to our elders learn that we are the keepers of the water, we are supposed to care for it. That's our role as women."[85] But the report reminds us that traditions are diverse. As Alex Wilson (Opaskwayak Cree Nation) notes, "In Cree, the land (aski) is not gendered. . . . Same for water. It's not gendered but it has the spirit of life and it's fluid."[86]

Violence on the Land, Violence on Our Bodies calls for responses to violence that resist appeals to the state for more policing. Legal measures, including policy and policing, often address effects, rather than root causes of violence. They are circular responses to violence that produce more violence. Instead, the focus is on reclaiming traditions, to focus on *transformative resurgence* rather than on legal tools. Transformative resurgence emphasizes practices of care for selves and communities, addressing trauma, and building *cultures of consent*. Yet while this politics resists appeals to the state, it does rely on invocations of rights. Building and rebuilding cultures of consent over land and bodies draws on traditions of rights to consent, grounded in the principle of Free Prior and Informed Consent (FPIC): "an internationally accepted principle that recognizes Indigenous peoples' inherent and prior rights to their lands and resources, and respects their

---

[84] The report quotes Vanessa Gray, Aamjiwnaang First Nation: "The land is our mother, so when we lose value for the land . . . people lose value for the women." And Melina Laboucan-Massimo Lubicon Cree): "The industrial system of resource extraction in Canada is predicated on systems of power and domination. This system is based on the raping and pillaging of Mother Earth as well as violence against women. The two are inextricably linked. With the expansion of extractive industries, not only do we see desecration of the land, we see an increase in violence against women. Rampant sexual violence against women and a variety of social ills result from the influx of transient workers in and around workers' camps." Women's Earth Alliance and the Native Youth Sexual Health Network, *Violence on the Land, Violence on our Bodies: Building an Indigenous Response to Environmental Violence*, 4, 31. http://landbodydefense.org/uploads/files/VLVBReportToolkit2016.pdf
[85] *Violence on the Land, Violence on our Bodies*, 19.
[86] *Violence on the Land, Violence on our Bodies*, 5.

legitimate authority to require that third parties enter into an equal and respectful relationship with them, based on the principle of informed consent."[87] This principle is extended to bodies, where consent is understood as "consensual ongoing agreement about the project/procedure/action on your land or your body." Body sovereignty, then, is seen as a fundamental right. Just as rights to consent over land are not respected by extractive industries, rights to consent over bodies are too often not respected by male workers. Too often, they are not respected by Indigenous leaders calling for land rights or by men within the environmental justice movement.

As Sarah Hunt asks:

> So what would happen if every time an Indigenous woman had her personal boundaries crossed without consent, we were moved to act in the same way as we've seen to the threat of a pipeline in our territories—the nonconsensual crossing of territorial boundaries? We would see our chiefs and elders, the language speakers, children and networks of kin, all in our regalia our allies and neighbors all across the generations show up outside the house of a woman who had been hurt to drum and sing her healing songs. What if we looked to the land for berries and to the ocean for fish and herring eggs and seaweed to help her body to heal? What if we put her within a circle of honor and respect to show her that we will not stand for this violence any longer. We would bring her food and song and story, we would truly protect her self-determination and defend the boundaries of her body which had been trespassed and violated.[88]

The invocation of the right to bodily sovereignty grounded in an ethic of reciprocity and consent and rooted in rights to land is indebted to a history of Indigenous women's claims to individual and collective rights that are inherent and fundamental, that are rooted in relations to land, and that are recognized in Aboriginal customary law as well as Canadian and international law. These invocations of rights have a central place in the politics of resurgence.

Indigenous Feminist Rights Claims Have Generated Unique Formulations of Relational Rights

To summarize, then, Indigenous feminist rights claims are made in the context of the ethic of relationality that is specific to Indigenous law. These rights claims

---

[87] *Violence on the Land, Violence on our Bodies*, 16.
[88] Sarah Hunt, "Violence, Law and the Everyday Politics of Recognition," presented at the Native American and Indigenous Studies Association (NAISA) conference, Washington, DC, June 6, 2015.

are not, then, reducible to Western rights discourses. The rights discourses used by the NWAC and Indigenous feminists are rooted in Indigenous philosophies of relationality. They are arguments for inclusion and belonging: for full citizenship and rights to participate in Indigenous communities and Indigenous governance. They are often grounded in claims to women's specific relations to and responsibilities for land and water, and in traditions of women's power, autonomy, and rights. They are grounded in arguments for Indigenous self-determination understood in terms of rights to individual and collective wellbeing. They advance critiques of violations of relationship, often grounded in explicit claims of traditions of Indigenous relationality and reciprocity, and in reformulations of nation and sovereignty.

Against the politics of control and noninterference, Indigenous feminist rights politics focus on land not as a right to property that serves as a basis of exclusion, but as the basis of a right to a relation of belonging and inclusion, and a right to participate in relations of responsibility. Claims of rights to freedom from violence are framed as a sovereignty issue, in recognition that colonization and patriarchal dominance have worked together to undermine women's power, to break relations among Indigenous people and between Indigenous people and land. Indigenous feminist approaches to violence focus on violations of relations of consent and reciprocity. They focus on building cultures of consent, grounded in inherent and prior rights to land.

Indigenous feminist rights discourses are formulated through an attunement to the complexity of relations. Claims to rights are grounded in critically analyzed and interpreted traditions of Indigenous and Western law, state and international law, producing hybrid discourses of rights, including rights to have rights. The aim of Indigenous feminist rights claims is to restructure and transform relations: to shift from relations of patriarchal colonization to relations of reciprocity.

Hybrid Discourses, Hybrid Laws, and Multiple Addressees

Indigenous feminist and queer rights claims draw on multiple discourses of rights. Rights to belong to their communities and to participate in governance, both within communities and internationally, are rooted in Indigenous traditions, in international human rights, and in the constitutional laws of Canada and of Indigenous nations. As noted earlier, the *Final Report of the National Inquiry into Missing and Murdered Indigenous Women and Girls* asserts that Indigenous women and girls and 2SLGBTQQISA people are holders of multiple forms of rights with multiple sources, including inherent Indigenous rights, constitutional rights, and international and domestic human rights. The rights to consent invoked in *Violence on the Land, Violence on our Bodies* are rooted in internationally recognized inherent and prior Indigenous rights to land. In other words, Indigenous feminist and queer politics draw on Indigenous traditions as essential components of hybrid combinations of rights rooted in multiple traditions that support the claims of Indigenous women and gender-diverse people to self-determination as individuals and collectives.

Just as rights are rooted in multiple traditions, invocations of rights are addressed to multiple addressees. They are sometimes addressed to states and to international bodies, including the United Nations. They are also addressed to white men and to Indigenous men and to male-dominated Indigenous organizations and bands. Making claims to the state does not entail an assumption of the rightful authority of state power, any more than making claims to men and male leaders assumes the rightful authority of patriarchal power. Rights claims can assert the agency and power of the claimant and can invoke the normative ideal of reciprocal relations to criticize an imbalance of power between claimant and addressee.[89]

The politics of resurgence addresses a *we* of Indigenous communities, in a call to turn away from fruitless battles for state recognition and to turn toward rebuilding communities through revaluing traditions. Indigenous feminist and queer politics are more complicated politics of resurgence: they sometimes choose to turn away from fruitless battles for recognition by both colonizing states and Indigenous heteropatriarchal power, to rebuild communities of Indigenous women and gender-diverse people. They also work to rebuild Indigenous communities and organizations that will center the leadership of women and gender-diverse people. Sometimes this involves asserting rights to a range of addressees. For Indigenous feminist and queer communities, *transformative resurgence* is a complex politics that includes *critical* interpretation and revaluing of diverse Indigenous traditions. Just as there is no single addressee of rights claims, there is no simple *we* of resurgence.

Transformative resurgence includes the reinstitution of Indigenous law encoding rights, responsibilities, and freedoms of individuals and of nations. As Kiera Ladner notes, "As with other constitutional orders, Indigenous orders establish and maintain political systems, provide citizens with rights, responsibilities, legal systems and traditions, and outline the interrelationship of society, politics and religion."[90] In many communities Indigenous law is still operative; others are beginning to do the work of research and retrieval. Decolonization will require nation-to-nation recognition of Indigenous constitutional orders. As

---

[89] As Valeria del Toro argues in her analysis of rights discourses in Puerto Rico, the success of rights claims is not necessarily tied to recognition by the state (Pelet Del Toro, "Beyond the Critique of Rights").

[90] Ladner, "Gendering Decolonization, Decolonizing Gender," 74.

Ladner argues, decolonization must be a gendered project: this will depend on the institution of Indigenous constitutional orders that are "gender-neutral and gender-positive."[91]

Emily Snyder, Val Napoleon, and John Borrows argue that Indigenous constitutional orders must be assessed on a case-by-case basis, to ensure that Indigenous law is critically interpreted to address gendered violence. This will require an understanding of law as "dynamic, contested, deliberated," including multiple, competing, and contradictory discourses.[92] The politics of retrieval of Indigenous law must avoid "dangerous dualisms," including the dualisms of Indigenous versus feminist and authentic versus colonized. It will require attention to the ways in which Indigenous laws are gendered. For example, Snyder's research indicates that Cree law is a resource that can both challenge and perpetuate gendered oppression.[93] Addressing gendered violence involves what Snyder, Napoleon, and Borrows call *process pluralism*, to include a plurality of political strategies and systems, including but not limited to legal systems.[94]

Just as Indigenous feminist political theories and politics draw on multiple discourses of rights, addressed to multiple addressees, some Indigenous feminist legal theorists affirm the reinstitution of Indigenous law in combination with revised Canadian legal systems. John Borrows has long argued that Canadian legal systems are already hybrid systems that have combined Indigenous, British, and new Canadian laws. If nation-to-nation relations are to include overlapping sovereignties, they will also require the development and recognition of hybrid legal systems, through assessing and combining Indigenous and Canadian laws. As Borrows argues, all Canadians could benefit from the recognition of Indigenous law.

The relational conceptions of rights formulated through Indigenous feminist and queer thought and activism are part of a practice of freedom in resurgence grounded in relations to land: in reciprocal relations of interdependence. These relational rights are formulated through attunement to multiple forms of violence and negotiation with competing discourses of resistance, to create expansive politics of decolonization. As Joanne Barker writes, "Indigenous feminism has asserted *the polity of the Indigenous*: the unique governance, territory, and culture of an Indigenous people in a system of (non)human relationships and

---

[91] Ladner, "Gendering Decolonization, Decolonizing Gender," 74.
[92] Snyder, Napoleon, and Borrows, "Gender and Violence."
[93] Snyder, Gender, Power, and Representations of Cree Law.
[94] Snyder, Napoleon, and Borrows, "Gender and Violence," 597. The authors argue that legal resources for dealing with gendered violence can be found in historic accounts of responses to gendered violence. These can be accessed through precedent in "Indigenous stories, songs, dances, teachings, practices, customs, and kinship relationships." And they point out that these resources will become invisible if we narrate the past as if it were free from violence. See also Napoleon and Friedland, "An Inside Job."

responsibilities to one another. In doing so, Indigenous feminisms rearticulate the futurity of indigeneity in political coalition with non-Indigenous peoples against the ongoing social forces of U.S. imperialism, racism, and sexism."[95]

In his analysis of the activism at Standing Rock, Benjamin P. Davis argues that Indigenous rights claims can be sites of *theoretical innovations* in contemporary understandings of human rights. As he writes, "Human rights claims, without a taken-for-granted orientation to the state, can become a shared language for protecting, imagining, and realizing alternative political communities, alternative self-authorized forms of social organization."[96] The aim of Indigenous feminist rights claims is to restructure and transform relations: to shift from relations of patriarchal colonization to relations of reciprocity. These reformulations of rights and of collectivity are sources of Indigenous resurgence. They can also provide models for all of us, in coalitional politics of transformative reconciliation with each other and with the earth.

---

[95] Barker, "Indigenous Feminisms."
[96] Davis argues that approaches to rights can be divided into three categories: paradigmatic, critical, and organizational. Davis, "The Promises of Standing Rock."

Conclusion

Critical Theory and the Spirit of Freedom

Freedom is a place.
—Ruth Wilson Gilmore

We are remaking the whole world.
—Leanne Betasamosake Simpson

When we talk about these losses and these traumas it's important that it is not to impart a sense of guilt. It's to impart a sense of *freedom from denial*. So the Native peoples' objective is to heal; the non-native peoples' objective is to come out of denial. When that happens . . . Then they can start to come together on common ground.
—Faith Spotted Eagle[1]

What would it mean for a state and a people to emerge from denial—from colonial unknowing—into some kind of freedom? Emerging from denial would require taking responsibility for a violent history, and engaging in a transformation of relationship.

For settler states, this would involve honoring treaties, making reparations—and questioning state sovereignty. But remaking the relationship between settlers and Indigenous peoples requires more than law and policy. It would involve a transformation of who we are, by reencountering the other, encountering another worldview. Transformation of who we are would involve changing how we understand and experience and practice freedom. The point of self-transformation and transformation of relationship is to create just relations, but it's also to create freedom: if we are suffering from colonial unknowing, we do it for our own freedom from denial, our own freedom in relations.

---

[1] Opening quotations are from Gilmore, *Abolition Geography*; Maynard and Simpson, *Rehearsals for Living*; Dakota Oyate elder and activist Faith Spotted Eagle (Yankton Sioux Nation), a leader of the Standing Rock resistance to the Dakota Access Pipeline. https://www.youtube.com/watch?v=bqd_gYAhBII

If all of us are enchained in relations of colonization, how do we find a way out? That is a very big question. I'm going to address a smaller one: what would be required for a critical theory of freedom from relations of colonization? I want to suggest that a critical theory of freedom from colonization needs to be a theory of resistance to all forms of domination, oriented to relational freedom as both an ideal and a practice. This critical theory needs to be a practice of self-transformation through transformative encounters with the other. If self-transformation is a practice of freedom, openness to self-transformation *through encounter with the other* is a defining practice of *relational* freedom. For Western Eurocentric critical theories, this will involve a practice of freedom from colonial unknowing, through encounters with Indigenous critical theories. A critical theory of freedom from colonization also needs to move beyond the binary of settler/Indigenous, through critical engagement with what Leanne Simpson calls *constellations of co-resistance*: encounters with the theories, ideals, and practices of a wide range of critical theories and movements of resistance to all forms of domination.

A critical theory of freedom from relations of colonization requires a model of *critique* as a practice of encounter with the other, oriented toward transformation of ourselves and our relations, guided by an ethos of relational freedom: freedom in relations of reciprocity. This is a method of critical theory as a practice both *of* and *for* freedom: a practice of critique that is both engaged in resistance and oriented toward an ideal of relational freedom emergent from our shared and intersecting histories.[2] This is a practice of self-transformation that includes questioning and testing limits, engagement in agonistic struggle, and orientation toward an ideal; but its focus is on reencountering and engaging in reparative relations. In this critical theory, the means and the end are conjoined in a practice of relational freedom oriented toward the end of relational freedom.

Critical Theories and Freedom from Colonization

In his classic essay, "Traditional and Critical Theory," Max Horkheimer defined the aim of critical theory as the emancipation of human beings from slavery, and the realization of freedom.[3] The critical theory of the Frankfurt School, situated

---

[2] Tully, "The Struggles of Indigenous Peoples for and of Freedom." I return to this formulation repeatedly, to thematize the interconnection between a procedural conception of agonistic freedom and a substantive ideal of freedom.
[3] Horkheimer, "Traditional and Critical Theory." Horkheimer was not thematizing racialized slavery, but he also was not using the term *slavery* just as a metaphor. The essay, written in 1937, was an attempt to clarify the aims and methodology of a group of Jewish scholars confronting the Nazi regime in Germany. Members of the Frankfurt School analyzed fascism as the culmination of systems of domination that enslaved not only the victims but the victors.

in a history of modern Western theories of freedom, takes its point of departure from Marx: the aim of critical theory is not just to interpret the world but to change it. As James Bohman writes:

> a "critical" theory may be distinguished from a "traditional" theory according to a specific practical purpose: a theory is critical to the extent that it seeks human "emancipation from slavery", acts as a "liberating . . . influence," and works "to create a world which satisfies the needs and powers of" human beings (Horkheimer 1972b [1992, 246]). Because such theories aim to explain and transform *all* the circumstances that enslave human beings, many "critical theories" in the broader sense have been developed. They have emerged in connection with the many social movements that identify varied dimensions of the domination of human beings in modern societies. In both the broad and the narrow senses, however, a critical theory provides the descriptive and normative bases for social inquiry aimed at decreasing domination and increasing freedom in all their forms.[4]

If the aim of critical theory is the realization of freedom, a critical theory of freedom from colonial unknowing would require resisting the assumption that we already know what freedom is. It would require a reencounter and deep engagement with colonized others, to understand what freedom might be from the perspective of the colonized.[5] Saba Mahmood has made this point:

> Critique, I believe, is most powerful when it leaves open the possibility that we might also be remade in the process of engaging another's worldview that we might come to learn things that we did not already know before we undertook the engagement. This requires that we occasionally turn the critical gaze upon

---

[4] Bohman, "Critical Theory," *Stanford Encyclopedia of Philosophy*.
[5] This project of self-transformation through encounter with the other takes us back to the roots of Frankfurt School critical theory. The early Frankfurt School theorists drew on psychoanalytic and aesthetic theories, not just to elucidate forms of domination and subordination, and not to affirm the aspiration of given subjects to given regulative norms, but to imagine paths for individual and social transformation. Marcuse's *Eros and Civilization*, Horkheimer and Adorno's *Dialectic of Enlightenment*, Benjamin's essays, Adorno's work on aesthetics, all argued for projects of self-transformation through the encounter with the other. For them the other was typically an object: most often nature, including inner nature, the object world, the work of art, sometimes the feminine. Habermas's argument for a shift from theories of relations to objects to intersubjective theories could potentially ground a critical theory of encounter with othered subjects. If the basis of critique in critical theory is an appeal to standards of normativity that are immanent in existing social and political relations, discourses, and institutions, then decolonizing critical theory would involve considering standards of normativity in a wide range of social worlds, beyond the Eurocentric frame. If self-transformation is a practice of freedom, openness to self-transformation *through encounter with the other* is a defining practice of *relational* freedom.

ourselves, to leave open the possibility that we may be remade through an encounter with the other.[6]

For many Indigenous critical theorists, freedom would be the decolonizing resurgence of a life lived according to what Glen Coulthard calls grounded normativity: a life oriented to relations of reciprocity with all our relations. I have argued that this is a *political* conception of freedom in participation in democratic relations. It is a conception of freedom as a practice of *world-creation*. It is also a *substantive* conception of freedom: a normative ideal of freedom in relations of reciprocity, grounded in an ontology of the world as a system of gift relations.

Contemporary Euro-American critical and political theorists tend to resist a substantive understanding of freedom. Yet substantive theories of freedom constitute the essential but disavowed background of critical theories. Marx's early work imagined an ideal of a nonalienated life: a dream of freedom not only as shared ownership of the means of production but as the realization of ourselves through sustaining relations with self, nature, and our "species being." The ideal of an unalienated life, the Kantian ideal of what Habermas calls an unconstrained communication community, and Rousseau's ideal of the general will—all live on in contemporary theories of freedom as collective participation in self-governance. Against the totalitarian tendencies of those early theories, contemporary critical and democratic theories resist substantive theories of freedom, arguing instead for the need to hold together democratic and negative freedoms in tension with each other, or to affirm more open-ended and procedural conceptions of freedom as political action and public participation, as agonistic politics of contestation and resistance to oppression within relations of power.

While the work of the early Frankfurt School theorists suggested the possibility of freedom in a redemptive relationship of humans with nature, including our own natures, that possibility was typically disavowed as dangerously romantic. In his shift to the analysis of intersubjective communicative practices, Habermas has argued for a discourse ethics oriented toward Western conceptions of universal normative ideals, grounded not in natural or rational foundations but in history. These historically produced ideals, including the liberal ideals of individual rights, autonomy, equality, and freedom, and the ideal of rational consensus as the unattainable yet guiding ideal of democracy, are understood to be achievements of the modern world. The task is to attempt to realize these ideals more fully in our practices.

Most contemporary critical theories, broadly construed, are more critical of liberal ideals, and of the history of the modern Western world as a history of

[6] Mahmood, *Politics of Piety*, 37.

progress toward those ideals. Postcolonial, poststructuralist, and deconstructive theories are theories of demystification of liberal ideals. If freedom remains a guiding ideal, it's an ideal of freedom in practice, in relations of power, in resistance to domination. For Foucault, the guiding ideal of Enlightenment modernity is freedom *as* critique, understood as an open-ended practice of experiment, questioning, testing limits, and self-transformation. If individuals and collectives are deeply constituted through relations of power, then it makes no sense to advocate the liberation of the individual or of a people. The paradox of the subject is the paradox of freedom: our agency and freedom are grounded in the very relations of power that subject us.

If freedom is constituted only in and through relations of power, then freedom can only be a practice of critique and of struggles for change within those relations.[7] The understanding of freedom as critique, as political struggle in agonistic relations of power, has displaced more substantive theories and ideals. Reflecting on the "abandoned radicalism" of contemporary feminist theory, Wendy Brown writes that ambitions to overthrow relations of domination have been replaced by "projects of resistance, reform, or resignification, on the one hand, and normative political theory abstracted from conditions for its realization, on the other."[8] From our contemporary historical perspective, the dreams of an embodied feminist freedom expressed in the early socialist feminist critical theories of Marcuse and Angela Davis can appear quaint and naïve.[9] And yet, she writes, we have lost the qualities exemplified in those early theories: "openhearted, hopeful, vulnerable, imaginative, revolutionary." Brown appears here to be on the verge of nostalgia for the feminist revolution, but she briskly shakes that off. "But," she writes, "to rescind an investment in revolutionary change does not require revoking the elaborate commitment to *critique* represented by Critical Theory."[10] Brown's call, in the absence of an investment in liberation, for a commitment to critique, feels quite sad in comparison. What is critique—and what is critical theory—without a dream of freedom? And what does critique without a dream of freedom *do to us*?

But do we really need to choose between naïve dreams of perfect freedom or just critique? That opposition reflects the assumption that there is no

---

[7] Foucault does affirm the struggles of colonized peoples for liberation from domination, but he argues that this practice of liberation will not be enough to define "the practices of freedom that will still be needed if this people, this society, and these individuals are to be able to define admissible and acceptable forms of existence or political society" (Foucault, "The Ethics of the Concern of the Self as a Practice of Freedom, 282).

[8] Brown, "Feminist Theory and the Frankfurt School," 2. Brown is referring to the opposed positions in feminist critical theory represented by Benhabib and Butler in Feminist Contentions, which mirror the opposed positions of Habermas and Foucault. I discuss this exchange in Weir, "Feminist Critical Theory."

[9] Brown cites Marcuse but not Davis.

[10] Brown, "Feminist Theory and the Frankfurt School," 1, 3.

alternative—that ideals of freedom can only be nostalgic dreams of origin stories, lost paradises, repressed desires. These dreams of unity and harmony must be replaced with the hard-headed realism: politics is about struggles for power. Or could this binary be seen as one form of denial? There is no history to redeem—or to redream. I would call this a wounded critique.

Amy Allen has argued that (feminist) critical theory should abandon its attachment to modern anticipatory-utopian norms of positive freedom and instead affirm a Foucaultian vision of a negativistic nonutopian vision of emancipation as the transformation of a state of (gender) domination into a mobile field of power relations.[11] The contrast between orientation toward utopian ideals and a negativistic conception of emancipation excludes the possibility of an ideal of positive freedom that is not a utopian dream of a conflict-free harmony. Yet ideals of positive freedom are not necessarily utopian. As Charles Taylor has argued, the difference between negative and positive freedoms is the difference between an *opportunity concept* and an *exercise concept*. If negative freedom is the absence of constraint to action, positive freedom is the exercise or *practice* of a substantive ideal.[12] And theories of freedom as democratic participation are theories of positive freedom insofar as they define freedom as the practice of collective self-governance.

A substantive ideal is not necessarily a conflict-free utopia. The conception of relational freedom in Indigenous philosophies of grounded normativity is not an ideal of perfect harmony. It's a conception and practice of freedom in relations among diverse beings, "deeply informed by what land as a system of reciprocal relations and obligations can teach us about living our lives in relation to one another and the natural world in nondominating and nonexploitative terms."[13] The understanding of land as a system of reciprocal relations and obligations does not assume that relations are or can be simply harmonious. It assumes that relations of power must be continually balanced by relations of reciprocity. Fear, aggression, and violence must be continually balanced by practices that take responsibility for interconnectedness and interdependence. Relations of reciprocity are gift relations. They are practices of exchange organized not around acquisition but around gratitude and responsibility. Relational freedom is a practice that involves *risking connection* with and against potentially dangerous others, through the continual development of skills of conflict resolution and cooperative action. It's a practice of reciprocity, of gift exchanges that work to create and maintain sustainable relationships. This requires an engagement in

---

[11] Allen, "Emancipation without Utopia." Allen is referring to Seyla Benhabib's argument that critical theory must include both explanatory-diagnostic and anticipatory-utopian dimensions. See Benhabib, *Critique, Norm, and Utopia*.

[12] Taylor, "What's Wrong with Negative Liberty?"

[13] Coulthard, *Red Skin, White Masks*, 13.

the endless complexity of dynamic and changing relations among a diversity of strange others, who can be dangerous and frightening, but who are also our relations—and parts of ourselves.

Allen's vision of emancipation draws on the queer utopianism articulated by José Muñoz, and on Foucault's conception of *heterotopia*. In contrast to imagined utopias, heterotopias are real spaces that serve as "counter-sites," in which the larger society can be "represented, contested, and inverted." Such sites open up lines of fragility and fracture, creating a distance between ourselves and our forms of life. This distance is the space of freedom.[14] From the perspective of the dominant society, the space of Indigenous relational freedom might be a heterotopia in Foucault's sense: a counter-site that opens up a distance between ourselves and our forms of life—a possibility of another form of life. From the perspective of Indigenous people, heterotopia might have a different meaning: a way of life in which human beings are situated and engaged in relations of radical heterogeneity and complexity. This understanding of heterotopia opens up, for all of us, the possibility of freedom in relations, including relations to place, rather than in gaps, distance, and exit.

As Leanne Betasamosake Simpson writes, Indigenous normativity is essentially queer, because it is rooted in the land that provides endless examples of queerness and diversity. Simpson affirms a queer Indigeneity as a web of supportive, reciprocal, generative relationships.[15]

The difference between Simpson's Indigenous queer normativity and Allen's Foucaultian negativistic vision of emancipation is that Simpson does not understand relations of interdependence solely as relations of power. Relations of interdependence are much more complex. They include relations of power but also include relations of mutuality and reciprocity.[16] And relational freedom foregrounds the normative ethical responsibility of human beings to practice relations of reciprocity.

Allen's negativistic model of emancipation is an attempt to move out of the paradox of freedom with a more realistic vision, consistent with the recognition that human freedom is conditioned by relations of power. This recognition is part of the self-understanding of critical theory: critical theory is a method of theorizing from within relations of power, by drawing on glimpses of ideals that are historically produced and that are present in our situated lives. Critique is a practice of analyzing history and analyzing the present, with an orientation to the future grounded in an appeal to those immanent ideals.[17]

---

[14] Allen, "Emancipation without Utopia," 524 (citing Foucault, "Of Other Spaces: Utopias and Heterotopias," *Diacritics* 16(1) 1986: 22–27, p. 24).
[15] Simpson, *As We Have Always Done*, 134.
[16] I develop this understanding of relations of freedom in Weir, Identities and Freedom.
[17] As Allen writes elsewhere, "critical theory understands itself to be rooted in and constituted by an existing social reality that is structured by power relations that it therefore also aims to critique by

Yet the understanding of freedom as the imagining of an exit through fractured glimpses of otherness still assumes that we are caught in a single story of history. And the assumption that we can find freedom only in relations of power still assumes that we are caught in a single form of relationship. The series of dichotomies that characterize Western modernity—that we must affirm either modern Western norms or modern Western negativistic forms of freedom; either abstract ideals or just critique; either perfect harmony and consensus or fields of agonistic power relations; either a totalizing regime or just action—all assume that there is no alternative. Both sides of each of these dichotomies can be seen as forms of *denial of alternatives*: there is nothing here but us and our story. Despite the self-understanding of critical theory as situated in and drawing from the analysis of history, there is a surprising resistance to history in critical theory. Or there is an assumption that history is *our history* and a resistance to hearing alternative stories.

> You know, when you've experienced a lot of trauma, you repress memories, just to deal with life. But unless you deal with those repressed memories as a person, in this case as a country, we will never move on.[18]

Critical theory should be able to point to a way out of the paralysis of the binaries of modernity and the paradox of freedom by recognizing that we are situated within multiple histories, and multiple kinds of relations: relations of power but also heterogeneous relations of mutuality, care, and solidarity, gift relations of love and reciprocity. A critical theory of freedom from colonization can do this by drawing on the immanent ideals and actual practices of relational freedom in our diverse and shared histories. A critical theory of freedom from colonization would need not only to recognize and theorize the history of colonization. It would also need to assume that we could find in our diverse and heterogeneous histories some resources for a better future. In a broader conception of history that includes *all* of our diverse histories, we can find a diversity of immanent normative ideals, including diverse ideals of relational freedom, that have guided actual practices of freedom.

appealing to immanent standards of normativity and rationality.... what is distinctive about critical theory is its conception of the critical subject as self-consciously rooted in and shaped by the power relations in the society that she nevertheless aims self-reflexively and rationally to critique" (Allen, The End of Progress, xiii). Iris Young writes: "the method of critical theory, as I understand it, reflects on existing social relations and processes to identify what we experience as valuable in them, but as present only intermittently, partially, or potentially" (Young 2000:10).

[18] Wesley Enoch, Sydney Festival Director. From the documentary *Firestarter: The Story of Bangarra*.

Indigenous critical theories affirm a substantive ideal of freedom, rooted in stories of history that find traditions of freedom already practiced in a diversity of ancient Indigenous cultures: multiple and diverse traditions of relational freedom that have been attacked and disavowed by colonization. This understanding of history is not a story of progression from unfreedom to freedom, nor is it a story of the fall from innocence to corruption. It's a more complicated web of stories of heterogeneous ways of life, alternative formations of freedom, knowledge, and power, in relations with each other and with waves of settlement and movement. These stories acknowledge long histories of conflict and violence but also long histories of democratic practices modeled on earth democracies. They serve as alternative sources for understanding and practicing freedom today. Freedom from colonial unknowing would involve taking those histories seriously and learning from the encounter.

In her account of critical theory, Nancy Fraser returns to Marx, to define critical theory as "the self-clarification of the struggles and wishes of the age."[19] A critical theory of freedom from colonial unknowing would need to respond directly to the critical theories that strive to clarify the struggles and wishes of the colonized.

Struggles and Wishes of the Age

"No one is free until all are free." The assertion is attributed to Martin Luther King, Jr., and to the love and justice tradition of Black America, but it expresses a conception of freedom with a long and wide history. It doesn't mean just that everyone would be free to follow their own path without constraint. Freedom would be found in the transformation of relations of domination into relations of reciprocity. So freedom and equality are not opposed values. That formulation relies on a conception of freedom that corresponds to an understanding of ourselves as atomistic individuals in competition with each other. If we understand ourselves as social and political beings—beings whose freedom can be found only in social and political relations—then our freedom is a practice of relationship. The practice of relationship is a practice *of* freedom. And it is a practice *for* freedom in reciprocal relations.[20]

This interrelation between struggles of and for freedom is central to many young political movements today. For the Movement for Black Lives, the project

---

[19] Fraser, "What's Critical About Critical Theory?" 31.
[20] This conception of freedom is part of the "love and justice tradition of Black America" invoked by Patricia Hill Collins, who draws on work by Audre Lorde and other Black feminist theorists, along with the Hegelian-Marxist tradition, and feminist theories of relational identity, to argue for a conception of freedom in relationship.

of resistance to a continuing history of oppression, focused on the abolition of the prison-industrial complex and on social, economic, and political justice, requires struggles of freedom within relations of power and against structures of domination. The aim is to break those structures. Yet the Black Lives Matter principle of restorative and transformative justice sustains the love and justice tradition of struggle for freedom with and for a beloved community.

> We are committed to collectively, lovingly and courageously working vigorously for freedom and justice for Black people and, by extension, all people. As we forge our path, we intentionally build and nurture a beloved community that is bonded together through a beautiful struggle that is restorative, not depleting.[21]

For Frederick Douglass, freedom was found in a social and ethical force that he called "spirit." As Cynthia Willett writes, for Douglass, "freedom does not reside primarily in individual or collective forms of ownership or control . . . Freedom lives or dies in the relations forged between persons."[22] In his story, *Conduction*, Ta-Nehisi Coates articulates this freedom, in an exchange between Otha, a former slave who now works for the Underground Railroad, and Mary Bronson, who has just been freed, on arrival in Philadelphia.

> "It's a good city, ma'am," Otha said. "And we are strong here. But I understand if you don't want to stay. . . . As you will soon see, finding freedom is only the first part. Living free is a whole other." Mary Bronson responds that while she is grateful for being freed from slavery, her husband and sons remain enslaved, and she cannot live free until they are found and reunited with her: "Ain't no living free, less I'm living with my boys."
>
> "Mrs. Bronson," Otha said. "We just ain't set up like that. That just ain't in our power."
>
> "Then you ain't got the power of freedom," she said. "If you can't put us back together, then your freedom is thin and your city hold nothing for me."[23]

This sense that *living* free in relations is much more than breaking the chains that shackle an individual is expressed in the concept of relational freedom in Indigenous philosophies: living well in relations. It's an experience of freedom that isn't stopped by others but is only found *with* them. This is a freedom beyond both private freedom and the public freedom of participation in political

---

[21] https://blacklivesmatter.com/guiding-principles/. See also Davis et al., *Abolition. Feminism. Now.*
[22] Willett, *The Soul of Justice*, 190.
[23] Coates, "Conduction." The story is included in Coates's novel *The Water Dancer*.

institutions and political contestation. It's the freedom of social beings in their everyday embodied practices in relation with each other, themselves, and the world: a social associational freedom that is a political freedom, essential to the practices of democratic life. Just as breaking the chains of slavery does not give the power of freedom—of living free—so legal claims to land as property do not realize freedom for Indigenous communities. When freedom means living well in relations with the land, with all beings in an animate universe, struggles for land as property can sometimes be experienced as struggles not for but away from freedom.[24]

In *Notes Toward a Performative Theory of Assembly*, Judith Butler affirms an ideal of freedom as *a relation among us*, oriented toward an ideal of equality. "Freedom does not come from me or you; it can and does happen as a relation between us, or, indeed, among us." This understanding of freedom means "understanding the human as a relational and social being, one whose action depends upon equality and articulates the principle of equality."[25] This ideal of agency in concert, of freedom as a relation among us, oriented toward an ideal of equality, is one understanding of what I'm calling *relational freedom*. This understanding of freedom is essential to critical theory and to democratic conceptions of freedom as political participation.

Loving Freedom: Political Activism and the Spirit of Transformation

How do we scaffold and support our wellbeing through direct action and confrontation?

How do we begin to draw energy from naming and sourcing our visions more often than our wounds?
 —Healing in Action: A Toolkit for Black Lives Matter[26]

As civil rights activist, academic, and public theologian Ruby Sales says, we have to remember not just what we hate, but what we love.[27] This grounding in a commitment to what we love is essential for a transformative politics that resists the

---

[24] Within Western legal systems, within states that have systematically denied their freedoms and destroyed their ways of life, Indigenous communities asserting treaty rights are pushed to fight for rights to land as property, and rights to use or sell that land for profit: so they are caught between dispossession and fighting for a freedom that breaks relations. Glen Coulthard discusses this dilemma in *Red Skin, White Masks*.
[25] Butler, *Notes Toward a Performative Theory of Assembly*, 88.
[26] https://blacklivesmatter.com/wp-content/uploads/2018/01/BLM_HealingAction_r1.pdf
[27] Sales, "Where Does It Hurt?"

spiral of violence, to practice and generate relations of freedom. A politics of love draws its energy from a vision of freedom in a beloved community: love for land, love for the world, love for ourselves in relations of freedom.

The connection between freedom and love is central to Hannah Arendt's *amor mundi* and to Leanne Betasamosake Simpson's *love of land*. Both understand freedom as involving a practice of love for the world. But how do we hold together love for the world with the necessary anger that fuels political critique and resistance?

As Robyn Wiegman notes, in America outrage has become "our national affective glue . . . the thing that is shared across the political spectrum."[28] Rage against the enemy is commonly advocated as a politics of resistance. But a politics of hate directed toward an object-enemy is a naïve form of politics and is ultimately self-destructive. An effective politics of resistance to domination requires something more intelligent than hatred of the other. It requires careful analysis of political systems, and it requires an intentional exemplary practice of an alternative mode of life. Domination can be resisted only through a practice that enacts an alternative, nondominating way of being. In a politics of nonviolence, anger is grounded in commitment to that alternative way of being, in a challenging practice of love for the world—for all our relations. The politics of love are not politics of niceness or avoidance of confrontation. Anger and love are not opposed. Anger does not have to take the form of hate, directed toward an individualized object-enemy. Anger can be an expression of love: love of land, love of the world, love of relations, love of freedom. These are the forms of love that motivate and sustain revolutionary anger toward systems of colonization.

Black, Indigenous, and People of Color (BIPOC) movements are increasingly embracing and refining politics that combine rage with love. Idle No More activists speak of organizing "from a place of love and rage."[29] Of Black Lives Matter, Patrisse Cullors says "It's both rage and love at the center of our work."[30] These young political movements are becoming increasingly attuned to the politics of emotions, to understand how affects shape our politics and our critiques. Addressing the destructive legacies of colonization requires attending to the wellbeing of communities and individuals by creating a politics that is "restorative, not depleting."[31] Against a machismo politics that meets hate with hate, and that perpetuates cycles of violence, organizations and movements like Idle No More, the Native Youth Sexual Health Network, and Black Lives Matter are developing queer feminist politics of revolutionary freedom grounded in a politics

---

[28] Wiegman, "Outrage."
[29] Sleydo' (Molly Wickham), Wet'suwet'en activist, quoted by Pitts, "From a Place of Love and Rage."
[30] Cullors and Ross, "The Spiritual Work of Black Lives Matter."
[31] See note 26.

of love that supports individual and collective wellbeing. The spirit of relational freedom informs these movements, as source and end of critique: for Black Lives Matter, the ideal of a beloved community, for Indigenous resurgence movements, land-based spiritualities. The politics of love and the ethos of relational freedom are essential to struggles that go beyond resistance, and beyond the attempt to replace one form of dominant power with another, to transform relations.

The idea of love as a revolutionary force is not new. bell hooks writes that all of the great social movements for freedom and justice have promoted an ethic of love.[32] Black feminist theorists in the "love and justice" tradition have long argued that love is essential to political movements. Audre Lorde criticized the false dichotomy between the spiritual and the political, arguing that the bridge that connects them is formed by the erotic: "the passions of love, in its deepest meanings," including "the sharing of joy."[33] In mainstream political theory, the idea of revolutionary love has been taken up in several books by Michael Hardt and Antonio Negri. But the conception of love proposed by Hardt and Negri is a rather vague "romanticisation of the undifferentiated multitude."[34] While they argue for an ideal of love that can infuse a broad-based revolution, Hardt and Negri assume that we can simply generalize from love in the private sphere to the public and fail to problematize the complex relations between private and public, intersectional identities. And while they criticize the "love of the same" that is the basis of nationalism, racism, and fundamentalism, and argue that that love must be extended to embrace others and strangers, they give no indication as to how this might be possible.[35]

As I've argued in Chapter 3, the philoxenic love central to Indigenous philosophies and politics of love for land—love for all our relations, in all of their strangeness and diversity—is the form of love that grounds intelligent responses to the fear and hatred of the strange other, and works to accept and include that otherness within us. This kind of love is not a feeling but an intentional attitude that works to counteract the fear and hostility provoked by our dependence on the other, and to transform that dependence into relations of interdependence.

Central to a politics of love for all our relations is a politics of care for individual and collective wellbeing. As Indigenous feminist and queer theorists and activists argue, community and individual wellbeing must be addressed directly as part of Indigenous political struggles for self-governance. If struggles for self-determination focus on political sovereignty without addressing the wellbeing

---

[32] hooks, *All About Love*. As I've argued, this is not just a Christian ethic. Indigenous relational freedom is animated by a philoxenic ethic, and that ethic is central to politics of resurgence.
[33] Lorde, *Sister Outsider*, 56.
[34] Ferguson and Jónasdóttir, *Love*, 6.
[35] Wilkinson, "Love in the Multitude?"; Ferguson, "Feminist Love Politics"; Hennessey, "Bread and Roses in the Common."

of communities traumatized by the legacy of colonization, they are bound to fail. Civil rights activist Ruby Sales says: "one of the greatest trigger fingers of the Empire has been to destroy intimacy: to destroy how we know each other."[36] Sales argues that politics of freedom must address both the erosion of a beloved community and the loss of public space that could bring people together. In response, movements for political transformation are developing politics of healing justice, transformative justice, transformative resurgence: spiritual political practices of transformation of selves and collectives, transformation of relations. These are politics that directly address the need to restore individuals and collectives, restoring a sense of selves in connection, to heal trauma and to build resilient movements.

Indigenous politics of transformative resurgence ground political struggles for self-determination in land-based spiritualities.[37] The term "Native spiritualities" can be misused to generalize about a wide range of specific practices that are often appropriated by new age and self-help industries. Indigenous land-based spiritualities are practices of ways of life; they are "spiritual" insofar as they are rooted in and oriented toward a sense of the sacredness of the relations among all beings in an animate world. Land-based spiritualities ground a politics of transformation that centers on remaking Indigenous communities, focusing on individual and community wellbeing. They also support very effective politics of resistance. In the Water Protectors camps at Standing Rock, resistance to the Dakota Access Pipeline was led with prayer circles and rituals that sustained the protests through several years. In such protests, Indigenous sovereignty is asserted in a practice of spiritual resistance: the protection of water is understood not just as conservation of a resource but as a sacred trust.

Patrisse Cullors says the work of Black Lives Matter is deeply spiritual work: it's healing justice work. "I believe that this work of Black Lives Matter is actually healing work. It's not just about policy. It's why, I think, some people get so confused about us. They're like, where's the policy? And I'm like, you can't policy your racism away. We no longer have Jim Crow laws, but we still have Jim Crow hate."[38] The Black Lives Matter Healing Justice Working Group addresses the need to integrate care for selves and each other into political action, arguing

---

[36] "The Black community has been under this assault ever since enslavement, where Black people's families were sold away from each other." Paradoxically, Black communities were further eroded with integration, as children were thrust out into a public world with no protection from hate (Sales, "Where Does It Hurt?"). Faith Spotted Eagle talks about layers of trauma, beginning with theft of land, starvation, and criminalization of language and ceremony. The most damage, she argues, was done by the removal of children into residential schools, which destroyed communities and produced a downward spiral of abuse, self-sedation, and violence (Faith Spotted Eagle, "Trauma and Resiliency," https://www.youtube.com/watch?v=nb_yXly4sDw).

[37] Dian Million writes that the politics of resurgence have developed through a reciprocal play between land-based spiritualities and politics of self-determination (Million, *Therapeutic Nations*, 121).

[38] Cullors and Ross, "The Spiritual Work of Black Lives Matter."

that "Healing justice needs to be at the very center of how we work together.... We hold this space together as sacred to our learning and practice of how to collectively enter into an embodied, restorative and transformative practice towards Black liberation."[39]

The Black Lives Matter movement has made the principles and practices of *healing justice* and *transformative justice* central to their practices of freedom. The movement consciously addresses the historical and generational trauma Black people have endured at the hands of the state, which "unresolved and unhealed lives on in our bodies, in our relationships and in what we create together."[40] The work of social and political transformation thus requires embodied and collective practices and rituals that heal and transform individuals and collectives. The practices of healing justice and transformative justice are embodied practices that cultivate habits of reparative relationship with bodies and with each other, and cultivate affects of openness, curiosity, and "rigorous love" that risks confronting and intelligently working through trauma and conflict. These are practices that inhabit ideals of freedom and embody relational freedom: engaging in self and social transformation through openness to the other: to bodies, to each other, to ideals. Against the appropriation of self-care by neoliberal policies that support the restoration of individuals only to render them more productive and conformist, these are practices of self-care and collective care, within a politics of reworking and reimagining freedom in social and political relationships and institutions. Healing justice and transformative justice are practiced in response to a history of heroic activism that prides itself on self-denial and on a reckless and destructive disregard for bodies and for relationships. As Cara Page writes, "Our movements themselves need to be healing or there is no point to them."[41]

Like discourses of spirituality, discourses of trauma and healing can, of course, be problematic. As Dian Million argues, psychologizing discourses of trauma, disconnected from a politics that addresses Indigenous governance, can support a neoliberal politics of adaptation to "reality." A focus on violence and abuse in

---

[39] Healing in Action: A Toolkit for Black Lives Matter, https://blacklivesmatter.com/wp-content/uploads/2018/01/BLM_HealingAction_r1.pdf
[40] https://blacklivesmatter.com/healing-justice/
[41] Cara Page, at the 2010 USSF Healing Justice People's Movement Assembly, quoted by Leah Lakshmi Piepzna-Samarinha. Cara Page, a Black and Indigenous, queer femme organizer, is a founder of healing justice movements, through her work with the Kindred: Southern Healing Justice Collective. Leah Lakshmi Piepzna-Samarasinha writes that *healing justice* as a movement and a term was created by queer and trans people of color and in particular Black and brown femmes, centering working-class, poor, disabled, and Southern/rural healers. Leah Lakshmi Piepzna-Samarasinha, "A Not-So-Brief Personal History of the Healing Justice Movement 2010–2016," *Mice Magazine* (http://micemagazine.ca/issue-two/not-so-brief-personal-history-healing-justice-movement-2010-2016). As Diane Winston writes, "Black Lives Matter's chapters and affiliated groups are expressing a type of spiritual practice that makes use of the language of health and wellness to impart meaning, heal grief and trauma, combat burnout, and encourage organizational efficiency" (Winston, *Religion Dispatches*).

Indigenous communities can serve as justification for government intervention. Million problematizes the discourse of trauma and healing in Indigenous communities, and criticizes "development" discourses that psychologize legacies of colonization as individual and community trauma. Community development programs can provide support for self-management as a means of assimilation and incorporation of individuals through acceptance of individualized responsibility and a muting of critique. When this framework is taken up by Indigenous organizations, "a certain script is offered where 'what happened' leads to a larger diagnosis of trauma with a prescription for healing. This diagnosis is most often identified with large scale personal 'healing' from dysfunctionality, rather than a discussion of 'how we govern.'" Thus, "the larger goal of healing trauma, reconciliation, now pulls toward reconciliation with the state."[42] In contrast, Indigenous women's activism and queer activism offer "a specific vision of polity that encompasses diverse alliances, one that is informed by practices of *naw'qinwixw* [collective decision-making] in political struggles for land, food, and environmental justice. In these performed affective acts, an alternate vision of polity and justice emerges that potentially performs self-determined autonomy rather than self-management."[43] These are practices of *political* healing that center wellbeing as integral to political transformation, and integral to a reformulation of Indigenous *governance*: healing as a practice of resurgence that includes recognition of historical political trauma, and that works through revaluing restorative relations with land and with one another. The practice of *transformative resurgence* focuses on issues of health and harm reduction in relation to sexuality, gender identity, and embodiment, in the context of relations to bodies, each other, and land: "reclaiming our bodies and restoring our cultures are part of the process" of responding to oppression: "the land speaks through our bodies."[44] Dian Million cites examples of Indigenous decolonizing methodologies that develop Indigenous spiritual practices not by psychologizing trauma but by revitalizing relations with land. These are spiritual practices insofar as they revive meaningful relations among communities with land, governance practices that heal by bringing people together to develop and articulate responsibility for sustainable practices, understood as protection of a sacred alliance with land.[45]

---

[42] Million, *Therapeutic Nations*, 144.
[43] Million, *Therapeutic Nations*, 31–32. Million references Jeanette Armstrong's use of the Syilx term *naw'quinwixw* as a collective practice of decision-making that draws on diverse views and allows them to permeate through the collective.
[44] Native Youth Sexual Health Network website: https://www.nativeyouthsexualhealth.com
[45] Such actions protect treaties, but in their assertions of a sacred trust to protect a sacred alliance, they claim an authority prior to treaties: "This is a statement that claims its own authority beyond that of treaties but protects the treaty—by articulating their rights as sacred and part of what they seek to protect, by assuming them and performing them. It is also a statement that reaches out inclusively

All of these practices are spiritual practices that involve transformation of selves in relation to each other and to ideals, transformation of relations of power and reciprocity. These are the transformations that settlers need to take up in a practice of freedom from colonial unknowing. As James Baldwin wrote:

> White people in this country will have quite enough to do in learning how to accept and love themselves and each other, and when they have achieved this—which will not be tomorrow and may very well be never—the Negro problem will no longer exist, for it will no longer be needed.[46]

For settlers, freedom from colonial unknowing would involve a transformation of who we are through engaging in transformative relations with Indigenous peoples and in embodied and affective relations with the locations in which we live: with earth others, with land. This would be a practice of transformation of our relations with ourselves, with our bodies, with our fears and hatreds—with the parts of ourselves that we have projected onto colonized others. It would be a location of ourselves within the world. This involves both an acceptance of a nondominant position and an expansion of ourselves to include whatever we have othered. Learning to love ourselves and each other: for those of us who want to transform the world, it's a vital, difficult, and necessary *political* practice.

Freedom as a Spiritual Exercise: Foucault and Hadot

If critical theory has been oriented toward freedom, then critical theory has always been spiritual. It just means we have a sense of what critique is *for:* what it means for us. Holding together freedom with critique involves affirming an ethos or spirit that motivates and animates political struggle: a sense of meaning that pervades our habits and our practices. Albrecht Wellmer has argued that freedom in the modern world is conceivable only as a democratic form of ethical life. Freedom can exist, he writes, "only as a form of ethical life [*Sittlichkeit*], that is, as a communal practice pervading the institutions of society at all levels and habitualized in the character, the customs, and the moral sentiments of its citizens."[47]

For Michel Foucault, the spirit or ethos of modernity is the practice of critique oriented toward freedom. Critique is not only historical analysis but experiment,

---

to portray that their responsibility should be shared, should be everyone's" (Million, *Therapeutic Nations*, 169).

[46] Baldwin, "Letter from a Region of my Mind."
[47] Wellmer, "Models of Freedom in the Modern World," 237, 238.

questioning, testing of limits, finding exits, ways out of the stories that produce and limit us as historical beings. The spirit of modernity, or (the) enlightenment, is "an attitude, an ethos, a philosophical life in which the critique of what we are is at one and the same time the historical analysis of the limits that are imposed on us and an experiment with the possibility of going beyond them."[48] "I shall thus characterize the philosophical ethos appropriate to the critical ontology of ourselves as a historico-practical test of the limits that we may go beyond, and thus as work carried out by ourselves upon ourselves as free beings."[49]

To think about the work carried out by ourselves upon ourselves, Foucault drew on Pierre Hadot's argument that the central focus of ancient philosophy was the practice of *spiritual exercises*. Hadot argues that the primary focus of ancient Greek and Roman philosophies was not the development of reason or knowledge but the transformation of the self: philosophy as a way of life. The point of spiritual exercises was to bring about "a transformation of our vision of the world, and to a metamorphosis of our personality."[50]

> "Spiritual exercises." The expression is a bit disconcerting for the contemporary reader. . . . It is nevertheless necessary to use this term, I believe, because none of the other adjectives we could use—"psychic," "moral," "ethical," "intellectual," "of thought," "of the soul"—covers all the aspects of the reality we want to describe.[51]

Foucault prefers to call these exercises ethical practices or techniques of the self. But he does occasionally use the terms *spirituality* and *spiritual practice*. When asked about the relation between philosophy and spirituality in the context of the care of the self, Foucault replies: "By spirituality I mean—but I'm not sure this definition can hold for very long—the subject's attainment of a certain mode of being and the transformations that the subject must carry out on itself to attain this mode of being." Following Hadot, he adds, "I believe that spirituality and philosophy were identical or nearly identical in ancient spirituality."[52]

The practices of self-transformation that define the spirit of modernity can be understood, then, as spiritual practices. And they are spiritual insofar as they are practices of self-transformation oriented toward an ideal. It's commonly assumed that in affirming a practice of experimentation, Foucault resisted any orientation

---

[48] Foucault, "What Is Enlightenment?" 50.
[49] Foucault, "What Is Enlightenment?" 47. In this essay Foucault positions his argument with and against Kant, who, he says, defines the "essential conditions under which mankind can escape from its immaturity. And these two conditions are at once spiritual and institutional, ethical and political" (35).
[50] Hadot, *Philosophy as a Way of Life*, 82.
[51] Hadot, *Philosophy as a Way of Life*, 81.
[52] Foucault, "The Ethics of Concern for Self as a Practice of Freedom," 294.

toward an endpoint, a fixed ideal or telos of that practice. According to this understanding, Foucault offers *practices* of freedom, but not orientation to an end or *ideal* of freedom: struggles *of* but not *for* freedom. It's true that the spirit of an open-ended practice of freedom is the attitude or ethos that Foucault affirmed as the definitive attitude of modernity—the attitude that is worth reclaiming, as opposed to the orientation to normative morality, which is not. And yet in his discussions of the ethics of the self, Foucault both describes and affirms a practice of care of the self that involves orientation to a *telos* or ideal. He argues that all such practices are related to some *telos* or ideal self: for the Greeks, the beautiful self. Foucault's critique of normative morality as a "mode of subjection" is a critique of a universal moral law that is enforced, regulated, and policed. And his understanding of practices of freedom is distinguished from an understanding of liberation as a normative end of freedom: Foucault criticized discourses of liberation, with their illusion of a perfect freedom achievable by casting off external oppression to liberate natural selves in harmony with each other. Yet Foucault does affirm a shared collective modern normative ideal of freedom as experimentation and self-transformation.[53] This normative ideal bears some relation to what Habermas means by regulative norms: ideals that orient and guide our practices.

Pierre Hadot argues that Foucault's understanding of the spiritual exercises of the ancients as a therapeutic ethics focused on the self misses what is distinctive to ancient Greek and Roman philosophies: the understanding of the self as belonging to a communal and cosmic whole. "In my view, the feeling of belonging to a whole is an essential element [in the philosophical practice of the Stoics and Platonists]: belonging, that is, both to the whole constituted by the human community, and to that constituted by the cosmic whole. Seneca sums it up in four words: *Toti se inserens mundo*, 'Plunging oneself into the totality of the world.' "[54] It's in plunging into the totality of the world that the self transforms itself, through conscious relation to that whole. The practice of *spiritual exercises* is a practice not of attention to the self, but of attention to the self's relation to the whole. It involves transcendence of the particularity of the self, through a consciousness of relation with the universal. "Above all, the word 'spiritual' reveals the true dimensions of these exercises. By means of them, the individual raises himself up to the life of the objective Spirit; that is to say, he re-places himself within the perspective of the Whole."[55] "In fact, the goal of Stoic exercises is to go beyond the self, and think and act in unison with universal reason."[56] Foucault does argue that the techniques of the self are developed in relation with others,

---

[53] See Butler, "What Is Critique?
[54] Hadot, *Philosophy as a Way of Life*, 208.
[55] Hadot, *Philosophy as a Way of Life*, 82.
[56] Hadot, *Philosophy as a Way of Life*, 207.

with mentors, and in consideration of one's social roles and responsibilities. But Hadot is saying something very different. For the ancients, the point of philosophy was to transform oneself by becoming aware of oneself as belonging to a cosmic Whole and to align with the cosmos.

For the Epicureans, the importance of the *hypomnemata* was that it connects the self with the whole. "Writing, like the other spiritual exercises, *changes the level of the self*, and universalizes it.... A person writing feels he is being watched; he is no longer alone, but is part of the silently present human community. When one formulates one's personal acts in writing, one is taken up by the machinery of reason, logic, and universality. What was confused and subjective becomes thereby objective."[57] Philosophy as a way of life meant not just the development of individuality; "This is a new way of being-in-the-world, which consists in becoming aware of oneself as a part of nature, and a portion of universal reason.... one identifies oneself with an "Other": nature, or universal reason, as it is present within each individual. This implies a radical transformation, and contains a universalist, cosmic dimension."[58] Hadot's understanding of the term *spiritual* differs, then, from Foucault's. Where Foucault understands spiritual exercises as practices of self-transformation, Hadot understands them as practices of self-transformation oriented toward a shared natural, cosmic, and social and political whole.

Hadot recognizes that Foucault's reading of the ancients for an ethics of the self is a distinctly modern reading. But while the focus on the ethics of the self *qua* self is specific to modernity, Hadot argues that it does not do justice to the possibility of modernity. "I believe firmly—albeit perhaps naively—that it is possible for modern man to live, not as a sage (Sophos)—most of the ancients did not hold this to be possible—but as a practitioner of the ever-fragile *exercise* of wisdom."[59] For Hadot, this would mean beginning from the lived experience of the concrete, living, and perceiving subject, to follow the practice described by Marcus Aurelius: to attempt to practice objectivity of judgment, to live according to justice, in the service of the human community, and to become aware of our situation as a part of the universe—to be open to the universal. These spiritual exercises, he argues, are practiced in diverse cultures and are justified by diverse philosophical discourses. What they share is a location of the self within the natural, human, and cosmic whole. They also share an attention to the present moment. This is why the spiritual exercises are so important. For the ancients, philosophy was not discourse *about* a way of life; it *was* a way of life. And the fundamental philosophic attitude consisted in *living in the present*: practicing

---

[57] Hadot, *Philosophy as a Way of Life*, 211.
[58] Hadot, *Philosophy as a Way of Life*, 211.
[59] Hadot, *Philosophy as a Way of Life*, 211.

philosophy as a way of life in the present moment. Living in the present is not, then, a particularly modern form of life. Focus on the present moment is the practice of all ancient spiritual exercises—and of all ancient philosophies. This understanding of philosophy as a way of life is distinct from philosophy as a practice of justification through defensive denial of the other.[60] It goes beyond a practice of critique limited to demystification, and beyond a practice of open-ended experimentation. For the ancients, living in the present meant experiencing and understanding one's place and location in a world of relations. This was a practice of freedom from the particularity of the self and from the weight of the past and the future: a practice of freedom found only in relations to self, others, and the world.

For Foucault, the modern individual could live philosophy as a way of life—a way of freedom—only through glimpses of ways *out*—through counter-sites, heterotopias, experimental practices of other ways of being. Modern freedom would require an escape route from what he understood to be the linear story of our history. He couldn't see a way out through reencountering our multiple and diverse histories and ways of life, not conquered, in the present. Or could he? In his visit to a Zen temple, Foucault said this:

> European thought finds itself at a turning point . . . (which) is nothing other than the end of imperialism. The crisis of Western thought is identical to the end of imperialism. . . .There is no philosopher who marks out this period. For it is the end of the era of Western philosophy. Thus, if philosophy of the future exists, it must be born outside of Europe, or equally born in consequence of meetings and impacts between Europe and non-Europe.[61]

Foucault used the term *political spirituality* to refer to "the will to discover a different way of governing oneself"—a different mode of being.[62] As Karen Vintges notes, in his essays on the Iranian Revolution and in his interest in Buddhism, Foucault sought forms of political spirituality in "freedom practices opposing truth regimes, and involving the whole of peoples' ways of life.[63]" Foucault, then, was still looking for large-scale social and political transformation. But he understood that this would have to be a transformation of all of our selves. When Foucault used the term *political spirituality*, he was invoking a guiding principle for practices of transformation in our modes of being. His interest in Buddhist

---

[60] See Dotson, "How Is This Essay Philosophy?" and Salamon, "Justification and Queer Method, or Leaving Philosophy."

[61] The text is an interview originally published in the Japanese Buddhist review *Shunju* and included in translation in Foucault, *Dits et Écrits*. This translation is from Carrette, "Michel Foucault and Zen," 113.

[62] Foucault, "Questions of Method," 82; quoted by Vintges, "Freedom and Spirituality," 106.

[63] Vintges, "Freedom and Spirituality," 107.

and Islamic spirituality was an interest in an experience of and orientation toward something we call *spirit*: some kind of sacred value or ideal or meaning that guides our practices.

I would suggest that "spiritual" is just a sense of connection. It's a lived experience of relationship. A political spirituality for critical theory would involve the transformation of our selves through the transformation of our relations with each other, oriented toward a guiding ideal of freedom.

Philosophy as a way of life in the modern world requires, I think, that we transform ourselves through a practice of critique and a practice of life oriented around a freedom in which we understand ourselves as belonging to the world. Central to this transformative practice is a model of critique that foregrounds openness and curiosity toward the radically other in our explanatory-diagnostic methods, and reciprocity as an anticipatory-utopian ideal. Critical theory, then, can be understood as a practice of encountering and engaging in reparative relations with diverse and strange others, to learn and to practice a radically new way of life.

Reparative Theorizing: Toward a Reparative Relation to an Ideal of Relational Freedom

Has critical theory lost its aim: a dream of freedom that we can love? We could say that Eurocentric critical theories are often caught in the vicious circle of a dream of freedom and its disappointment—of attachment to abstract ideals and attachment their brokenness. So we either cling to our defining ideals, or we demystify them. This is a central binary of Western critical theories, and it is central to the paradox of freedom: either we have perfect freedom, or we retreat into negativistic critique, or stoical engagement in relations of power.

What does it mean for us to remember not only what we hate, but what we love? We hate the enemy. But we also hate the stupid naïve ideals we once had. What would it mean to hold together love and critique: love of the world, and love of an ideal and practice of relational freedom, with critique of colonization? It would mean holding together careful analyses of all of the dimensions of colonization with a constant remembrance of what critique is *for*.

I want to suggest that Eve Sedgwick's model of reparative theorizing offers a way to repair the relation between critique and freedom, by repairing our relation to a world we can love, and to a normative ideal of relational freedom. Sedgwick makes a distinction, drawing on Melanie Klein, between what she calls *paranoid* and *reparative* theorizing. She argues that theories of demystification, of unmasking and exposure of systems of domination, can be paranoid theories, insofar as knowledge is understood as exposure of truth, and the practice of knowledge involves an obsessive, defensive and suspicious vigilance against any surprise. Paranoia, she suggests, has become a kind of sanctioned and privileged *methodology*. Obsessively fixated on unmasking and exposing the truth, paranoid theories shield us against the shame of humiliation that could befall a more hopeful vision. This defensive position blocks more open and receptive affects, blocking curiosity about other ways of thinking and being, and blocking openness to the possibility of surprise. I would say that it blocks freedom. Paranoid theory requires "a certain disarticulation, disavowal, and misrecognition of other ways of knowing, ways less oriented around suspicion, that are actually being practiced, often by the same theorists and as part of the same projects."[64]

Sedgwick is not saying that we should stop unmasking and exposing oppression and domination. Obviously demystifying theories are exposing important truths. She is thinking about how we *do* theories and what theories *do* to us. Drawing on Silvan Tomkins, Sedgwick argues that paranoia is a "strong negative affect theory"—in this case, a strong humiliation-fear theory. The term *theory* here refers to a way of approaching the world, a way of doing one's life, and a way of thinking, such that affects are construed *as* theories. Paranoia is a strong negative affect theory insofar as it is reductive and totalizing, compulsively seeking the same truth everywhere. Sedgwick argues, then, that we also need *reparative theories*, which open up to a middle range of affects. Here she draws on Klein's contention that we have the capacity to move between paranoid and reparative *positions*, rather than being stuck in fixed personality types. Sedgwick's argument for reparative critical *practices* is an argument for a particular *relational stance*— or rather, for "changing and heterogeneous relational stances."[65] She suggests that we can shift from theorizing that deploys relentlessly negative affects that shield against humiliation to theorizing that takes the risk of being open to curiosity and surprise, and of moving toward a sustained seeking of pleasure.

While Sedgwick's critique of paranoid theorizing is focused on demystifying theories, I would argue that both theories obsessed with demystification and theories obsessed with defensive justification of the regulative norms that are

---

[64] Sedgwick, "Paranoid Reading and Reparative Reading," 144. Sedgwick's alternative model of theorizing has been taken up in queer literary and cultural studies, founding a whole industry of affect theory, but has had little impact on critical political theory. Robyn Wiegman discusses the importance of reparative methodology as "a critical practice that seeks to love and nurture its objects of study" (Wiegman, "The Times We're in). Jana Sawicki has suggested that Sedgwick's model of reparative theorizing can be taken up as a guiding practice of a queer feminism that cultivates practices of freedom "an eccentric, provocative and unruly feminist practice, one able to risk, challenge, and transform itself, any static sense of its beloved objects and self-understandings, its sense of temporal and spatial orders." Sedgwick, she writes, "extends Foucault's project of 'thinking [and being] otherwise'. . . [and] offers us a way of thinking about how to undo our attachments to particular self-understandings and practices and create others in the midst of subjection, normalization and the intensification of neoliberalism" (Sawicki, "Queer Feminism," 75).

[65] Sedgwick, "Paranoid Reading and Reparative Reading," 128.

supposed to be the achievements of Western modernity are narrow and rigid conceptions of critique, offering diminished understandings of freedom in relation to ideal norms: as either allegiance or subversion, conformity or resistance, to given abstract ideals of autonomy and emancipation. Neither of these alternatives allows for curiosity about other possibilities. Both alternatives preclude relationship—to the other, and to another way of being.

Could a reparative critical theory move beyond the opposed projects of defensive justification or demystification, to replace our abandoned dreams with something more than dreamless critique? To reclaim a stance that could be, despite everything, openhearted, hopeful, vulnerable, imaginative, revolutionary? With the idea of the reparative stance, Sedgwick was proposing an approach to theorizing—but she was also proposing an approach to thinking, politics, and life. I think that Sedgwick was offering a particular conception of *freedom*: a movement from a defensive practice of vigilant critique to a practice of freedom characterized by curiosity and openness, from a form of defensive resistance to a practice of freedom involving a different affect and a different methodology. I would argue that critical theory requires a reparative method of critique that involves curiosity and openness to being surprised in an extended encounter with those we have othered.

Reparative methodology involves a particular kind of relation to *objects*. In Klein's object relations theory, the relation to the loved object is split between love and hate: the loved object is divided into the beloved object we desire, and the feared, hated object that disappoints and abandons us. Development to maturity and the capacity for mature relationship requires that we put together the loved and hated objects into some kind of whole. Following Klein, reparative theories are facilitated by moving from the paranoid position to the depressive position, from which it is possible to assemble or repair the "murderous part-objects" into something like a whole, which then becomes available for *identification*, and which then can be a source of sustenance. Among Klein's names for the reparative process is love.[66]

I want to suggest that a reparative critical theory requires reparative relations to two kinds of objects. Reparative theory allows us to understand the object of critique—the world—in all of its complexity, so that we can remake it into an ambiguous, complex object to which we can reattach. By remembering our love for the world, we can combine that love with critique that is reparative, rather than paranoid. This means, further, that we can take a reparative stance toward an object or ideal of relational freedom. Reparative theorizing is a *practice of* freedom, and it can orient us in struggles *for* freedom—toward a normative

---

[66] Bonnie Honig has drawn on Melanie Klein for a theory of relation to public things as loved objects (Honig, *Public Things*).

ideal of freedom as loved object. Reparative theorizing can guide our practices of embodied and affective relation to that normative ideal.

What would it mean to take relational freedom as a loved ideal? When Sedgwick argued for a reparative relation to loved objects, she was perhaps insufficiently attentive to the conflictual nature of that love, and to the ambiguity of the loved object. For Klein, the reparative position is possible only when we mourn the loss of the idealized object, heal the splitting between the beloved and the enemy, and are able to recreate a loved object that is a composite of the good and bad, loved and hated objects—a recognition of the ambiguity and complexity of the object-other, and a capacity to sustain love for that imperfect other. If we are going to sustain an ideal of relational freedom, our broken dreams of perfect freedom will have to be mourned. But rather than renouncing our ideals as naïve and immature, and moving to the paranoid defensive position, a reparative stance will allow us to be guided by an ideal of relational freedom, of active and continual engagement in cultivating relations of mutuality and reciprocity.

The disavowal of orientation toward an ideal of relational freedom is the effect of paranoid theory: no one wants to be caught stupidly believing, and humiliated by failure. What would it mean for critical theory *not* to be paranoid? I think it would mean taking the risk of attachment to the beloved ideal of freedom, in all of its ambiguity and complexity, but in a way that that is open to surprise—that does not assume we already know what freedom is or might be. To emerge from colonial unknowing, to decolonize critical theory, we would need to detach from paranoid attachments to certainties, self-understandings, and practices that may no longer serve us, and reattach to an ideal of relational freedom that supports practices of transformation. We would need to take a relational stance in an encounter with Indigenous critical theories of relational freedom. Critical theory requires, then, an intersubjective method: a method that shifts from disavowal of particular objects to an encounter with other subjects.

This method would be a practice of self-transformation through taking a reparative stance toward the knowledge of others, a curiosity and openness to surprise that can counteract our paranoid stances. This self-transformation through encounter with the other and this expansion of critique would involve retraining our sensibilities, affects, desires, and sentiments, cultivating habits of curiosity, to inhabit relational freedom. And it would involve reconsidering and remaking our embodied and affective attachments. In these practices freedom is constructed as not just the obverse of oppression. The dream of absolute freedom has to be grieved, its impossibility accepted, its loss mourned. In its place is a capacity for freedom in and through relations of power, and relations of love, meaning, and solidarity. This is a freedom that must be endlessly re-created in and through mourning, in and through the acceptance of loss and the work of repair.

Inhabiting Relational Freedom: Decolonizing Critical Theory

Given the multiple critiques of the liberal ideal of freedom, we won't repair our relation to the ideal of freedom by just reasserting regulative norms of autonomy and rights. Yet being stuck in the stance of critique and resistance, without orienting ideals, is self-destructive. The stance of resistance is oriented only toward the oppressor, or the system of oppression, and can only mirror that object. This stance produces only resentment and aggression, which are turned not only toward the oppressor but toward the self and others. Many of the world's philosophical traditions offer resources for dealing with this dilemma: traditions of relationality and relational freedom. Central to philosophies of relationality is the concept of the person-in-relationship, a critique of violation of sustaining relationships, and a recognition of vulnerability to violation within relations of power. Freedom is possible only in and through continued practices of repair of relationships. There is no illusion that all that is broken can be repaired to produce a seamless harmonious whole. Reparative practices must be ongoing and continually transformative.

In Australia the First Nations National Constitutional Convention Uluru Statement from the Heart has invoked the Yolngu concept of Makarrata: coming together after a struggle. This is a call for treaty, and it acknowledges irreparable and ongoing damage, but affirms a willingness to work together to repair and to re-create relationships. "The Uluru Statement from the Heart is an invitation to the Australian people to work with First Nations people to create a better future. It is a gift: a strategic roadmap to peace, where First Nations peoples take a rightful place in our own land."[67] Indigenous peoples around the world are extending the invitation to treaty. This is an extraordinarily generous invitation to practice relational freedom: to decolonize ourselves.

In his reflective essay, "*Hoquotist*: Reorienting through Storied Practice," Johnny Mack asks how taking stories seriously could transform treaty negotiations. If settlers were to take their story seriously, he writes, "it seems that they would have to confront the inherent injustice in their claim of any rights or authority over indigenous peoples and to their unconquered and unceded territory." They would have to accept a story of thievery and show a willingness to return what was stolen. He holds out little hope that this will happen.

Then he turns to the corresponding question: "*what would we as Nuu-chah-nulth do differently if we took our stories seriously?*" When he consults with Elder Wickaninnish, the answer is clear: "we must turn to our own stories with a

---

[67] Uluru Statement from the Heart. https://ulurustatement.org/the-statement/view-the-statement/

posture of respect and an imperative toward balance" and draw on those stories in a practice of cultural regeneration, to improve individual and collective wellbeing, and to support a capacity to make fair compromises. Yet there is a formidable obstacle to that task. As Mack himself writes, even though he grew up in his home village, he hasn't been raised in those stories. His attempt to reconnect to those stories produces a state of disorientation. As Wickaninnish puts it, "Our people are lost." In Nuu-chah-nulth, the metaphor used to describe that state of disorientation is *hoquotist*: a person whose canoe has been overturned. This term describes a people who no longer know their stories, or who, even if they know them, have become, in Mack's words, "disconnected from the perceptual orientation and responsibilities that flowed from those stories." Again, Wickaninnish offers a solution that is simple—at least conceptually. The stories are still there. Just tend to them and practice. Mack writes, "I am beginning to understand that what was lost was not an essence or thing. Of course, we have lost a vast amount of knowledge, but that knowledge was acquired through practice. . . . It is not a matter of returning to an old and almost lost story. It is a matter of looking back to those stories through practice. These practices will provide the inspiration and instruction as we move to rebuild a canoe that can help us navigate the currents we encounter in the present."[68]

Settlers, too, need to reorient ourselves through storied practice. We need to take seriously our own stories—including stories of theft and genocide, freedom and redemption —to allow ourselves to be disoriented, and reoriented. We need to start telling, and practicing, stories of relationship.

---

[68] Mack, "*Hoquotist.*"

References

Adams, Carol J., and Lori Gruen. 2014. *Ecofeminism: Feminist Intersections with Other Animals and the Earth*. London: Bloomsbury.
Ahmed, Sara. 2005. *The Cultural Politics of Emotion*. London: Routledge.
Aikau, Hokulani K., Maile Arvin, Mishuana Goeman, and Scott Morgensen. 2015. "Indigenous Feminisms Roundtable." *Frontiers: A Journal of Women Studies* 36(3): 84–106.
Alfred, Gerald (Taiaiake). 1995. *Heeding the Voices of Our Ancestors: Kahnawake and the Rise of Native Nationalism*. Toronto: Oxford University Press.
Alfred, Taiaiake. 1999. *Peace, Power, Righteousness: An Indigenous Manifesto*. Toronto: Oxford University Press.
Alfred, Taiaiake. 2005. "Sovereignty." In *Sovereignty Matters: Locations of Contestation and Possibility in Indigenous Struggles for Self-Determination*, edited by Joanne Barker, 33–50. Lincoln: Nebraska University Press.
Alfred, Taiaiake. 2005. *Wasáse: Indigenous Pathways of Action and Freedom*. Peterborough: Broadview Press.
Alfred, Taiaiake, and Jeff Corntassel. 2005. "Being Indigenous: Resurgences Against Contemporary Colonialism." *Government and Opposition* 40(4): 597–614.
Allen, Amy. 2008. *The Politics of Our Selves. Power, Autonomy, and Gender in Contemporary Critical Theory*. New York: Columbia University Press.
Allen, Amy. 2015. "Emancipation without Utopia: Subjection, Modernity, and the Normative Claims of Feminist Critical Theory." *Hypatia* 30(3): 513–529.
Allen, Amy. 2016. *The End of Progress: Decolonizing the Normative Foundations of Critical Theory*. New York: Columbia University Press.
Allen, Paula Gunn. 1984. "Who Is Your Mother? Red Roots of White Feminism." *Sinister Wisdom* 25: 34–36.
Altamirano-Jiménez, Isabel. 2013. *Indigenous Encounters with Neoliberalism: Place, Women, and the Environment in Canada and Mexico*. Vancouver: UBC Press.
Anaya, S. James. 1996. *Indigenous Peoples in International Law*. New York: Oxford University Press.
Anderson, Kim. 2000. *A Recognition of Being: Reconstructing Native Womanhood*. Toronto: Second Story Press.
Anderson, Kim, and Bonita Lawrence. 2003. *Strong Women Stories: Native Vision and Community Survival*. Toronto: Sumach Press.
Arendt, Hannah. (1951) 2004. *The Origins of Totalitarianism*. New York: Schocken Books.
Arendt, Hannah. (1958) 1998. *The Human Condition*. 2nd ed. Chicago: University of Chicago Press.
Arendt, Hannah. 1961. *Between Past and Future*. New York: Viking.
Arendt, Hannah. 1963. *On Revolution*. New York: Penguin.
Arendt, Hannah. 1968. *Men in Dark Times*. New York: Harcourt Brace Jovanovich.
Arendt, Hannah. 1978. *The Life of the Mind*. Vol. 2: *Willing*. New York: Harcourt.
Arendt, Hannah. 1996. *Love and Saint Augustine*. Chicago: University of Chicago Press.

Arendt, Hannah. 2007. *The Jewish Writings*. Edited by Jerome Kohn and Ron Feldman. New York: Schocken Books.
Arvin, Maile, Eve Tuck, and Angie Morrill. 2013. "Decolonizing Feminism: Challenging Connections between Settler Colonialism and Heteropatriarchy." *Feminist Formations*. 25(1): 8–34.
Asad, Talal. 2003. *Formations of the Secular: Christianity, Islam, Modernity*. Stanford, CA: Stanford University Press.
Asad, Talal. 2009. "Free Speech, Blasphemy, and Secular Criticism." In *Is Critique Secular?* edited by Talal Asad et al., 20–63. Berkeley: University of California Press.
Asad, Talal, Wendy Brown, Judith Butler, and Saba Mahmood. 2009. *Is Critique Secular? Blasphemy, Injury, and Free Speech*. Berkeley: University of California Press.
Asch, Michael. 2014. *On Being Here to Stay: Treaties and Aboriginal Rights in Canada*. Toronto: University of Toronto Press.
Asch, Michael. 2018. "Confederation Treaties and Reconciliation: Stepping Back into the Future." In *Resurgence and Reconciliation: Indigenous-Settler Relations and Earth Teachings*, edited by Michael Asch, John Borrows, and James Tully, 29–48. Toronto: University of Toronto Press.
Asch, Michael, John Borrows, and James Tully, eds. 2018. *Resurgence and Reconciliation: Indigenous-Settler Relations and Earth Teachings*. Toronto: University of Toronto Press.
Baier, Annette. 1985. *Postures of the Mind*. Minneapolis: University of Minnesota Press.
Baldwin, James. 1962. "Letter from a Region in My Mind." *The New Yorker*, November 17.
Baldwin, James. 1963. *The Fire Next Time*. New York: The Dial Press.
Barker, Joanne, ed. 2005. *Sovereignty Matters: Locations of Contestation and Possibility in Indigenous Struggles for Self-Determination*. Lincoln: Nebraska University Press.
Barker, Joanne. 2006. "Gender, Sovereignty, and the Discourse of Rights in Native Women's Activism." *Meridians: Feminism, Race, Transnationalism* 7(1): 127–161.
Barker, Joanne. 2011. *Native Acts: Law, Recognition, and Cultural Authenticity*. Durham, NC: Duke University Press.
Barker, Joanne. 2015. "Indigenous Feminisms." In *Oxford Handbook of Indigenous Peoples Politics*, edited by José Antonio Lucero, Dale Turner, and Donna Lee VanCott.
Basso, Keith. 1996. *Wisdom Sits in Places: Landscape and Language Among the Western Apache*. Albuquerque: University of New Mexico Press.
Battiste, Marie, and James Youngblood Henderson. 2000. *Protecting Indigenous Knowledge and Heritage: A Global Challenge*. Saskatoon: Purich.
Baum, Bruce, and Robert Nichols, eds. 2013. *Isaiah Berlin and the Politics of Freedom*. New York: Routledge.
Behrendt, Larissa. 1993. "Aboriginal Women and the White Lies of the Feminist Movement: Implications for Aboriginal Women in Rights Discourse." *Australian Feminist Law Journal* 1: 27–44.
Belcourt, Billy-Ray. 2017. *This Wound Is a World*. Okotoks, Alberta: Frontenac House.
Bell, Catherine, and Val Napoleon, eds. 2008. *First Nations Cultural Heritage and Law: Case Studies, Voices, and Perspectives*. Vancouver: UBC Press.
Benhabib, Seyla. 1992. *Situating the Self*. New York: Routledge.
Benhabib, Seyla. 2002. *The Claims of Culture: Equality and Diversity in the Global Era*. Princeton, NJ: Princeton University Press.
Benhabib, Seyla, Judith Butler, Drucilla Cornell, Nancy Fraser, Linda Nicholson. 1995. *Feminist Contentions: A Philosophical Exchange*. New York: Routledge.

Benveniste, Emile. 1973. *Indo-European Language and Society.* Translated by Elizabeth Palmer. London: Faber and Faber.
Berlin, Isaiah. 2008. "Two Concepts of Liberty." In *Liberty*, edited by Henry Hardy, 166–217. Oxford: Oxford University Press.
Bhambra, Gurminder K. 2021. "Decolonizing Critical Theory? Epistemological Justice, Progress, Reparations." *Critical Times* 4(1): 73–89.
Bilgrami, Akeel. 2014. *Secularism, Identity, and Enchantment.* Cambridge, MA: Harvard University Press.
Bilgrami, Akeel. 2020. "Value and Alienation: A Revisionist Essay on our Political Ideals." In *Nature and Value*, edited by Akeel Bilgrami, 68–88. New York: Columbia University Press.
Bird, Alyssa. 2014. [Untitled]. In *The Winter We Danced.* Edited by the Kino-nda-niimi Collective, 440. Winnipeg: ARP Books.
Birmingham, Peg. 2003. "The Pleasure of Your Company: Arendt, Kristeva, and an Ethics of Public Happiness." *Research in Phenomenology* 33: 53–73.
Biskowski, Lawrence. 1993. "Practical Foundations for Political Judgment: Arendt on Action and World." *Journal of Politics* 55(4): 867–887.
Bohman, James. 2005. "Critical Theory." In *Stanford Encyclopedia of Philosophy*, edited by Edward Zalta.
Borrows, John. 2002. *Recovering Canada: The Resurgence of Indigenous Law.* Toronto: University of Toronto Press.
Borrows, John. 2016. *Freedom and Indigenous Constitutionalism.* Toronto: University of Toronto Press.
Borrows, John. 2018. "Earth Bound: Indigenous Resurgence and Environmental Reconciliation." In *Resurgence and Reconciliation: Indigenous-Settler Relations and Earth Teachings*, edited by Michael Asch, John Borrows, and James Tully, 49–82. Toronto: University of Toronto Press.
Brandon, William. 1986. *New Worlds for Old: Reports from the New World and Their Effect on the Development of Social Thought in Europe, 1600–1800.* Athens: Ohio University Press.
Brant, Clare. 1990. "Native Ethics and Rules of Behavior." *Canadian Journal of Psychiatry* 35(6): 535–539.
Brown, Adrienne Marie. 2017. *Emergent Strategy: Shaping Change, Changing Worlds.* Chico, CA: AK Press.
Brown, Wendy. 1995. *States of Injury: Power and Freedom in Late Modernity.* Princeton, NJ: Princeton University Press.
Brown, Wendy. 2006. "Feminist Theory and the Frankfurt School: Introduction." *Differences* 17(1): 1–5.
Brown, Wendy. 2018a. "Neoliberalism's Frankenstein: Authoritarian Freedom in Twenty-First Century 'Democracies.'" *Critical Times* 1(1): 60–79.
Brown, Wendy. 2018b. "Where the Fires Are." Interview with Jo Littler in *Soundings* 68: 14–25.
Brundige, Lorraine (Mayer). 1997. "Continuity of Native Values: Cree and Ojibwa." MA thesis, Lakehead University, Thunder Bay, Ontario.
Brundige, Lorraine (Mayer). 1997. "Ungrateful Indian: Continuity of Native Values." *Ayaangwaamizin: The International Journal of Indigenous Philosophy* 1(1): 44–54.
Bruyneel, Kevin. 2007. *The Third Space of Sovereignty: The Postcolonial Politics of U.S.-Indigenous Relations.* Minneapolis: University of Minnesota.

Bryant-Bertell, Sarah. 2009. "Old Spirits in a New World: Pacific Northwest Performance." In *Native American Performance and Representation*, edited by S. E. Wilmer, 40–60. Tucson: University of Arizona Press.

Buck-Morss, Susan. 2009. *Hegel, Haiti, and Universal History*. Pittsburgh: University of Pittsburgh Press.

Burkhart, Brian Yazzie. 2004. "What Coyote and Thales Can Teach Us: An Outline of American Indian Epistemology." In *American Indian Thought: Philosophical Essays*, edited by Anne Waters, 15–26. Malden, MA: Blackwell.

Butler, Judith. 1990. *Gender Trouble*. New York: Routledge.

Butler, Judith. 2001. "What Is Critique? An Essay on Foucault's Virtue." *Transversal Texts*. https://transversal.at/transversal/0806/butler/en

Butler, Judith. 2015. *Notes Toward a Performative Theory of Assembly*. Cambridge, MA: Harvard University Press.

Byrd, Jodi. A. 2011. *The Transit of Empire. Indigenous Critiques of Colonialism*. Minneapolis: University of Minnesota Press.

Byrd, Jodi A., Alyosha Goldstein, Jodi Melamed, and Chandan Reddy. 2018. "Predatory Value: Economies of Dispossession and Disturbed Relationalities." *Social Text* 36(2): 1–18.

Cajete, Gregory. 2000. *Native Science: Natural Laws of Interdependence*. Santa Fe, NM: Clear Light.

Cameron, Angela. 2006. "Sentencing Circles and Intimate Violence: A Canadian Feminist Perspective." *Canadian Journal of Women and the Law* 18(2): 479–512.

Cameron, Angela, Sari Graben and Val Napoleon, eds. 2020. *Creating Indigenous Property: Power, Rights, and Relationships*. Toronto: University of Toronto Press.

National Inquiry into Missing and Murdered Indigenous Women and Girls (Canada). 2019. *Reclaiming Power and Place: The Final Report of the National Inquiry into Missing and Murdered Indigenous Women and Girls*. https://www.mmiwg-ffada.ca/final-report/.

Canadian Royal Commission on Aboriginal Peoples. 1996. *Restructuring the Relationship*. Ottawa: Supply and Services.

Carrette, Jeremy. 1999. "Michel Foucault and Zen: A Stay in a Zen Temple." In *Religion and Culture: Michel Foucault*, edited by J. Carrette, 110–114. London: Routledge.

CBC Winnipeg. "Round Dance: Why it's the Symbol of Idle No More." January 28, 2013.

Chiba, Shin. 1995. "Hannah Arendt on Love and the Political: Love, Friendship, and Citizenship." *The Review of Politics* 57(3): 505–535.

Churchill, Ward. 2004. *Kill the Indian, Save the Man: The Genocidal Impact of American Residential Schools*. San Francisco: City Lights.

Coates, Ta-Nehisi. 2019. "Conduction." *New Yorker*, June 10 and 17.

Coffey, Wallace, and Rebecca Tsosie. 2001. "Rethinking the Tribal Sovereignty Doctrine: Cultural Sovereignty and the Collective Future of Indian Nations." *Stanford Law and Policy Review* 12(2): 191–221.

Collins, Patricia Hill. 1990. *Black Feminist Thought*. London: Harper Collins.

Cordova, Viola. 2004. "Ethics: The We and the I." In *American Indian Thought: Philosophical Essays*, edited by Anne Waters, 173–181. Malden, MA: Blackwell.

Coulthard, Glen S. 2007. "Subjects of Empire: Indigenous Peoples and the 'Politics of Recognition' in Canada." *Contemporary Political Theory* 6: 437–460.

Coulthard, Glen Sean. 2014. *Red Skin, White Masks: Rejecting the Colonial Politics of Recognition*. Minneapolis: University of Minnesota Press.

Coulthard, Glen, and Leanne Betasamosake Simpson. 2016. "Grounded Normativity / Place-Based Solidarity." *American Quarterly* 68(2): 249–255.
Cover, Robert M. 1983. "Nomos and Narrative." *Harvard Law Review* 97(1): 4–69.
Cullors, Patrisse, and Robert Ross. 2016. "The Spiritual Work of Black Lives Matter." *On Being* interview, February 18.
Dalmiya, Vrinda. 1998. "The Indian Subcontinent." In *A Companion to Feminist Philosophy*, edited by Alison M. Jaggar and Iris Marion Young, 118–127. Oxford: Blackwell.
Davis, Angela Y. 1977. "Women and Capitalism: Dialectics of Oppression and Liberation." In *Marxism, Revolution, and Peace*, edited by Howard Parsons and John Sommerville, 139–171. Amsterdam: B.R. Grülner.
Davis, Angela Y. 1981. *Women, Race, and Class*. New York: Random House.
Davis, Angela Y., Gina Dent, Erica R. Meiners, and Beth E. Richie. 2022. *Abolition. Feminism. Now.* Chicago: Haymarket.
Davis, Benjamin P. 2021. "The Promises of Standing Rock: Three Approaches to Human Rights." *Humanity: An International Journal of Human Rights, Humanitarianism, and Development* 12(2): 205–225.
Deer, Sarah. 2009. "Decolonizing Rape Law: A Native Feminist Synthesis of Safety and Sovereignty." *Wicazo Sa Review* 24(2).
Deer, Sarah. 2015. *The Beginning and End of Rape: Confronting Sexual Violence in Native America*. Minneapolis: University of Minnesota Press.
Deer, Sarah. 2019. "(En)gendering Indian Law: Indigenous Feminist Legal Theory in the United States." *Yale Journal of Law and Feminism* 31(1): 1–34.
Deloria, Vine Jr. 1994. *God is Red: A Native View of Religion*. Golden, CO: North American Press.
Denetdale, Jennifer Nez. 2009. "Securing the Navajo National Boundaries: War, Patriotism, Tradition, and the Diné Marriage Act of 2005. *Wicazo Sa Review* 24(2).
Desai, Gauruv. 2007. "Editor's Column: The End of Postcolonial Theory?" *PMLA* 122(3): 633–651.
Dotson, Kristie. 2012. "How Is This Essay Philosophy?" *Comparative Philosophy* 3(1): 3–29.
Dotson, Kristie, and Kyle Whyte. 2013. "Environmental Justice, Unknowability, and Unqualified Affectability." *Ethics and the Environment* 18(2): 55–79.
Driskill, Qwo-Li, Chris Finley, Brian Joseph Gilley, and Scott Lauria Morgensen, eds. 2011. *Queer Indigenous Studies: Critical Interventions in Theory, Politics, and Literature*. Tucson: University of Arizona Press.
Ehrenreich, Barbara. 2007. *Dancing in the Streets: A History of Collective Joy*. London: Granta.
Ervin, Maile, Eve Tuck, and Angie Morrill. 2013. "Decolonizing Feminism: Challenging Connections between Settler Colonialism and Heteropatriarchy." *Feminist Formations* 25(1): 8–34.
Estes, Nick. 2019. *Our History Is the Future: Standing Rock Versus the Dakota Access Pipeline, and the Long Tradition of Indigenous Resistance*. London: Verso.
Ferguson, Ann, and Anna Jónasdóttir, eds. 2014. *Love: A Question for Feminism in the Twenty-First Century*. New York: Routledge.
Ferguson, Ann. 2014. "Feminist Love Politics: Romance, Care, and Solidarity." In *Love: A Question for Feminism in the Twenty-First Century*, edited by Ann Ferguson and Anna Jónasdóttir, 250–264. New York: Routledge.

Ferreira da Silva, Denise. 2007. *Toward a Global Idea of Race*. Minneapolis: University of Minnesota Press.

Fiske, Jo-Anne. 1996. "'The Womb Is to the Nation as the Heart Is to the Body': Ethnopolitical Discourses of the Canadian Indigenous Women's Movement." *Studies in Political Economy* 51: 65–95.

Flannery, Tim. 2016. Introduction to Peter Wohlleben, *The Hidden Life of Trees: What They Feel, How They Communicate*. Melbourne: Black.

Foucault, Michel. 1984. "What Is Enlightenment?" In *The Foucault Reader*, edited by Paul Rabinow, 32–50. New York: Pantheon.

Foucault, Michel. 1997. "The Ethics of Concern for Self as a Practice of Freedom." In *Ethics, Subjectivity and Truth: The Essential Works of Michel Foucault*, edited by Paul Rabinow, 281–302. New York: New Press.

Foucault, Michel. 2000. "Michel Foucault and Zen: A Stay in a Zen Temple." In *Religion and Culture: Michel Foucault*, edited by Jeremy Carrette, 110–114. London: Routledge.

Foucault, Michel. 2003. *Society Must Be Defended*. Lectures at the Collège de France 1975–76. Edited by Mauro Bertani and Alessandro Fontana. Translated by David Macey. New York: Penguin Books.

Fox Keller, Evelyn. 1985. *Reflections on Gender and Science*. New Haven, CT: Yale University Press.

Fraser, Nancy. 1987. "What's Critical About Critical Theory? The Case of Habermas and Gender." In *Feminism as Critique*, edited by Seyla Benhabib and Drucilla Cornell, 31–55. Minneapolis: University of Minnesota Press.

Fraser, Nancy. 1989. *Unruly Practices: Power, Discourse and Gender in Contemporary Social Theory*. Minnesota: University of Minnesota Press.

Fraser, Nancy. 1997. *Justice Interruptus: Critical Reflections on the "Postsocialist" Condition*. New York: Routledge.

Gammage, Bill. 2011. *The Biggest Estate on Earth: How Aborigines Made Australia*. Melbourne: Allen and Unwin.

Gandhi, Leela. 2006. *Affective Communities: Anticolonial Thought, Fin-de-Siècle Radicalism, and the Politics of Friendship*. Durham, NC: Duke University Press.

Gilmore, Ruth Wilson. 2022. *Abolition Geography: Essays Toward Liberation*. London: Verso.

Goeman, Mishuana. 2013. *Mark My Words: Native Women Mapping Our Nations*. Minneapolis: University of Minnesota Press.

Goeman, Mishuana. 2015. "Land as Life: Unsettling the Logics of Containment." In *Native Studies Keywords*, edited by Stephanie Nohelani Teves, Andrea Smith, and Michelle H. Raheja, 71–89. Tucson: University of Arizona Press.

Goeman, Mishuana R., and Jennifer Nez Denetdale. 2009. "Native Feminisms: Legacies, Interventions, and Indigenous Sovereignties." *Wicazo Sa Review* (Special Issue) 24(2): 9–13.

Goldman, Emma. 1934. *Living My Life*. New York: Knopf.

Goodman, A., Morgan, R., Kuehlke, R., Kastor, S., Fleming, K., Boyd, J., and Aboriginal Harm Reduction Society. 2018. "'We've Been Researched to Death': Exploring the Research Experiences of Urban Indigenous Peoples in Vancouver, Canada." *The International Indigenous Policy Journal* 9(2).

Graeber, David, and David Wengrow. 2021. *The Dawn of Everything: A New History of Humanity*. New York: Farrar, Straus and Giroux.

Green, Joyce. 2007. "Balancing Strategies: Aboriginal Women and Constitutional Rights in Canada." In *Making Space for Indigenous Feminism*, edited by Joyce Green, 140–159. Winnipeg: Fernwood.
Green, Joyce. 2017. *Making Space for Indigenous Feminism*. 2nd ed. Halifax: Fernwood.
Grenville, Kate. 2005. *The Secret River*. Melbourne: Text.
Goodin, Robert. 2003. "Folie Républicaine." *Annual Review of Political Science* 6: 55–76.
Grinde, Donald A., and Bruce E. Johansen. 1991. *Exemplar of Liberty: Native America and the Evolution of Democracy*. Los Angeles: American Indian Studies Centre, UCLA.
Guerrero, M. Annette Jaimes. 2003. "'Patriarchal Colonialism' and Indigenism: Implications for Native Feminist Spirituality and Native Womanism." *Hypatia* 18(2): 58–69.
Hadot, Pierre. 1995. *Philosophy as a Way of Life: Spiritual Exercises from Socrates to Foucault*. Edited by Arnold Davidson. Translated by Michael Chase. Oxford: Blackwell.
Hardt, Michael, and Antonio Negri. 2004. *Multitude: War and Democracy in the Age of Empire*. New York: Penguin.
Hart, Michael Anthony. 1996. "Sharing Circles: Utilizing Traditional Practice Methods for Teaching, Helping, and Supporting." In *From Our Eyes: Learning from Indigenous Peoples*, edited by Sylvia O'Meara, 59–72. Toronto: Garamond.
Held, Virginia. 1987. "Non-Contractual Society: A Feminist View." *Canadian Journal of Philosophy* 13: 111–137.
Henderson, James (Sákéj) Youngblood. 2000. "Postcolonial Ghost Dancing: Diagnosing European Colonialism." In *Reclaiming Indigenous Voice and Vision*, edited by Marie Battiste, 88–108. Vancouver: UBC Press.
Hennessey, Rosemary. 2014. "Bread and Roses in the Common." In *Love: A Question for Feminism in the Twenty-First Century*, edited by Ann Ferguson and Anna Jónasdóttir, 265–278. New York: Routledge.
Hill Collins, Patricia. 1990. *Black Feminist Thought*. London: Harper Collins.
Hirschmann, Nancy J. 2003. *The Subject of Liberty. Toward a Feminist Theory of Freedom*. Princeton, NJ: Princeton University Press.
Hobbes, Thomas. (1651) 1991. *Leviathan*. Edited by Richard Tuck. Cambridge: Cambridge University Press.
Honig, Bonnie. 2017. *Public Things: Democracy in Disrepair*. New York: Fordham University Press.
hooks, bell. 2000. *All About Love: New Visions*. New York: William Morrow.
Horkheimer, Max. 1972. "Traditional and Critical Theory." In Max Horkheimer, *Critical Theory: Selected Essays*. Translated by Matthew O'Connell et al. New York: Continuum.
Irigaray, Luce. 1985. *Speculum of the Other Woman*. Translated by Gillian C. Gill. Ithaca, NY: Cornell University Press.
Jacobs, Sue-Ellen, Wesley Thomas, and Sabine Lang, eds. 1997. *Two-Spirit People. Native American Gender Identity, Sexuality and Spirituality*. Urbana: University of Illinois.
Jaggar, Alison. 1983. *Feminist Politics and Human Nature*. Totowa, NJ: Rowman and Allanheld.
Jaimes, Annette M. 1995. "Some Kind of Indian: On Race, Eugenics, and Mixed-Bloods." In *American Mixed Race: The Culture of Microdiversity*, edited by Naomi Zack. Totowa, NJ: Rowman and Littlefield.
Jamieson, Kathleen. 1978. *Indian Women and the Law in Canada: Citizens Minus*. Ottawa: Canadian Advisory Council on the Status of Women and Indian Rights for Indian Women.

Johnston, Basil. 1976. *Ojibway Heritage*. Toronto: McClelland and Stewart.
Keller, Catherine. 1986. *From a Broken Web: Separation, Sexism, and Self*. Boston: Beacon Press.
Khader, Serene. 2019. *Decolonizing Universalism*. New York: Oxford University Press.
Kimmerer, Robin Wall. 2013. *Braiding Sweetgrass: Indigenous Wisdom, Indigenous Knowledges, and the Teachings of Plants*. Minneapolis, MN: Milkweed Editions.
King, Hayden. "We Natives Are Deeply Divided. There's Nothing Wrong with That." In *The Winter We Danced*, edited by The Kino-nda-niimi Collective, 150–151. Winnipeg: ARP Books.
King, Thomas. 2003. *The Truth About Stories: A Native Narrative*. (Massey Lectures Series.) Toronto: Anansi Press.
The Kino-nda-niimi Collective. 2014.*The Winter We Danced: Voices from the Past, the Future, and the Idle No More Movement*. Winnipeg: ARP Books.
Klein, Melanie. 1975. *Collected Works*. London: Hogarth Press.
Kompridis, Nikolas. 2020. "Nonhuman Agency and Human Normativity." In *Nature and Value*, edited by Akeel Bilgrami, 240–260. New York: Columbia University Press.
Kovach, Margaret. 2009. *Indigenous Methodologies: Characteristics, Conversations, and Contexts*. Toronto: University of Toronto Press.
Kramer, Matthew. 2008. "Liberty and Domination." In *Republicanism and Political Theory*, edited by Cécile Laborde and John Maynor, 31–57. Malden, MA: Blackwell.
Kristeva, Julia. 1991. *Strangers to Ourselves*. Translated by Leon S. Roudiez. New York: Columbia University Press.
Kristeva, Julia. 2001. *Hannah Arendt: Life Is a Narrative*. Translated by Frank Collins. Toronto: University of Toronto Press.
Kuokkanen, Rauna. 2019. *Restructuring Relations: Indigenous Self-Determination, Governance, and Gender*. New York: Oxford University Press.
Ladner, Kiera. 2003. "Governing within an Ecological Context: Creating an AlterNative Understanding of Blackfoot Governance." *Studies in Political Economy* 70(1): 125–152.
Ladner, Kiera. 2009. "Gendering Decolonisation, Decolonising Gender." *Australian Indigenous Law Review* 13(1): 62–77.
Ladner, Kiera. 2009. "Understanding the Impact of Self-Determination on Communities in Crisis." *Journal of Aboriginal Health* 5(2): 88–101.
LaDuke, Winona. 1999. *All our Relations: Native Struggles for Land and Life*. Cambridge, MA: South End Press.
Larmore, Charles. 2001. "A Critique of Philip Pettit's Republicanism." *Philosophical Issues* 11(1): 229–243.
LaRocque, Emma. 2007. "Métis and Feminist: Ethical Reflections on Feminism, Human Rights and Decolonization." In *Making Space for Indigenous Feminism*, edited by Joyce Green, 53–71. Winnipeg: Fernwood.
Lawrence, Bonita. 2004. *"Real" Indians and Others: Mixed-Blood Urban Native Peoples and Indigenous Nationhood*. Lincoln: University of Nebraska Press.
Lepecki, André. 2014. "Performance and Corporeality." Lecture. https://artmuseum.pl/en/doc/video-performans-i-cielesnosc
Littlebear, Leroy. 2000. "Jagged Worldviews Colliding." In *Reclaiming Indigenous Voice and Vision*, edited by Marie Battiste, 77–85. Vancouver: University of British Columbia Press.
Lorde, Audre. 1984. *Sister Outsider*. Freedom, CA: Crossing Press.

Lugones, Maria. 2007. "Heterosexualism and the Colonial/Modern Gender System." *Hypatia* 22(1): 186–209.
Lugones, Maria. 2008. "The Coloniality of Gender." *Worlds and Knowledges Otherwise* 2: 1–17.
Lyons, Scott Richard. 2010. *X-Marks: Native Signatures of Assent*. Minneapolis: University of Minnesota Press.
Maaka, Roger, and Augie Fleras. 2000. "Engaging with Indigeneity: Tino Rangatiratanga in Aotearoa." In *Political Theory and the Rights of Indigenous Peoples*, edited by Duncan Ivison, Paul Patton, and Will Sanders, 89–112. Cambridge: Cambridge University Press.
Mack, Johnny. 2011. "*Hoquotist:* Reorienting through Stories Practice." In *Storied Communities: Narratives of Contact and Arrival in Constituting Political Community*, edited by Hester Lessard, Rebecca Johnson, and Jeremy Webber, 287–307. Vancouver: UBC Press.
Macpherson, C. B. 1962. *The Political Theory of Possessive Individualism: Hobbes to Locke*. Oxford: Oxford University Press.
Mahmood, Saba. 2005. *Politics of Piety: The Islamic Revival and the Feminist Subject*. Princeton, NJ: Princeton University Press.
Mahmood, Saba. 2009. "Religious Reason and Secular Affect: An Incommensurable Divide?" In *Is Critique Secular? Blasphemy, Injury, and Free Speech*, edited by Talal Asad et al., 64–100. Berkeley: University of California Press.
Mamdani, Mahmood. 2012. *Define and Rule: Native as Political Identity*. Cambridge. MA: Harvard University Press.
Maracle, Lee. 1988. *I Am Woman: A Native Perspective on Sociology and Feminism*. Vancouver: Press Gang.
Marcuse, Herbert. 1974. "Marxism and Feminism." *Women's Studies* 2(3).
Margulis, Lynn. 1998. *Symbiotic Planet: A New Look at Evolution*. New York: Basic Books.
Markell, Patchen. 2006. "The Rule of the People: Arendt, *Arché*, and Democracy." *American Political Science Review* 100(1): 1–14.
Markell, Patchen. 2008. "The Insufficiency of Non-Domination." *Political Theory* 36(1): 9–36.
Martin, Karen. 2008. *Please Knock Before You Enter: Aboriginal Regulation of Outsiders and the Implications for Researchers*. Teneriffe, Qld.: Post Pressed.
Mayer, Lorraine. 2007. "A Return to Reciprocity." *Hypatia* 22(3): 22–42.
Maynard, Robyn, and Leanne Betasamosake Simpson. 2022. *Rehearsals for Living*. Toronto: Alfred A. Knopf.
McClintock, Anne. 1995. *Imperial Leather: Race, Gender, and Sexuality in the Colonial Context*. New York: Routledge.
McGregor, Deborah. 2005. "Traditional Ecological Knowledge: An Anishnabe Woman's Perspective." *Atlantis* 29(2): 103–109.
McIvor, Sharon Donna. 1995. "Aboriginal Women's Rights as 'Existing Rights.'" *Canadian Woman Studies/Les Cahiers de la Femme* 15(2&3): 34–38.
McIvor, Sharon Donna. 2004. "Aboriginal Women Unmasked: Using Equality Litigation to Advance Women's Rights." *Canadian Journal of Women and the Law/Revue femmes et droit* 16(1): 106–136.
McLean, Sheelah. 2014. "Idle No More: Re-Storying Canada." In *The Winter We Danced*, edited by The Kino-nda-niimi Collective. Winnipeg: ARP Books.

McMahon, Ryan. 2014. "The Round Dance Revolution: Idle No More." In *The Winter We Danced*. Winnipeg: ARP Books.
McPherson, Dennis H., and J. Douglas Rabb. 2011. *Indian from the Inside: Native American Philosophy and Cultural Renewal*. 2nd ed. Jefferson, NC: McFarland.
Medina, José. 2013. *The Epistemology of Resistance*. New York: Oxford University Press.
Mendez, Xhercis. 2015. "Notes Toward a Decolonial Feminist Methodology: Revisiting the Race/Gender Matrix." *Trans-Scripts* 5: 41–59.
Million, Dian. 2013. *Therapeutic Nations. Healing in an Age of Indigenous Human Rights*. Tuscon: University of Arizona Press.
Million, Dian. 2014. "There Is a River in Me: Theory from Life." In *Theorizing Native Studies*, edited by Audra Simpson and Andrea Smith, 31–42. Durham, NC: Duke University Press.
Mills, Charles W. 1997. *The Racial Contract*. Ithaca, NY: Cornell University Press.
Mondal, Anshuman. 2014. *Islam and Controversy: The Politics of Free Speech After Rushdie*. New York: Palgrave Macmillan.
Monture, Patricia. 1996. *Thunder in My Soul: A Mohawk Woman Speaks*. Halifax: Fernwood Press.
Monture-Angus, Patricia. 1999. *Journeying Forward*. Halifax: Fernwood Press.
Mooney, James. (1896) 1973. *The Ghost Dance: Religion and Wounded Knee*. New York: Dover.
Moreton-Robinson, Aileen. 2000. *Talkin' Up to the White Woman. Indigenous Women and Feminism*. Queensland: University of Queensland Press.
Moreton-Robinson, Aileen. 2007. *Sovereign Subjects. Indigenous Sovereignty Matters*. Melbourne: Allen and Unwin.
Moreton-Robinson, Aileen. 2013. "Towards an Australian Indigenous Women's Standpoint Theory: A Methodological Tool." *Australian Feminist Studies* 28(78): 331–347.
Moreton-Robinson, Aileen. 2015. *The White Possessive. Property, Power, and Indigenous Sovereignty*. Minneapolis: University of Minnesota Press.
Morgensen, Scott Lauria. 2010. "Settler Homonationalism: Theorizing Settler Colonialism within Queer Modernities." *GLQ: A Journal of Lesbian and Gay Studies* 16(1–2): 106–131.
Morgensen, Scott Lauria. 2011. *Spaces Between Us: Queer Settler Colonialism and Indigenous Colonization*. Minneapolis: University of Minnesota.
Morin, SkyBlue Mary. 2014. "A Healing Time." In The Kino-nda-niimi Collective, *The Winter We Danced: Voices from the Past, the Future, and the Idle No More Movement*, 7–9. Winnipeg: ARP Books.
Myers, Ella. 2013. *Worldly Ethics: Democratic Politics and Care for the World*. Durham, NC: Duke University Press.
Napoleon, Val. 2005. "Aboriginal Self-Determination: Individual Self and Collective Selves." *Atlantis* 29(2): 31–46.
Napoleon, Val. 2009. "Aboriginal Discourse: Gender, Identity and Community." In *Indigenous Peoples and the Law: Comparative and Critical Perspectives*, edited by Benjamin J. Richardson, Shin Imai, and Kent McNeil, 235–236. Portland, OR: Hart.
Napoleon, Val. "What Is Indigenous Law? A Small Discussion." Indigenous Law Research Unit, University of Victoria. https://www.uvic.ca/law/assets/docs/ilru/What%20is%20 Indigenous%20Law%20Oct%2028%202016.pdf
Napoleon, Val, and Hadley Friedland. 2016. "An Inside Job: Engaging with Indigenous Legal Traditions through Stories." *McGill Law Journal* 61(4): 725–754.

Narayan, Uma. 1997. *Dislocating Cultures: Identities, Traditions, and Third World Feminism*. New York: Routledge.
Nason, Dory. 2014. "We Hold Our Hands Up: On Indigenous Women's Love and Resistance." In *The Winter We Danced*, edited by The Kino-nda-niimi Collective, 186–190. Winnipeg: ARP Books.
Native Women's Association of Canada. 1991. *Aboriginal Women, Self Government and The Canadian Charter of Rights and Freedoms*. Ottawa: Native Women's Association of Canada.
Native Women's Association of Canada. 1992. *An Aboriginal Charter of Rights and Freedoms*. Ottawa: Native Women's Association of Canada.
Nedelsky, Jennifer. 2011. *Law's Relations: A Relational Theory of Self, Autonomy, and Law*. New York: Oxford University Press.
Nedelsky, Jennifer. Forthcoming. *A Care Manifesto: (Part)Time for All*. New York: Oxford University Press.
Nichols, Robert. 2005. "Realizing the Social Contract: The Case of Colonialism and Indigenous Peoples." *Contemporary Political Theory* 4: 42–62.
Nichols, Robert. 2013. "Indigeneity and the Settler Contract Today." *Philosophy and Social Criticism* 39(2): 165–186.
Nichols, Robert. 2014. "Contract and Usurpation." In *Theorizing Native Studies*, edited by Audra Simpson and Andrea Smith, 99–121. Durham, NC: Duke University Press.
Nichols, Robert. 2020. *Theft Is Property! Dispossession and Critical Theory*. Durham, NC: Duke University Press.
Norton-Smith, Thomas. 2010. *The Dance of Person and Place: One Interpretation of American Indian Philosophy*. Albany: SUNY Press.
Okin, Susan Moller. 1989. *Justice, Gender, and the Family*. New York: Basic Books.
Oksala, Johanna. 2005. *Foucault on Freedom*. Cambridge: Cambridge University Press.
Olaveson, Tim. 2001. "Collective Effervescence and Communitas: Processual Models of Ritual and Society in Emile Durkheim and Victor Turner." *Dialectical Anthropology* 26: 89–124.
Olson, Kevin. 2016. *Imagined Sovereignties: The Power of the People and Other Myths of the Modern Age*. Cambridge: Cambridge University Press.
Onians, Richard Broxton. 1951. *The Origins of European Thought: About the Body the Mind, the Soul, the World, Time, and Fate*. Cambridge: Cambridge University Press.
Palmater, Pamela. 2011. *Beyond Blood: Rethinking Indigenous Identity*. Saskatoon: Purich.
Palmater, Pamela. 2020. *Warrior Life: Indigenous Resistance and Resurgence*. Halifax: Fernwood Press.
Palmer, Vera B. 2014. "The Devil in the Details: Controverting an American Indian Conversion Narrative." In *Theorizing Native Studies*, edited by Audra Simpson and Andrea Smith, 266–296. Durham, NC: Duke University Press.
Pateman, Carole. 2007. "The Settler Contract." In Carole Pateman and Charles W. Mills, *Contract and Domination*, 35–78. Cambridge: Polity.
Patterson, Orlando. 1991. *Freedom in the Making of Western Culture*. New York: Basic Books.
Parekh, Biku. 2006. *Rethinking Multiculturalism*. 2nd ed. London: Palgrave Macmillan.
Parisi, Laura, and Jeff Corntassel. 2007. "In Pursuit of Self-Determination: Indigenous Women's Challenges to Traditional Diplomatic Spaces." *Canadian Foreign Policy* 13(3): 81–98.

Pelet Del Toro, Valeria M. 2019. "Beyond the Critique of Rights: The Puerto Rico Legal Project and Civil Rights Litigation in America's Colony." *The Yale Law Journal* 128(3): 792–842.

Perez, Hiram. 2005. "You Can Have My Brown Body and Eat It, Ioo!" *Social Text* 85: 171–191.

Pettit, Philip. 1997. *Republicanism: A Theory of Freedom and Government*. Oxford: Oxford University Press.

Pettit, Philip. 2000. "Minority Claims Under Two Conceptions of Democracy." In *Political Theory and the Rights of Indigenous Peoples*, edited by Duncan Ivison, Paul Patton, and Will Sanders, 199–215. Cambridge: Cambridge University Press.

Pettit, Philip. 2012. *On the People's Terms: A Republican Theory and Model of Democracy*. Cambridge: Cambridge University Press.

Pettit, Philip. 2014. *Just Freedom*. New York: W.W. Norton.

Pitkin, Hanna Fenichel. 1988. "Are Freedom and Liberty Twins?" *Political Theory* 16(4): 523–552.

Pitkin, Hanna Fenichel. 1995. "Conformism, Housekeeping, and the Attack of the Blob: The Origins of Hannah Arendt's Concept of the Social." In *Feminist Interpretations of Hannah Arendt*, edited by Bonnie Honig, 51–82. Pennsylvania State University Press.

Pitkin, Hanna Fenichel. 1998. *The Attack of the Blob: Hannah Arendt's Concept of the Social*. Chicago: University of Chicago Press.

Pitts, Phillippa. 2020. "From a Place of Love and Rage: Idle No More's Cancel Canada Day Program." *Cultural Survival*, July 8.

Potter, Elizabeth. 1993. "Gender and Epistemic Negotiation." In *Feminist Epistemologies*, edited by Linda Alcoff and Elizabeth Potter, 161–186. New York: Routledge.

Povinelli, Elizabeth. 2006. *The Empire of Love*. Durham, NC: Duke University Press.

Prattes, Riikka. 2019. "'I Don't Clean Up after Myself': Epistemic Ignorance, Responsibility, and the Politics of Outsourcing Domestic Cleaning." *Feminist Theory* 21(1): 25–45.

Puar, Jasbir. 2007. *Terrorist Assemblages: Homonationalism in Queer Times*. Durham, NC: Duke University Press.

Quijano, Anibal. 2000. "Coloniality of Power, Eurocentrism, and Latin America." *Neplanta: Views from the South* 1(3): 533–580.

Ramirez, Renya. 2007. *Native Hubs: Culture, Community, and Belonging in Silicon Valley and Beyond*. Durham, NC: Duke University Press.

Red Nation. 2021. *The Red Deal: Indigenous Action to Save Our Earth*. Brooklyn, NY: Common Notions.

Rifkin, Mark. 2011. *When Did Indians Become Straight? Kinship, the History of Sexuality, and Native Sovereignty*. Oxford: Oxford University Press.

Rifkin, Mark. 2014. "Making Peoples into Populations: The Racial Limits of Tribal Sovereignty." In *Theorizing Native Studies*, edited by Audra Simpson and Andrea Smith, 149–187. Durham, NC: Duke University Press.

Robinson, Cedric J. 2019. *On Racial Capitalism, Black Internationalism, and Cultures of Resistance*. London: Pluto Press.

Roscoe, Will. 1998. *Changing Ones: Third and Fourth Genders in Native North America*. New York: St. Martin's Press.

Salamon, Gayle. 2009. "Justification and Queer Method, or Leaving Philosophy." *Hypatia* 24(1): 225–230.

Sawicki, Jana. 2013. "Queer Feminism: Cultivating Ethical Practices of Freedom." *Foucault Studies* 16: 74–87.

Sales, Ruby. 2016. "Where Does It Hurt?" *On Being* interview, September 15.
Sayers, Judith F., Kelly A. MacDonald, Jo-Anne Fiske, Melonie Newell, Evelyn George, and Wendy Cornet. 2001. *First Nations Women, Governance and the Indian Act: A Collection of Policy Research Reports*. Ottawa: Status of Women Canada.
Scott, Craig. 1996. "Indigenous Self-Determination and Decolonization of the International Imagination: A Plea." *Human Rights Quarterly* 18(4): 814–820.
Sedgwick, Eve Kosofsky. 2003. *Touching Feeling: Affect, Pedagogy, Performativity*. Durham, NC: Duke University Press.
Shea Murphy, Jacqueline. 2016. "Editor's Note: Doing Indigenous Dance Today." *Dance Research Journal* 48(1): 1–8.
Shiva, Vandana. 2014. *The Vandana Shiva Reader*. Lexington: University Press of Kentucky.
Simard, Suzanne. 2016. "Notes from a Forest Ecologist." In Peter Wohlleben, *The Hidden Life of Trees: What They Feel, How They Communicate*, 247–250. Melbourne: Black.
Simpson, Audra. 2000. "Paths Toward a Mohawk Nation: Narratives of Citizenship and Nationhood in Kahnawake." In *Political Theory and the Rights of Indigenous Peoples*, edited by Duncan Ivison, Paul Patton, and Will Sanders, 113–136. Cambridge: Cambridge University Press.
Simpson, Audra. 2014. *Mohawk Interruptus: Political Life Across the Borders of Settler States*. Durham, NC: Duke University Press.
Simpson, Audra. 2016. "The State Is a Man: Theresa Spence, Loretta Saunders and the Gender of Settler Sovereignty." *Theory and Event* 19(4): 1–15.
Simpson, Audra, and Andrea Smith, eds. 2014. *Theorizing Native Studies*. Durham, NC: Duke University Press.
Simpson, Leanne (Betasamosake). 2011. *Dancing on Our Turtle's Back*. Winnipeg: Arbeiter Ring.
Simpson, Leanne Betasamosake. 2015. "The Place Where We All Live and Work Together: A Gendered Analysis of 'Sovereignty'." In *Native Studies Keywords*, edited by Stephanie Nohelani Teves, Andrea Smith, and Michelle H. Raheja, 18–24. Tucson: University of Arizona Press.
Simpson, Leanne Betasamosake. 2017. *As We Have Always Done: Indigenous Freedom Through Radical Resistance*. Minneapolis: University of Minnesota Press.
Skinner, Quentin. 1998. *Liberty Before Liberalism*. Cambridge: Cambridge University Press.
Skinner, Quentin. 2002. "A Third Conception of Liberty." *Proceedings of the British Academy* 117: 237–268.
Skinner, Quentin. 2008. *Hobbes and Republican Liberty*. Cambridge: Cambridge University Press.
Smith, Andrea. 2008. "American Studies without America: Native Feminisms and the Nation-State." *American Quarterly* 60(2): 309–315.
Smith, Andrea. 2010. "Queer Theory and Native Studies: The Heteronormativity of Settler Colonialism." *GLQ: A Journal of Lesbian and Gay Studies* 16(1–2): 41–68.
Smith, Andrea. 2014. "Native Studies at the Horizon of Death: Theorizing Ethnographic Entrapment and Settler Self-Reflexivity." In *Theorizing Native Studies*, edited by Audra Simpson and Andrea Smith, 207–234. Durham, NC: Duke University Press.
Smith, Andrea, and J. Kēhaulani Kauanui. 2008. "Native Feminisms Engage American Studies." *American Quarterly* 60(2): 309–315.
Snyder, Emily. 2018. *Gender, Power, and Representations of Cree Law*. Vancouver: UBC Press.

Snyder, Emily, Val Napoleon, and John Borrows. 2015. "Gender and Violence: Drawing on Indigenous Legal Resources." *UBC Law Review* 48(2): 593–654.

Sprankling, John G. 2014. "The Right to Destroy." In *The International Law of Property*. Oxford: Oxford University Press.

Starblanket, Gina, and Heidi Kiiwetinepinesiik Stark. 2018. "Towards a Relational Paradigm—Four Points for Consideration: Knowledge, Gender, Land, and Modernity." In *Resurgence and Reconciliation: Indigenous-Settler Relations and Earth Teachings*, edited by Michael Asch, John Borrows, and James Tully, 175–208. Toronto: University of Toronto Press.

Stoler, Ann. 2002. *Carnal Knowledge and Imperial Power: Race and the Intimate in Colonial Rule*. Berkeley: University of California Press.

Stoller Miller, Barbara. 1996. *Yoga. Discipline of Freedom. The* Yoga Sutra *Attributed to Patanjali*. Berkeley: University of California Press.

Strahilevitz, Lior Jacob. 2005. "The Right to Destroy." *Yale Law Journal* 114(4): 781–854.

Stubben, Jerry D. 2000. "The Indigenous Influence Theory of American Democracy." *Social Science Quarterly* 81(3): 716–731.

Sullivan, Shannon, and Nancy Tuana, eds. 2007. *Race and Epistemologies of Ignorance*. Albany: SUNY Press.

Suzack, Cheryl, Shari M. Huhndorf, Jeanne Perreault, and Jean Barman, eds. 2010. *Indigenous Women and Feminism. Politics, Activism, Culture*. Vancouver: University of British Columbia Press.

Tailfeathers, Elle-Máijá. 2012. "Fractured Land: A First-Hand Account of Resistance to Fracking on Blood Land." *Briarpatch*, February 28.

Taylor, Charles. 1985. "What's Wrong With Negative Liberty" In *Philosophy and the Human Sciences: Philosophical Papers 2*, edited by Charles Taylor, 211–229. Cambridge: Cambridge University Press.

Tomsons, Sandra, and Lorraine Mayer, eds. 2013. *Philosophy and Aboriginal Rights. Critical Dialogues*. Toronto: Oxford University Press.

Tsosie, Rebecca. 2010. "Native Women and Leadership: An Ethics of Culture and Relationship." In *Indigenous Women and Feminism*, edited by Cheryl Suzack, Shari M. Huhndorf, Jeanne Perreault, and Jean Barman, 29–42. Vancouver: UBC Press.

Tuck, Eve, and K. Wayne Yang. 2012. "Decolonization Is Not a Metaphor." *Decolonization: Indigeneity, Education and Society* 1(1): 1–40.

Tuhiwai Smith, Linda. 2012. *Decolonizing Methodologies. Research and Indigenous Peoples*. 2nd ed. London: Zed Books.

Tully, James. 1993. *An Approach to Political Philosophy: Locke in Contexts*. Cambridge: Cambridge University Press.

Tully, James. 1995. *Strange Multiplicity: Constitutionalism in an Age of Diversity*. Cambridge: Cambridge University Press.

Tully, James. 2008. *Democracy and Civic Freedom*. Cambridge: Cambridge University Press.

Tully, James. 2008. "The Struggles of Indigenous Peoples for and of Freedom." In *Public Philosophy in a New Key, vol. 1: Democracy and Civic Freedom*, edited by James Tully, 257–288. Cambridge: Cambridge University Press.

Tully, James. 2012. "Reconciliation Here on Earth." In *Resurgence and Reconciliation: Indigenous-Settler Relations and Earth Teachings*, edited by Michael Asch, John Borrows, and James Tully, 83–132. Toronto: University of Toronto Press.

Tully, James. 2013. "'Two Concepts of Liberty' in Context." In *Isaiah Berlin and the Politics of Freedom*, edited by Bruce Baum and Robert Nichols, 23–51. New York: Routledge.

Tully, James. 2018. "Introduction." In Richard Gregg, *The Power of Nonviolence*. Cambridge: Cambridge University Press.

Tully, James. 2020. "Life Sustains Life 1: Value, Social and Ecological" and "Life Sustains Life 2: The Ways of Reengagement with the Living Earth." In *Nature and Value*, edited by Akeel Bilgrami, 163–204. New York: Columbia University Press.

Turner, Dale. 2006. *This Is Not a Peace Pipe: Towards a Critical Indigenous Philosophy*. Toronto: University of Toronto Press.

Turner, Edith. 2012. *Communitas: The Anthropology of Collective Joy*. New York: Palgrave-Macmillan.

Turner, Victor. 1969. *The Ritual Process: Structure and Anti-Structure*. Ithaca, NY: Cornell University Press.

Turner, Victor. 1983. "*Carnaval* in Rio: Dionysian Drama in an Industrializing Society." In *The Celebration of Society: Perspectives on Contemporary Cultural Performance*, edited by Frank E. Manning, 103–124. Bowling Green, OH: Bowling Green State University Popular Press.

Ungunmerr-Bauman, Miriam Rose. 2015. Miriam Rose Foundation videos. https://www.youtube.com/watch?v=pkY1dGk-LyE

United Nations. 2007. *United Nations Declaration on the Rights of Indigenous Peoples*. New York: United Nations.

Verancini, Lorenzo. 2010. *Settler Colonialism: A Theoretical Overview*. New York: Palgrave Macmillan.

Vimalassery, Manu, Juliana Hu Pegues, and Alyosha Goldstein. 2016. "On Colonial Unknowing." *Theory and Event* 19(4).

Vintges, Karen. 2011. "Freedom and Spirituality." In *Michel Foucault: Key Concepts*, edited by Dianna Taylor, 99–110. New York: Routledge.

von Redecker, Eva. 2020. "Ownership's Shadow: Neoauthoritarianism as Defense of Phantom Possession." *Critical Times* 3(1): 33–67.

Wagner, Sally Roesch, ed. 2019. *The Women's Suffrage Movement*. New York: Penguin Classics.

Walcott, Rinaldo, and Harsha Idil Abdillahi. 2019. *BlackLife: Post-BLM and the Struggle for Freedom*. Winnipeg: ARP Books.

Walia, Harsha. 2021. *Border and Rule. Global Migration, Capitalism, and the Rise of Racist Nationalism*. Halifax: Fernwood.

Warrior, Robert. 1994. *Tribal Secrets: Recovering American Indian Intellectual Traditions*. Minneapolis: University of Minnesota Press.

Waters, Anne. 2004. *American Indian Thought: Philosophical Essays*. Malden, MA: Blackwell.

Waters, Anne. 2004. "Language Matters: Nondiscrete Nonbinary Dualism." In *American Indian Thought*, edited by Anne Waters, 97–115. Blackwell.

Watson, Irene. 2007. "Settled and Unsettled Spaces: Are We Free to Roam?" In *Sovereign Subjects: Indigenous Sovereignty Matter*, edited by Aileen Moreton-Robinson, 15–32. Melbourne: Allen and Unwin.

Watson, Irene. 2014. *Aboriginal Peoples, Colonialism, and International Law: Raw Law*. Oxfordshire: Routledge.

Weir, Allison. 1996. *Sacrificial Logics. Feminist Theory and the Critique of Identity.* New York: Routledge.
Weir, Allison. 2013. *Identities and Freedom.* New York: Oxford University Press.
Weir, Allison. 2017. "Decolonizing Feminist Freedom: Indigenous Relationalities." In *Decolonizing Feminism. Transnational Feminism and Globalization,* edited by Margaret A. McLaren, 257–288. London: Rowman and Littlefield.
Weir, Allison. 2017. "Feminism and Freedom." In *The Routledge Companion to Feminist Philosophy,* edited by Ann Garry, Serene J. Khader, and Alison Stone, 655–677. New York: Routledge.
Weir, Allison. 2021. "Feminist Critical Theory." In *The Oxford Handbook of Feminist Philosophy,* edited by Kim Q. Hall and Ásta, 50–62. New York: Oxford University Press.
Welch, Shay. 2013. "Radical-cum-Relation: Bridging Feminist Ethics and Native Individual Autonomy." *Philosophical Topics* 41(2): 203–222.
Welch, Shay. 2019. *The Phenomenology of a Performative Knowledge System: Dancing with Native American Epistemology.* New York: Palgrave Macmillan.
Wellmer, Albrecht. 1990. "Models of Freedom in the Modern World." In *Hermeneutics and Critical Theory in Ethics and Politics,* edited by Michael Kelly, 227–252. Cambridge, MA: MIT.
West, M. L. 2007. *Indo-European Poetry and Myth.* Oxford: Oxford University Press.
Whitt, Laurelyn. 2013. "Transforming Sovereignties." In *Philosophy and Aboriginal Rights. Critical Dialogues,* edited by Sandra Tomsons and Lorraine Mayer, 181–197. Toronto: Oxford University Press.
Whyte, Kyle. 2018. "Settler Colonialism, Ecology, and Environmental Injustice." *Environment and Society* 9(1): 125–144.
Wiegman, Robyn. 2014. "The Times We're in: Queer Feminist Criticism and the Reparative 'Turn.'" *Feminist Theory* 15(1): 4–25.
Wiegman, Robyn. 2019. "Outrage: Feeling the Political Present." Eve Sedgwick Memorial Lecture in Gender and Sexuality Studies. Duke University, March 21, 2019.
Wilkins, David E., and Heidi Kiiwetinepinesiik Stark. 2017. *American Indian Politics and the American Political System.* 4th ed. Lanham, MD: Rowman and Littlefield.
Wilkinson, Eleanor. 2014. "Love in the Multitude? A Feminist Critique of Love as a Political Concept." In *Love: A Question for Feminism in the Twenty-First Century,* edited by Ann Ferguson and Anna Jónasdóttir, 237–249. New York: Routledge.
Willett, Cynthia. 2001. *The Soul of Justice: Social Bonds and Racial Hubris.* Ithaca, NY: Cornell University Press.
Willett, Cynthia. 2008.*Irony in the Age of Empire: Comic Perspectives on Democracy and Freedom.* Bloomington: Indiana University Press.
Williams, Robert A. Jr. 1990. *The American Indian in Western Legal Thought: The Discourses of Conquest.* New York: Oxford University Press.
Williams, Robert A. Jr. 1997. *Linking Arms Together: North American Treaty Visions of Law and Peace 1600–1800.* New York: Routledge.
Williams, Robert A. Jr. 2012. *Savage Anxieties: The Invention of Western Civilization.* New York: Palgrave Macmillan.
Wilson, Nina. 2014. "Kisikew Iskwew, the Woman Spirit." In *The Winter We Danced,* edited by The Kino-nda-niimi Collective, 102–107. Winnipeg: ARP Books.
Wilson, Shawn. 2008. *Research Is Ceremony. Indigenous Research Methods.* Halifax: Fernwood.

Wohlleben, Peter. 2016. *The Hidden Life of Trees: What They Feel, How They Communicate.* Melbourne: Black.

Wolfe, Patrick. 1999. *Settler Colonialism and the Transformation of Anthropology.* London: Continuum.

Wolfe, Patrick. 2006. "Settler Colonialism and the Elimination of the Native." *Journal of Genocide Research* 8(4): 387–409.

Women's Earth Alliance and the Native Youth Sexual Health Network. *Violence on the Land, Violence on our Bodies: Building an Indigenous Response to Environmental Violence.* http://landbodydefense.org/uploads/files/VLVBReportToolkit2016.pdf

Wynter, Sylvia. 2003. "Unsettling the Coloniality of Being/Power/Truth/Freedom: Towards the Human, After Man, Its Overrepresentation—An Argument." *CR: The New Centennial Review* 3(3): 257–333.

Young, Iris. 1990. *Justice and the Politics of Difference.* Princeton, NJ: Princeton University Press.

Young, Iris. 2000. *Inclusion and Democracy.* New York: Oxford.

Young, Iris. 2007. *Global Challenges: War, Self-Determination, and Responsibility for Justice.* Cambridge: Polity Press.

Zerilli, Linda. 2005. *Feminism and the Abyss of Freedom.* Chicago: University of Chicago Press.

Index

For the benefit of digital users, indexed terms that span two pages (e.g., 52–53) may, on occasion, appear on only one of those pages.

Abdillahi, Idil, 194–96
AFN (Assembly of First Nations), 214, 218–19.
  See also National Indian Brotherhood (NIB)
agency
  decolonizing freedom and, 21–22, 31–32
  feminisms and, 206, 215, 228–31, 232
  grounded normativity and, 175–76
  human and nonhuman boundaries and, 31–32, 81, 86, 94
  land as pedagogy and, 89
  law and, 70–71
  love of land and, 81, 86–90, 97
  paradox of freedom and, 246–47
  as participation in web of relations, 81, 90
  political agency, 97, 184–85, 230–31, 253
  as response to gifts, 81, 86–90
  rights claims and, 240
Ahmed, Sara, 180–81
Alfred, Taiaiake
  anarcho-indigenism and, 107–8
  indigeneity and, 184–85
  Kahnawa:ke and, 191
  nationhood and, 185–86
  relational freedom and, 75
  resurgence and, 7, 75–76, 77, 107–8, 193
  sovereignty and, 72
Allen, Amy, 64, 248
Allen, Paula Gunn, 229–30
amor mundi, 29, 31, 80, 81–86, 129–35, 254
Anishinaabe
  law and, 70–71
  nationhood and, 102
  relational freedom and, 7–9, 67–68
  treaties and, 102–3
Anzaldua, Gloria, 181–82
Arendt, Hannah
  amor mundi and, 29, 31, 80, 81–86, 129–35, 254
  Baldwin's exchange with, 110–14
  being with and, 134–35
  on claim she lacks love of the Jewish people, 103–4, 106–7

  collective participation and, freedom as, 29, 81–82
  contestation and, 84, 89–90
  democratic governance and, 134–35, 151–52
  equality and, 81–82
  love and freedom and, relationship between, 110–14, 150–54
  love of land and, 81–82, 89–90, 103, 110–14
  love of nation and, 31–32, 80, 81, 103, 110
  love of self and, 104–5
  natality and, 130, 133, 134–36, 151–52
  philia politikē and, 32–33, 130–33, 151
  philoxenic relations and, 131–35
  practices of freedom and, 82–86
  public happiness and, 133–35
  relational freedom and, 81–82
  resistance movements and, 110
  right to have rights and, 220–21
  round dance and, 128, 129–35
  self-interest and, 32, 81, 104–5, 106–7
  slavery's connection to freedom and, 82
  "tribal" nationalisms and, 103–4
  world-creation and, 129
Aristotle, 27–28, 104, 130–32, 134–35, 220–21
arrivants, 194, 196–98
Arvin, Maile, 163
Asad, Talal, 178
Asch, Michael, 198–99
Assembly of First Nations (AFN). See National Indian Brotherhood (NIB)
autonomy, 8–9, 15–16, 28, 30–31, 40–41, 43, 50, 65–69, 185–86, 225–26

Baldwin, James
  on gospel in white church, 111–12
  love and freedom and, relationship between, 110–14
  love of the same and, 111–13
  ressentiment and, 112–13
  self-hatred of whites and, 112–13, 137–38, 259

Barker, Joanne, 21n.51, 72, 161–62, 184, 210, 215
Bédard, Yvonne, 209–10
Belcourt, Billy-Ray, 141
Benveniste, Emile, 148
Berlin, Isaiah, 9, 29–30, 38–39, 48, 62, 81–82, 152
Bhabha, Homi, 42
Bilgrami, Akeel, 142, 171
Bill of Rights (Canada), 209–10, 221–22
Birmingham, Peg, 135–36
Biskowski, Lawrence, 83
Black Elk, 69–70
Black Lives Matter movement, 125–26, 251–52, 254–55, 256–57
Blaney, Fay, 226–27
Bohman, James, 244–45
Borrows, John
    Anishinaabe and, 7–9, 67–68, 70–73
    colonial unknowing and, 187–88
    freedom of movement and, 68–69, 122–23, 182
    gendered violence and, 232
    Indigenous relational freedom and, 67–69
    law and, 70–73, 77–78, 200, 241
    Ojibwe and, 109–10
    ownership and, 109–10
    reconciliation and, 19, 78, 100–1
    relational freedom and, 7–9, 67–68, 91
    resurgence and, 77, 78
    right of prior occupancy and, 199
    round dance and, 122–23
    sovereignty and, 77–78
Brandon, William, 53
Brant, Clare, 65–66
Brown, Wendy, 22–23, 62–63
Buber, Martin, 126–27
Buck-Morss, Susan, 11
Burkhart, Brian Yazzie, 173
Butler, Judith, 22–23
Byrd, Goldstein, 24–25
Byrd, Jodi
    arrivants and, 194, 196–98
    economies of dispossession and, 24–25, 194–96
    essentialism and, 179–80, 193
    kinship sovereignties and, 27, 192–93, 197–98
    resurgence and, 192–93

Canada. *See also* Indian Act (1876) (Canada)
    Bill of Rights in, 209–10, 221–22
    Canadian Constitution Act, 236
    feminisms and, 207–11
    "Indian problem" in, 35, 207
    missing and murdered Indigenous women and girls in, 116–17, 156–58, 217–19, 228
    MMIWG in, 156–57, 217–19, 228
    NWAC in, 35, 156–57, 210, 211–15, 228, 230–31, 238–39
    Royal Commission on Aboriginal Peoples of, 18
    treaties and, 116, 157, 198–99
    Truth and Reconciliation Commission of, 18, 160n.14
care for the world. *See* love of land
Cherokee Nation, 188, 192–93
Chiba, Shin, 130
Choctaw, 83–84, 192
Christianity and Christian beliefs, 107–8, 111–12, 114, 119, 124, 159–61, 177–78
coalitional politics, 188–202
Coffey, Wallace, 74–75
Colden, Cadwallader, 63
collective identities, 21–22, 34, 183–88, 222–23, 232–33
collective participation, 29, 38–39, 81–82, 246
collective rights. *See* rights claims
colonial unknowing, 12–14. *See also* epistemologies
    ambivalent freedoms and, 59–63
    constitution of freedom through, 52–57
    constitutive exclusions and, 59–63
    critical theory and, 243, 245–46, 259
    decolonizing freedom and, 13–16
    democratic governance and, 38–39
    disavowals and, 52–57, 161
    epistemologies and, 158–62, 179–88
    epistemic ignorance and, 12–14, 161
    Eurocentrism and, 63–64
    exemplars of liberty and, 40, 41–42, 57–58
    historical progress and, 63–64
    internalization of, 187–88
    negative freedom and, 38
    neoliberalism and, 62
    nondomination and, 38–40
    noninterference and, 38–49, 53–55, 57–58
    overview of, 33–34, 38–41
    Pettit and, 45–49
    process of colonization and, 52–57
    racialization and, 59–60
    relational freedom and, 52–57, 65–69
    from relation freedom to noninterference and, 41–45
    republican freedom and, 45–49
    resurgence and, 75–76

romantic identifications and, 59–63
savage freedom and, 52–57
self-determination and, 49–51
settler contract and, 61
social contract and, 59–61
state of nature and, 52–55, 56–57, 59–61, 62, 63, 64
treaties and, 161–62
Young and, 41–45
communitas, 33, 115, 123–25, 126–28, 133n.52, 141–42
Conduction (Coates), 252
Constant, Benjamin, 52
constellations of co-resistance, 25, 80–81, 92–93, 101, 103, 244
Constitution Act (1982), 211–12
constitutive exclusions, 1–3, 10–11, 12, 13–14, 15–16, 59–63, 228–29
Cordova, V. F., 65–66
co-resistance, constellations of, 25, 80–81, 92–93, 101, 103, 244
Corntassel, Jeff, 184–85
Coulthard, Glen
　coalitional politics and, 141
　critically revitalized traditions and, 144
　culture as a mode of life and, 185–86
　direct action and, 140
　essentialism and, 193
　feminisms and, 215–16
　grounded normativity and, 9, 175–76, 201, 246
　identity politics and, 201
　internalized domination and, 140–41
　land as field of relationships and, 15, 87–88, 175–76
　modes of life and, 185–86
　resurgence and, 7, 19, 75, 76–77, 193, 216–17, 233–34
　rights claims and, 215–16
Courchene, David, Jr., 117–18
creation of the world. *See* world-creation
critical theory
　aims of, 176, 244–46
　belonging and, 261–62
　BIPOC movements and, 254–55
　colonial unknowing and, 243, 245–46, 259
　competing forms of, 244–51
　decolonizing freedom and, 6, 13–16, 23
　decolonizing of, 193–94, 268–69
　definition of, 251
　development of, 244–51
　Foucault and, 259–64
　Frankfurt School and, 244–45, 246

　grounded normativity and, 246
　Hadot and, 259–64
　healing justice and, 255–57
　love of land and, 255
　loving freedom and, 253–59
　models of critique and, 244–51
　nationhood and, 201
　nondomination and, 82, 244
　overview of, 36–37, 243–44
　paranoid theorizing and, 264–67
　philoxenic relations and, 255
　political activism and, 253–59
　practice of relationship as practice of freedom and, 251–53
　relational freedom and, 244, 249, 250–51, 253, 254–55, 264–69
　reparative theorizing and, 264–67
　resistance and, 244
　resurgence and, 256
　self-transformation and, 244, 253–59
　spiritual exercise and, freedom as, 259–64
　struggles and wishes of the age and, 251–53
　transformative justice and, 257
　treaties and, 268
　world-creation and, 246
Cullors, Patrisse, 256–57

Dakota Access Pipeline, 87, 115, 121–22, 231, 256
dance. *See* round dance
Dancing in the Streets (Ehrenreich), 123–24
Dancing on Our Turtle's Back (Simpson), 118
"Decolonizing Feminism" (Ervin, Tuck, & Morrill), 163
decolonizing freedom
　agency and, 21–22, 31–32
　collective identities and, 20–25
　colonial unknowing and, 13–16
　colonization and, entangled relations of, 20–25
　constellations of co-resistance and, 25
　constitutive exclusions and, 1–3, 10–11, 12, 15–16
　critical theory and, 6, 13–16, 23
　definition of freedom and, 1–3
　democratic governance and, 3–5, 15–16, 27–28
　economies of dispossession and, 24–25
　egalitarian views of freedom and, 3
　equality and, 3, 10, 21–22, 29–30, 31, 35
　genealogies of freedom and, 10–12
　grounded normativity and, 3–4, 19
　guiding argumentation on, 4–6

decolonizing freedom (*cont.*)
  identity of author and, 6
  identity politics and, 22–23
  land as pedagogy and, 3–4
  land as property and, 13–15
  methodological approach to, 3–4
  nationhood and, 26–27
  negative freedom and, 2–3
  overview of, 1–6
  philoxenic relations and, 3–4
  politics of freedom from colonization and, 16–20
  private freedom and, 2–3
  racial and gender dimensions of freedom and, 1–3
  reconciliation and, 17–20
  relational freedom and, 3–10, 15, 16–37
  resurgence and, 18–20, 23
  rights claims and, 17–18, 36
  savage freedom and, 12, 13–14
  self-determination and, 20–24
  settler contract and, 13–14
  slavery's connection to freedom and, 1–3, 10–11
  social contract and, 13–16
  sovereignty and, 6–7, 10, 13–14, 16–17, 18, 20, 23–24, 32, 35–36, 260
  state of nature and, 13–14
  Statue of Liberty and, 1–3
  structure of current volume on, 29–37
  transformative theories and, 25–28
  treaties and, 16–17, 26–28
  universalism and, 1–2
  Western conception of freedom and, 1–2, 11–12, 21–22
  Westphalian state and, 23–24, 26–27
  world-creation and, 3–4, 28
Deloria, Vine, Jr., 74–75, 175, 177–78
democratic governance. *See also* law; nationhood; politics; rights claims; self-determination
  colonial unknowing and, 38–39
  consensus as orientation of, 143
  decolonizing freedom and, 3–5, 15–16, 27–28
  epistemologies and, 156, 167–68
  grounded normativity and, 217
  law as system of, 71
  philoxenic relations and, 27–28
  rational argument and, 69–70
  relational freedom and, 69–72
  round dance and, 143–44
  self-interest and, 133–34
  traditions of, 69–72

disavowals
  colonial unknowing and, 52–57, 161
  epistemologies and, 158–59
  noninterference and, 30, 55
  relational freedom and, 15–16, 267
Douglass, Frederick, 252
Dutcher, Jeremy, 160n.14

economies of dispossession, 24–25, 194–96, 201–2
Ehrenreich, Barbara, 33, 115, 123–28, 149–50
Epicureans, 131–32, 262
epistemic ignorance, 12–14, 161
epistemologies. *See also* colonial unknowing
  alternative formations of freedom and, 163–79
  axiology and, 171–76
  being with and, 163–65, 176–77
  breath and, 165–66
  colonial unknowing and, 158–62, 179–88
  decolonization through, 162, 163–79
  definition of knowledge and, 168–70
  democratic governance and, 156, 167–68
  disavowals and, 158–59
  ecological knowledge and, 168–70, 171–72
  emergent normativity and, 171
  epistemic vice and, 168
  essentialism and, 161–62, 179–88, 193
  expansive conception of persons and, 167–68
  feminisms and, 158–60, 163–64, 168–70, 177, 187
  Gaia Hypothesis and, 171
  grounded normativity and, 175–76
  heterogenous relational selves and, 180–83
  identity politics and, 183
  individualist model of knowledge and, 178–79
  infinite regress and, 173–74
  kinship as polity and, 160
  knowing with and, 165–67
  land as pedagogy and, 94–95, 96–97, 165–70
  law and, 161–62
  legal femicide and, 157–59
  limits of knowledge and, 173–75
  lived dimension of knowledge and, 171–73
  metaphysics and, 165–66
  nationhood and, 162, 183–86
  normative practices and, 171–76
  overview of, 33–35, 155–58
  politics and, 156–62, 171–76
  polycentric knowledge and, 165–70
  queerness and, 160, 180–82

racialization and, 158–62
relational freedom and, 165–70, 174–75, 179–80, 182
relativism and universalism in, 166–67, 170, 178–79, 186–87
resistance and, 184
responding to critiques of essentialism and, 180–83
resurgence and, 162
skepticism and, 175, 179
sovereignty and, 157–58, 160–61
spirituality and secular myths and, 176–79
treaties and, 161–62
undermining of Indigenous political orders and, 156–62
use of Indigenous people as objects of research and, 171–72
whiteness and, 161, 180–81
world-creation and, 174
equality and decolonizing freedom, 3, 10, 21–22, 29–30, 31, 35
essentialism, 29, 34, 64, 161–62, 179–88, 193
ethics of reciprocity, 9, 19, 94–95, 106, 175–76, 232
Eurocentrism, 63–64, 129
Exemplarity, 3–5, 28, 33, 115–16, 141–44
 as a politics of freedom, 31–32
 and democracy, 32–33
 and political action, 144
Exemplar of Liberty (Grinde and Johansen), 42, 57–58, 69
exemplars of liberty, 11–12, 40, 41–42, 57–58

Faith Spotted Eagle, 243
feminisms
 agency and, 206, 215, 228–31, 232
 belonging and, 235–36
 breaking relations and, 207–11
 citizenship and, 221–22
 collective rights and, 211–14, 231–33
 colonization, gendered politics of, 207–11
 connection between individual and collective rights and, 226–27
 constitutional struggles and, 211–14
 decolonizing of, 158–59, 163
 denial of rights and, effects of, 224–25
 epistemologies and, 158–60, 163–64, 168–70, 177, 187
 gendered violence and, 218–19, 227, 232–33, 236–38, 241
 gender justice and, 205–6, 217
 gender roles and, 189–90, 216–17, 230–32
 grounded normativity and, 226

Indian Act and, 208–12, 217, 222, 223–25, 226–27, 230–31
law and, 208, 239–42
male opposition to, 210
MMIWG report and, 228
nationhood and, 206–7, 233–36
neo-colonialism and, 205–6
noninterference and, 204, 210–11, 225
NWAC and, 228, 230–31
overview of, 35–36, 203–7
patriarchal leadership and, 20–21, 67, 207, 208, 210, 211–14, 216–17, 230–31, 234–35, 240
politics and, 222–39
racialization and, 204
restorative justice and, 218–19
resurgence and, 215–17, 233–38
rights claims and, 36, 205, 210, 211–39
self-determination and, 225–27, 234–36, 239–40
sovereignty and, 204, 206–7, 208–9
struggles for rights are struggles to restructure relations and, 225–26
traditions and struggles for decolonization and, 228–33
treaties and, 157, 208, 229–30
undermining of Indigenous women and, 157–58
unique formulations of relational rights and, 238–39
as Western idea, 210, 214
white feminism and, 229–30
Ferreira da Silva, Denise, 8n.23, 182
Fiske, Joanne, 215
Flannery, Tim, 168–69
Fleras, Augie, 72
Fort Laramie Treaty (1868), 121–22
Foucault, Michel
 boomerang effect of colonialism and, 56
 conquest and, 54–55
 counterhistory of rebellion and, 55–56
 critique as spirit of modernity for, 37, 246–47, 259–60
 disavowals and, 55–56
 dividing practices and, 208–9
 freedom as spiritual exercise and, 259–64
 heterotopia and, 249
 political spirituality and, 263–64
 practices of freedom and, 260–61
 self-transformation and, 37
 sovereignty and, 56–57
Frankfurt School, 244–45, 246
Fraser, Nancy, 97, 251

freedom. *See also* decolonizing freedom; nondomination; noninterference; relational freedom; self-determination; sovereignty
   of movement, 68–69, 120–23, 182
   negative freedom, 2–3, 9, 38–40, 47, 148, 151, 152, 180, 246, 248
   politics of, 18, 25, 33, 75, 130, 141–44, 201, 255–56
   positive freedom, 12, 43, 47–48, 148, 152, 248
   republican freedom, 40, 43, 45–49, 52
   savage freedom, 12, 13–14, 52–57
Fugitive Slave Act (1850), 194–96

Gage, Matilda Joslyn, 12, 229–30
Gaia Hypothesis, 171
Gandhi, Leela, 100–1, 131–32
Gandhi, Mohandas, 108, 142
Garfinkel, Yosef, 123–24
gendered violence, 116–17, 156–58, 217–19, 227, 228, 232–33, 236–38, 241
Ghost Dance. *See* round dance
God is Red (Deloria), 177–78
Goeman, Mishuana, 199
Goldstein, Alyosha, 194, 197
Gordon, Jess, 116
governance. *See* democratic governance; law; nationhood; politics; sovereignty
Gray, Vanessa, 236–37
Great Law of Peace of the Iroquois Federation (Haudenosaunee Confederacy), 42–43
Great Sioux Reservation, 121–22
Greek and Roman conceptions of freedom, 1–2, 16, 81–85, 124, 126, 145, 261–62
Green, Joyce, 227
grounded normativity
   agency and, 175–76
   critical theory and, 246
   decolonizing freedom and, 3–4, 19
   definition of, 9
   democratic governance and, 217
   epistemologies and, 175–76
   ethics of reciprocity and, 19, 94–95, 106, 176, 232
   feminisms and, 226
   internationalism and, 106
   land as pedagogy and, 3–4
   land as source of, 87–88, 175–76, 232
   love of land and, 87–88, 93–95, 99–100
   philoxenic relations and, 100, 106
   relational freedom and, 9, 248–49
   resurgence and, 23, 108, 110, 233–34, 246
Guerrero, M. Annette James, 5–6n.10

Habermas, Jürgen, 15–16, 64, 246, 260–61
Hadot, Pierre, 37, 259–64
Half Caste Act (1886) (Australia), 183n.84
Hardt, Michael, 255
Harper, Stephen, 116
Harris, Cheryl, 161
Hart, Michael A., 166–67
Haudenosaunee Confederacy, 42–43, 158, 190, 198, 229–30
Hegel, G. W. F., 11, 13, 15–16, 38–39, 55, 64, 82
Henderson, James (Sákéj) Youngblood, 129
Hennessey, Rosemary, 125–26
Hidden Life of Trees, The (Wohlleben), 168–69
Hill Collins, Patricia, 164n.22
Hirschmann, Nancy, 1–2
History of the Five Indian Nations (Colden), 63
Hobbes, Thomas
   disavowals and, 54–57
   fear and, 9
   homo economicus and, 59
   ideal theory and, 54–55
   noninterference and, 29, 38, 39–40, 45–46, 47–48, 52, 54–55, 59
   private property and, 105
   register of argumentation and, 54–55
   right to destroy and, 105
   savage freedom and, 52–54
   settler contract and, 54–55
   state of nature and, 13–14, 52–54
Honig, Bonnie, 83–84
Honneth, Axel, 15–16, 64
hooks, bell, 255
"*Hoquotist*" (Mack), 268
Horkheimer, Max, 176
"How to Stop an Oil and Gas Pipeline" (video), 108
Human Condition, The (Arendt), 82–83, 89–90, 130–31
Hunt, Sarah, 238
Huron-Wendat, 190
Huson, Freda, 108–9

identity politics, 20, 22–24, 29, 106, 179–80, 183–85, 187, 189, 201
Idle No More (2012-2013) (Canada)
   Bill C-45 and, 116–17
   context for, 116
   critical theory and, 254–55
   decentralized nature of, 116–17
   diversity of participants in, 116–17
   initiation of, 116
   organizers of, 116
   overview of, 115

as re-storying Canada, 121
round dances as central in, 115–18, 122–23, 125–26, 137
women's role in, 231
Indian Act (1876) (Canada)
abolishment of, 210–11
amendments to, 116, 214
continued effects of, 157
feminisms and, 208–12, 217, 222, 223–25, 226–27, 230–31
gendered violence and, 156–57, 218–19
membership status rules imposed by, 106
nationhood and, 218–19
property rights and, 223–24
rights claims and, 222, 223–25, 230–31
women excluded by, 188, 207, 208–10, 212, 215, 217, 224–25, 226–27, 230–31
Indian Rights for Indian Women, 210
indigeneity, 5–6n.10, 159, 184–85, 187, 241–42
Indigenous democracy. *See* democratic governance
Indigenous epistemologies. *See* epistemologies
Indigenous feminisms. *See* feminisms
Indigenous Law Research Unit (University of Victoria), 71n.107
Indigenous nationhood. *See* nationhood
Indigenous relational freedom. *See* relational freedom
Indigenous sovereignty. *See* sovereignty
Iroquois Confederacy, 42, 63

Jaggar, Alison, 54–55
Jesuit Relations, 167
Johnston, Basil, 70–71
justice (gender), 205–6, 217
justice (healing), 218–19, 251–52, 255–57
justice (transformative), 37, 251–52, 255–57

Kahnawa:ke, 24, 27, 107, 184–85, 189, 191, 197–98
Kanehsata:ke/ Oka, 231–32
Kant, Immanuel, 1–2, 13–14, 38–39, 63, 65, 137–38, 246
Khader, Serene, 228n.59
Kimmerer, Robin Wall, 88–89
King, Hayden, 184
King, Martin Luther, Jr., 251
King, Thomas, 165–66
kinship sovereignties, 27, 192–93, 197–98
Klein, Melanie, 135–36, 264–66
Kristeva, Julia, 26, 33, 135–38, 139
Kuokkanen, Rauna, 26, 219, 225–26, 227, 234–35
Kwakwaka'wakw Thunderbird dance, 120–21

Ladner, Kiera, 26, 36, 70, 77–78, 203, 205–6, 234, 240–41
LaDuke, Winona, 7, 171–72
land, love of. *See* love of land
land as pedagogy
agency and, 89
decolonizing freedom and, 3–4
definition of, 31
epistemologies and, 94–95, 96–97, 165–70
grounded normativity and, 3–4
love of land and, 31, 81, 89
lovingly coming to know and, 92–93
reciprocal relations and, 89
resurgence and, 92
land as property, 13–15, 16–17, 23–25, 158, 168, 176, 207–8, 252–53
land as system of reciprocal relations and obligations, 9, 15, 87–89, 97, 109, 232, 248–49
Lavell, Jeanette Corbière, 209–10, 221–22
law. *See also* democratic governance; nationhood; rights claims; self-determination
agency and, 70–71
arrivants and, 197–98
democratic governance and, 71
direct action and, 140
epistemologies and, 161–62
feminisms and, 208, 238–42
pluralism and, 73–74
property rights and, 26, 199
reconciliation and, 19
relational freedom and, 69–72
resurgence and, 18, 36, 205, 218–19, 240–42
rights claims and, 219–20, 222
whiteness and, 161
Lawrence, Bonita, 190, 207, 211
le Jeune, Father, 58
"Letter from a Region in My Mind" (Baldwin), 111
Light, Andrew, 93–94
Locke, John
constitutive exclusions and, 60
land as property and, 13–15
political society and, 60
self as property and, 13
settler contract and, 13–15
social contract and, 60–61
Lorde, Audre, 255
love. *See also* love of land; love of nation; love of self
agape, 130–31, 152
Arendt and, 110–14, 150–54

love (*cont.*)
  caritas, 130–31, 152
  critical theory and, 253–59
  eros, 114, 147–48, 149, 151–52
  etymology of, 146–51
  freedom's relation to, 110–14, 145–54
  mysticism and, 152–53
  negative freedom and, 148, 151
  noninterference and, 148
  philia politikē and, 27–28, 32–33, 106–7, 130–32, 151
  political freedom and, 150–54
  relational freedom and, 82, 84–86
  round dance and, 124–25, 127–29
  of the same, 111–13
  slavery's connection to freedom and, 145–48
  speculative genealogy of, 145–54
Lovelace, Sandra, 209–10
Lovelock, James, 171
love of land
  agency and, 81, 86–90, 94, 97
  amor mundi and, 31, 80–86
  Arendt and, 81–82, 103, 110–14
  authoritarianism and, 105
  Baldwin and, 110–14
  care for the world as, 84–85, 86–90
  coalitional politics of solidarity and, 99–101
  coda on, 110–14
  constellations of co-resistance and, 101
  contested of meaning of land and, 87–88
  critical theory and, 255
  decolonization as risking connection and, 91–93
  generative refusal and, 107–10
  grounded normativity and, 87–88, 93–95, 99–100
  land as pedagogy and, 31, 81, 89
  land as web of relationships, 88
  love and freedom and, relationship between, 110–14
  love of nation and, 102–7
  nationhood and, 102–7
  overview of, 80–81
  ownership and, 109–10
  philoxenic relations and, 32, 81, 99–101
  pipeline protests and, 108–9
  political nationalism and, 102–7
  as practice of relational freedom, 91–93
  practices of freedom and, 91–93
  racialization and, 105
  radiating responsibilities and, 102–7
  reconciliation and, 81, 100–1
  resurgence and, 107–8
  rethinking public/private split and, 95–99
  right to destroy and, 102–7
  round dance and, 139–40
  self-interest and, 105
  sovereignty and, 102–3
  thing as gathering and, 90
  treaties and, 87, 92, 102–3
  wordly ethics and, 80–81, 84–85, 93–95
  world-creation and, 106, 129
love of nation, 31–32, 80, 81, 102–7, 110
love of self, 104–5

Maaka, Roger, 41, 72
Macpherson, C. B., 13
Mahmood, Saba, 245–46
Maitland, F. W., 53–54
Mamdani, Mahmood, 20n.49, 194
Maracle, Lee, 234n.71
Marcus Aurelius, 262–63
Margulis, Lynn, 171
Markell, Patchen, 89
Martínez-Cobo, José R., 5–6n.10
Marx, Karl, 11, 13, 38–39, 55–56, 63, 82, 185–86, 244–45, 246
Massacre at Wounded Knee, 121–22
McAdam, Sylvia, 116
McGregor, Deborah, 171–72
McIvor, Sharon, 209–10, 213–14, 224–25, 229–30, 236
McLean, Sheelah, 116
McMahon, Ryan, 137
McPherson, Dennis, 65, 166–67, 177
Medina, José, 168
migration, 194–98, 201
Mi'kmaq, 167
Million, Dian, 165–66, 186, 215, 230–31, 257–58
Mills, Charles, 12–13n.33, 13–14, 54–55, 60–61
Milmore, Ruth Wilson, 243
Minobimaatisiiwin, 171–72
MMIWG (Report on Missing and Murdered Indigenous Women and Girls), 156–57, 217–19, 228
Mohawk Interruptus (Simpson), 106
Monture-Angus, Patricia, 26, 73, 215–16, 222
Moreton-Robinson, Aileen, 8–9, 161, 163–64, 170, 180
Morrill, Angie
Morton, Thomas, 58
Muñoz, José, 249
Murphy, Jacqueline Shea, 120–21
Musqua, Danny, 105n.67

Myers, Ella
  amor mundi and, 84–85
  anthropocentrism and, 93–94
  democratic governance and, 31, 84–85
  self-interest and, 93–94
  solidarity and, 89
  wordly ethics and, 80–81, 84–85, 93–95
  worldy things and, 85, 87, 89

Napoleon, Val, 71, 227, 241
natality, 130, 133, 134–36, 151–52
National Indian Brotherhood (NIB), 210–12, 215, 218–19, 252
National Inquiry into Missing and Murdered Women and Girls (2016-2019), 18
nationhood. *See also* democratic governance; law; politics; rights claims; self-determination; sovereignty
  addressing conflicting imaginaries and, 200–2
  arrivants and, 197–98
  coalitional politics of decolonization and, 188–202
  collective identities as heterogeneous polities and, 183–88
  critical theory and, 201
  decolonizing freedom and, 26–27
  destabilizing binaries and, 193–96
  entangled relations of dispossession and, 193–96
  epistemologies and, 162, 183–86
  essentialism and, 188–89, 193
  family as polity and, 160
  feminisms and, 206–7, 233–36
  as form of political identity, 185–86
  heterogenous relationalities and, 188–202
  identity politics and, 183, 185–86, 187, 189, 197–98, 201
  Indian Act and, 218–19
  kinship and, 188–202
  legal culture and, 200
  love of land and, 102–7
  migration and, 194–98, 201
  mixedness and, 190
  narratives of freedom and, 200–2
  politics of exclusion, traditions of inclusion and, 188–202
  polity of the Indigenous and, 161–62, 184, 241–42
  queerness and, 189–90
  racialization and, 188, 194–97
  relational freedom and, 26–27, 102
  resurgence and, 193
  self-determination and, 26
  as series of radiating responsibilities, 26, 32, 102, 103
  settlers distinguished from migrants and, 194–96
  sovereignty and, 72, 102–3, 184, 196–97, 198
  theorizing coalitions and, 196–200
  toward a coalitional politics and, 200–2
  treaties and, 26–27, 74–75, 102–3, 198–99
  varying conceptions of, 188–202
  Westphalian state and, 23–24, 26, 72–73, 210–11
Nations National Constitutional Convention Uluru Statement from the Heart, 268
Native Women's Association of Canada (NWAC), 35, 156–57, 210, 211–15, 228, 230–31, 238–39
Nedelsky, Jennifer, 43, 95–96, 223–24, 225–26
negative freedom. *See* freedom
Negri, Antonio, 255
neo-colonialism, 36, 205–6
neoliberalism, 16, 62–63
Nichols, Robert, 13–14, 26n.73, 52, 54–55, 61, 184–85
Nietzsche, Friedrich, 112–13, 126–27
Nishnaabeg, 88–127, 128–29, 141, 176–77, 198
nondomination
  colonial unknowing and, 38–40
  critical theory and, 82, 244
  definition of, 30
  interdependence assumed in, 67
  noninterference and, 44–49
  relational freedom and, 67, 73
  republican freedom as, 40, 43, 45–46, 52
noninterference
  as an ideal, 57–58
  autonomy and, 43
  colonial unknowing and, 38–49, 53–55, 57–58
  decolonizing freedom and, 29
  disavowals and, 30, 55
  exemplars of liberty and, 30, 57–58
  feminisms and, 204, 210–11, 225
  love and, 148
  nondomination and, 44–49
  overview of, 29–30
  relational freedom and, 30–31, 41–45, 51, 72–73, 78–79
  savage freedom and, 53
  self-determination and, 30, 41–45, 50
  slavery's connection to freedom and, 1–3, 10–11, 82, 145–48
nonviolence, 67, 108, 142, 144, 254
normativity, grounded. *See* grounded normativity

Norton-Smith, Thomas, 4n.8, 33, 119–20, 127–28, 129, 167–68, 172–75, 178–79
Notes Toward a Performative Theory of Assembly (Butler), 253
NWAC (Native Women's Association of Canada), 35, 156–57, 210, 211–15, 228, 230–31, 238–39

Onians, Richard Broxton, 147–48
On Revolution (Arendt), 81–82, 133–34
Origins of Totalitarianism, The (Arendt), 103, 104–5

Palmater, Pamela, 231
Patterson, Orlando, 11
pedagogy, land as. *See* land as pedagogy
Pegues, Hu, 197
Peter Martyr of Anghiera, 53
Pettit, Philip, 29–30, 40, 43, 45–50, 51–52, 57, 73
philia politikē, 27–28, 32–33, 106–7, 130–33, 151
philoxenic relations
　critical theory and, 255
　decolonizing freedom and, 3–4
　democratic governance and, 27–28
　grounded normativity and, 100, 106
　love of land and, 32, 81, 99–101
　round dance and, 115, 128, 129–35, 138, 139–40
　solidarity and, 33, 138
Pitkin, Hanna, 133
Plato, 84–85, 173, 261–62
politics. *See also* democratic governance; nationhood; rights claims; self-determination; sovereignty
　coalitional politics, 99–101, 188–202
　of decolonization, 16–20, 222–39
　epistemologies and, 156–62, 171–76
　of freedom, 16–20, 25, 33, 75, 130, 141–44, 201, 255–56
　gendered politics of colonization and, 207–11
　identity politics, 20, 22–24, 29, 106, 179–80, 183–85, 187, 189, 201
　love and, 150–54
　love of land and, 99–101
　philia politikē, 27–28, 32–33, 106–7, 130–33, 151
　political agency, 97, 184–85, 230–31, 253
　political nationalism, 102–7
　of racialization, 160–61, 194–97
　of reconciliation, 17–18
　of relational freedom, 7, 9, 67, 77–79, 110, 162

　relational freedom and, 7, 9, 77–79
　of resurgence, 18, 77–79, 240
　round dance and, 121–23, 141–44
　of self-determination, 15–16, 20–21, 23–24, 184
　solidarity and, 99–101
　polity of the Indigenous, 161–62, 184, 241–42
positive freedom. *See* freedom
Potter, Elizabeth, 169–70
Povinelli, Elizabeth, 155, 190–91
property, land as. *See* land as property
Puar, Jasbir, 180–81
public freedom, 6–9, 10, 32–33, 80, 115–16, 119–20, 127, 130–40, 142, 144
public things, 83–85
public/private split, 6–7, 32, 67–68, 81, 106, 231, 252–53, 255
　care for the world and, 95–99

queerness, 141, 160, 180–82, 189–90, 201, 249

Rabb, Douglas, 65, 166–67, 177
racialization
　colonial unknowing and, 59–60
　epistemologies and, 158–62
　feminisms and, 204
　love of land and, 105
　nationhood and, 188, 194–97
　politics of, 160–61, 194–97
　relational freedom and, 72
　sovereignty and, 72
　whiteness and, 161
radiating responsibilities, nationhood as series of, 26, 32, 102, 103
Ramirez, Renya, 187n.99
reciprocal relations and obligations, land as system of, 9, 15, 87–89, 97, 109, 232, 248–49
reciprocity, ethics of, 9, 19, 175–76
Recollet, Karyn, 120–21, 123
reconciliation. *See also* self-determination
　constitutional reconciliation, 77–78
　decolonizing freedom and, 19–20
　dominant models of freedom and, 78
　ethical reconciliation, 77–78
　ethical transformation required for, 78
　love of land and, 81, 100–1
　politics of, 17–18
　relational freedom and, 77–79
　round dance and, 144
　transformative reconciliation, 6–7, 10, 19–20, 32, 77–79
　treaty constitutionalism and, 78

"Reconciliation Here on Earth" (Tully), 138
relational freedom. *See also* round dance
   autonomy and, 65–69
   childrearing practices and, 65–67
   colonial unknowing and, 52–57, 65–69
   critical theory and, 244, 249, 250–51, 253, 254–55, 264–69
   decolonizing freedom and, 3–10, 15, 16–37
   definition of, 6–7
   democratic governance and, 69–72
   disavowals and, 15–16, 267
   empowerment and, 75–76
   encountering of, 29–37
   epistemologies and, 165–70, 174–75, 179–80, 182
   ethic of interventive-noninterference and, 66
   freedom of movement and, 68–69
   grounded normativity and, 9, 248–49
   instrumental relations contrasted with, 70
   law and, 69–72
   love and, 82, 84–86
   love of land as practice of, 91–93
   nationhood and, 26–27, 102
   negative freedom and, 9
   nondomination and, 67, 73
   noninterference and, 30–31, 41–45, 51, 65–67, 72–73, 75–76, 78–79
   overview of, 3–10
   peace pipe and, 70
   politics of, 7, 9, 67, 77–79, 110, 162
   racialization and, 72
   reconciliation and, 77–79
   relationality as root of, 8–9
   resurgence and, 7, 18, 75–79
   revaluation of, 4–6
   rites of making relatives and, 69–70
   rooted dynamism of, 7–9
   round dance and, 115, 119–20, 132–33, 143
   self-determination and, 26, 30, 41–45, 68
   sovereignty and, 72–75
   terminological note on, 5–6n.10
   treaties and, 69–70
   Westphalian state and, 72–73
   world-creation and, 25, 27–28, 115
"Remnants of the Five Nations, The" (Gage), 229–30
Report on Missing and Murdered Indigenous Women and Girls (MMIWG), 156–57, 217–19, 228
Republicanism (Pettit), 45–46, 57n.64
republican freedom. *See* freedom
reservations, 16–17, 24–25, 50, 122–23

residential schools, 16–17, 18, 122–23, 157, 159, 160–61
resistance, constellations of co-, 25, 80–81, 92–93, 101, 103, 244
resurgence. *See also* self-determination
   colonial unknowing and, 75–76
   critical resurgence, 19, 23–24, 193, 205, 236–37
   critical theory and, 256
   decolonizing freedom and, 18–20, 23
   epistemologies and, 162
   essentialism and, 193
   feminisms and, 215–17, 233–38
   grounded normativity and, 23, 108, 110, 233–34, 246
   land as pedagogy and, 92
   law and, 18, 36, 205, 218–19, 240–42
   love of land and, 107–8
   nationhood and, 193
   politics of, 18, 77–79, 240
   round dance and, 117–19, 144
   transformative resurgence, 19–20, 77–79, 240–41, 256
Rifkin, Mark, 159–60, 180–81
rights claims. *See also* democratic governance; law; nationhood; politics
   agency and, 240
   collective rights, 20–21, 24, 35, 60, 203, 205–7, 210, 211–14, 226–27, 231–33
   decolonizing freedom and, 17–18, 36
   feminisms and, 36, 205, 210, 211–40
   law and, 219–20, 222
   precontact rights and, 236–40
   restructuring relations through, 225–26
   resurgence and, 233–38
   right to have rights and, 220–22
   self-determination and, 35, 226–27, 232–33
   struggles for, 225–26
Roman and Greek conceptions of freedom, 1–2, 16, 81–85, 124, 126, 145, 261–62
round dance
   amor mundi and, 129–31, 139–40
   Arendt and, 129–35
   being the change through, 33, 139, 141–42
   being the other through, 137–41
   communitas and, 123–25, 126–28, 141–42
   as decolonial gesture, 120–21, 123, 136
   democratic governance and, 143–44
   Ehrenreich and, 127–29
   exemplarity and, 141–44
   freedom of movement and, 122–23
   function of, 127–28
   hierarchy resisted through, 127–28

round dance (cont.)
    historical use in political protests of, 121–23
    Idle No More and, 115–18, 122–23, 125–26, 137
    internalized domination and, 140–41
    Klein and, 135–37
    Kristeva and, 135–37
    love and, 124–25, 127–29, 149–50
    love of land and, 139–40
    misinterpretation of, 129, 141–42
    mourning and gratitude and, 135–37
    nonviolence and, 142, 144
    oneself as a stranger and, 140–41
    origin and significance of, 117–18
    overview of, 115–16
    performativity and, 119
    philoxenic relations and, 115, 128, 129–35, 138, 139–40
    pleasure and danger and, 125–27
    politics and, 121–23, 141–44
    as practices of collective love, 123–25
    reconciliation and, 144
    relational freedom and, 115, 119–20, 132–33, 143
    resistance through, 115–18, 125–28, 144
    resurgence and, 117–19, 144
    ritual dimensions of dance and, 120, 127–28, 129–35, 136
    solidarity and, 138
    terminology of, 120–21
    theorizing of, 135–37
    vice in public life and, 135–36
    world-creation and, 118–23, 128–35, 141–42, 149–50
Royal Commission on Aboriginal Peoples, The (1991–1996), 18

Sales, Ruby, 253–54, 255–56
Satyagraha, 142
savage freedom, 12, 13–14, 52–57
Scott, Craig, 41
Secret River, The (Grenville), 14–15, 15n.40
Sedgwick, Eve, 37, 264–66, 267
self-determination. *See also* democratic governance; law; nationhood; politics; reconciliation; resurgence; sovereignty
    collective self-determination, 17–18, 26, 35, 50, 73, 204–5, 226–27, 232–33
    colonial unknowing and, 49–51
    decolonizing freedom and, 20–24
    essentialism and, 183, 188–89
    feminisms and, 35, 225–27, 234–36, 239–40
    individual and women's rights as essential for, 226–27

    nationhood and, 23–24, 26
    noninterference and, 30, 41–45, 50
    politics of, 15–16, 20–21, 23–24, 184
    as practice of restructuring relations, 44, 225–26
    relational freedom and, 26, 30, 41–45, 68
    rights claims and, 35, 226–27, 232–33
    self-interest, 32, 81, 104–5, 106–7, 133–34
    self-transformation, 7, 10, 37, 75, 76–77, 244, 246–47, 253–59, 260–62, 267
Seneca, 261–62
settler colonialism. *See* colonial unknowing; decolonizing freedom
settler contract, 13–14, 54–55, 61
Shawnee Bread Dances, 119
Simpson, Audra
    alternative formations and, 155
    belonging and, 108
    gender roles and, 231
    identity politics and, 24, 189
    kinship and, 191, 197–98
    legal femicide and, 157–59
    love of land and, 29
    nationhood and, 27, 184–85
    nested sovereignties and, 198
    reconciliation and, 18
    refusal and, 107
    relational selves and, 182
    settler colonialism and, 161–62
Simpson, Leanne Betasamosake
    belonging and, 108
    biiskabiyang and, 92
    constellations of co-resistance and, 101
    epistemologies and, 165
    family as polity and, 160
    generative refusal and, 106
    heteropatriarchy and, 203
    identity politics and, 201
    Idle No More and, 233–34
    land as pedagogy and, 81, 89, 92–93, 96–97, 165
    love of land and, 31, 80–81, 88–89, 91–93, 129, 254
    love of nation and, 102–7
    natality and, 92–93
    nationhood and, 102–7
    political nationalism and, 102–3
    politics of generative refusal and, 108
    queerness and, 141, 189–90, 249
    relational freedom and, 91
    resistance and, 91–92
    resurgence and, 7, 19, 75, 76, 91–92, 110, 118–19, 141, 233–34

round dance and, 119
sovereignty and, 73–74
treaties and, 102–3
world-creation and, 129, 243
Sioui, Georges, 190
Sitting Bull, 121–22
Skinner, Quentin, 29–30, 39–40, 49, 52, 54
Skull Valley Goshutes, 50
slavery's connection to freedom, 1–3, 10–11, 24–25, 39–40, 59–61, 82, 105, 145–48
Smith, Andrea, 161–62, 181–82
Smith, Linda Tuhiwai, 172, 177, 183–84n.85
Snyder, Emily, 241
social contract, 13–16, 59–61, 63
Society Must Be Defended (Foucault), 40, 54–55
sovereignty. *See also* law; politics; self-determination
 decolonizing freedom and, 6–7, 10, 13–14, 16–17, 18, 20, 23–24, 32, 35–36, 260
 definition of, 73
 epistemologies and, 157–58, 160–61
 feminisms and, 204, 206–7, 208–9
 kinship sovereignties, 27, 192–93, 197–98
 love of land and, 102–3
 nationhood and, 72, 102–3, 184, 196–97, 198
 nested sovereignties, 198
 noninterference and, 210–11
 racialization and, 72
 relational freedom and, 72–75
 treaties and, 74–75
 Westphalian state and, 23–24, 26, 72–73, 210–11
spiritual exercise, freedom as, 259–64
Spivak, Gayatri, 196–97
Stanton, Elizabeth Cady, 229–30
Starblanket, Gina, 198–99, 201, 230–31
Stark, Heidi Kiiwetinepinesiik, 198–99, 201, 230–31
state of nature, 13–14, 52–55, 56–57, 59–61, 62, 63, 64
Stevenson, Ray "Coco," 117–18
Stoics, 261–62
Strangers to Ourselves (Kristeva), 137
Stubben, Jerry D., 69

Tailfeathers, Elle-Máijá Apiniskim, 234–35
Tataman, Lucy, 129–30
Taylor, Charles, 248
Thass-Thienemann, Theodore, 147–48
Tomkins, Silvan, 265
"Traditional and Critical Theory" (Horkheimer), 244–45
treaties
 colonial unknowing and, 161–62

critical theory and, 268
decolonizing freedom and, 16–17, 26–28
epistemologies and, 161–62
feminisms and, 157, 208, 229–30
kindship and, 74
love of land and, 87, 92, 102–3
meaning-making and, 199
nationhood and, 26–27, 74–75, 102–3, 198–99
property and, 199
relational freedom and, 69–70
as rites of making relatives, 69–70
sovereignty and, 74–75
treaties among nations, 69–70, 102–3
treaty constitutionalism, 17, 26, 78, 184, 229–30
Truth and Reconciliation Commission of Canada, 18, 160n.14
Tsosie, Rebecca, 74–75
Tucker, T. G., 147–48, 163
Tully, James
 being the change and, 139
 constitutive exclusions and, 60
 Eurocentrism and, 63
 Gaia Hypothesis and, 171
 governance and, 77–78
 political freedom and, 14
 practices of and for freedom and, 36n.81
 public autonomy and, 8
 reconciliation and, 19
 resurgence and, 77, 78
 savage freedom and, 14
Turner, Victor, 33, 124–25, 126–27
2SLGBTQQIA persons, 156–57, 159, 218–19, 228

Ungunmerr-Baumann, Miriam-Rose, 165–66
Unist'ot'en resistance, 108–10, 115, 231
United Nations Declaration of the Rights of Indigenous Peoples, 5–6n.10, 41, 184, 203
United Nations Human Rights Committee, 35, 209–10
Universal Declaration of Human Rights, 220–21
unknowing, colonial. *See* colonial unknowing

Veracini, Lorenzo, 194
Vimalassery, Manu, 194, 197
violence against women and girls, 218–19, 227, 232–33, 236–38, 241
Violence on the Land, Violence on Our Bodies (Women's Earth Alliance and the Native Youth Sexual Health Network), 19, 236–38, 239–40
von Redecker, Eva, 105

Wagner, Sally Roesch, 229–30
Walcott, Rinaldo, 194–96
Walia, Harsha, 24–25, 194–96
Warrior, Robert, 74–75
Wasase (Alfred), 107–8
Waters, Anne, 165
Welch, Shay, 119–20
Wellmer, Albrecht, 259
Wendat, 167
Western conception of freedom, 1–4, 11–12, 21–22, 29–30, 246. *See also* decolonizing freedom; nondomination; noninterference
Westphalian state, 23–24, 26–27, 72–73, 210–11
whiteness, 59–60, 161, 180–81
Whitt, Laurelyn, 74–75
Wickannish, Elder, 268–69
Wiegman, Robyn, 254
Willett, Cynthia, 252
Williams, Doug, 26, 102
Williams, Robert A., Jr., 69–70, 74
Wilson, Alex, 236–37
Wilson, Nina, 116
Winter We Danced, The (Kino-nda-niimi Collective), 116–17
Wodziwob (Northern Paiute), 121–22
Wolfe, Patrick, 7n.15, 160–61
women's movements. *See* feminisms
world-creation
  critical theory and, 246
  decolonizing freedom and, 3–4, 28
  epistemologies and, 174
  love of land and, 106, 129
  relational freedom and, 25, 27–28, 115
  ritual as practice of, 33
  round dance and, 118–23, 128–35, 141–42, 149–50
Worster, Donald, 171
Wovoka (Jack Wilson, Northern Paiute), 121–22

Yidindji, Murrumu Walubara, 168–69
Yoga Sutra, 152–53
Young, Iris Marion
  arbitrary inference and, 51
  autonomy and, 43
  collective self-determination and, 50
  colonial unknowing and, 41–45
  constitutionalism and, 43
  decentered diverse democratic federalism and, 42–43
  democratic governance and, 42–43, 45, 50n.43
  exemplars of liberty and, 41–42
  inspiration for, 40
  limitations of, 51
  nondomination and, 44–45, 50–51
  noninterference and, 43–45, 50–51
  from relational freedom to noninterference and, 41–45
  Skull Valley Goshutes and, 50–51
  sovereignty and, 30

The manufacturer's authorised representative in the EU for product safety is Oxford University Press España S.A. of El Parque Empresarial San Fernando de Henares, Avenida de Castilla, 2 – 28830 Madrid (www.oup.es/en or product.safety@oup.com). OUP España S.A. also acts as importer into Spain of products made by the manufacturer.

Printed in the USA/Agawam, MA
January 31, 2025

881971.009